A Guide to the Lexington and Harrisburg Yearling Sales

By Carl Palumbo

Mane Street Publications LLC

First Editon: 2012
ISBN 978-0615669816

Cover photograph courtesy USTA

Published by
Mane Street Publications LLC
Plantsville, CT

manestpub.com

For My Three Daughters: Adrienne, Jessica and Melissa

Acknowledgments

Ron Palumbo, who designed the cover and the interior of the book. Without his contribution, this book would not exist.

Adrienne Palumbo did a significant amount of accurate data entry, which allowed me to devote more time to research.

Phyllis Palumbo read and provided advice regarding grammar, sentence structure and chart flow.

Ann Chunko, of the USTA, has provided the data for the $50,000 two-year olds and $100,000 three-year olds to me for the past three years. She has been very dependable and professional.

Jean and Marthe Drolet, who have rekindled my enthusiasm for racing, have been exceptional mentors and supportive friends.

Table of Contents

Introduction

Each year buyers spend over *$60 million* at the Lexington and Harrisburg Yearling Sales. They are the two biggest and most prestigious sale venues, selling about 1,900 youngsters in the fall. In the 2008, 2009, and 2010 sales, 5,685 yearlings, aspiring to race as two-year olds in 2009, 2010 and 2011, were auctioned.

Yet most buyers will attend this year's sales with very little statistical information about the rate of success attained by these sales graduates. Do prospective buyers know how many of these 5,685 youngsters earned $200,000, $100,000 or even $50,000 as two-year olds? Do they know which sires, broodmare sires, or farms produced the most elite freshmen performers? If buyers had this historical information would they be better prepared for the sales?

Naturally, we see advertisements about the half-dozen or so big winners emerging from these sales. That gets everyone dreaming of buying that elusive champion. But the champions are not alone in their scarcity. In doing the research for this book, we found that only 86 (1.51%) of the 5,685 yearlings sold from the 2008–2010 Harrisburg and Lexington Sales earned $200,000 or more at two. Just 195 (3.43%) two-year olds achieved $100,000 or more. And only 406 (7.14%) attained the $50,000 plateau as freshmen. Therefore, buyers who attended these sales had a 1 in 14 chance of purchasing a $50,000 winning two-year old. Those odds diminished to 1 in 29 for a $100,000 earner, and fell to 1 in 66 for a $200,000 winner. Traditionally, these two sale venues have given buyers the best chance of purchasing a high earning two-year old. In fact, in the years 2009 through 2011, HB and LEX graduates have comprised over 38% of the $50,000+ two-year olds recorded by the USTA.

Most yearling buyers are not aware of these numbers. Even experienced horse people we have interviewed thought that the odds of purchasing a yearling that earns $50,000 at two from HB or LEX would be 15% to 20%. That estimate is more than double reality. And many of them considered a two-year old with earnings of $50,000 quite pedestrian. However, if we look at the 406 HB and LEX two-year olds that reached the $50,000 threshold, their average earnings were $154,323. There's nothing pedestrian about that. In fact, we would call them *elite performers.*

In my earlier book, *Profiles of Two-Year-Old Standardbreds Earning $50,000 and Up,* we used that metric to define an elite performer. The book detailed, by gait and gender, the most prolific sires, broodmare sires, crosses, dams, and birth order of the 1,373 two-year olds that had won $50,000 or more from 1993–1998. In his review of that book, our industry sage, the late Stan Bergstein wrote: "...[H]arness racing is woefully short on those indicators of profitable operation. [It] is poverty stricken when it comes to statistics and data on which informed judgments can be made." He continued: "So, dismayed with what's currently out there in the way of meaningful statistics, Carl Palumbo created his own. And they are both extremely interesting and extremely valuable…The book represents a huge step forward as a statistical and common sense approach to yearling selection and it represents a tremendous amount of valuable research on Palumbo's part."

Therefore, the scope of this book is the quantification and analysis of the two-year olds that earned $50,000 or more that were sold at the 2008, 2009, and 2010 Lexington and Harrisburg Sales. This is a macro approach. The names of these elite horses are not important. Examining their sires, broodmare sires, crosses, farms/consignors, mares, birth order, and price will provide the data we need to consider historical performance in the yearling selection process.

Most horse people employ a micro approach that is obsessed with physicality, which is certainly the most important consideration. Yet, in reviewing the 5,685 pages in the LEX and HB catalogs, there were many horses that sold for far more than the sire's, mare's, or farm's historical production warranted. They must have been striking individuals. But, basing a purchase on looks alone is rather shortsighted. As we'll see in Chapter 2, if conformation and pedigree were such prescient indicators of success, why have over 82% of the high priced ($100,000 and up) yearlings failed to earn $50,000 at two?

The odds are overwhelmingly against purchasing an elite performer. A staggering 92.9% of the horses sold at HB and LEX from 2008–2010 did not earn $50,000 at two. So how do you improve your chances of buying an elite performer at these sale venues? It can be distilled to *Success Rate*. If the 2008–2010 historical Success Rate was 7.14% (1 in 14), we need to scrutinize the data to find niches where the Success Rate was significantly higher. Obtaining this information should give us an advantage.

The prospective buyer should be able to develop a check-list for each of the youngsters he/she considers for purchase by gait, gender and sale venue, based upon the following Success Rates:

Sire
Farm/Consignor
Broodmare Sire
Cross of Sire and Broodmare Sire
Raced and Unraced Mares
Grand-dam
Yearling's Birth Order
Age and Birth Order of Mares
Sale Position – Hip Number Range
Estimated Price

Of course, this statistical assessment shouldn't stand alone. It must be used in concert with a physical evaluation. The opinion of your trainer and vet are vital in the process.

For our initial exposure to the application of some of these historical statistics, let's review two examples:

Example 1

From Chart 2 in Chapter 4, top trotting sire *Yankee Glide* had 99 fillies sold at HB and LEX from 2008–2010. From those 99, eight (8) went on to earn $50,000 or more at two. If you're shopping for a *Yankee Glide* filly, did you know that there has been a big disparity between sale venues? Lexington sold 72 fillies, but only two (2) became elite performers. Harrisburg sent 27 *Yankee Glide* fillies through the ring, with six (6) earning an average of $131,515. That's an extraordinary 22.2% (or 1 in 4.5) Success Rate that was 699% better than Lexington's 2.8% (or 1 in 36).

Will this past performance continue in the future? Who can predict? LEX might sell half a dozen of them this year. We are not advocating a course of action. We're just reporting what has transpired.

Example 2

Let's imagine we belong to a partnership trying to buy a moderately priced ($20,000–$30,000) Pennsylvania sired trotting filly. With *Andover Hall, Yankee Glide* and *Donato Hanover* fillies most likely out of our price range, some partners are looking at *Broadway Hall* and *SJ's Caviar*. We, on the other hand, prefer *Cantab Hall, Tom Ridge* or *Glidemaster*. How can we reach an agreement? Let's compare each sire's Success Rate with fillies sold at HB and LEX from 2008–2010:

Sire	Fillies Sold	$50,000 2 Year Olds	Success Rate	Average Sale Price
Broadway Hall	52	4	7.7%	$18,186
Cantab Hall	99	8	8.1%	31,904
Glidemaster	42	1	2.4%	33,464
SJ's Caviar	50	0	0.0%	19,880
Tom Ridge	31	5	16.1%	14,048

From the data listed above, it's obvious that we should pursue *Cantab Hall, Broadway Hall* and *Tom Ridge* fillies. We should exclude *Glidemaster* and *SJ's Caviar*, two sires that have had a combined Success Rate of 1.1% (1 out of 92). The three sires we will follow have had an aggregated Success Rate of 9.3%, which is 750% better than the two sires we eliminated. Could *SJ's Caviar* and *Glidemaster* improve their output in 2012 or 2013? Absolutely they can. But, why would we bet $20,000 or more on such a reversal?

In these two examples the aspirant yearling buyer can apply historical statistics to put the percentages in his/her favor. Is it foolproof or guaranteed? No, it's not. But, it provides the buyer with another dimension, another angle to consider when making his/her selections. For the most part, the yearling selection process is two-dimensional: *conformation* and *pedigree*. And for most budgets, getting both is very difficult. Our statistical dimension of historical Success Rates will give the informed buyer an edge over his/her competitors when making those difficult compromises regarding conformation and pedigree.

Some people go to the Yearling Sales hoping to get lucky, hoping that their trainer might find a real gem at a bargain price. We've all heard the stories of a trainer or owner spotting a horse that caught his/her fancy, purchasing it for $10,000 or $15,000, and having it earn $500,000 at two. Good luck with that!

The Lexington and Harrisburg Sales are highly competitive. Anyone going to these sales must be at the top of his/her game. Here's the proof: The average price of the 5,685 yearlings auctioned at HB and LEX from 2008 to 2010 was $32,698. The average price of the 406 *elite performers* was *53%* higher at $50,070. The people bidding are very knowledgeable and very sophisticated.

Here's a breakdown of the average price and average earnings of the 406 elite two-year olds by gender, gait and sale venue:

Sale	Sex/Gait	$50,000 2 Year Olds	Average Sale Price	Average Earnings at 2
Harrisburg	C/P	67	$45,709	$178,787
Harrisburg	F/P	53	38,991	150,809
Harrisburg	C/T	54	61,648	155,948
Harrisburg	F/T	53	50,538	166,078
TOTAL	–	**227**	**49,059**	**163,854**
Lexington	C/P	54	59,204	145,722
Lexington	F/P	46	41,152	151,611
Lexington	C/T	46	50,196	148,872
Lexington	F/T	33	54,333	114,208
TOTAL	–	**179**	**51,352**	**142,235**
GRAND TOTAL	–	**406**	**$50,070**	**$154,323**

It's obvious that the competition is fierce. In order to compete in this arena, it's going to take much more than luck. It's also going to take more than the pursuit of physical appearance.

The tables presented in this book will illustrate which Sires, Consignors, Farms, Broodmare Sires, Mares, Crosses, Selling-Price, Sales Position, Birth Order etc. have had the highest percentage of success in producing *elite performers*. We will uncover disparities of performance between colts and fillies by sire, farm, broodmare sire, price range, birth order etc. Seeing this information in black and white should give the reader cause to reflect more critically than his/her uninformed counterparts.

The approach is, very simply, agnostic. The purpose is to help you prepare for the Lexington and Harrisburg Yearling Sales. This book will arm you with historical statistics that can help increase your odds of purchasing an *elite performer*. We have no affiliations or relationships with any farms, consignors or sale venues. We're not passing judgment; just reporting data regarding the production of two-year olds earning $50,000 or more that have emanated from the HB and LEX Sales of 2008–2010.

Like all data and analysis of prior year's statistics, previous results can't guarantee future success or continued failure.

What about three-year old performance?

Some people may think we've been a bit myopic by confining the data and analysis to only two-year olds. After all, there are great three-year old performers that don't earn $50,000 at two.

Firstly, the earnings bar must be raised for three-year olds since the owner incurs another year of expenses. In our opinion a three year old must have $100,000 in lifetime earnings to be considered an *elite performer*. Applying that metric to two years of history, the 2008 and 2009 HB and LEX Sales for three-year olds that raced in 2010 and 2011, here are the numbers:

Out of 3,769 yearlings sold, 359 three-year olds achieved lifetime earnings of $100,000 or more. In order to retrieve the Success Rate of three-year olds who did not earn $50,000 at two, we must extract the elite freshmen from these numbers:

279 yearlings of the 3,769 earned $50,000 at two.
232 (83%) of those 279 achieved $100,000 through three.

Therefore:
Yearlings Sold w/o $50,000 Two Year Olds = 3,490 (3,769 minus 279)
$100,000 Three Year Olds w/o $50,000 Two Year Olds = 127 (359 minus 232)

The Success Rate for $100,000 three-year olds that did not earn $50,000 at two is *3.6%* (127/3,490).

The odds of purchasing a yearling that did not achieve $50,000 at two, but blossomed into a $100,000 lifetime earner at three, were *1 in 27.5*. Put another way, 96.4% failed to do it in the two years we've chronicled. Admittedly, two years of history is not a very long time, but 3,490 horses is not a small sample. It appears that the best route to success is getting an elite two-year old.

Chapter 1: Success Rates by Sale Venue

There are interesting disparities between Harrisburg and Lexington that will become more magnified when we review performance by sire, farm/consignor, and broodmare sire.

Chart 1: $50,000 Winners

HARRISBURG, 2008-2010

Sale	Sold	$50,000 2 Year Olds	Gait	Sex	Year	Average Earnings	Success Rate
HB	343	19	P	C	2008	$192,545	5.5%
HB	342	26	P	C	2009	170,582	7.6%
HB	345	22	P	C	2010	176,601	6.4%
Total	1030	67	P	C	All	178,787	6.5%
HB	298	24	P	F	2008	136,012	8.1%
HB	282	17	P	F	2009	142,361	6.0%
HB	285	12	P	F	2010	192,370	4.2%
Total	865	53	P	F	All	150,809	6.1%
All Pacers	1895	120	P	F	–	166,016	6.3%
HB	244	20	T	C	2008	154,378	8.2%
HB	212	16	T	C	2009	155,519	7.5%
HB	265	18	T	C	2010	158,074	6.8%
Total	721	54	T	C	All	155,948	7.5%
HB	208	21	T	F	2008	211,204	10.1%
HB	243	17	T	F	2009	176,603	7.0%
HB	229	15	T	F	2010	90,974	6.6%
Total	680	53	T	F	All	166,078	7.8%
All Trotters	1401	107	T	F	All	160,966	7.6%
TOTAL HB	3296	227	ALL	ALL	ALL	$163,854	6.9%

LEXINGTON, 2008-2010

Sale	Sold	$50,000 2 Year Olds	Gait	Sex	Year	Average Earnings	Success Rate
LEX	211	17	P	C	2008	$133,742	8.1%
LEX	219	14	P	C	2009	155,176	6.4%
LEX	214	23	P	C	2010	148,822	10.7%
Total	**644**	**54**	**P**	**C**	–	**145,722**	**8.4%**
LEX	210	21	P	F	2008	163,924	10.0%
LEX	172	10	P	F	2009	161,112	5.8%
LEX	173	15	P	F	2010	128,038	8.7%
Total	**555**	**46**	**P**	**F**	–	**151,611**	**8.3%**
All Pacers	**1199**	**100**	**P**	**ALL**	–	**$148,431**	**8.3%**
LEX	220	14	T	C	2008	167,175	6.4%
LEX	217	20	T	C	2009	145,997	9.2%
LEX	213	12	T	C	2010	132,310	5.6%
Total	**650**	**46**	**T**	**C**	–	**$148,872**	**7.1%**
LEX	156	11	T	F	2008	98,029	7.1%
LEX	192	12	T	F	2009	102,787	6.3%
LEX	192	10	T	F	2010	145,709	5.2%
Total	540	33	T	F	–	114,208	6.1%
All Trotters	**1190**	**79**	**T**	**ALL**		**$134,392**	**6.6%**
Total LEX	**2389**	**179**	**ALL**	**ALL**	**ALL**	**$142,235**	**7.5%**

HARRISBURG AND LEXINGTON COMBINED

Sold	$50,000 2 Year Olds	Gait	Sex	Year	Average Earnings	Success Rate
1674	121	P	C	ALL	$164,031	7.2%
1420	99	P	F	ALL	151,182	7.0%
3094	220	P	ALL	ALL	$158,249	7.1%
1371	100	T	C	ALL	152,693	7.3%
1220	86	T	F	ALL	146,174	7.1%
2591	186	T	ALL	ALL	$149,679	7.2%
5685	**406**	**ALL**	**ALL**	**ALL**	**$154,323**	**7.1%**

Chart 2: Success Rates by Year

HARRISBURG

Sale	Year	Sold	$50,000 2 Year Olds	Success Rate	Odds
HB	2008	1093	84	7.7%	1 in 13.0
HB	2009	1079	76	7.0%	1 in 14.2
HB	2010	1124	67	6.0%	1 in 16.8
Total	All	3296	227	6.9%	1 in 14.5

LEXINGTON

Sale	Year	Sold	$50,000 2 Year Olds	Success Rate	Odds
LEX	2008	797	63	7.9%	1 in 12.7
LEX	2009	800	56	7.0%	1 in 14.3
LEX	2010	792	60	7.6%	1 in 13.2
LEX	All	2389	179	7.5%	1 in 13.3

Immediately we see a decrease in both quantity and Success Rate at Harrisburg from the high of 2008 to 2009 and 2010. The 2010 Sale was particularly sparse in the production of $50K pacing filly two-year olds (12 out of 285). That's a 4.2% Success Rate which is 41% below the overall three year average of 7.1%

Just like Harrisburg, Lexington had its most productive year in quantity and Success Rate in 2008. Unlike Harrisburg, Lexington bounced back in 2010 from its 2009 lows. That recovery was fueled by pacers. There were 23 elite two-year old pacing colts racing in 2011 out of 214 sold at the 2010 Lexington Sale. That's a 10.8% Success Rate. Lexington pacing fillies did nicely also. There were 15 elite fillies out of 173 sold for an 8.7% Success Rate.

Trotters from the 2010 Lexington Sale performed below the average. Trotting colts were 12 out of 213 for a 5.6% Success Rate. Trotting fillies were weaker with just 10 elites out of 192 sold for just 5.2%.

Chart 3: Success Rates by Gait and Gender, 2008–2010

Venue	Sex/Gait	Sold	$50,000 2 Year Olds	Success Rate	Odds
HB	C/P	1030	67	8.5%	1 in 15.4
LEX	C/P	644	54	8.4%	1 in 11.9
HB	F/P	865	53	6.1%	1 in 16.3
LEX	F/P	555	46	8.3%	1 in 12.1
HB	C/T	721	54	7.5%	1 in 13.4
LEX	C/T	650	46	7.1%	1 in 14.1
HB	F/T	680	53	7.8%	1 in 12.8
LEX	F/T	540	33	6.1%	1 in 16.4
Total	**All**	**5685**	**406**	**7.1%**	**1 in 14**

Considering the average success rate of 7.1% (or 1 in 14), pacing colts sold at Lexington have been best, while trotting fillies at Lexington were the worst. From this high level it appears that the best chance of getting elite pacers is at Lexington; for trotters, it's Harrisburg. But, we need to examine this data in much more detail.

Chapter 2: Success Rates by Price Range

Let's take a look at the correlation between price and Success Rate:

Chart 1: Harrisburg and Lexington Yearlings by Price, 2008-2010

Price Range	Sold	$50,000 2 Year Olds	Success Rate	Odds	% Sold	% of $50,000 2 Year Olds
Under $10,000	1198	30	2.5%	1 in 40.0	21.1%	7.4%
10,000 to $19,999	1220	56	4.6%	1 in 21.8	21.5%	13.8%
$20,000 to $29,999	960	61	6.4%	1 in 15.8	16.9%	15.0%
$30,000 to $39,999	703	60	8.5%	1 in 11.7	12.4%	14.8%
$40,000 to $49,999	436	44	10.1%	1 in 9.9	7.7%	10.8%
$50,000 to $59,999	325	31	9.5%	1 in 10.5	5.7%	7.6%
$60,000 to $74,999	293	37	12.6%	1 in 7.9	5.2%	9.1%
$75,000 to $99,999	262	37	14.1%	1 in 7.1	4.6%	9.1%
$100,000 to $149,999	204	35	17.2%	1 in 5.8	3.6%	8.6%
$150,000 and above	84	15	17.9%	1 in 5.6	1.5%	3.7%
TOTALS	5685	406	7.1%	1 in 14.0	100.0%	100.0%

Price Range vs. Success Rate

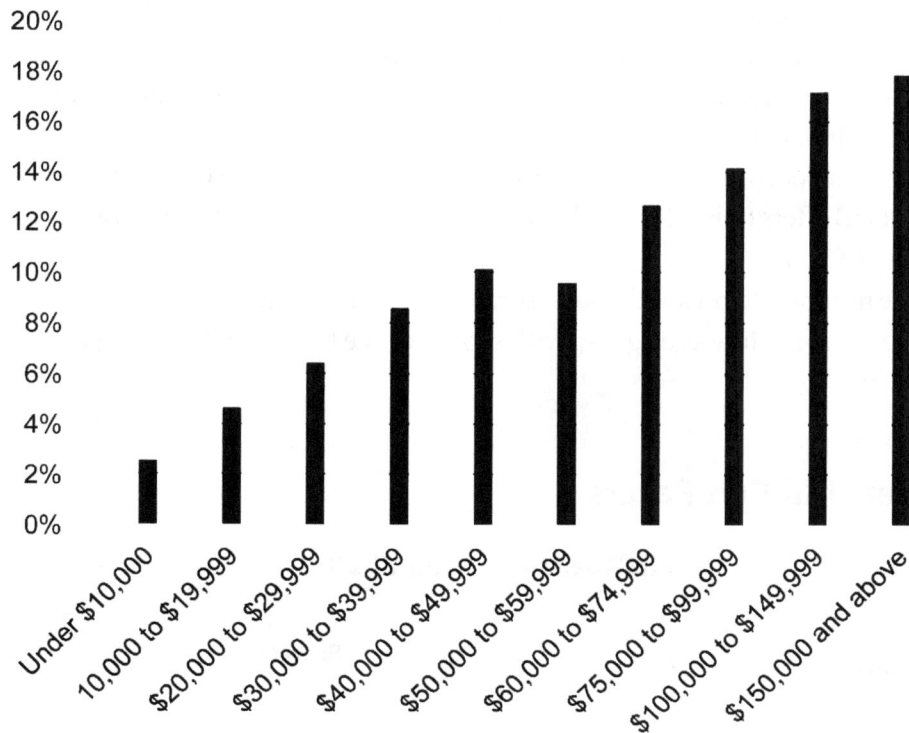

There is almost a straight-line correlation between price and Success Rate: the higher the price, the better the Success Rate. This demonstrates the expertise of the trainers and purchasers. Let's consolidate these price ranges in order to obtain a clearer picture:

Price Range	Yearlings Sold	$50,000 2 Year Olds	Success Rate	Odds
$0 – $29,999	3378	147	4.4%	1 in 23
$30,000 – $59,999	1464	135	9.2%	1 in 10.8
$60,000 – $99,999	555	74	13.3%	1 in 7.5
$100,000 and up	288	50	17.4%	1 in 5.8

Remembering that the Success Rate average was 7.1% (406 out of 5685), we can see that yearlings bought for less than $30,000 at Harrisburg and Lexington under-produced the average by 39%. Conversely, buying yearlings between $30,000 and $59,999 produced a 29% better result. The group between

$60,000 and $99,999 were 86% better than average. And finally, the expensive youngsters that sold for $100,000 and up were 143% better than the average.

As mentioned in the introduction, even though the horses purchased for $100,000 and up had the best Success Rate at 17.4% (1 in 5.8), 82.6% of them (238 out of 288) failed to earn $50,000 at two. Considering that these youngsters usually have the best *pedigrees* and *conformations*, those are not very good odds—especially for a $100,000+ investment.

At the other end of the spectrum, the prospective buyer must realize that spending under $20,000 for a yearling at LEX and HB offers only a 1 in 28 chance of bringing home an elite two-year old. That's 50% less than the average of 1 in 14.

Let's go inside the numbers to review the success rates by gait and gender for each Sale Venue. As you might imagine, there are some interesting disparities to note. We'll begin with pacing colts.

Chart 2: Two-Year Old Colt Pacers

HARRISBURG, 2008-2010

Price	Sold	$50,000 2 Year Olds	Success Rate	Odds
$0 - $9,999	173	3	1.7%	1 in 57.8
$10,000 - $19,999	211	5	2.4%	1 in 42.2
$20,000 - $29,999	209	11	5.3%	1 in 19.0
$30,000 - $39,999	136	14	10.3%	1 in 9.7
$40,000 - $49,999	88	9	10.2%	1 in 9.8
$50,000 - $59,999	69	5	7.3%	1 in 13.8
$60,000 - $74,999	52	7	13.5%	1 in 7.4
$75,000 - $99,999	47	9	19.2%	1 in 5.2
$100,000 - $149,999	38	4	10.5%	1 in 9.5
$150,000 and above	7	0	0%	0
ALL	1030	67	6.5%	1 in 15.3

LEXINGTON, 2008-2010

Price	Sold	$50,000 2 Year Olds	Success Rate	Odds
$0 - $9,999	111	4	3.6%	1 in 27.8
$10,000 - $19,999	117	5	4.3%	1 in 23.4
$20,000 - $29,999	108	8	7.4%	1 in 13.5
$30,000 - $39,999	83	7	8.4%	1 in 11.9
$40,000 - $49,999	46	4	8.7%	1 in 11.5
$50,000 - $59,999	44	4	9.1%	1 in 11.0
$60,000 - $74,999	52	10	19.2%	1 in 5.2
$75,000 - $99,999	42	3	7.1%	1 in 14.0
$100,000 - $149,999	29	6	20.7%	1 in 4.8
$150,000 and above	12	3	25.0%	1 in 4.0
ALL	**644**	**54**	**8.4%**	**1 in 11.9**

Pacing colts that sold for under $20,000 at Harrisburg from 2008–2010 had a Success Rate of only 2.1% (8 out of 384). That's just 1 in 48 and 70% below the average. The $30,000 to $49,999 range was the sweet spot for moderate budgets. There were 23 elite performers out of 224 sold for a 10.3% Success Rate, or 1 in 9.7. For those who opened their wallets a bit wider, the $60,000 to $99,999 range was the most propitious. That group produced 16 elite two-year olds out of 99 sold for a 16.2% Success Rate, or 1 in 6.2. The group that sold for $100,000 and above had 4 out of 45 for an 8.9% Success Rate (1 in 11.3).

Pacing colts selling for under $20,000 did better at Lexington. Out of 228 sold, 9 became elite two-year olds for a Success Rate of 4%, or 1 in 25. Despite being 44.7% below the average, they were 89% better than their Harrisburg compatriots.

The pacing colts selling for $20,000–$29,999 at Lexington had a 7.4% Success Rate compared to the Harrisburg group at 5.3%. That's over 40% better. One strange group at Lexington was the $60,000 to $74,999 price range. It produced only 3 elite performers out of 42 for a 7.1% Success Rate, which just met the overall average. Of the 41 pacing colts that sold for $100,000 and up at LEX, 9 became elite performers for a 22% Success Rate, or 1 in 4.5.

Now let's take a look at the pacing fillies.

Chart 3: Two-Year Old Filly Pacers

HARRISBURG, 2008-2010

Price	Sold	$50,000 2 Year Olds	Success Rate	Odds
$0 - $9,999	278	8	2.9%	1 in 34.8
$10,000 - $19,999	180	11	6.1%	1 in 16.4
$20,000 - $29,999	130	9	6.9%	1 in 14.4
$30,000 - $39,999	97	3	3.1%	1 in 32.3
$40,000 - $49,999	60	4	6.7%	1 in 15.0
$50,000 - $59,999	42	5	11.9%	1 in 8.4
$60,000 - $74,999	33	4	12.1%	1 in 8.3
$75,000 - $99,999	26	6	23.1%	1 in 4.3
$100,000 - $149,999	13	3	23.1%	1 in 4.3
$150,000 and above	6	0	0%	0
ALL	865	53	6.1%	1 in 16.3

LEXINGTON, 2008-2010

Price	Sold	$50,000 2 Year Olds	Success Rate	Odds
$0 - $9,999	167	3	1.8%	1 in 55.7
$10,000 - $19,999	133	7	5.3%	1 in 19.0
$20,000 - $29,999	72	5	6.9%	1 in 14.4
$30,000 - $39,999	49	7	14.3%	1 in 7.0
$40,000 - $49,999	47	9	19.2%	1 in 5.2
$50,000 - $59,999	26	4	15.4%	1 in 6.5
$60,000 - $74,999	26	5	19.2%	1 in 5.2
$75,000 - $99,999	21	5	23.8%	1 in 4.2
$100,000 - $149,999	11	1	9.1%	1 in 11.0
$150,000 and above	3	0	0%	0
ALL	555	46	8.3%	1 in 12.1

Filly pacers that sold for under $20,000 at Harrisburg had a Success Rate of 4.2%, with 19 elite performers from 458 sold, or 1 in 24.1. This was 23% better than Lexington, which produced 10 elites from 300 for a Success Rate of 3.3%, or 1 in 30. However, in the moderate price levels, $30,000–$49,999, Lexington's Success Rate was 16.7% (16 in 96), or 1 in 6. This was *273%* superior to Harrisburg's 4.5% (7 out of 157), or 1 in 22.4.

All pacing fillies selling between $50,000 and $99,999 were *133%* better than the average, with a Success Rate of 16.7%, or 1 in 6. Fillies in this price range at LEX had a 19.2% Success Rate, or 1 in 5.2 (14 out of 73). That was 29% better than HB's strong showing of 14.9% (15 out of 101), or 1 in 6.7.

Now let's review Chart 4 to compare trotting colts.

Chart 4: Two-Year Old Colt Trotters

HARRISBURG, 2008-2010

Price	Sold	$50,000 2 Year Olds	Success Rate	Odds
$0 - $9,999	132	4	3.0%	1 in 33.0
$10,000 - $19,999	160	5	3.1%	1 in 32.0
$20,000 - $29,999	135	6	4.4%	1 in 22.5
$30,000 - $39,999	90	9	10.0%	1 in 10.0
$40,000 - $49,999	50	9	18.0%	1 in 5.6
$50,000 - $59,999	29	1	3.5%	1 in 29.0
$60,000 - $74,999	32	2	6.3%	1 in 16.0
$75,000 - $99,999	41	6	14.6%	1 in 6.8
$100,000 - $149,999	37	7	18.9%	1 in 5.3
$150,000 and above	15	5	33.3%	1 in 3.0
ALL	**721**	**54**	**7.5%**	**1 in 13.4**

LEXINGTON, 2008-2010

Price	Sold	$50,000 2 Year Olds	Success Rate	Odds
$0 - $9,999	108	3	2.8%	1 in 36.0
$10,000 - $19,999	139	8	5.8%	1 in 17.4
$20,000 - $29,999	104	7	6.7%	1 in 14.9
$30,000 - $39,999	94	7	7.5%	1 in 13.4

$40,000 - $49,999	38	1	2.6%	1 in 38.0
$50,000 - $59,999	44	7	15.9%	1 in 6.3
$60,000 - $74,999	24	4	16.7%	1 in 6.0
$75,000 - $99,999	40	2	5.0%	1 in 20.0
$100,000 - $149,999	36	4	11.1%	1 in 9.0
$150,000 and above	23	3	13.0%	1 in 7.7
ALL	**650**	**46**	**7.1%**	**1 in 14.1**

There seems to be a real bargain here. Harrisburg trotting colts that sold between $40,000 and $49,999 produced 9 elite two-year olds from just 50 offered. That's an 18% Success Rate, or 1 in 5.6. Lexington trotting colts in the same price range were only 1 for 38. But, almost the exact opposite happened in the $50,000–$59,999 range. Lexington had 7 elites out of 44 sold for 15.9%, while Harrisburg had just 1 out of 29 for 3.5%.

Trotting colts selling above $75,000 at Harrisburg had a Success Rate of 19.4%, or 1 in 5.2, with 18 elite performers from 93 sold. Lexington graduates in this price range had 9 elites out of 99 for a 9.1% Success Rate (1 in 11). Therefore, Harrisburg had a 112% better Success Rate with high-end trotting colts.

Our last group is trotting fillies.

Chart 4: Two-Year Old Filly Trotters

HARRISBURG, 2008-2010

Price	Sold	$50,000 2 Year Olds	Success Rate	Odds
$0 - $9,999	132	3	2.3%	1 in 44.0
$10,000 - $19,999	169	8	4.7%	1 in 21.1
$20,000 - $29,999	126	11	8.7%	1 in 11.5
$30,000 - $39,999	87	8	9.2%	1 in 10.9
$40,000 - $49,999	63	7	11.1%	1 in 9.0
$50,000 - $59,999	32	3	9.4%	1 in 10.7
$60,000 - $74,999	31	3	9.7%	1 in 10.3
$75,000 - $99,999	18	3	16.7%	1 in 6.0
$100,000 - $149,999	13	4	30.8%	1 in 3.3
$150,000 & up	9	3	33.3%	1 in 3.0
ALL	**680**	**53**	**7.8%**	**1 in 12.8**

LEXINGTON, 2008-2010

Price	Sold	$50,000 2 Year Olds	Success Rate	Odds
$0 - $9,999	97	2	2.1%	1 in 48.5
$10, 000 - $19,999	111	7	6.3%	1 in 15.9
$20,000 - $29,999	76	4	5.3%	1 in 19.0
$30, 000 - $39,999	67	5	7.5%	1 in 13.4
$40,000 - $49,999	44	1	2.3%	1 in 44.0
$50,000 - $59,999	39	2	5.1%	1 in 19.5
$60,000 - $74,999	43	2	4.7%	1 in 21.5
$75,000 - $99,999	27	3	11.1%	1 in 9.0
$100,000 - $149,999	27	6	22.2%	1 in 4.5
$150,000 & up	9	1	11.1%	1 in 9.0
ALL	540	33	6.1%	1 in 16.4

Harrisburg has had a good Success Rate among filly trotters selling at moderate price points. Trot fillies that sold from $20,000 to $49,999 had 26 elites out of 276 for a 9.4% success rate, or 1 in 10.6. That's basically the same as the fillies that sold for $50,000 to $74,999, which were 6 out of 63 (9.5%) or 1 in 10.5. Distaff trotters selling for $75,000 and up at HB had an exceptional Success Rate of 25% (10 out of 40), or 1 in 4.

Lexington trotting fillies were not as prolific. The group that sold between $40,000 and $74,999 was especially sparse. It produced only 5 elites out of 126 (4%), or 1 in 25. That's 44% below the average. In fact, aside from the trotting fillies that sold for $75,000 and up, only those in the $30,000 to $39,999 price range were better than average.

Chapter 3: Success Rates of Hip Numbers

Not many people are going to buy horses based upon Hip Number. The purpose of this chapter is to give the reader a familiarity with the selling patterns of the Lexington and Harrisburg Sales from 2008–2010.

Chart 1: Success Rate by HIP Number Range

LEXINGTON, 2008-2010

Hip Range	Sold	$50,000 2 Year Olds	Success Rate	Odds	Avg Price
1 - 49	141	18	12.8%	1 in 7.8	$70,050
50 - 99	145	31	21.4%	1 in 4.7	93,641
100 - 149	145	6	4.1%	1 in 24.2	48,814
150 - 199	148	15	10.1%	1 in 9.9	59,473
200 - 249	147	10	6.8%	1 in 14.7	54,551
250 - 299	139	10	7.2%	1 in 13.9	34,144
300 - 349	148	14	9.5%	1 in 10.6	38,054
350 - 399	147	10	6.8%	1 in 14.7	34,238
400 - 449	138	10	7.2%	1 in 13.8	24,630
450 - 499	146	8	5.5%	1 in 18.3	24,459
500 - 549	148	9	6.1%	1 in 16.4	23,959
550 - 599	142	7	4.9%	1 in 20.3	18,162
600 - 649	145	15	10.3%	1 in 9.7	13,207
650 - 699	143	4	2.8%	1 in 35.8	16,028
700 - 749	146	6	4.1%	1 in 24.3	12,733
750 - 799	144	6	4.2%	1 in 24.0	12,146
800 - 849	77	0	0%	0	10,455
TOTAL	**2389**	**179**	**7.5%**	**1 in 13.3**	**35,362**

HARRISBURG, 2008–2010

Hip Range	Sold	$50,000 2 Year Olds	Success Rate	Odds	Average Price
1 - 49	139	15	10.8%	1 in 9.3	$35,450
50 - 99	140	10	7.1%	1 in 14.0	49,393
100 - 149	149	15	10.1%	1 in 9.9	55,470
150 - 199	147	10	6.8%	1 in 14.7	61,286
200 - 249	146	12	8.2%	1 in 12.2	48,312
250 - 299	141	22	15.6%	1 in 6.4	43,477
300 - 349	146	7	4.8%	1 in 20.9	37,310
350 - 399	145	16	11.0%	1 in 9.1	31,128
400 - 449	147	14	9.5%	1 in 10.5	34,129
450 - 499	144	11	7.6%	1 in 13.1	35,493
500 - 549	147	7	4.8%	1 in 21.0	33,357
550 - 599	139	11	7.9%	1 in 12.6	29,032
600 - 649	144	7	4.9%	1 in 20.6	20,580
650 - 699	144	14	9.7%	1 in 10.3	21,538
700 - 749	145	5	3.4%	1 in 29.0	24,045
750 - 799	139	9	6.5%	1 in 15.4	18,468
800 - 849	147	9	6.1%	1 in 16.3	19,884
850 - 899	146	6	4.1%	1 in 24.3	15,545
900 - 949	145	8	5.5%	1 in 18.1	21,107
950 - 999	148	5	3.4%	1 in 29.6	16,635
1000 - 1049	145	6	4.1%	1 in 24.2	18,014
1050 - 1099	146	4	2.7%	1 in 36.5	18,507
1110 +	117	4	3.4%	1 in 29.3	18,162
TOTAL	**3296**	**227**	**6.9%**	**1 in 14.5**	**$30,768**

Lexington's Hip Range history is not very complicated. The first 99 Hip Numbers account for 27.4% of their elite performers while representing only 12% of the youngsters offered. The average price of the first 99 horses was a stratospheric $82,010! The balance of the Lexington Sale, in this three year amalgam, averages only a 6.2% Success Rate, or 17% below the sale average of 7.5%.

We were surprised to see such a low Success Rate for Hip Range 100–149. The average price dropped to $48,814, but the Success Rate plunged to 4.1%, or 1 out of 24. The $48,814 represents the fifth highest average price of all 17 Hip Ranges. However, it ranks 14th in elite performer production.

On the other side of the coin, look at Hip Range 600–649. Here we have a Success Rate of 10.3%, which was 38% better than the LEX average. But the average selling price of $13,207 was 62% lower than the $35,362 LEX average. This Hip Range was the bargain hunters' dream.

However, after Hip Range 600–649, we encounter the last 200 Hip Numbers. They have had a 3.14% Success Rate, or 1 in 31.9.

At Harrisburg, we can see that Hip Numbers 250–299 have been 126% more successful than the HB average: 15.6% versus 6.9%. The average price of the yearlings sold in this range was $43,477. That's 41% above the Harrisburg average of $30,768. Hip Range 350–399 was 59% better than average with an 11% Success Rate. This range averaged only 1% more in price than the HB average. For the bargain seekers, Hip Range 650–699 offered the most value. This Range's Success Rate of 9.7% is 40% better than the HB average and sold at 30% less than the average.

Interestingly, Hip Range 150–199 had the highest average selling price at $61,286, which is double the HB average. Yet this Range only produced 10 elites out of 147 sold. Its Success Rate of 6.8% was slightly below the HB average of 6.9%.

As anyone who has attended the HB Sale has surmised, the last 250–300 horses sold have had low Success Rates. If we look at Hip numbers 850 to the end, there have been 847 yearlings sold. Only 33 of them have earned $50,000 or more at two. Their Success Rate is 3.9%, or 1 in 25.6.

In conclusion, we must repeat that having the performance of the Hip Ranges quantified is probably helpful for a sense of perspective. Our next chapters, detailing the Success Rates of Sires and Farms, are far more important.

Chapter 4: Sire Success Rates

Our scope regarding sire Success Rates is confined to the 2008–2010 Harrisburg and Lexington Sales. Therefore, yearlings sold at other venues and home-breds are not part of this analysis. One aspect of sire performance is a numbers game. The more mares a sire covers, the more chances it has to have a great offspring. Just one great performer will garner publicity for a sire and farm. But, it's important to be aware of the overall production record of sires and farms.

Our focus here is to define the Success Rates of each sire. This is also a bit of a numbers game. For example, *Astreos*, the Ontario Sire, has a Success Rate of 20% compared to *Art Major* at 15.2%. But, there have been only 10 *Astreos* yearlings sold at HB and LEX versus 244 for *Art Major*. Therefore, *Art Major's* Success Rate with 37 elite two-year olds out of 244 is much more impressive than the 2 out of 10 for *Astreos*.

Speaking of *Art Major*, you will notice a big disparity between sale venues. At Harrisburg, 162 *Art Major* youngsters went under the gavel. Of those 162, an impressive 18 have been elite two-year olds with average earnings at a patrician $173,000. His 11.1% (1 in 9) Success Rate is almost 50% above the average of 7.1%. However, *Art Major's* progeny at Lexington were even better. Of his 82 yearlings sold, an astounding *19* became elite performers averaging $104,000 in their freshman campaigns. His 19 out of 82 is a remarkable 23.2% (1 in 4.3) Success Rate. That's more than double Harrisburg and 224% above the average.

Here are five more examples of disparities to note:

Dragon Again has a Success Rate of 5.4%, or 1 in 18.5. However, his colts are 10 out of 119 for a respectable 8.4% or 1 in 11.9. His fillies have been disappointing with only 2 out of 104 for a 1.9% Success Rate or 1 in 52. Knowing this sire's gender production disparity should be a prerequisite for any prospective buyer.

Yankee Cruiser has had 4 elite fillies out of only 17 for a 23.5% Success Rate (1 in 4.25). With colts he has had only one (1) elite performer out of 22 sold. Even though that one colt earned $686,647 and has been impressive in his initial three year old contests, *Yankee Cruiser* has been better at producing elite fillies.

Certainly *Western Ideal* has taken up the mantle from his sire, *Western Hanover*. He has had an 8.7% Success Rate with 16 elite two-year olds out of 185 sold. However, if you eliminate the performance of his colts at Harrisburg, his Success Rate jumps to 12.1% or 1 in 8.3. His HB colts have been just 1 out of 61 for a microscopic Success Rate of 1.6%. Some of you may remember that one colt, since he earned $827,000 at two. But, I'm sure the people who purchased the other 60 colts at HB haven't derived much consolation from his success.

Rocknroll Hanover has made his presence felt since becoming a stud. The average price for his colts has been $56,526. His fillies have averaged $47,993. Looking at *Rocknroll Hanover* fillies, he has had a much better Success Rate at Lexington. He has had 7 elite two-year olds out of 61 offered at LEX for 11.5%. That's 210% better than Harrisburg's 3.7% (3 elite fillies out of 81 sold).

If you're shopping for a *Muscles Yankee* colt, the following information may be of interest. In our three-year aggregation, Lexington has sold 34 *Muscles Yankee* colts. *None* has earned $50,000 at two. Conversely, Harrisburg has hammered down 53 of his colts. Six (6) of those colts have been elite two-year olds earning an average of $133,358. Muscles Yankee colts that sold at HB had an 11.3% Success Rate, or 1 in 8.8.

Below is a summary of each Sire's Success Rate:

Chart 1: Sire Success Rates from the HB and LEX 2008-2010 Sales

Sire	Sold	$50,000 2 Year Olds	Success Rate
Allamerican Ingot	28	0	0%
Allamerican Native	71	4	5.6%
Allstar Hall	1	0	0%
American Ideal	105	10	9.5%
American Winner	1	0	0%
Amigo Hall	10	0	0%
Andover Hall	210	24	11.4%
Angus Hall	118	4	3.4%
Armbro Deuce	5	1	20.0%
Art Major	244	37	15.2%
Artiscape	107	3	2.8%
Artsplace	87	5	5.8%
Astreos	10	2	20.0%
Badlands Hanover	6	2	33.3%
Bettor's Delight	197	21	10.7%
Blissful Hall	8	0	0%
Broadway Hall	105	6	5.7%
Cambest	41	1	2.4%
Camluck	74	3	4.1%

Sire	Sold	$50,000 2 Year Olds	Success Rate
Cam's Card Shark	106	8	7.6%
Cantab Hall	203	17	8.4%
Cash Hall	38	3	7.9%
Chip Chip Hooray	9	0	0%
Chocolatier	83	1	1.2%
Conway Hall	171	17	9.9%
CR Excalibur	1	0	0%
Credit Winner	209	21	10.1%
Daguet Rapide	6	1	16.7%
Donato Hanover	81	7	8.6%
Donerail	8	0	0%
Dragon Again	223	12	5.4%
Dream Vacation	22	1	4.6%
E Dee's Cam	5	1	20.0%
Equinox Bi	4	0	0%
Four Starzzz Shark	62	6	9.7%
Glidemaster	84	3	3.6%
Grinfromeartoear	4	0	0%
Here Comes Herbie	6	0	0%
I Am A Fool	68	1	1.5%
Jate Lobell	10	0	0%
Jenna's Beach Boy	16	1	6.3%
Jereme's Jet	19	2	10.5%
Justice Hall	2	0	0%
Kadabra	73	6	8.2%
Ken Warkentin	26	3	11.5%
Like A Prayer	33	4	12.1%
Lis Mara	32	0	0%
Mach Three	41	4	9.8%
Majestic Son	22	0	0%
Malabar Man	23	3	13.0%
Malabar Maple	1	0	0%
Master Glide	11	0	0%
Mcardle	73	6	8.2%
Metropolitan	14	0	0%
Modern Art	21	1	4.8%
Mr Feelgood	8	0	0%

Sire	Sold	$50,000 2 Year Olds	Success Rate
Mr Lavec	2	0	0%
Muscles Yankee	198	13	6.6%
No Pan Intended	24	1	4.2%
Pacific Fella	1	0	0%
Peruvian Hanover	1	0	0%
Plesac	1	0	0%
Ponder	40	3	7.5%
Pro Bono Best	2	0	0%
Quik Pulse Mindale	16	1	6.3%
Real Artist	45	2	4.4%
Real Desire	100	7	7.0%
Red River Hanover	27	0	0%
Revenue S	48	1	2.1%
Riverboat King	5	0	0%
Rocknroll Hanover	330	26	7.9%
Royal Mattjesty	18	0	0%
Rustler Hanover	1	0	0%
SJ's Photo	17	0	0%
Sand Vic	6	0	0%
Shark Gesture	7	1	14.3%
SJ's Caviar	118	2	1.7%
Stonebridge Regal	6	0	0%
Striking Sahbra	39	3	7.7%
Tagliabue	4	1	25.0%
Taurus Dream	2	1	50.0%
Tell All	54	1	1.9%
The Panderosa	140	5	3.6%
Tom Ridge	75	10	13.3%
Totally Western	1	0	0%
Valley Victor	89	8	9.0%
Varenne	2	0	0%
Village Jolt	76	0	0%
Western Hanover	174	17	9.8%

Sire	Sold	$50,000 2 Year Olds	Success Rate
Western Ideal	185	16	8.7%
Western Terror	116	4	3.5%
Windsong's Legacy	106	4	3.8%
Yankee Cruiser	39	5	12.8%
Yankee Glide	225	16	7.1%
TOTAL	**5685**	**406**	**7.1%**

There are sires with very low Success Rates. Unless you are aware of their historically weak production, you may buy one based upon conformation, pedigree or "inside information." As you can see, there is one sire that has had *76* of his progeny go to auction without producing *one* elite performer. What are the odds that *you'll* be the person to purchase *the* yearling that breaks this sire's streak?

As an aside, I have deliberately avoided the topic of times. I believe that earnings supersede fast marks. For example, there are sires that have produced some mercurial two-year performers. I saw four freshmen colts by *Western Terror* that took marks of 1:52:3s, 1:52:4f, 1:53f and 1:54f in 2011. They sold for $47,000, $52,000, $40,000 and $125,000 respectively. However, only one of them made our list. He was the slowest, but most expensive of the four, earning $66,723. The three faster colts failed to make our list since their earnings were $31,671, $19,540 and $27,655.

One caveat to remember is that times have become virtually meaningless in our sport. In May, 2012 at half-mile oval, Yonkers Raceway, we witnessed $15,000 claiming races that went in 1:51:2 and 1:52:3!

Examine the chart detailing Sire Success Rates by sale venue and gender to find more disparities.

Chart 2: Sire Success Rates by Gender and Sales Venue

Sire	Sale	Sex	Sold	$50,000 2 Year Olds	Success Rate	Average Price	Avg Earnings of $50,000 2 Year Olds
Allamerican Ingot	LEX	C	18	0	0%	$10,333	
	LEX	F	10	0	0%	8,700	
			28	**0**	**0%**	**9,750**	
Allamerican Native	HB	C	24	0	0%	12,146	
	HB	F	30	3	10.0%	17,767	$132,143
	LEX	C	6	1	16.7%	11,667	91,977
	LEX	F	11	0	0%	15,909	
			71	**4**	**5.6%**	**15,063**	**122,101**
Allstar Hall	LEX	C	1	0	0%	8,000	
American Ideal	HB	C	42	6	14%	30,417	120,136
	HB	F	27	1	3.7%	22,148	78,057
	LEX	C	17	1	5.9%	48,412	189,253
	LEX	F	19	2	10.5%	19,895	465,101
			105	**10**	**9.5%**	**29,300**	**191,833**
American Winner	LEX	F	1	0	0%	26,000	
Amigo Hall	HB	C	1	0	0%	30,000	
	HB	F	4	0	0%	19,500	
	LEX	C	4	0	0%	20,750	
	LEX	F	1	0	0%	6,000	
			10	**0**	**0%**	**19,700**	
Andover Hall	HB	C	73	7	9.6%	53,212	118,681
	HB	F	55	8	14.5%	51,982	120,942
	LEX	C	48	5	10.4%	51,979	107,970
	LEX	F	34	4	11.8%	65,265	130,136
			210	**24**	**11.4%**	**54,560**	**119,112**
Angus Hall	HB	C	33	1	3.0%	36,030	136,013
	HB	F	34	1	2.9%	35,926	112,899
	LEX	C	27	2	7.4%	30,630	136,533
	LEX	F	24	0	0%	29,583	
			118	**4**	**3.4%**	**33,453**	**130,495**
Armbro Deuce	HB	C	1	0	0%	$5,000	
	HB	F	2	0	0%	10,000	
	LEX	F	2	1	50.0%	12,500	$75,166
			5	**1**	**20.0%**	**10,000**	**75,166**

Sire	Sale	Sex	Sold	$50,000 2 Year Olds	Success Rate	Average Price	Avg Earnings of $50,000 2 Year Olds
Art Major	HB	C	85	11	12.9%	37,582	170,769
	HB	F	77	7	9.1%	32,208	177,730
	LEX	C	45	10	22.2%	51,022	113,326
	LEX	F	37	9	24.3%	33,216	94,860
			244	**37**	**15.2%**	**37,703**	**138,097**
Artiscape	HB	C	35	0	0%	27,686	
	HB	F	29	0	0%	16,483	
	LEX	C	27	1	3.7%	29,852	111,279
	LEX	F	16	2	12.5%	14,125	168,185
			107	**3**	**2.8%**	**23,168**	**149,216**
Artsplace	HB	C	32	2	6.3%	29,047	436,950
	HB	F	23	2	8.7%	21,652	94,050
	LEX	C	16	0	0%	56,438	
	LEX	F	16	1	6.3%	25,875	133,301
			87	**5**	**5.7%**	**31,546**	**239,060**
Astreos	HB	C	4	1	25.0%	21,875	178,811
	HB	F	5	1	20.0%	20,000	89,443
	LEX	C	1	0	0%	150,000	
			10	**2**	**20.0%**	**33,750**	**134,127**
Badlands Hanover	HB	C	3	2	66.7%	58,333	84,842
	HB	F	1	0	0%	19,000	
	LEX	F	2	0	0%	12,500	
			6	**2**	**33.3%**	**36,500**	**84,842**
Bettor's Delight	HB	C	64	6	9.4%	39,094	212,283
	HB	F	65	6	9.2%	37,538	138,802
	LEX	C	36	6	16.7%	53,139	109,456
	LEX	F	32	3	9.4%	47,250	113,541
			197	**21**	**10.7%**	**42,472**	**147,803**
Blissful Hall	HB	C	1	0	0%	13,000	
	HB	F	2	0	0%	7,750	
	LEX	C	3	0	0%	19,333	
	LEX	F	2	0	0%	7,500	
			8	**0**	**0%**	**12,687**	
Broadway Hall	HB	C	40	2	5.0%	18,450	480,527
	HB	F	37	3	8.1%	17,181	167,597
	LEX	C	13	0	0%	33,000	
	LEX	F	15	1	6.7%	20,667	70,675
			105	**6**	**5.7%**	**20,121**	**255,753**

Sire	Sale	Sex	Sold	$50,000 2 Year Olds	Success Rate	Average Price	Avg Earnings of $50,000 2 Year Olds
Cambest	HB	C	5	0	0%	20,300	
	HB	F	2	0	0%	7,250	
	LEX	C	17	0	0%	18,235	
	LEX	F	17	1	5.9%	12,176	105,000
			41	**1**	**2.4%**	**15,439**	**105,000**
Camluck	HB	C	27	1	3.7%	48,222	271,793
	HB	F	27	1	3.7%	28,815	52,617
	LEX	C	14	1	7.1%	38,857	63,311
	LEX	F	6	0	0%	15,833	
			74	**3**	**4.1%**	**36,743**	**129,240**
Cam's Card Shark	HB	C	53	4	7.5%	31,340	284,791
	HB	F	24	2	8.3%	16,042	154,803
	LEX	C	15	2	13.3%	26,733	112,130
	LEX	F	14	0	0%	16,500	
			106	**8**	**7.5%**	**25,264**	**209,129**
Cantab Hall	HB	C	62	6	9.7%	27,548	116,323
	HB	F	56	5	8.9%	28,473	119,472
	LEX	C	42	3	7.3%	48,690	369,642
	LEX	F	43	3	7.0%	36,372	132,051
			203	**17**	**8.4%**	**34,047**	**164,728**
Cash Hall	HB	C	18	0	0%	19,444	
	HB	F	16	2	12.5%	16,469	66,722
	LEX	C	3	1	33.3%	25,000	65,757
	LEX	F	1	0	0%	10,000	
			38	**3**	**7.9%**	**18,382**	**66,400**
Chocolatier	HB	C	19	1	5.3%	39,974	61,517
	HB	F	17	0	0%	28,500	
	LEX	C	22	0	0%	52,773	
	LEX	F	25	0	0%	37,640	
			83	**1**	**1.2%**	**40,313**	**61,517**
Classic Photo	HB	C	19	2	10.5%	18,132	59,573
	HB	F	15	0	0%	11,967	
	LEX	C	37	3	8.1%	15,135	67,357
	LEX	F	28	1	3.6%	13,750	56,694
			99	**6**	**6.1%**	**14,838**	**62,985**

Sire	Sale	Sex	Sold	$50,000 2 Year Olds	Success Rate	Average Price	Avg Earnings of $50,000 2 Year Olds
Conway Hall	HB	C	51	3	5.9%	33,020	86,863
	HB	F	43	4	9.3%	28,070	128,228
	LEX	C	46	5	10.9%	39,826	111,228
	LEX	F	31	5	16.1%	31,516	76,103
			171	**17**	**9.9%**	**33,333**	**100,597**
CR Excalibur	**HB**	**F**	**1**	**0**	**0%**	**19,000**	
Credit Winner	HB	C	59	7	11.9%	64,983	98,172
	HB	F	55	5	9.1%	37,009	79,866
	LEX	C	50	4	8.0%	68,660	156,308
	LEX	F	45	5	11.1%	54,733	152,968
			209	**21**	**10.0%**	**56,294**	**117,934**
Daguet Rapide	HB	C	1	0	0%	40,000	
	HB	F	1	0	0%	11,000	
	LEX	C	2	0	0%	21,000	
	LEX	F	2	1	50.0%	37,500	91,740
			6	**1**	**16.7%**	**28,000**	**91,740**
Donato Hanover	HB	C	26	3	11.5%	60,385	336,473
	HB	F	22	1	4.5%	43,773	76,574
	LEX	C	20	1	5.0%	74,200	84,300
	LEX	F	13	2	15.4%	61,923	71,150
			81	**7**	**8.6%**	**59,531**	**187,513**
Donerail	HB	F	5	0	0%	12,300	
	LEX	C	1	0	0%	8,000	
	LEX	F	2	0	0%	10,000	
			8	**0**	**0%**	**11,188**	
Dragon Again	HB	C	97	7	7.2%	35,299	113,848
	HB	F	78	1	1.3%	23,688	81,443
	LEX	C	22	3	13.6%	41,045	265,055
	LEX	F	26	1	3.8%	27,038	108,228
			223	**12**	**5.4%**	**30,842**	**148,481**
Dream Vacation	HB	C	3	0	0%	13,333	
	LEX	C	8	0	0%	11,250	
	LEX	F	11	1	9.1%	29,091	97,334
			22	**1**	**4.5%**	**20,455**	**97,334**
E Dee's Cam	HB	C	3	0	0%	15,667	
	HB	F	2	1	50.0%	12,000	143,344
			5	**1**	**20.0%**	**14,200**	**143,344**

Sire	Sale	Sex	Sold	$50,000 2 Year Olds	Success Rate	Average Price	Avg Earnings of $50,000 2 Year Olds
Equinox Bi	HB	C	2	0	0%	41,000	
	LEX	C	2	0	0%	15,500	
			4	**0**	**0%**	**28,250**	
Four Starzzz Shark	HB	C	16	2	12.5%	18,500	85,753
	HB	F	15	2	13.3%	20,500	165,779
	LEX	C	12	2	16.7%	41,417	121,184
	LEX	F	19	0	0%	19,947	
			62	**6**	**9.7%**	**23,863**	**124,238**
Glidemaster	HB	C	25	2	8.0%	38,340	298,298
	HB	F	19	0	0%	22,711	
	LEX	C	17	0	0%	50,294	
	LEX	F	23	1	4.3%	42,348	155,594
			84	**3**	**3.6%**	**38,321**	**250,730**
Grinfromeartoear	LEX	C	2	0	0%	16,500	
	LEX	F	2	0	0%	8,000	
			4	**0**	**0%**	**12,250**	
Here Comes Herbie	HB	C	1	0	0%	35,000	
	HB	F	4	0	0%	59,750	
	LEX	C	1	0	0%	31,000	
			6	**0**	**0%**	**50,833**	
I Am A Fool	HB	C	13	1	7.7%	10,808	52,667
	HB	F	9	0	0%	4,722	
	LEX	C	28	0	0%	12,250	
	LEX	F	18	0	0%	14,167	
			68	**1**	**1.5%**	**11,485**	**52,667**
Jate Lobell	LEX	C	6	0	0%	19,667	
	LEX	F	4	0	0%	18,250	
			10	**0**	**0%**	**19,100**	
Jenna's Beach Boy	HB	C	1	0	0%	20,000	
	HB	F	1	0	0%	11,500	
	LEX	C	8	1	12.5%	20,625	91,981
	LEX	F	6	0	0%	19,333	
			16	**1**	**6.3%**	**19,531**	**91,981**
Jereme's Jet	HB	C	8	0	0%	59,375	
	HB	F	8	2	25.0%	51,625	205,021
	LEX	F	3	0	0%	36,000	
			19	**2**	**10.5%**	**52,421**	**205,021**

Sire	Sale	Sex	Sold	$50,000 2 Year Olds	Success Rate	Average Price	Avg Earnings of $50,000 2 Year Olds
Justice Hall	LEX	C	1	0	0%	1,000	
	LEX	F	1	0	0%	1,000	
			2	**0**	**0%**	**1,000**	
Kadabra	HB	C	23	3	13.0%	30,522	183,299
	HB	F	33	2	6.1%	28,242	550,246
	LEX	C	10	0	0%	45,000	
	LEX	F	7	1	14.3%	58,571	480,234
			73	**6**	**8.2%**	**34,164**	**355,104**
Ken Warkentin	HB	C	6	0	0%	24,667	
	HB	F	5	2	40.0%	41,600	96,359
	LEX	C	8	1	12.5%	51,500	83,858
	LEX	F	7	0	0%	20,143	
			26	**3**	**11.5%**	**34,962**	**92,192**
Like A Prayer	HB	C	1	0	0%	22,000	
	HB	F	1	0	0%	3,000	
	LEX	C	19	3	15.8%	13,000	133,740
	LEX	F	12	1	8.3%	10,833	60,444
			33	**4**	**12.1%**	**12,182**	**115,416**
Lis Mara	HB	C	7	0	0%	14,929	
	HB	F	12	0	0%	11,500	
	LEX	C	8	0	0%	14,875	
	LEX	F	5	0	0%	10,400	
			32	**0**	**0%**	**12,922**	
Mach Three	HB	C	17	1	5.9%	33,706	52,575
	HB	F	16	2	12.5%	22,156	150,120
	LEX	C	4	1	25.0%	22,750	124,365
	LEX	F	4	0	0%	72,250	
			41	**4**	**9.8%**	**31,890**	**119,295**
Majestic Son	HB	C	10	0	0%	20,250	
	HB	F	11	0	0%	14,318	
	LEX	C	1	0	0%	110,000	
			22	**0**	**0%**	**21,364**	
Malabar Man	HB	C	5	2	40.0%	32,000	78,279
	HB	F	5	0	0%	24,800	
	LEX	C	10	1	10.0%	21,400	63,575
	LEX	F	3	0	0%	10,667	
			23	**3**	**13.0%**	**23,043**	**73,378**
Malabar Maple	LEX	C	1	0	0%	55,000	

Sire	Sale	Sex	Sold	$50,000 2 Year Olds	Success Rate	Average Price	Avg Earnings of $50,000 2 Year Olds
Master Glide	LEX	C	6	0	0%	7,167	
	LEX	F	5	0	0%	12,200	
			11	**0**	**0%**	**9,455**	
Mcardle	HB	C	22	2	9.1%	18,341	58,178
	HB	F	24	1	4.2%	13,521	240,904
	LEX	C	15	1	6.7%	26,400	69,967
	LEX	F	12	2	16.7%	26,083	200,861
			73	**6**	**8.2%**	**19,685**	**138,158**
Metropolitan	HB	C	2	0	0%	6,000	
	LEX	C	5	0	0%	17,800	
	HB	F	2	0	0%	6,000	
	LEX	C	5	0	0%	26,800	
			14	**0**	**0%**	**17,643**	
Modern Art	HB	C	10	1	10.0%	18,900	87,551
	HB	F	6	0	0%	13,833	
	LEX	C	2	0	0%	25,000	
	LEX	F	3	0	0%	13,000	
			21	**1**	**4.8%**	**17,190**	**87,551**
Mr Feelgood	LEX	C	4	0	0%	20,750	
	LEX	F	4	0	0%	5,250	
			8	**0**	**0%**	**13,000**	
Mr Lavec	HB	F	1	0	0%	4,500	
	LEX	C	1	0	0%	60,000	
			2	**0**	**0%**		
Muscles Yankee	HB	C	53	6	11.3%	60,075	133,358
	HB	F	73	6	8.2%	30,479	298,723
	LEX	C	34	0	0%	70,059	
	LEX	F	38	1	2.6%	43,842	115,449
			198	**13**	**6.6%**	**47,763**	**208,303**
No Pan Intended	HB	C	9	0	0%	12,611	
	HB	F	8	0	0%	13,500	
	LEX	C	4	1	25.0%	6,500	53,178
	LEX	F	3	0	0%	6,000	
			24	**1**	**4.2%**	**11,062**	**53,178**
Pacific Fella	LEX	C	1	0	0%	13,000	
Peruvian Hanover	HB	F	1	0	0%	3,000	
Plesac	HB	C	1	0	0%	23,000	

Sire	Sale	Sex	Sold	$50,000 2 Year Olds	Success Rate	Average Price	Avg Earnings of $50,000 2 Year Olds
Ponder	HB	C	12	1	8.3%	19,917	214,058
	HB	F	5	0	0%	16,000	
	LEX	C	17	1	5.9%	18,000	191,073
	LEX	F	6	1	16.7%	16,667	164,705
			40	**3**	**7.5%**	**18,125**	**189,945**
Pro Bono Best	**HB**	**F**	**2**	**0**	**0%**	**18,250**	
Quik Pulse Mindale	HB	C	6	0	0%	26,167	
	HB	F	4	1	25.0%	15,000	128,875
	LEX	C	4	0	0%	24,250	
	LEX	F	2	0	0%	15,000	
			16	**1**	**6.3%**	**21,500**	**128,875**
Real Artist	HB	C	13	1	7.7%	14,308	116,333
	HB	F	16	0	0%	20,406	
	LEX	C	9	1	11.1%	23,111	72,422
	LEX	F	7	0	0.00%	12,286	
			45	**2**	**4.4%**	**17,922**	**94,378**
Real Desire	HB	C	25	0	0%	17,200	
	HB	F	19	2	10.5%	13,737	103,916
	LEX	C	30	3	10.0%	28,367	216,617
	LEX	F	26	2	7.7%	22,269	57,230
			100	**7**	**7.0%**	**21,210**	**138,877**
Red River Hanover	HB	C	4	0	0%	11,000	
	HB	F	11	0	0%	6,045	
	LEX	C	2	0	0%	2,500	
	LEX	F	10	0	0%	8,600	
			27	**0**	**0%**	**7,463**	
Revenue S	HB	C	17	1	5.9%	13,882	104,532
	HB	F	17	0	0%	18,353	
	LEX	C	10	0	0%	11,700	
	LEX	F	4	0	0%	20,000	
			48	**1**	**2.1%**	**15,521**	**104,532**
Riverboat King	HB	C	2	0	0%	15,500	
	HB	F	2	0	0%	11,500	
	LEX	C	1	0	0%	30,000	
			5	**0**	**0%**	**16,800**	

Sire	Sale	Sex	Sold	$50,000 2 Year Olds	Success Rate	Average Price	Avg Earnings of $50,000 2 Year Olds
Rocknroll Hanover	HB	C	108	8	7.4%	53,435	212,684
	HB	F	81	3	3.7%	45,519	185,668
	LEX	C	80	8	10.0%	60,700	269,147
	LEX	F	61	7	11.5%	51,279	199,314
			330	**26**	**7.9%**	**52,855**	**223,340**
Royal Mattjesty	HB	C	8	0	0%	33,500	
	HB	F	4	0	0%	22,250	
	LEX	C	4	0	0%	19,750	
	LEX	F	2	0	0%	21,500	
			18	**0**	**0%**	**26,611**	
Rustler Hanover	LEX	C	1	0	0%	17,000	
SJ's Photo	HB	C	3	0	0%	20,667	
	HB	F	2	0	0%	60,000	
	LEX	C	10	0	0%	20,400	
	LEX	F	2	0	0%	10,500	
			17	**0**	**0%**	**23,941**	
Sand Vic	HB	C	1	0	0%	11,000	
	HB	F	2	0	0%	22,500	
	LEX	C	2	0	0%	8,500	
	LEX	F	1	0	0%	12,000	
			6	**0**	**0%**	**14,167**	
Shark Gesture	HB	C	4	0	0%	28,750	
	LEX	C	3	1	33.3%	48,333	78,029
			7	**1**	**14.3%**	**37,143**	**78,029**
SJ's Caviar	HB	C	52	1	1.9%	16,173	55,527
	HB	F	38	0	0%	19,421	
	LEX	C	16	1	6.3%	22,125	210,581
	LEX	F	12	0	0%	21,333	
			118	**2**	**1.7%**	**18,551**	**133,054**
Stonebridge Regal	HB	C	1	0	0%	67,000	
	LEX	C	4	0	0%	7,000	
	LEX	F	1	0	0%	9,000	
			6	**0**	**0%**	**17,333**	
Striking Sahbra	HB	C	9	1	11.1%	32,500	63,379
	HB	F	11	1	9.1%	31,364	289,068
	LEX	C	13	1	7.7%	34,154	155,106
	LEX	F	6	0	0%	15,333	
			39	**3**	**7.7%**	**30,090**	**169,184**

Sire	Sale	Sex	Sold	$50,000 2 Year Olds	Success Rate	Average Price	Avg Earnings of $50,000 2 Year Olds
Tagliabue	HB	C	1	0	0%	12,000	
	HB	F	3	1	33.3%	17,667	114,436
			4	**1**	**25.0%**	**16,250**	**114,436**
Taurus Dream	**HB**	**F**	**2**	**1**	**50.0%**	**34,500**	**584,392**
Tell All	HB	C	15	0	0%	11,933	
	HB	F	10	0	0%	3,800	
	LEX	C	13	1	7.7%	19,154	50,132
	LEX	F	16	0	0%	6,563	
			54	**1**	**1.9%**	**10,574**	**50,132**
The Panderosa	HB	C	58	2	3.4%	24,379	119,940
	HB	F	50	2	4.0%	17,650	63,940
	LEX	C	16	1	6.3%	29,063	84,962
	LEX	F	16	0	0%	16,313	
			140	**5**	**3.6%**	**21,589**	**90,544**
Tom Ridge	HB	C	31	2	6.5%	17,645	93,203
	HB	F	25	4	16.0%	14,380	75,381
	LEX	C	13	3	23.1%	24,462	110,295
	LEX	F	6	1	16.7%	12,667	82,656
			75	**10**	**13.3%**	**17,340**	**90,147**
Totally Western	**HB**	**C**	**1**	**0**	**0%**	**4,000**	
Valley Victor	HB	C	4	0	0%	28,250	
	HB	F	3	0	0%	19,333	
	LEX	C	39	5	12.8%	18,641	82,514
	LEX	F	43	3	7.0%	15,047	75,482
			89	**8**	**9.0%**	**17,360**	**79,877**
Varenne	HB	C	1	0	0%	2,500	
	LEX	C	1	0	0%	29,000	
			2	**0**	**0%**	**15,750**	
Village Jolt	HB	C	36	0	0%	20,250	
	HB	F	25	0	0%	12,160	
	LEX	C	9	0	0%	20,889	
	LEX	F	6	0	0%	12,333	
			76	**0**	**0%**	**17,039**	
Western Hanover	HB	C	67	6	9.0%	38,761	68,201
	HB	F	61	5	8.2%	25,254	138,306
	LEX	C	23	2	8.7%	62,565	139,216
	LEX	F	23	4	17.4%	40,304	248,258
			174	**17**	**9.8%**	**37,376**	**139,541**

Sire	Sale	Sex	Sold	$50,000 2 Year Olds	Success Rate	Average Price	Avg Earnings of $50,000 2 Year Olds
Western Ideal	HB	C	61	1	1.6%	35,590	827,204
	HB	F	53	5	9.4%	36,443	225,549
	LEX	C	38	4	10.5%	50,526	99,273
	LEX	F	33	6	18.2%	36,212	112,038
			185	**16**	**8.6%**	**39,014**	**189,017**
Western Terror	HB	C	14	0	0%	34,536	
	HB	F	18	1	5.6%	26,361	296,156
	LEX	C	41	1	2.4%	41,488	66,723
	LEX	F	43	2	4.7%	22,047	63,562
			116	**4**	**3.4%**	**31,095**	**122,501**
Windsong's Legacy	HB	C	33	3	9.1%	24,864	319,815
	HB	F	37	1	2.7%	32,568	335,250
	LEX	C	18	0	0%	20,611	
	LEX	F	18	0	0%	26,611	
			106	**4**	**3.8%**	**27,127**	**323,674**
Yankee Cruiser	HB	C	14	1	7.1%	20,179	686,647
	HB	F	8	2	25.0%	11,000	78,575
	LEX	C	8	0	0%	18,375	
	LEX	F	9	2	22.2%	9,667	111,507
			39	**5**	**12.8%**	**15,500**	**213,362**
Yankee Glide	HB	C	37	1	2.7%	28,108	185,081
	HB	F	27	6	22.2%	41,130	131,515
	LEX	C	89	7	7.9%	41,213	247,854
	LEX	F	72	2	2.8%	53,222	63,619
			225	**16**	**7.1%**	**42,891**	**177,274**
Grand Total	**HB/LEX**		**5685**	**406**	**7.1%**	**32,698**	**$154,323**

Now let's look at Sire Performance through the prism of consignors and farms.

For the buyer looking for low to moderate yearlings, it is especially difficult. We've seen that the lower price ranges have had low Success Rates. However, here are a few gems that can be found when sifting through the next chart. *Allamerican Native* has an overall success rate of 5.6% (4 out of 71). His fillies are better at 7.3% (3 out of 41). If we break down these numbers by sale venue, we find that *Allamerican Native* is 3 out of 30, or 10.0%, with fillies sold at Harrisburg. If we look further, we see that all three fillies were sold by Hanover out of a consignment of only 17. The Success Rate for *Allamerican Native* fillies, sold by Hanover at Harrisburg, was 17.6%, or 1 in 5.7. That's 146% better than average. Even though *Allamerican Native* has been moved to Ontario, hopefully some will be offered at HB.

We've already discovered that *Dragon Again* has had a much better Success Rate with his colts. He's 10 out of 119 for 8.4% or 1 in 11.9. However, *Dragon Again* colts sold by Vieux Carre Farms are 3 out of 13 for a 23.1% Success Rate (1 in 4.33). The average price of the three *Dragon Again* elite colts was a modest $27,667. They attained average earnings of $142,746.

Another moderately priced sire has been *Mcardle*. He's had 6 elite two-year olds from 73 yearlings sold at HB and LEX. That's an 8.2% Success Rate. Getting into the numbers we find that Perretti Farms has sold 5 of the 6 elite performers out of a consignment of 28. Perretti's *Mcardle* yearlings have had a 17.9% Success Rate (1 in 5.6). The five elites averaged $154,452 in earnings while selling for an average of $25,400.

We've discussed *Art Major's* excellent Success Rate at both HB and LEX. Kentuckiana has sold 5 elite *Art Major* youngsters out of only 13 for a spectacular 38.5% Success Rate, or 1 in 2.6. Winbak has also been a good source for Art Major yearlings. They have sold 3 elite two-year olds out of 10 for a 30% Success Rate.

Earlier in this chapter we discussed *Muscles Yankee's* 6 elite colts at Harrisburg. Looking at the following chart, you will notice that 4 of those 6 elite colts were sold by Peninsula Farm. Their total consignment at Harrisburg from 2008–2010 consisted of 9 *Muscles Yankee* colts. Thus, Peninsula was 4 out of 9 for an amazing 44.4% Success Rate. Note that three colts were raised at Peninsula Farm and one was raised at Three Crow Farm.

If you're shopping for a *Credit Winner* you may want to review Diamond Creek's consignment. They have sold 3 elite Credit *Winners* out of only 9 for a 33.3% Success Rate.

New Sire *American Ideal* has had 10 elite performers from 105 sold for a 9.5% Success Rate. *American Ideal* yearlings emanating from Hunterton have had 3 elites out of 11 for a 27.3% Success Rate or 1 in 3.7.

White Birch has the exact same record (3 out of 11) with *American Ideal's* Sire, *Western Ideal* and with New York Sire *Bettor's Delight*.

Sire and farm relationships can be an important angle to review in the purchasing process. Looking at Chart 3 we can identify both the potent sire-farm combinations and, just as important, the unproductive ones by gender and Sale Venue. Note: the column labeled "Avg $ Won" refers to the amount earned by $50,000 two-year olds only.

Chart 3: Sire Performance By Consignor and Farm

Consignor: Farm or auspices which offered the horse for sale. Farm: Per catalog–the place where the horse was raised

Sire	Consignor	Farm	Sex	Sold	$50,000 2 YOs	Sale	Avg Price	Avg $ Won
Allamerican Ingot	Cameo Hills	Blue Ridge	C	1	0	LEX	$4,000	
Allamerican Ingot	Hunterton	Hunterton	F	1	0	LEX	11,000	
Allamerican Ingot	Kentuckiana	Kentuckiana	C	10	0	LEX	11,300	

Sire	Consignor	Farm	Sex	Sold	$50,000 2 YOs	Sale	Avg Price	Avg $ Won
Allamerican Ingot	Kentuckiana	Kentuckiana	F	4	0	LEX	9,250	
Allamerican Ingot	Preferred	Emerald Highlands	C	1	0	LEX	7,000	
Allamerican Ingot	Preferred	Emerald Highlands	F	1	0	LEX	10,000	
Allamerican Ingot	Saga	Blue Ridge	C	1	0	LEX	7,000	
Allamerican Ingot	Saga	Victory Hill	C	5	0	LEX	11,000	
Allamerican Ingot	Saga	Victory Hill	F	3	0	LEX	6,667	
Allamerican Ingot	Winbak	Winbak	F	1	0	LEX	9,000	
Allamerican Ingot				**28**	**0**			
Allamerican Native	Allamerican	Allamerican	F	1	0	HB	9,000	
Allamerican Native	Boxwood	Boxwood	C	1	0	HB	8,000	
Allamerican Native	Boxwood	Shadowbrook	C	1	0	HB	5,500	
Allamerican Native	Cameo Hills	Blue Ridge	C	1	0	LEX	2,000	
Allamerican Native	Diamond Creek	Diamond Creek	F	1	0	LEX	47,000	
Allamerican Native	Fox Den	Stoltzfus	C	1	0	HB	25,000	
Allamerican Native	Hanover	Hanover	C	7	0	HB	19,643	
Allamerican Native	Hanover	Hanover	F	17	3	HB	19,971	132,143
Allamerican Native	Hempt	Barefoot	F	1	0	HB	14,000	
Allamerican Native	Hunterton	Lebo	C	1	0	HB	14,000	
Allamerican Native	Kentuckiana	Kentuckiana	C	4	1	LEX	16,500	91,977
Allamerican Native	Kentuckiana	Kentuckiana	F	2	0	LEX	24,000	
Allamerican Native	Northstar	Northstar	F	1	0	HB	7,000	
Allamerican Native	Northwood	Nandi	C	2	0	HB	4,500	
Allamerican Native	Peninsula	Lindwood	F	1	0	HB	9,000	
Allamerican Native	Saga	Victory Hill	F	3	0	LEX	6,333	
Allamerican Native	Spring Haven	Lmn Bred	F	1	0	LEX	2,000	
Allamerican Native	Spring Haven	Rails Edge	F	2	0	LEX	12,000	
Allamerican Native	Spring Haven	Spring Haven	F	1	0	LEX	32,000	
Allamerican Native	Twinbrook	Archie Downey	C	1	0	HB	6,000	
Allamerican Native	Vieux Carre	Vieux Carre	C	3	0	HB	2,000	
Allamerican Native	Vieux Carre	Vieux Carre	F	4	0	HB	25,500	
Allamerican Native	Winbak	Winbak	C	6	0	HB	10,083	
Allamerican Native	Winbak	Winbak	F	3	0	HB	12,333	
Allamerican Native	Winbak	Winbak	C	1	0	LEX	2,000	
Allamerican Native	Winbak	Winbak	F	1	0	LEX	3,000	
Allamerican Native	Winterwood	Cashelmara	C	1	0	HB	20,000	
Allamerican Native	Winterwood	Cashelmara	F	1	0	HB	6,500	
Allamerican Native	Winterwood	Morrowland	F	1	0	HB	9,000	

Sire	Consignor	Farm	Sex	Sold	$50,000 2 YOs	Sale	Avg Price	Avg $ Won
Allamerican Native				71	4			
Allstar Hall	Kentuckiana	Kentuckiana	C	1	0	LEX	8,000	
American Ideal	Blue Chip	Blue Chip	C	11	2	HB	38,955	216,695
American Ideal	Blue Chip	Blue Chip	F	6	0	HB	19,917	
American Ideal	Blue Chip	Blue Chip	C	2	0	LEX	45,000	
American Ideal	Boxwood	Shadowbrook	C	3	0	HB	55,667	
American Ideal	Boxwood	Shadowbrook	F	1	1	HB	45,000	78,057
American Ideal	Brittany	Brittany	C	5	1	LEX	82,400	189,253
American Ideal	Brittany	Brittany	F	2	0	LEX	18,500	
American Ideal	Cameo Hills	Cameo Hills	C	1	0	LEX	85,000	
American Ideal	Cameo Hills	Cameo Hills	F	2	0	LEX	20,000	
American Ideal	Cameo Hills	Forty Hill	F	1	0	LEX	15,000	
American Ideal	Concord	Concord	C	2	0	HB	21,000	
American Ideal	Concord	Concord	F	2	0	HB	66,000	
American Ideal	Fair Winds	Fair Winds	C	1	0	HB	35,000	
American Ideal	Fair Winds	Fair Winds	F	1	0	HB	32,000	
American Ideal	Fox Den	Stoltzfus	F	1	0	HB	7,500	
American Ideal	Hanover	Hanover	C	3	0	HB	46,333	
American Ideal	Hunterton	Brittany	C	1	0	HB	17,000	
American Ideal	Hunterton	Ernie Martinez	C	1	0	LEX	9,000	
American Ideal	Hunterton	High Stakes	F	1	0	HB	40,000	
American Ideal	Hunterton	Hunterton	C	4	1	HB	16,500	53,188
American Ideal	Hunterton	Hunterton	F	2	0	HB	23,000	
American Ideal	Hunterton	Hunterton	F	5	2	LEX	25,600	465,101
American Ideal	Hunterton	Martinez Equine	C	1	0	HB	10,000	
American Ideal	Hunterton	Sunrise	F	1	0	LEX	15,000	
American Ideal	Kentuckiana	Kentuckiana	C	2	0	LEX	18,000	
American Ideal	Kentuckiana	Kentuckiana	F	4	0	LEX	20,250	
American Ideal	Northwood	Andray	C	1	1	HB	42,000	58,108
American Ideal	Northwood	Bluestone	F	1	0	LEX	10,000	
American Ideal	Northwood	Century Spring	C	1	1	HB	15,000	119,182
American Ideal	Northwood	Snowball Hill	F	1	0	HB	12,000	
American Ideal	Peninsula	Equine Center	F	1	0	LEX	7,000	
American Ideal	Peninsula	Holly Gate	C	1	0	HB	15,000	
American Ideal	Perretti	Perretti	C	1	0	LEX	22,000	
American Ideal	Preferred	Brittany	C	1	0	HB	26,000	
American Ideal	Preferred	Dr. Robert Milkey's	C	1	0	HB	10,000	

Sire	Consignor	Farm	Sex	Sold	$50,000 2 YOs	Sale	Avg Price	Avg $ Won
American Ideal	Preferred	Lindy	C	1	0	HB	4,000	
American Ideal	Preferred	Lindy	F	1	0	HB	11,000	
American Ideal	Preferred	Lindy	C	1	0	LEX	32,000	
American Ideal	Preferred	Millcreek	F	1	0	HB	6,000	
American Ideal	Preferred	Morrison	C	1	0	HB	55,000	
American Ideal	Preferred	Southwind	C	1	0	HB	21,000	
American Ideal	Preferred	Southwind	F	1	0	LEX	30,000	
American Ideal	Preferred	Warrawee	C	1	0	HB	50,000	
American Ideal	Preferred	Warrawee	F	1	0	HB	9,000	
American Ideal	Preferred	White Birch	F	4	0	HB	15,750	
American Ideal	Preferred	White Birch	C	1	0	LEX	60,000	
American Ideal	Spring Haven	Lmn Bred	C	1	0	LEX	9,000	
American Ideal	Spring Haven	Mindale	C	1	0	LEX	18,000	
American Ideal	Steiner Stock	Steiner Stock	C	1	0	LEX	50,000	
American Ideal	Stonegate	Stonegate	C	2	0	HB	13,500	
American Ideal	Stonegate	Stonegate	F	1	0	HB	3,000	
American Ideal	Twinbrook	Twinbrook	C	1	0	HB	13,000	
American Ideal	Walnridge	Walnridge	C	1	0	HB	9,000	
American Ideal	Walnut Hall Ltd	Walnut Hall Ltd	F	1	0	HB	2,500	
American Ideal	Winbak	Winbak	C	3	1	HB	28,667	56,949
American Ideal	Winbak	Winbak	F	2	0	HB	30,750	
American Ideal	Winbak	Winbak	F	1	0	LEX	15,000	
American Ideal	Winterwood	Winterwood	F	1	0	HB	8,000	
American Ideal				**105**	**10**			
American Winner	Saga	Saga	F	1	0	LEX	26,000	
Amigo Hall	Brittany	Brittany	C	1	0	LEX	37,000	
Amigo Hall	Hunterton	Crawford	F	1	0	HB	12,000	
Amigo Hall	Hunterton	Crawford	C	1	0	LEX	12,000	
Amigo Hall	Hunterton	Hunterton	C	1	0	HB	30,000	
Amigo Hall	Hunterton	Hunterton	F	3	0	HB	22,000	
Amigo Hall	Hunterton	Hunterton	C	1	0	LEX	22,000	
Amigo Hall	Hunterton	Hunterton	F	1	0	LEX	6,000	
Amigo Hall	Walnut Hall Stock	Walnut Hall Stock	C	1	0	LEX	12,000	
Amigo Hall				**10**	**0**			
Andover Hall	Blue Chip	Blue Chip	C	1	0	HB	130,000	
Andover Hall	Blue Chip	Blue Chip	F	4	0	HB	49,250	
Andover Hall	Blue Chip	Blue Chip	F	1	1	LEX	105,000	54,607

Sire	Consignor	Farm	Sex	Sold	$50,000 2 YOs	Sale	Avg Price	Avg $ Won
Andover Hall	Cane Run	Cane Run	C	1	0	LEX	60,000	
Andover Hall	Concord	Concord	C	4	0	HB	56,000	
Andover Hall	Concord	Concord	F	1	0	HB	22,000	
Andover Hall	Concord	Hanover	C	4	1	HB	67,750	98,250
Andover Hall	Concord	Hanover	F	1	1	HB	37,000	65,257
Andover Hall	Diamond Creek	Diamond Creek	C	3	1	HB	34,667	114,682
Andover Hall	Diamond Creek	Diamond Creek	F	5	0	HB	75,000	
Andover Hall	Diamond Creek	Diamond Creek	C	4	2	LEX	77,750	122,174
Andover Hall	Diamond Creek	Diamond Creek	F	3	0	LEX	146,667	
Andover Hall	Fair Winds	Fair Winds	C	2	0	HB	51,000	
Andover Hall	Fox Den	Avonlea	F	1	0	HB	10,000	
Andover Hall	Fox Den	Three Cedars	C	1	0	HB	14,000	
Andover Hall	Hanover	Hanover	C	26	2	HB	49,692	158,559
Andover Hall	Hanover	Hanover	F	27	5	HB	43,944	125,531
Andover Hall	Hanover	Hanover	C	2	0	LEX	86,000	
Andover Hall	Hanover	Hanover	F	2	0	LEX	30,000	
Andover Hall	Hempt	Hempt	C	1	1	HB	12,000	50,057
Andover Hall	Hunterton	Glassford Equine	F	1	0	LEX	30,000	
Andover Hall	Hunterton	Hunterton	F	1	0	HB	12,000	
Andover Hall	Hunterton	Hunterton	C	1	0	LEX	17,000	
Andover Hall	Hunterton	Hunterton	F	1	0	LEX	200,000	
Andover Hall	Hunterton	Venture	F	1	0	LEX	15,000	
Andover Hall	Hunterton	Walco	C	6	2	LEX	71,667	82,686
Andover Hall	Hunterton	Walco	F	3	0	LEX	51,667	
Andover Hall	Kentuckiana	Kentuckiana	C	6	0	LEX	27,833	
Andover Hall	Kentuckiana	Kentuckiana	F	1	0	LEX	65,000	
Andover Hall	Northwood	Allerage	C	1	0	LEX	30,000	
Andover Hall	Northwood	Allerage	F	2	1	LEX	36,000	188,788
Andover Hall	Northwood	Bluestone	C	2	0	LEX	48,000	
Andover Hall	Northwood	Deo Volente	F	1	0	HB	9,500	
Andover Hall	Northwood	Jonalee	C	2	0	HB	13,500	
Andover Hall	Northwood	Jonalee	F	1	0	HB	15,000	
Andover Hall	Northwood	White Hollow	C	1	0	HB	4,500	
Andover Hall	Northwood	White Hollow	F	1	1	HB	18,000	72,989
Andover Hall	Peninsula	Cool Creek	F	1	0	LEX	70,000	
Andover Hall	Peninsula	Deo Volente	C	1	0	HB	10,000	
Andover Hall	Peninsula	Peninsula	C	12	0	HB	90,750	

Sire	Consignor	Farm	Sex	Sold	$50,000 2 YOs	Sale	Avg Price	Avg $ Won
Andover Hall	Peninsula	Peninsula	F	7	1	HB	109,714	201,632
Andover Hall	Peninsula	Peninsula	C	9	1	LEX	52,333	130,133
Andover Hall	Peninsula	Peninsula	F	1	0	LEX	17,000	
Andover Hall	Peninsula	Pheasant Hill	C	1	0	LEX	80,000	
Andover Hall	Peninsula	Pin Oak Lane	F	1	0	LEX	25,000	
Andover Hall	Peninsula	Quad	C	2	0	HB	52,000	
Andover Hall	Peninsula	Quantum	C	1	0	HB	5,000	
Andover Hall	Peninsula	Quantum	C	1	0	LEX	20,000	
Andover Hall	Peninsula	Wizard Heights	C	2	0	LEX	40,000	
Andover Hall	Peninsula	Wizard Heights	F	1	0	LEX	23,000	
Andover Hall	Perretti	Perretti	C	1	0	HB	120,000	
Andover Hall	Preferred	Anderson	C	2	0	LEX	108,500	
Andover Hall	Preferred	Anderson	F	3	1	LEX	80,667	187,438
Andover Hall	Preferred	Bennett	C	1	0	LEX	30,000	
Andover Hall	Preferred	D Farm	C	2	0	LEX	35,000	
Andover Hall	Preferred	D Farm	F	4	0	LEX	78,000	
Andover Hall	Preferred	David Miller's	C	1	0	HB	50,000	
Andover Hall	Preferred	Don Lamontagne	F	1	0	LEX	67,000	
Andover Hall	Preferred	Dumain Haven	C	1	1	HB	57,000	120,289
Andover Hall	Preferred	Fair Winds	C	1	0	LEX	87,000	
Andover Hall	Preferred	Joie De Vie	C	1	0	LEX	40,000	
Andover Hall	Preferred	Lindy	F	1	0	LEX	50,000	
Andover Hall	Preferred	Southwind	F	2	1	LEX	19,000	89,710
Andover Hall	Preferred	Stonehenge	C	1	0	LEX	17,000	
Andover Hall	Preferred	Tara Hills	F	1	0	HB	35,000	
Andover Hall	Preferred	White Birch	C	1	0	HB	14,000	
Andover Hall	Spring Haven	Cool Creek	F	1	0	LEX	48,000	
Andover Hall	Spring Haven	FJD	C	2	0	LEX	18,000	
Andover Hall	Spring Haven	FJD	F	1	0	LEX	45,000	
Andover Hall	Spring Haven	Hickory Lane	C	1	0	LEX	12,000	
Andover Hall	Stonegate	Stonegate	C	1	0	HB	6,000	
Andover Hall	Vieux Carre	Vieux Carre	C	6	1	HB	37,000	130,371
Andover Hall	Vieux Carre	Vieux Carre	F	3	0	HB	28,000	
Andover Hall	Walnridge	Photo Mountain	F	1	0	HB	90,000	
Andover Hall	Walnut Hall Stock	Walnut Hall Stock	C	1	0	LEX	52,000	
Andover Hall	Winbak	Winbak	F	2	0	LEX	70,000	
Andover Hall	Winterwood	Winterwood	C	1	0	HB	27,000	

Sire	Consignor	Farm	Sex	Sold	$50,000 2 YOs	Sale	Avg Price	Avg $ Won
Andover Hall				210	24			
Angus Hall	Allamerican	Allamerican	F	2	0	HB	21,750	
Angus Hall	Boxwood	Boxwood	F	1	0	HB	32,000	
Angus Hall	Brittany	Brittany	C	1	0	LEX	15,000	
Angus Hall	Brittany	Brittany	F	4	0	LEX	26,750	
Angus Hall	Cameo Hills	Cameo Hills	F	1	0	LEX	17,000	
Angus Hall	Cane Run	Cane Run	C	1	0	LEX	11,000	
Angus Hall	Concord	Concord	C	1	0	HB	30,000	
Angus Hall	Concord	Concord	F	1	0	HB	55,000	
Angus Hall	Diamond Creek	Diamond Creek	C	1	0	LEX	30,000	
Angus Hall	Dunroven	Dunroven	C	1	0	LEX	35,000	
Angus Hall	Dunroven	Dunroven	F	1	0	LEX	20,000	
Angus Hall	Fox Den	Avonlea	F	1	0	HB	10,000	
Angus Hall	Hanover	Hanover	C	3	0	HB	29,667	
Angus Hall	Hanover	Hanover	F	5	0	HB	32,400	
Angus Hall	Hempt	Hempt	C	4	1	HB	15,000	136,013
Angus Hall	Hempt	Hempt	F	3	0	HB	25,667	
Angus Hall	Hunterton	Brittany	C	1	0	HB	50,000	
Angus Hall	Hunterton	Hunterton	C	1	0	HB	10,000	
Angus Hall	Hunterton	Hunterton	C	1	0	LEX	65,000	
Angus Hall	Hunterton	Hunterton	F	1	0	LEX	35,000	
Angus Hall	Hunterton	Walco	F	1	0	LEX	10,000	
Angus Hall	Kentuckiana	Kentuckiana	C	1	0	LEX	11,000	
Angus Hall	Kentuckiana	Kentuckiana	F	2	0	LEX	41,000	
Angus Hall	Kentuckiana	Wilt Standardbreds	C	1	1	LEX	37,000	190,174
Angus Hall	Midland Acres	Midland Acres	F	1	0	LEX	30,000	
Angus Hall	Northwood	Allerage	C	1	0	HB	22,000	
Angus Hall	Northwood	Allerage	C	4	0	LEX	33,000	
Angus Hall	Northwood	Allerage	F	2	0	LEX	35,000	
Angus Hall	Northwood	Bluestone	C	1	0	LEX	5,000	
Angus Hall	Northwood	Kurt Hansen's	C	1	0	HB	37,000	
Angus Hall	Northwood	Skyhaven	F	1	0	HB	40,000	
Angus Hall	Peninsula	Peninsula	C	3	0	HB	62,333	
Angus Hall	Peninsula	Peninsula	F	2	0	HB	67,500	
Angus Hall	Peninsula	Pheasant Hill	F	1	0	LEX	6,000	
Angus Hall	Peninsula	Quantum	F	1	0	HB	26,000	
Angus Hall	Peninsula	Shawnee Run	C	1	0	LEX	20,000	

Sire	Consignor	Farm	Sex	Sold	$50,000 2 YOs	Sale	Avg Price	Avg $ Won
Angus Hall	Peninsula	Sholty's Farm	C	1	0	HB	62,000	
Angus Hall	Preferred	Hamstan	C	3	0	HB	56,667	
Angus Hall	Preferred	Hamstan	F	1	0	HB	37,000	
Angus Hall	Preferred	Joie De Vie	F	1	0	HB	13,000	
Angus Hall	Preferred	Joie De Vie	C	1	0	LEX	25,000	
Angus Hall	Preferred	Joie De Vie	F	1	0	LEX	32,000	
Angus Hall	Preferred	Lindy	C	3	1	LEX	72,333	82,892
Angus Hall	Preferred	Morrison	C	1	0	HB	29,000	
Angus Hall	Preferred	Northstar	C	1	0	HB	70,000	
Angus Hall	Preferred	Seelster	C	1	0	HB	57,000	
Angus Hall	Preferred	Talbot Creek	C	1	0	HB	6,000	
Angus Hall	Saga	Saga	C	1	0	LEX	6,000	
Angus Hall	Saga	Saga	F	1	0	LEX	62,000	
Angus Hall	Spring Haven	Doug Millard	C	1	0	LEX	15,000	
Angus Hall	Spring Haven	FJD	C	2	0	LEX	7,000	
Angus Hall	Spring Haven	FJD	F	1	0	LEX	42,000	
Angus Hall	Spring Haven	Seufert	F	1	0	LEX	10,000	
Angus Hall	Spring Haven	Spring Haven	C	1	0	LEX	10,000	
Angus Hall	Spring Haven	Wilbur Stoll Lang	F	1	0	LEX	25,000	
Angus Hall	Spring Haven	Windswept Valley	C	1	0	LEX	90,000	
Angus Hall	Stonegate	Stonegate	F	1	1	HB	40,000	112,899
Angus Hall	Vieux Carre	Vieux Carre	C	1	0	HB	30,000	
Angus Hall	Vieux Carre	Vieux Carre	F	1	0	HB	42,000	
Angus Hall	Walnridge	Golden Gait	C	1	0	HB	20,000	
Angus Hall	Walnridge	Marion	C	1	0	HB	12,000	
Angus Hall	Westwind	Rich Thompson's	F	1		HB	23,000	
Angus Hall	Winbak	Winbak	C	7	0	HB	35,429	
Angus Hall	Winbak	Winbak	F	12	0	HB	40,500	
Angus Hall	Winbak	Winbak	C	4	0	LEX	22,250	
Angus Hall	Winbak	Winbak	F	5	0	LEX	32,400	
Angus Hall				**118**	**4**			
Armbro Deuce	Saga	Gold Star	F	1	1	LEX	13,000	75,166
Armbro Deuce	Winbak	Winbak	C	1	0	HB	5,000	
Armbro Deuce	Winbak	Winbak	F	1	0	LEX	12,000	
Armbro Deuce	Winterwood	Winterwood	F	2	0	HB	10,000	
Armbro Deuce				**5**	**1**			
Art Major	Allamerican	Allamerican	C	3	0	HB	19,333	

Sire	Consignor	Farm	Sex	Sold	$50,000 2 YOs	Sale	Avg Price	Avg $ Won
Art Major	Allamerican	Allamerican	F	2	0	HB	40,000	
Art Major	Blue Chip	Blue Chip	C	23	3	HB	43,522	133,210
Art Major	Blue Chip	Blue Chip	F	14	1	HB	39,286	75,664
Art Major	Blue Chip	Blue Chip	C	2	0	LEX	81,000	
Art Major	Blue Chip	Blue Chip	F	4	2	LEX	61,750	70,189
Art Major	Boxwood	Boxwood	C	1	0	HB	50,000	
Art Major	Boxwood	Shadowbrook	C	1	1	HB	30,000	104,579
Art Major	Cameo Hills	Cameo Hills	C	4	1	LEX	57,500	74,342
Art Major	Cameo Hills	Cameo Hills	F	4	0	LEX	31,500	
Art Major	Cameo Hills	Forty Hill	C	2	1	LEX	37,500	102,858
Art Major	Concord	Concord	F	1	0	HB	30,000	
Art Major	Concord	Crosscountry	F	1	0	HB	7,000	
Art Major	Diamond Creek	Diamond Creek	C	1	0	HB	110,000	
Art Major	Diamond Creek	Diamond Creek	F	3	0	HB	48,000	
Art Major	Diamond Creek	Diamond Creek	C	2	0	LEX	38,500	
Art Major	Dunroven	Dunroven	F	4	0	LEX	10,500	
Art Major	Fair Winds	Fair Winds	C	3	1	HB	44,000	60,818
Art Major	Fair Winds	Fair Winds	F	4	0	HB	36,750	
Art Major	Fox Den	Burnt Cabins	C	1	0	HB	30,000	
Art Major	Hanover	Hanover	C	11	1	HB	46,000	137,086
Art Major	Hanover	Hanover	F	9	2	HB	49,222	99,318
Art Major	Hanover	Hanover	C	2	0	LEX	87,500	
Art Major	Hanover	Hanover	F	2	0	LEX	37,500	
Art Major	Hempt	Hempt	C	1	0	HB	10,000	
Art Major	Hunterton	Hunterton	F	6	0	HB	29,833	
Art Major	Hunterton	Hunterton	C	1	1	LEX	52,000	56,827
Art Major	Hunterton	Hunterton	F	1	0	LEX	22,000	
Art Major	Hunterton	Ilazue	C	1	0	HB	34,000	
Art Major	Hunterton	Jeff S. Jones	F	1	0	LEX	27,000	
Art Major	Hunterton	Martinez Equine	C	1	0	HB	23,000	
Art Major	Hunterton	Meadow Creek	C	1	0	HB	6,500	
Art Major	Hunterton	Meadow Creek	F	1	1	HB	40,000	72,843
Art Major	Hunterton	Meadow Creek	C	1	0	LEX	31,000	
Art Major	Hunterton	Shady Lane Meadows	C	1	0	LEX	17,000	
Art Major	Hunterton	Starmaker	F	1	0	LEX	8,000	
Art Major	Hunterton	Walco	C	1	1	LEX	60,000	60,106
Art Major	Kentuckiana	Big Al's	C	1	0	LEX	20,000	

Sire	Consignor	Farm	Sex	Sold	$50,000 2 YOs	Sale	Avg Price	Avg $ Won
Art Major	Kentuckiana	Kentuckiana	C	8	4	LEX	55,750	144,405
Art Major	Kentuckiana	Kentuckiana	F	5	1	LEX	34,200	89,835
Art Major	Midland Acres	Midland Acres	F	1	1	LEX	47,000	109,746
Art Major	Northwood	Nandi	C	1	0	HB	32,000	
Art Major	Northwood	Olive Branch	F	1	1	HB	65,000	205,303
Art Major	Peninsula	Cinder Lane	C	1	0	HB	50,000	
Art Major	Peninsula	Holly Gate	F	3	0	HB	26,667	
Art Major	Peninsula	Marvin Kuhn's	C	1	0	HB	35,000	
Art Major	Peninsula	Peninsula	C	1	0	LEX	20,000	
Art Major	Peninsula	Robert Newman	C	1	0	LEX	32,000	
Art Major	Perretti	Perretti	F	1	0	HB	15,000	
Art Major	Perretti	Perretti	F	1	0	LEX	42,000	
Art Major	Pin Oak Lane	Pin Oak Lane	F	1	0	HB	26,000	
Art Major	Preferred	BJ's	F	1	0	HB	2,500	
Art Major	Preferred	Charlotte Ranch	F	1	0	HB	51,000	
Art Major	Preferred	D C P M Racing Stable	C	1	0	HB	4,000	
Art Major	Preferred	Dr. Robert Milkey's	C	1	0	LEX	27,000	
Art Major	Preferred	Dumain Haven	C	1	0	HB	5,000	
Art Major	Preferred	Heritage Hill	C	2	0	HB	36,000	
Art Major	Preferred	Heritage Hill	F	1	0	HB	37,000	
Art Major	Preferred	Lee Taylor's	F	1	0	HB	25,000	
Art Major	Preferred	Lindy	C	1	0	HB	35,000	
Art Major	Preferred	Lindy	C	3	0	LEX	52,333	
Art Major	Preferred	Lindy	F	2	1	LEX	37,000	129,998
Art Major	Preferred	Mulberry Meadows	C	2	0	HB	11,500	
Art Major	Preferred	Oak Knoll	C	1	1	HB	72,000	212,133
Art Major	Preferred	Oak Knoll	F	1	0	HB	15,000	
Art Major	Preferred	Rolling Acres	C	2	0	HB	93,500	
Art Major	Preferred	Rolling Acres	F	1	0	LEX	28,000	
Art Major	Preferred	Schunk Stables	C	1	0	LEX	82,000	
Art Major	Preferred	Southwind	C	2	0	HB	50,000	
Art Major	Preferred	Southwind	F	3	0	HB	8,333	
Art Major	Preferred	Southwind	C	1	0	LEX	32,000	
Art Major	Preferred	Southwind	F	3	2	LEX	30,667	132,578
Art Major	Preferred	Twin Willows	F	1	0	LEX	29,000	
Art Major	Preferred	White Birch	C	1	1	HB	60,000	79,362
Art Major	Preferred	White Birch	F	7	0	HB	26,286	

Sire	Consignor	Farm	Sex	Sold	$50,000 2 YOs	Sale	Avg Price	Avg $ Won
Art Major	Preferred	White Birch	C	4	1	LEX	66,750	209,916
Art Major	Preferred	White Birch	F	2	1	LEX	50,000	55,409
Art Major	Spring Haven	Aquatic	C	1	0	LEX	20,000	
Art Major	Spring Haven	Lyle Slabach's	C	1	0	HB	12,000	
Art Major	Spring Haven	Spring Haven	C	2	0	HB	17,500	
Art Major	Spring Haven	Spring Haven	C	3	1	LEX	59,000	51,590
Art Major	Steiner Stock	Steiner Stock	C	1	0	LEX	30,000	
Art Major	Steiner Stock	Steiner Stock	F	1	0	LEX	15,000	
Art Major	Stonegate	Stonegate	C	2	0	HB	35,500	
Art Major	Stonegate	Stonegate	F	4	0	HB	30,875	
Art Major	Twinbrook	Twinbrook	C	2	1	HB	40,000	65,484
Art Major	Twinbrook	Twinbrook	F	4	0	HB	16,750	
Art Major	Vieux Carre	Vieux Carre	C	7	1	HB	16,429	568,786
Art Major	Vieux Carre	Vieux Carre	F	3	0	HB	18,667	
Art Major	Walnridge	Cornerstone	C	1	0	HB	42,000	
Art Major	Walnridge	Walnridge	C	2	1	HB	60,000	250,586
Art Major	Walnut Hall Stock	Walnut Hall Stock	C	1	0	LEX	70,000	
Art Major	Westwind	JM Farm	F	1	0	HB	35,000	
Art Major	Winbak	Winbak	C	3	0	HB	14,667	
Art Major	Winbak	Winbak	F	2	2	HB	20,000	345,833
Art Major	Winbak	Winbak	C	2	0	LEX	18,500	
Art Major	Winbak	Winbak	F	3	1	LEX	28,000	63,217
Art Major	Winterwood	Cashelmara	F	1	0	HB	13,000	
Art Major	Winterwood	Winterwood	C	1	0	HB	10,000	
Art Major				**244**	**37**			
Artiscape	Allamerican	Allamerican	C	1	0	HB	32,000	
Artiscape	Allamerican	Allamerican	F	4	0	HB	10,250	
Artiscape	Blue Chip	Blue Chip	C	1	0	HB	25,000	
Artiscape	Brittany	Brittany	C	10	0	LEX	42,500	
Artiscape	Brittany	Brittany	F	3	0	LEX	10,333	
Artiscape	Cameo Hills	Crawford	C	1	0	LEX	3,000	
Artiscape	Concord	Concord	F	1	0	HB	2,000	
Artiscape	Concord	Crosscountry	C	2	0	HB	30,000	
Artiscape	Fair Winds	Fair Winds	C	6	0	HB	38,167	
Artiscape	Fair Winds	Stonehenge	C	1	0	HB	22,000	
Artiscape	Hunterton	Hunterton	F	2	0	LEX	7,000	
Artiscape	Kentuckiana	Kentuckiana	C	1	0	LEX	40,000	

Sire	Consignor	Farm	Sex	Sold	$50,000 2 YOs	Sale	Avg Price	Avg $ Won
Artiscape	Majestic View	Majestic View	C	1	0	HB	12,500	
Artiscape	Midland Acres	Midland Acres	C	1	0	LEX	21,000	
Artiscape	Midland Acres	Midland Acres	F	3	1	LEX	23,333	263,496
Artiscape	Northwood	Heritage Hill	C	1	0	HB	1,000	
Artiscape	Peninsula	Maple Lane	C	1	0	HB	17,000	
Artiscape	Peninsula	Maple Lane	C	1	0	LEX	10,000	
Artiscape	Peninsula	Shamrock	F	1	0	HB	30,000	
Artiscape	Perretti	Perretti	C	4	0	HB	43,750	
Artiscape	Perretti	Perretti	F	4	0	HB	12,750	
Artiscape	Perretti	Perretti	C	1	0	LEX	18,000	
Artiscape	Perretti	Perretti	F	3	1	LEX	12,667	72,874
Artiscape	Preferred	BJ's	F	1	0	HB	4,500	
Artiscape	Preferred	Brittany	C	1	0	HB	2,500	
Artiscape	Preferred	Brittany	F	2	0	HB	16,500	
Artiscape	Preferred	Heritage Hill	F	1	0	HB	9,000	
Artiscape	Preferred	White Birch	C	2	0	HB	16,000	
Artiscape	Preferred	White Birch	F	1	0	HB	20,000	
Artiscape	Steiner Stock	Steiner Stock	F	1	0	LEX	7,000	
Artiscape	Twinbrook	Killean Acres	F	1	0	HB	7,000	
Artiscape	Walnut Hall Ltd	Walnut Hall Ltd	C	1	0	HB	28,000	
Artiscape	Walnut Hall Ltd	Walnut Hall Ltd	F	1	0	HB	10,000	
Artiscape	Winbak	Winbak	C	13	0	HB	25,615	
Artiscape	Winbak	Winbak	F	12	0	HB	22,542	
Artiscape	Winbak	Winbak	C	12	1	LEX	24,083	111,279
Artiscape	Winbak	Winbak	F	4	0	LEX	16,500	
Artiscape				**107**	**3**			
Artsplace	Blue Chip	Blue Chip	C	2	0	HB	14,750	
Artsplace	Blue Chip	Blue Chip	F	2	0	HB	19,500	
Artsplace	Brittany	Brittany	C	2	0	LEX	72,000	
Artsplace	Brittany	Brittany	F	1	0	LEX	45,000	
Artsplace	Concord	Concord	F	2	0	HB	9,000	
Artsplace	Diamond Creek	Diamond Creek	C	2	0	HB	38,500	
Artsplace	Diamond Creek	Diamond Creek	C	1	0	LEX	40,000	
Artsplace	Diamond Creek	Diamond Creek	F	1	0	LEX	8,000	
Artsplace	Dunroven	Dunroven	F	1	0	LEX	40,000	
Artsplace	Fair Winds	Charlotte Ranch	F	1	0	HB	4,000	
Artsplace	Fair Winds	Fair Winds	C	3	1	HB	47,000	58,220

Sire	Consignor	Farm	Sex	Sold	$50,000 2 YOs	Sale	Avg Price	Avg $ Won
Artsplace	Fair Winds	Fair Winds	F	3	2	HB	27,000	94,050
Artsplace	Fashion	Fashion	C	1	0	HB	50,000	
Artsplace	Fox Den	Burnt Cabins	C	1	0	HB	25,000	
Artsplace	Hanover	Hanover	C	2	0	HB	36,000	
Artsplace	Hanover	Hanover	F	1	0	HB	14,000	
Artsplace	Hanover	Hanover	F	1	0	LEX	50,000	
Artsplace	Hunterton	Hunterton	F	1	0	HB	70,000	
Artsplace	Hunterton	Hunterton	F	1	0	LEX	25,000	
Artsplace	Hunterton	Meadow Creek	C	1	1	HB	50,000	815,680
Artsplace	Hunterton	Mike Clucas	C	1	0	LEX	25,000	
Artsplace	Kentuckiana	Kentuckiana	C	1	0	LEX	32,000	
Artsplace	Kentuckiana	Kentuckiana	F	1	0	LEX	13,000	
Artsplace	Northwood	Bonley	C	1	0	HB	5,000	
Artsplace	Northwood	Century Spring	C	1	0	HB	10,000	
Artsplace	Peninsula	Equine Center	C	1	0	LEX	8,000	
Artsplace	Peninsula	Peninsula	C	1	0	LEX	30,000	
Artsplace	Peninsula	Quad	C	1	0	HB	10,000	
Artsplace	Peninsula	Shamrock	F	1	0	HB	30,000	
Artsplace	Peninsula	Two Creeks	C	1	0	LEX	22,000	
Artsplace	Perretti	Perretti	C	2	0	HB	23,000	
Artsplace	Perretti	Perretti	F	1	0	LEX	5,000	
Artsplace	Preferred	Birch Creek	C	1	0	HB	13,000	
Artsplace	Preferred	Eternal	C	1	0	HB	9,000	
Artsplace	Preferred	Eternal	F	1	0	HB	4,000	
Artsplace	Preferred	Southwind	F	3	1	LEX	30,667	133,301
Artsplace	Preferred	Tara Hills	C	2	0	HB	47,000	
Artsplace	Preferred	Twin Willows	C	1	0	LEX	30,000	
Artsplace	Preferred	White Birch	C	4	0	HB	30,500	
Artsplace	Preferred	White Birch	C	2	0	LEX	103,500	
Artsplace	Preferred	White Birch	F	1	0	LEX	6,000	
Artsplace	Spring Haven	Cool Winds	F	1	0	LEX	7,000	
Artsplace	Spring Haven	FJD	C	1	0	LEX	150,000	
Artsplace	Spring Haven	Mindale	C	1	0	LEX	55,000	
Artsplace	Spring Haven	Something Special	C	1	0	LEX	10,000	
Artsplace	Spring Haven	Spring Haven	F	1	0	HB	11,000	
Artsplace	Spring Haven	Spring Haven	F	1	0	LEX	30,000	
Artsplace	Spring Haven	Spring Run	C	1	0	HB	11,000	

Sire	Consignor	Farm	Sex	Sold	$50,000 2 YOs	Sale	Avg Price	Avg $ Won
Artsplace	Spring Haven	Steiner Stock	C	1	0	LEX	65,000	
Artsplace	Stonegate	Stonegate	C	1	0	HB	20,000	
Artsplace	Stonegate	Stonegate	F	1	0	HB	20,000	
Artsplace	Twinbrook	Killean Acres	F	1	0	HB	37,000	
Artsplace	Twinbrook	Twinbrook	F	1	0	HB	15,000	
Artsplace	Vieux Carre	Vieux Carre	C	1	0	HB	20,000	
Artsplace	Vieux Carre	Vieux Carre	F	2	0	HB	20,500	
Artsplace	Walnridge	Walnridge	C	2	0	HB	19,000	
Artsplace	Winbak	Winbak	C	2	0	HB	43,500	
Artsplace	Winbak	Winbak	F	5	0	HB	22,800	
Artsplace	Winbak	Winbak	C	1	0	LEX	85,000	
Artsplace	Winbak	Winbak	F	3	0	LEX	31,000	
Artsplace				**87**	**5**			
Astreos	Concord	Concord	F	2	0	HB	32,500	
Astreos	Hanover	Hanover	C	1	0	HB	3,500	
Astreos	Hanover	Hanover	F	1	0	HB	10,000	
Astreos	Hempt	Hempt	C	2	1	HB	19,500	178,811
Astreos	Spring Haven	Rails Edge	C	1	0	LEX	150,000	
Astreos	Twinbrook	Twinbrook	C	1	0	HB	45,000	
Astreos	Vieux Carre	Vieux Carre	F	1	0	HB	5,000	
Astreos	Westwind	Westwind	F	1	1	HB	20,000	89,443
Astreos				**10**	**2**			
Badlands Hanover	Hanover	Hanover	C	1	1	HB	38,000	70,300
Badlands Hanover	Peninsula	Shady Side	F	1	0	LEX	20,000	
Badlands Hanover	Spring Haven	Executive Standardbred	F	1	0	LEX	5,000	
Badlands Hanover	Winbak	Winbak	C	2	1	HB	68,500	99,383
Badlands Hanover	Winbak	Winbak	F	1	0	HB	19,000	
Badlands Hanover				**6**	**2**			
Bettor's Delight	Allamerican	Allamerican	C	1	0	HB	42,000	
Bettor's Delight	Allamerican	Allamerican	F	4	0	HB	19,875	
Bettor's Delight	Blue Chip	Blue Chip	C	10	1	HB	35,700	510,555
Bettor's Delight	Blue Chip	Blue Chip	F	11	1	HB	51,909	115,889
Bettor's Delight	Blue Chip	Blue Chip	F	2	0	LEX	58,500	
Bettor's Delight	Brittany	Brittany	F	2	0	LEX	49,500	
Bettor's Delight	Cameo Hills	Cameo Hills	C	5	1	LEX	97,400	91,479
Bettor's Delight	Cameo Hills	Cameo Hills	F	3	1	LEX	66,667	133,746
Bettor's Delight	Cameo Hills	Crawford	C	1	0	LEX	10,000	

Sire	Consignor	Farm	Sex	Sold	$50,000 2 YOs	Sale	Avg Price	Avg $ Won
Bettor's Delight	Concord	Concord	C	2	0	HB	48,500	
Bettor's Delight	Concord	Concord	F	3	0	HB	40,667	
Bettor's Delight	Diamond Creek	Diamond Creek	F	1	0	HB	47,000	
Bettor's Delight	Diamond Creek	Diamond Creek	C	1	0	LEX	47,000	
Bettor's Delight	Dunroven	Dunroven	C	5	1	LEX	14,200	92,260
Bettor's Delight	Dunroven	Dunroven	F	4	0	LEX	10,750	
Bettor's Delight	Fair Winds	Fair Winds	C	10	1	HB	41,400	160,695
Bettor's Delight	Fair Winds	Fair Winds	F	9	0	HB	34,111	
Bettor's Delight	Fair Winds	Stonehenge	C	1	0	HB	22,000	
Bettor's Delight	Fair Winds	Stonehenge	F	1	0	HB	40,000	
Bettor's Delight	Hanover	Hanover	C	7	2	HB	52,286	111,835
Bettor's Delight	Hanover	Hanover	F	8	1	HB	35,438	204,089
Bettor's Delight	Hempt	Hempt	C	1	0	HB	10,000	
Bettor's Delight	Hempt	Hempt	F	3	0	HB	19,333	
Bettor's Delight	Hunterton	Hunterton	C	1	0	LEX	55,000	
Bettor's Delight	Hunterton	Hunterton	F	2	0	LEX	138,500	
Bettor's Delight	Hunterton	Richard Malone's	F	1	0	HB	15,000	
Bettor's Delight	Kentuckiana	C.M.T.	F	1	0	LEX	7,000	
Bettor's Delight	Kentuckiana	Kentuckiana	C	3	1	LEX	60,667	87,486
Bettor's Delight	Kentuckiana	Kentuckiana	F	5	0	LEX	64,800	
Bettor's Delight	Midland Acres	Midland Acres	C	1	0	LEX	65,000	
Bettor's Delight	Midland Acres	Midland Acres	F	1	0	LEX	30,000	
Bettor's Delight	Northwood	Cameo Hills	F	1	0	HB	19,000	
Bettor's Delight	Northwood	Olive Branch	F	1	0	HB	80,000	
Bettor's Delight	Peninsula	Equine Center	C	1	0	LEX	90,000	
Bettor's Delight	Peninsula	Glassford Equine	C	1	0	HB	25,000	
Bettor's Delight	Peninsula	Holly Gate	F	1	0	HB	35,000	
Bettor's Delight	Peninsula	Odds On Racing	C	1	0	HB	35,000	
Bettor's Delight	Peninsula	Pheasant Hill	C	1	0	HB	25,000	
Bettor's Delight	Peninsula	Pheasant Hill	F	1	0	HB	15,000	
Bettor's Delight	Peninsula	Shamrock	F	1	0	HB	3,000	
Bettor's Delight	Perretti	Perretti	C	2	0	HB	115,000	
Bettor's Delight	Preferred	Anderson	C	1	0	LEX	70,000	
Bettor's Delight	Preferred	Brittany	C	1	0	HB	22,000	
Bettor's Delight	Preferred	Chad Yoder	F	1	0	LEX	17,000	
Bettor's Delight	Preferred	Dumain Haven	F	2	0	HB	36,000	
Bettor's Delight	Preferred	Freedom Hill	C	1	0	LEX	26,000	

Sire	Consignor	Farm	Sex	Sold	$50,000 2 YOs	Sale	Avg Price	Avg $ Won
Bettor's Delight	Preferred	Freedom Hill	F	1	0	LEX	17,000	
Bettor's Delight	Preferred	Hada Dream	C	1	0	LEX	25,000	
Bettor's Delight	Preferred	Heritage Hill	C	3	1	HB	22,000	50,438
Bettor's Delight	Preferred	Heritage Hill	F	5	0	HB	44,800	
Bettor's Delight	Preferred	Heritage Hill	C	1	0	LEX	45,000	
Bettor's Delight	Preferred	Heritage Hill	F	1	0	LEX	8,000	
Bettor's Delight	Preferred	Joie De Vie	F	1	0	HB	15,000	
Bettor's Delight	Preferred	Lindy	C	1	0	HB	57,000	
Bettor's Delight	Preferred	Lindy	F	1	0	LEX	25,000	
Bettor's Delight	Preferred	Oak Knoll	C	1	0	HB	25,000	
Bettor's Delight	Preferred	Rolling Acres	F	1	0	LEX	80,000	
Bettor's Delight	Preferred	Seelster	C	1	0	HB	9,000	
Bettor's Delight	Preferred	Seelster	F	1	0	HB	18,000	
Bettor's Delight	Preferred	Southwind	C	3	0	HB	19,167	
Bettor's Delight	Preferred	Southwind	F	2	1	HB	31,000	256,478
Bettor's Delight	Preferred	Southwind	C	1	0	LEX	90,000	
Bettor's Delight	Preferred	Southwind	F	2	1	LEX	27,000	87,860
Bettor's Delight	Preferred	Stirling Brook	C	1	0	HB	15,000	
Bettor's Delight	Preferred	Stirling Brook	C	1	0	LEX	85,000	
Bettor's Delight	Preferred	White Birch	C	3	0	HB	45,667	
Bettor's Delight	Preferred	White Birch	F	1	1	HB	5,000	78,460
Bettor's Delight	Preferred	White Birch	C	5	2	LEX	65,400	98,410
Bettor's Delight	Preferred	White Birch	F	2	0	LEX	40,000	
Bettor's Delight	Spring Haven	Spring Haven	C	1	0	LEX	27,000	
Bettor's Delight	Steiner Stock	Steiner Stock	F	1	0	LEX	12,000	
Bettor's Delight	Stonegate	Stonegate	C	4	0	HB	21,875	
Bettor's Delight	Stonegate	Stonegate	F	2	0	HB	55,000	
Bettor's Delight	Twinbrook	Twinbrook	C	3	0	HB	48,667	
Bettor's Delight	Vieux Carre	Vieux Carre	C	1	1	HB	45,000	328,341
Bettor's Delight	Vieux Carre	Vieux Carre	F	1	1	HB	85,000	96,631
Bettor's Delight	Walnridge	Holly Gate	C	1	0	HB	110,000	
Bettor's Delight	Walnridge	Walnridge	C	1	0	HB	25,000	
Bettor's Delight	Walnut Hall Stock	Walnut Hall Stock	C	3	1	LEX	30,333	188,689
Bettor's Delight	Walnut Hall Stock	Walnut Hall Stock	F	1	0	LEX	52,000	
Bettor's Delight	Winbak	Winbak	C	3	0	HB	25,667	
Bettor's Delight	Winbak	Winbak	F	4	1	HB	43,500	81,264
Bettor's Delight	Winbak	Winbak	C	3	0	LEX	40,000	

Sire	Consignor	Farm	Sex	Sold	$50,000 2 YOs	Sale	Avg Price	Avg $ Won
Bettor's Delight	Winbak	Winbak	F	1	1	LEX	70,000	119,017
Bettor's Delight				197	21			
Blissful Hall	Northwood	Nandi	F	1	0	LEX	7,000	
Blissful Hall	Peninsula	Pheasant Hill	F	1	0	HB	9,000	
Blissful Hall	Preferred	Omar Beiler	C	1	0	LEX	17,000	
Blissful Hall	Spring Haven	Spring Haven	C	1	0	LEX	32,000	
Blissful Hall	Spring Haven	Spring Haven	F	1	0	LEX	8,000	
Blissful Hall	Stonegate	Stonegate	F	1	0	HB	6,500	
Blissful Hall	Vieux Carre	Vieux Carre	C	1	0	HB	13,000	
Blissful Hall	Winbak	Winbak	C	1	0	LEX	9,000	
Blissful Hall				8	0			
Broadway Hall	Brittany	Brittany	C	2	0	LEX	10,000	
Broadway Hall	Brittany	Brittany	F	2	0	LEX	14,500	
Broadway Hall	Cameo Hills	Cameo Hills	C	1	0	LEX	7,000	
Broadway Hall	Cameo Hills	Cameo Hills	F	1	0	LEX	20,000	
Broadway Hall	Concord	Concord	F	1	0	HB	20,000	
Broadway Hall	Concord	Hanover	C	1	0	HB	25,000	
Broadway Hall	Concord	Hanover	F	1	0	HB	11,000	
Broadway Hall	Concord	Marion	C	3	0	HB	8,167	
Broadway Hall	Fair Winds	Fair Winds	C	2	1	HB	15,000	223,427
Broadway Hall	Fair Winds	Fair Winds	F	3	0	HB	17,333	
Broadway Hall	Fashion	Fashion	C	10	1	HB	15,200	737,627
Broadway Hall	Fashion	Fashion	F	12	2	HB	12,042	207,646
Broadway Hall	Fox Den	Shaffer Standardbreds	F	1	0	HB	20,000	
Broadway Hall	Fox Den	Stoltzfus	F	1	0	HB	7,500	
Broadway Hall	Hanover	Hanover	C	3	0	HB	36,667	
Broadway Hall	Hanover	Hanover	F	2	0	HB	7,250	
Broadway Hall	Hunterton	Hunterton	C	1	0	HB	24,000	
Broadway Hall	Hunterton	Hunterton	C	1	0	LEX	120,000	
Broadway Hall	Hunterton	Hunterton	F	1	0	LEX	19,000	
Broadway Hall	Kentuckiana	Kentuckiana	C	1	0	LEX	43,000	
Broadway Hall	Millstream	Millstream	C	1	0	HB	8,000	
Broadway Hall	Millstream	Millstream	F	1	0	HB	26,000	
Broadway Hall	Northwood	Allerage	C	1	0	HB	18,000	
Broadway Hall	Northwood	Allerage	F	2	0	HB	27,500	
Broadway Hall	Northwood	Andray	F	1	0	LEX	12,000	

Sire	Consignor	Farm	Sex	Sold	$50,000 2 YOs	Sale	Avg Price	Avg $ Won
Broadway Hall	Northwood	Bluestone	F	1	0	LEX	30,000	
Broadway Hall	Northwood	Maple Hill	C	1	0	HB	7,000	
Broadway Hall	Northwood	Olive Branch	F	1	0	LEX	30,000	
Broadway Hall	Northwood	Starmaker	C	1	0	HB	7,000	
Broadway Hall	Northwood	Wollam	F	1	0	HB	1,500	
Broadway Hall	Peninsula	Andray	C	1	0	LEX	40,000	
Broadway Hall	Peninsula	Cedar Post	F	2	0	HB	24,000	
Broadway Hall	Peninsula	Dottie Morone	F	1	0	LEX	37,000	
Broadway Hall	Peninsula	Ironstone Spring	F	1	0	HB	3,500	
Broadway Hall	Peninsula	Ivan Sugg's	C	1	0	HB	25,000	
Broadway Hall	Peninsula	Peninsula	F	1	0	HB	70,000	
Broadway Hall	Peninsula	Pheasant Hill	F	4	0	HB	27,000	
Broadway Hall	Peninsula	Pheasant Hill	F	1	0	LEX	10,000	
Broadway Hall	Peninsula	Quantum	C	1	0	HB	17,000	
Broadway Hall	Peninsula	Silver Linden	C	1	0	HB	25,000	
Broadway Hall	Pin Oak Lane	Pin Oak Lane	C	3	0	HB	19,333	
Broadway Hall	Preferred	Joie De Vie	F	1	0	LEX	10,000	
Broadway Hall	Preferred	Southwind	F	1	0	HB	25,000	
Broadway Hall	Preferred	White Birch	C	1	0	HB	6,000	
Broadway Hall	Saga	New Pioneer	C	1	0	LEX	40,000	
Broadway Hall	Saga	Saga	F	1	0	LEX	30,000	
Broadway Hall	Spring Haven	Double Spring	F	1	1	LEX	15,000	70,675
Broadway Hall	Spring Haven	Leroy Keim's	C	1	0	HB	20,000	
Broadway Hall	Spring Haven	Mindale	C	1	0	LEX	17,000	
Broadway Hall	Spring Haven	Slabach Bros	C	1	0	HB	31,000	
Broadway Hall	Spring Haven	Spring Haven	C	2	0	LEX	20,000	
Broadway Hall	Spring Haven	Spring Haven	F	1	0	LEX	18,000	
Broadway Hall	Spring Haven	White Oak	C	1	0	LEX	30,000	
Broadway Hall	Steiner Stock	Steiner Stock	C	1	0	LEX	22,000	
Broadway Hall	Steiner Stock	Steiner Stock	F	1	0	LEX	10,000	
Broadway Hall	Stonegate	Stonegate	C	3	0	HB	17,833	
Broadway Hall	Twinbrook	Twinbrook	C	1	0	HB	9,000	
Broadway Hall	Vieux Carre	Vieux Carre	C	1	0	HB	55,000	
Broadway Hall	Vieux Carre	Vieux Carre	F	1	1	HB	13,000	87,499
Broadway Hall	Walnridge	Marion	C	1	0	HB	6,000	
Broadway Hall	Walnridge	Marion	F	1	0	HB	4,200	

Sire	Consignor	Farm	Sex	Sold	$50,000 2 YOs	Sale	Avg Price	Avg $ Won
Broadway Hall	Walnridge	Samuel Zook's	F	1	0	HB	12,000	
Broadway Hall	Walnridge	Walnridge	C	1	0	HB	27,000	
Broadway Hall	Walnut Hall Stock	Walnut Hall Stock	C	1	0	LEX	50,000	
Broadway Hall	Walnut Hall Stock	Walnut Hall Stock	F	1	0	LEX	40,000	
Broadway Hall				**105**	**6**			
Cambest	Brittany	Brittany	C	1	0	LEX	15,000	
Cambest	Brittany	Brittany	F	1	0	LEX	3,000	
Cambest	Dunroven	Dunroven	C	1	0	LEX	15,000	
Cambest	Hunterton	Outback	F	1	0	LEX	5,000	
Cambest	Peninsula	Al Tomlinson	C	1	0	LEX	12,000	
Cambest	Peninsula	Equine Center	F	1	0	LEX	9,000	
Cambest	Peninsula	October Lane	C	1	0	LEX	35,000	
Cambest	Peninsula	Peninsula	C	1	0	LEX	30,000	
Cambest	Peninsula	Shamrock	C	1	0	HB	13,000	
Cambest	Peninsula	Walstan	C	1	0	LEX	14,000	
Cambest	Preferred	Concord	F	1	0	LEX	18,000	
Cambest	Preferred	D Farm	C	1	0	LEX	60,000	
Cambest	Preferred	D Farm	F	1	0	LEX	7,000	
Cambest	Preferred	Lindy	C	1	0	LEX	7,000	
Cambest	Preferred	Lindy	F	1	0	LEX	37,000	
Cambest	Preferred	Walnut Hall Ltd	C	6	0	LEX	12,167	
Cambest	Preferred	Walnut Hall Ltd	F	8	1	LEX	8,875	105,000
Cambest	Saga	Oldfield	C	1	0	LEX	34,000	
Cambest	Saga	Saga	F	2	0	LEX	13,500	
Cambest	Spring Haven	Hickory Lane	F	1	0	LEX	30,000	
Cambest	Spring Haven	Rick Lewis	C	1	0	HB	10,000	
Cambest	Walnridge	Walnridge	C	1	0	HB	40,000	
Cambest	Westwind	Walnut Hall Ltd	C	1	0	HB	35,000	
Cambest	Westwind	Walnut Hall Ltd	F	1	0	HB	9,000	
Cambest	Winbak	Winbak	C	2	0	LEX	7,500	
Cambest	Winterwood	Cashelmara	F	1	0	HB	5,500	
Cambest	Winterwood	Winterwood	C	1	0	HB	3,500	
Cambest				**41**	**1**			
Camluck	Allamerican	Allamerican	C	3	0	HB	23,333	
Camluck	Brittany	Brittany	C	4	0	LEX	34,750	
Camluck	Concord	Concord	F	1	0	HB	17,000	

Sire	Consignor	Farm	Sex	Sold	$50,000 2 YOs	Sale	Avg Price	Avg $ Won
Camluck	Concord	Crosscountry	F	1	0	HB	14,000	
Camluck	Concord	Loconte	F	1	0	HB	40,000	
Camluck	Concord	Olive Branch	C	1	0	HB	55,000	
Camluck	Diamond Creek	Diamond Creek	C	1	0	HB	22,000	
Camluck	Diamond Creek	Diamond Creek	C	1	0	LEX	20,000	
Camluck	Diamond Creek	Diamond Creek	F	1	0	LEX	15,000	
Camluck	Fair Winds	Fair Winds	C	1	1	HB	45,000	271,793
Camluck	Fair Winds	Fair Winds	F	1	0	HB	35,000	
Camluck	Hanover	Hanover	C	4	0	HB	60,000	
Camluck	Hanover	Hanover	F	5	0	HB	13,000	
Camluck	Hempt	Hempt	C	1	0	HB	17,000	
Camluck	Hempt	Hempt	F	3	1	HB	10,000	52,617
Camluck	Hunterton	Hunterton	F	2	0	HB	51,000	
Camluck	Hunterton	Meadow Creek	C	2	0	HB	61,500	
Camluck	Hunterton	Meadow Creek	C	1	0	LEX	120,000	
Camluck	Northwood	Bonley	C	1	0	HB	22,000	
Camluck	Northwood	Hillsborough Stable	C	1	0	LEX	17,000	
Camluck	Peninsula	Glassford Equine	F	1	0	HB	17,000	
Camluck	Peninsula	Pheasant Hill	C	1	0	HB	32,000	
Camluck	Peninsula	Pheasant Hill	F	2	0	HB	41,000	
Camluck	Peninsula	Pheasant Hill	F	1	0	LEX	40,000	
Camluck	Peninsula	Shamrock	C	1	0	HB	47,000	
Camluck	Peninsula	Shamrock	F	1	0	HB	25,000	
Camluck	Preferred	Green Gables	C	1	0	HB	20,000	
Camluck	Preferred	Talbot Creek	F	1	0	HB	40,000	
Camluck	Saga	Saga	F	2	0	LEX	7,000	
Camluck	Spring Haven	Doug Millard	C	1	0	LEX	30,000	
Camluck	Spring Haven	FJD	C	1	0	LEX	15,000	
Camluck	Spring Haven	FJD	F	1	0	LEX	13,000	
Camluck	Spring Haven	Mindale	C	3	0	LEX	32,667	
Camluck	Spring Haven	Mindale	F	1	0	LEX	13,000	
Camluck	Spring Haven	Spring Haven	C	3	0	HB	61,333	
Camluck	Spring Haven	Spring Haven	F	2	0	HB	41,000	
Camluck	Spring Haven	Spring Run	F	1	0	HB	35,000	
Camluck	Twinbrook	Ken And Joan Bryant's	C	1	0	HB	40,000	
Camluck	Twinbrook	Killean Acres	C	3	0	HB	75,000	
Camluck	Twinbrook	Twinbrook	F	2	0	HB	48,500	

Sire	Consignor	Farm	Sex	Sold	$50,000 2 YOs	Sale	Avg Price	Avg $ Won
Camluck	Winbak	Winbak	C	3	0	HB	53,333	
Camluck	Winbak	Winbak	F	3	0	HB	32,333	
Camluck	Winbak	Winbak	C	2	1	LEX	52,500	63,311
Camluck				**74**	**3**			
Cam's Card Shark	Allamerican	Allamerican	C	3	0	HB	30,000	
Cam's Card Shark	Allamerican	Allamerican	F	4	0	HB	18,125	
Cam's Card Shark	Blue Chip	Blue Chip	C	2	0	HB	26,500	
Cam's Card Shark	Boxwood	Boxwood	F	2	0	HB	26,000	
Cam's Card Shark	Dunroven	Dunroven	C	3	0	LEX	4,333	
Cam's Card Shark	Dunroven	Dunroven	F	2	0	LEX	4,500	
Cam's Card Shark	Fair Winds	Charlotte Ranch	F	1	0	HB	3,500	
Cam's Card Shark	Fair Winds	Fair Winds	C	2	0	HB	12,500	
Cam's Card Shark	Fair Winds	Fair Winds	F	3	1	HB	15,000	102,118
Cam's Card Shark	Fox Den	Mel Kauffman's	C	1	0	HB	5,000	
Cam's Card Shark	Hanover	Hanover	C	13	3	HB	57,000	354,861
Cam's Card Shark	Hanover	Hanover	F	7	1	HB	16,143	207,488
Cam's Card Shark	Hunterton	Brittany	C	1	0	HB	25,000	
Cam's Card Shark	Hunterton	Hunterton	C	1	0	HB	27,000	
Cam's Card Shark	Hunterton	Hunterton	C	1	0	LEX	5,000	
Cam's Card Shark	Hunterton	Hunterton	F	1	0	LEX	30,000	
Cam's Card Shark	Kentuckiana	Kentuckiana	C	3	0	LEX	25,333	
Cam's Card Shark	Kentuckiana	Kentuckiana	F	1	0	LEX	21,000	
Cam's Card Shark	Majestic View	Majestic View	C	1	0	HB	7,000	
Cam's Card Shark	Northwood	Olive Branch	C	1	0	HB	6,000	
Cam's Card Shark	Northwood	Perretti	C	1	0	HB	12,000	
Cam's Card Shark	Peninsula	Peninsula	C	1	0	HB	40,000	
Cam's Card Shark	Peninsula	Peninsula	F	1	0	LEX	10,000	
Cam's Card Shark	Peninsula	Wizard Heights	F	1	0	LEX	8,000	
Cam's Card Shark	Perretti	Perretti	C	3	1	HB	46,000	74,580
Cam's Card Shark	Perretti	Perretti	F	1	0	HB	21,000	
Cam's Card Shark	Preferred	Freedom Hill	F	1	0	LEX	9,000	
Cam's Card Shark	Preferred	Heritage Hill	C	2	0	HB	9,250	
Cam's Card Shark	Preferred	Heritage Hill	F	1	0	HB	4,000	
Cam's Card Shark	Preferred	Schwartz Boarding	C	1	0	LEX	6,000	
Cam's Card Shark	Preferred	Southwind	C	1	0	HB	12,000	
Cam's Card Shark	Preferred	White Birch	C	3	0	HB	24,000	
Cam's Card Shark	Spring Haven	Hickory Lane	C	1	0	LEX	30,000	

Sire	Consignor	Farm	Sex	Sold	$50,000 2 YOs	Sale	Avg Price	Avg $ Won
Cam's Card Shark	Spring Haven	Mindale	F	1	0	LEX	1,000	
Cam's Card Shark	Vieux Carre	Vieux Carre	C	2	0	HB	12,750	
Cam's Card Shark	Vieux Carre	Vieux Carre	F	1	0	HB	5,000	
Cam's Card Shark	Winbak	Winbak	C	13	0	HB	26,308	
Cam's Card Shark	Winbak	Winbak	F	4	0	HB	17,250	
Cam's Card Shark	Winbak	Winbak	C	6	2	LEX	45,167	112,130
Cam's Card Shark	Winbak	Winbak	F	6	0	LEX	23,833	
Cam's Card Shark	Winterwood	Boyce	C	1	0	HB	8,000	
Cam's Card Shark	Winterwood	Winterwood	C	1	0	HB	14,000	
Cam's Card Shark				**106**	**8**			
Cantab Hall	Allamerican	Allamerican	F	2	0	HB	23,500	
Cantab Hall	Blue Chip	Blue Chip	F	2	0	HB	46,000	
Cantab Hall	Brittany	Brittany	C	15	1	LEX	52,600	653,748
Cantab Hall	Brittany	Brittany	F	5	0	LEX	45,400	
Cantab Hall	Concord	Concord	C	2	0	HB	9,250	
Cantab Hall	Concord	Concord	F	2	0	HB	18,500	
Cantab Hall	Concord	Hanover	C	3	1	HB	45,667	132,551
Cantab Hall	Concord	Hanover	F	1	0	HB	25,000	
Cantab Hall	Concord	Marion	C	1	0	HB	15,000	
Cantab Hall	Diamond Creek	Diamond Creek	C	2	0	HB	45,000	
Cantab Hall	Dunroven	Dunroven	C	2	0	LEX	50,500	
Cantab Hall	Dunroven	Dunroven	F	1	1	LEX	100,000	86,654
Cantab Hall	Fox Den	Avonlea	F	1	0	HB	18,000	
Cantab Hall	Fox Den	Hanover	C	1	0	HB	8,000	
Cantab Hall	Hanover	Hanover	C	23	2	HB	29,152	84,520
Cantab Hall	Hanover	Hanover	F	23	2	HB	30,957	205,652
Cantab Hall	Hanover	Hanover	C	1	0	LEX	17,000	
Cantab Hall	Hanover	Hanover	F	2	0	LEX	48,500	
Cantab Hall	Hempt	Hempt	C	2	1	HB	57,250	76,484
Cantab Hall	Hempt	Hempt	F	4	1	HB	28,750	50,481
Cantab Hall	Hunterton	Elam Esh	F	1	0	LEX	15,000	
Cantab Hall	Hunterton	Hunterton	C	2	0	HB	20,000	
Cantab Hall	Hunterton	Hunterton	C	6	0	LEX	21,000	
Cantab Hall	Hunterton	Hunterton	F	2	0	LEX	22,500	
Cantab Hall	Hunterton	Meadow Creek	F	1	0	LEX	35,000	
Cantab Hall	Hunterton	Oaklea	F	1	0	LEX	10,000	
Cantab Hall	Hunterton	Rupert	F	1	0	LEX	37,000	

Sire	Consignor	Farm	Sex	Sold	$50,000 2 YOs	Sale	Avg Price	Avg $ Won
Cantab Hall	Hunterton	Wilt Standardbreds	F	1	0	LEX	30,000	
Cantab Hall	Kentuckiana	Kentuckiana	C	3	0	LEX	53,333	
Cantab Hall	Kentuckiana	Kentuckiana	F	4	0	LEX	26,000	
Cantab Hall	Kentuckiana	Wilt Standardbreds	C	1	0	LEX	16,000	
Cantab Hall	Northwood	Allerage	C	1	0	HB	52,000	
Cantab Hall	Northwood	Allerage	F	2	0	LEX	46,000	
Cantab Hall	Northwood	Bluestone	C	3	0	LEX	33,000	
Cantab Hall	Northwood	Bluestone	F	1	0	LEX	17,000	
Cantab Hall	Peninsula	Oaklea	C	1	0	HB	20,000	
Cantab Hall	Peninsula	Peninsula	C	5	1	HB	24,600	50,398
Cantab Hall	Peninsula	Peninsula	F	3	1	HB	56,667	72,960
Cantab Hall	Peninsula	Peninsula	F	1	0	LEX	70,000	
Cantab Hall	Peninsula	Pheasant Hill	F	2	0	HB	17,500	
Cantab Hall	Peninsula	Pheasant Hill	C	1	0	LEX	10,000	
Cantab Hall	Peninsula	Quantum	F	1	0	HB	13,000	
Cantab Hall	Peninsula	Quantum	F	1	0	LEX	5,000	
Cantab Hall	Peninsula	Rupert	F	1	0	LEX	65,000	
Cantab Hall	Peninsula	Silver Linden	F	1	0	HB	31,000	
Cantab Hall	Peninsula	Winterwood	C	1	1	LEX	60,000	346,582
Cantab Hall	Perretti	Perretti	C	1	1	HB	62,000	269,466
Cantab Hall	Pin Oak Lane	Hanover	C	1	0	HB	19,000	
Cantab Hall	Preferred	Bloodstock	C	1	0	LEX	15,000	
Cantab Hall	Preferred	Bloodstock	F	2	0	LEX	47,500	
Cantab Hall	Preferred	Joie De Vie	C	1	0	HB	40,000	
Cantab Hall	Preferred	Joie De Vie	F	1	0	HB	50,000	
Cantab Hall	Preferred	Joie De Vie	F	2	0	LEX	60,000	
Cantab Hall	Preferred	Lindy	C	3	0	HB	20,667	
Cantab Hall	Preferred	Lindy	F	1	0	HB	9,000	
Cantab Hall	Preferred	Lindy	C	4	0	LEX	123,000	
Cantab Hall	Preferred	Lindy	F	8	1	LEX	31,625	115,892
Cantab Hall	Preferred	Mackenzie	C	1	0	HB	9,000	
Cantab Hall	Preferred	Phil Hunt's	C	1	0	HB	11,000	
Cantab Hall	Preferred	Southwind	F	2	0	HB	18,500	
Cantab Hall	Preferred	Southwind	C	2	0	LEX	47,500	
Cantab Hall	Preferred	Stirling Brook	C	1	0	HB	9,000	
Cantab Hall	Preferred	Stirling Brook	F	1	0	LEX	6,000	
Cantab Hall	Preferred	Stonehenge	F	1	0	LEX	13,000	

Sire	Consignor	Farm	Sex	Sold	$50,000 2 YOs	Sale	Avg Price	Avg $ Won
Cantab Hall	Preferred	White Birch	C	1	0	HB	38,000	
Cantab Hall	Preferred	White Birch	F	4	1	HB	23,375	62,615
Cantab Hall	Preferred	White Birch	F	1	1	LEX	80,000	193,607
Cantab Hall	Spring Haven	Double Spring	C	1	0	HB	35,000	
Cantab Hall	Spring Haven	Spring Haven	C	1	0	LEX	35,000	
Cantab Hall	Steiner Stock	Steiner Stock	F	2	0	LEX	16,500	
Cantab Hall	Stonegate	Stonegate	F	1	0	HB	30,000	
Cantab Hall	Vieux Carre	Vieux Carre	C	6	0	HB	13,250	
Cantab Hall	Vieux Carre	Vieux Carre	F	1	0	HB	25,000	
Cantab Hall	Walnridge	Marion	F	2	0	HB	12,000	
Cantab Hall	Walnridge	Nandi	C	1	0	HB	30,000	
Cantab Hall	Winbak	Winbak	C	1	0	HB	25,000	
Cantab Hall	Winbak	Winbak	F	2	0	HB	15,500	
Cantab Hall	Winbak	Winbak	C	1	1	LEX	30,000	108,596
Cantab Hall	Winbak	Winbak	F	1	0	LEX	15,000	
Cantab Hall				**203**	**17**			
Cash Hall	Cameo Hills	Crawford	F	1	0	LEX	10,000	
Cash Hall	Concord	Concord	C	1	0	HB	47,000	
Cash Hall	Concord	Concord	F	3	0	HB	14,667	
Cash Hall	Concord	Northway	C	1	0	HB	20,000	
Cash Hall	Hunterton	Dan Kuhns'	C	1	0	HB	3,500	
Cash Hall	Hunterton	Ernie Martinez	C	1	0	LEX	30,000	
Cash Hall	Hunterton	Hunterton	C	1	0	LEX	15,000	
Cash Hall	Hunterton	Ilazue	F	2	0	HB	12,500	
Cash Hall	Northstar	Northstar	C	1	0	HB	27,000	
Cash Hall	Northwood	Paisley	C	1	0	HB	6,500	
Cash Hall	Peninsula	Dottie Morone	C	1	1	LEX	30,000	65,757
Cash Hall	Peninsula	Peninsula	C	1	0	HB	47,000	
Cash Hall	Peninsula	Spruce Run	C	1	0	HB	9,000	
Cash Hall	Preferred	Kurt Hansen's	F	1	0	HB	7,000	
Cash Hall	Preferred	Northstar	F	1	0	HB	25,000	
Cash Hall	Preferred	White Birch	C	1	0	HB	1,500	
Cash Hall	Preferred	Windsun	F	1	1	HB	5,000	80,608
Cash Hall	Spring Haven	LMN Bred	C	1	0	HB	10,000	
Cash Hall	Walnridge	Nandi	C	1	0	HB	4,500	
Cash Hall	Walnut Hall Ltd	Walnut Hall Ltd	C	8	0	HB	21,750	
Cash Hall	Walnut Hall Ltd	Walnut Hall Ltd	F	5	1	HB	16,400	52,835

Sire	Consignor	Farm	Sex	Sold	$50,000 2 YOs	Sale	Avg Price	Avg $ Won
Cash Hall	Winbak	Winbak	F	3	0	HB	25,167	
Cash Hall				**38**	**3**			
Chip Chip Hooray	Cane Run	Cane Run	C	1	0	LEX	8,000	
Chip Chip Hooray	Dunroven	Dunroven	C	2	0	LEX	19,500	
Chip Chip Hooray	Midland Acres	Midland Acres	C	1	0	LEX	7,000	
Chip Chip Hooray	Midland Acres	Midland Acres	F	2	0	LEX	15,500	
Chip Chip Hooray	Peninsula	Peninsula	F	1	0	LEX	10,000	
Chip Chip Hooray	Saga	Saga	F	1	0	LEX	14,000	
Chip Chip Hooray	Spring Haven	C and V Spellmire	F	1	0	LEX	8,000	
Chip Chip Hooray				**9**	**0**			
Chocolatier	Blue Chip	Blue Chip	C	1	0	HB	15,000	
Chocolatier	Blue Chip	Blue Chip	F	1	0	LEX	60,000	
Chocolatier	Cameo Hills	Cameo Hills	F	3	0	LEX	26,000	
Chocolatier	Concord	Concord	C	1	0	HB	5,000	
Chocolatier	Concord	Concord	F	1	0	HB	45,000	
Chocolatier	Concord	Marion	F	2	0	HB	35,000	
Chocolatier	Diamond Creek	Diamond Creek	F	1	0	HB	65,000	
Chocolatier	Diamond Creek	Diamond Creek	F	1	0	LEX	85,000	
Chocolatier	Fair Winds	Fair Winds	C	2	1	HB	80,000	61,517
Chocolatier	Fair Winds	Fair Winds	F	1	0	HB	22,000	
Chocolatier	Hanover	Hanover	F	1	0	HB	38,000	
Chocolatier	Hempt	Hempt	C	1	0	HB	10,000	
Chocolatier	Hunterton	Ernie Martinez	C	1	0	LEX	19,000	
Chocolatier	Hunterton	Hunterton	C	1	0	HB	20,000	
Chocolatier	Hunterton	Hunterton	F	1	0	HB	45,000	
Chocolatier	Hunterton	Walco	C	4	0	LEX	46,250	
Chocolatier	Hunterton	Walco	F	2	0	LEX	37,500	
Chocolatier	Kentuckiana	Kentuckiana	F	1	0	LEX	35,000	
Chocolatier	Millstream	Millstream	C	1	0	HB	100,000	
Chocolatier	Northwood	Bluestone	F	1	0	HB	20,000	
Chocolatier	Northwood	Bluestone	C	1	0	LEX	65,000	
Chocolatier	Northwood	Bluestone	F	2	0	LEX	38,500	
Chocolatier	Peninsula	Deo Volente	C	1	0	LEX	75,000	
Chocolatier	Peninsula	Oaklea	F	1	0	HB	30,000	
Chocolatier	Peninsula	Peninsula	C	4	0	HB	79,750	
Chocolatier	Peninsula	Peninsula	F	2	0	HB	26,500	
Chocolatier	Peninsula	Peninsula	C	2	0	LEX	55,000	

Sire	Consignor	Farm	Sex	Sold	$50,000 2 YOs	Sale	Avg Price	Avg $ Won
Chocolatier	Peninsula	Quantum	C	1	0	HB	8,000	
Chocolatier	Peninsula	Quantum	C	1	0	LEX	10,000	
Chocolatier	Peninsula	Silver Linden	C	1	0	HB	24,000	
Chocolatier	Peninsula	Silver Linden	F	1	0	HB	16,000	
Chocolatier	Preferred	Heritage Hill	C	1	0	HB	4,000	
Chocolatier	Preferred	Heritage Hill	F	1	0	LEX	4,000	
Chocolatier	Preferred	Joie De Vie	F	1	0	HB	4,000	
Chocolatier	Preferred	Lindy	C	1	0	HB	13,000	
Chocolatier	Preferred	Lindy	C	4	0	LEX	100,000	
Chocolatier	Preferred	Lindy	F	3	0	LEX	29,000	
Chocolatier	Preferred	Morrison	C	1	0	HB	6,500	
Chocolatier	Preferred	Southwind	F	3	0	HB	17,833	
Chocolatier	Preferred	Southwind	C	5	0	LEX	28,000	
Chocolatier	Preferred	Southwind	F	7	0	LEX	57,286	
Chocolatier	Preferred	Walker	F	1	0	LEX	15,000	
Chocolatier	Preferred	White Birch	C	2	0	HB	20,000	
Chocolatier	Preferred	White Birch	C	1	0	LEX	100,000	
Chocolatier	Saga	Robert Kuhns'	F	1	0	LEX	9,000	
Chocolatier	Saga	Saga	C	1	0	LEX	10,000	
Chocolatier	Saga	Saga	F	2	0	LEX	7,500	
Chocolatier	Vieux Carre	Vieux Carre	C	1	0	HB	35,000	
Chocolatier	Walnridge	Marion	F	1	0	HB	23,000	
Chocolatier	Walnut Hall Stk	Walnut Hall Stock	C	1	0	LEX	47,000	
Chocolatier				**83**	**1**			
Classic Photo	Blue Chip	Blue Chip	F	1	0	LEX	45,000	
Classic Photo	Boxwood	Hucks Undercover	C	3	0	HB	12,667	
Classic Photo	Brittany	Brittany	C	2	0	LEX	15,000	
Classic Photo	Brittany	Brittany	F	1	0	LEX	7,000	
Classic Photo	Cameo Hills	Blue Ridge	C	1	0	LEX	2,000	
Classic Photo	Cameo Hills	Blue Ridge	F	1	0	LEX	22,000	
Classic Photo	Cane Run	Cane Run	C	1	0	LEX	3,000	
Classic Photo	Concord	Northway	F	1	0	HB	2,500	
Classic Photo	Dunroven	Dunroven	C	3	1	LEX	14,000	55,869
Classic Photo	Dunroven	Dunroven	F	1	0	LEX	5,000	
Classic Photo	Futurity Hill	Futurity Hill	C	2	0	LEX	3,500	
Classic Photo	Hempt	Hempt	F	4	0	HB	9,500	
Classic Photo	Hunterton	Hunterton	C	1	0	HB	12,000	

Sire	Consignor	Farm	Sex	Sold	$50,000 2 YOs	Sale	Avg Price	Avg $ Won
Classic Photo	Hunterton	Hunterton	F	1	0	HB	6,000	
Classic Photo	Hunterton	Oak Park	F	1	0	LEX	12,000	
Classic Photo	Hunterton	Pine Hill	C	1	1	LEX	40,000	96,016
Classic Photo	Kentuckiana	Benaire	C	1	0	LEX	12,000	
Classic Photo	Kentuckiana	Benaire	F	1	0	LEX	6,000	
Classic Photo	Kentuckiana	Kentuckiana	C	16	1	LEX	14,250	50,187
Classic Photo	Kentuckiana	Kentuckiana	F	15	0	LEX	13,067	
Classic Photo	Kentuckiana	Wilbur Eash	C	1	0	LEX	9,000	
Classic Photo	Kentuckiana	Wilt Standardbreds	C	2	0	LEX	16,000	
Classic Photo	Kentuckiana	Wilt Standardbreds	F	2	0	LEX	20,500	
Classic Photo	Northwood	Allerage	C	1	0	HB	10,000	
Classic Photo	Northwood	Allerage	F	2	0	HB	9,500	
Classic Photo	Northwood	Allerage	C	1	0	LEX	3,000	
Classic Photo	Northwood	Bluestone	C	1	0	HB	2,500	
Classic Photo	Northwood	Bluestone	F	2	0	LEX	7,500	
Classic Photo	Peninsula	Cedar Creek	C	1	0	LEX	97,000	
Classic Photo	Peninsula	Peninsula	C	1	1	HB	35,000	67,341
Classic Photo	Peninsula	Robert Detweiler's	C	1	0	HB	15,000	
Classic Photo	Preferred	Ecuries Vandenplas	C	1	0	HB	10,000	
Classic Photo	Preferred	Fair Winds	C	1	0	LEX	32,000	
Classic Photo	Preferred	Heritage Hill	C	1	0	HB	7,000	
Classic Photo	Preferred	Heritage Hill	F	1	0	HB	19,000	
Classic Photo	Preferred	Lindy	C	2	0	HB	8,250	
Classic Photo	Preferred	Schunk Stables	C	1	0	LEX	12,000	
Classic Photo	Saga	New Pioneer	F	1	1	LEX	12,000	56,694
Classic Photo	Saga	Saga	F	1	0	LEX	4,000	
Classic Photo	Spring Haven	Mindale	F	1	0	LEX	20,000	
Classic Photo	Spring Haven	Viking Meadows	C	1	0	LEX	4,000	
Classic Photo	Steiner Stock	Steiner Stock	C	1	0	LEX	3,000	
Classic Photo	Stonegate	Stonegate	C	2	0	HB	7,750	
Classic Photo	Stonegate	Stonegate	F	1	0	HB	4,000	
Classic Photo	Vieux Carre	Vieux Carre	C	3	0	HB	16,000	
Classic Photo	Vieux Carre	Vieux Carre	F	4	0	HB	5,250	
Classic Photo	Walnridge	Golden Gait	C	1	1	HB	45,000	51,804
Classic Photo	Walnridge	Walnridge	C	1	0	HB	90,000	
Classic Photo	Walnridge	Walnridge	F	1	0	HB	70,000	
Classic Photo	Winbak	Winbak	C	1	0	LEX	4,000	

Sire	Consignor	Farm	Sex	Sold	$50,000 2 YOs	Sale	Avg Price	Avg $ Won
Classic Photo				99	6			
Conway Hall	Allamerican	Allamerican	C	1	0	HB	30,000	
Conway Hall	Blue Chip	Blue Chip	C	3	0	HB	30,333	
Conway Hall	Blue Chip	Blue Chip	F	1	0	HB	70,000	
Conway Hall	Boxwood	Boxwood	C	1	0	HB	10,000	
Conway Hall	Boxwood	Boxwood	F	1	0	HB	24,000	
Conway Hall	Brittany	Brittany	C	4	1	LEX	36,500	206,231
Conway Hall	Brittany	Brittany	F	1	0	LEX	35,000	
Conway Hall	Cameo Hills	Cameo Hills	C	2	0	LEX	57,500	
Conway Hall	Cameo Hills	Cameo Hills	F	2	1	LEX	14,500	61,203
Conway Hall	Cane Run	Cane Run	F	1	0	LEX	15,000	
Conway Hall	Concord	Concord	C	2	0	HB	19,500	
Conway Hall	Concord	Concord	F	4	1	HB	28,000	94,182
Conway Hall	Concord	Hanover	C	1	0	HB	80,000	
Conway Hall	Concord	Hanover	F	1	0	HB	27,000	
Conway Hall	Concord	Marion	C	1	0	HB	15,000	
Conway Hall	Concord	Marion	F	2	0	HB	20,000	
Conway Hall	Concord	Orchard Farm	C	1	1	HB	25,000	113,953
Conway Hall	Concord	Perretti	C	1	0	HB	27,000	
Conway Hall	Diamond Creek	Diamond Creek	C	2	0	HB	45,000	
Conway Hall	Diamond Creek	Diamond Creek	F	1	0	HB	40,000	
Conway Hall	Diamond Creek	Diamond Creek	F	1	0	LEX	4,000	
Conway Hall	Dunroven	Dunroven	C	2	0	LEX	25,000	
Conway Hall	Dunroven	Dunroven	F	2	0	LEX	17,500	
Conway Hall	Fair Winds	Fair Winds	C	3	0	HB	20,333	
Conway Hall	Fair Winds	Fair Winds	F	1	0	HB	27,000	
Conway Hall	Fox Den	Fox Den	F	1	0	HB	6,000	
Conway Hall	Fox Den	Shaffer Standardbreds	C	1	0	HB	19,000	
Conway Hall	Futurity Hill	Futurity Hill	F	1	0	LEX	32,000	
Conway Hall	Hanover	Hanover	C	1	0	HB	45,000	
Conway Hall	Hunterton	Crawford	C	1	0	LEX	50,000	
Conway Hall	Hunterton	Green Creek	C	1	0	LEX	12,000	
Conway Hall	Hunterton	Hunterton	F	2	0	HB	23,000	
Conway Hall	Hunterton	Hunterton	C	3	1	LEX	33,000	79,044
Conway Hall	Hunterton	Leroy Kemp	C	1	0	LEX	33,000	
Conway Hall	Hunterton	Venture	C	1	0	LEX	25,000	
Conway Hall	Kentuckiana	Kentuckiana	C	5	0	LEX	25,400	

Sire	Consignor	Farm	Sex	Sold	$50,000 2 YOs	Sale	Avg Price	Avg $ Won
Conway Hall	Kentuckiana	Kentuckiana	F	10	1	LEX	33,600	98,251
Conway Hall	Midland Acres	Midland Acres	C	1	0	LEX	32,000	
Conway Hall	Millstream	Millstream	F	2	0	HB	22,000	
Conway Hall	Northwood	Allerage	C	2	0	HB	18,250	
Conway Hall	Northwood	Allerage	F	3	0	HB	27,000	
Conway Hall	Northwood	Beal	C	1	0	HB	5,500	
Conway Hall	Northwood	Beal	F	1	0	HB	25,000	
Conway Hall	Northwood	Bluestone	C	1	0	LEX	30,000	
Conway Hall	Northwood	Bluestone	F	3	2	LEX	21,333	74,131
Conway Hall	Northwood	Howard Stables	F	1	1	HB	20,000	80,593
Conway Hall	Northwood	Kentuckiana	F	1	0	HB	18,000	
Conway Hall	Northwood	Kurt Hansen's	F	1	0	HB	37,000	
Conway Hall	Northwood	Starmaker	C	1	0	HB	22,000	
Conway Hall	Peninsula	Deo Volente	C	4	0	HB	56,250	
Conway Hall	Peninsula	Deo Volente	C	2	0	LEX	90,000	
Conway Hall	Peninsula	Deo Volente	F	1	1	LEX	100,000	72,799
Conway Hall	Peninsula	Peninsula	C	3	0	HB	40,667	
Conway Hall	Peninsula	Peninsula	F	1	0	HB	31,000	
Conway Hall	Peninsula	Peninsula	C	1	0	LEX	45,000	
Conway Hall	Peninsula	Peninsula	F	1	0	LEX	35,000	
Conway Hall	Peninsula	Quantum	C	1	0	HB	22,000	
Conway Hall	Peninsula	Silver Linden	F	1	0	LEX	13,000	
Conway Hall	Perretti	Perretti	F	1	1	HB	33,000	254,663
Conway Hall	Perretti	Perretti	C	1	0	LEX	100,000	
Conway Hall	Preferred	Birch Creek	C	1	0	LEX	70,000	
Conway Hall	Preferred	Bloodstock	C	1	0	LEX	9,000	
Conway Hall	Preferred	Brittany	C	1	0	HB	50,000	
Conway Hall	Preferred	Kronos	F	1	0	LEX	30,000	
Conway Hall	Preferred	Lindy	C	1	0	HB	4,000	
Conway Hall	Preferred	Lindy	F	2	0	HB	17,000	
Conway Hall	Preferred	Lindy	C	3	0	LEX	57,667	
Conway Hall	Preferred	Lindy	F	2	0	LEX	27,500	
Conway Hall	Preferred	Meadowbranch	C	1	0	LEX	12,000	
Conway Hall	Preferred	Southwind	C	1	0	HB	10,000	
Conway Hall	Preferred	Southwind	F	2	1	HB	20,500	83,475
Conway Hall	Preferred	Southwind	C	1	1	LEX	22,000	166,708
Conway Hall	Preferred	Stirling Brook	C	1	0	LEX	50,000	

Sire	Consignor	Farm	Sex	Sold	$50,000 2 YOs	Sale	Avg Price	Avg $ Won
Conway Hall	Preferred	Stirling Brook	F	1	0	LEX	50,000	
Conway Hall	Preferred	White Birch	C	1	0	LEX	32,000	
Conway Hall	Preferred	Wildewood	C	1	1	HB	10,000	62,353
Conway Hall	Preferred	Wildewood	F	1	0	HB	24,000	
Conway Hall	Saga	Saga	C	3	1	LEX	50,000	51,051
Conway Hall	Spring Haven	Jonas Schlabach's	C	1	0	HB	20,000	
Conway Hall	Spring Haven	Jonas Schlabach's	F	1	0	HB	45,000	
Conway Hall	Spring Haven	Martin Miller's	F	1	0	HB	30,000	
Conway Hall	Spring Haven	Mindale	F	1	0	LEX	22,000	
Conway Hall	Spring Haven	Spring Run	C	1	0	HB	30,000	
Conway Hall	Stonegate	Stonegate	C	1	0	HB	40,000	
Conway Hall	Vieux Carre	Vieux Carre	C	2	0	HB	27,500	
Conway Hall	Vieux Carre	Vieux Carre	F	1	0	HB	45,000	
Conway Hall	Walnridge	Maple Hill	F	1	0	HB	35,000	
Conway Hall	Walnridge	Marion	C	1	0	HB	17,000	
Conway Hall	Walnridge	Marion	F	1	0	HB	7,000	
Conway Hall	Walnridge	Walnridge	C	1	0	HB	110,000	
Conway Hall	Walnut Hall Ltd	Walnut Hall Ltd	C	7	1	HB	39,429	84,283
Conway Hall	Walnut Hall Ltd	Walnut Hall Ltd	F	4	0	HB	37,750	
Conway Hall	Walnut Hall Stock	Walnut Hall Stock	C	3	0	LEX	19,000	
Conway Hall	Walnut Hall Stock	Walnut Hall Stock	F	1	0	LEX	60,000	
Conway Hall	Westwind	Walnut Hall Ltd	C	1	0	HB	25,000	
Conway Hall	Westwind	Walnut Hall Ltd	F	3	0	HB	24,000	
Conway Hall	Winbak	Winbak	C	2	0	HB	36,000	
Conway Hall	Winbak	Winbak	F	1	0	HB	42,000	
Conway Hall	Winbak	Winbak	C	5	1	LEX	42,600	53,106
Conway Hall	Winbak	Winbak	F	1	0	LEX	62,000	
Conway Hall				171	17			
CR Excalibur	Winterwood	Winterwood	F	1	0	HB	19,000	
Credit Winner	Allamerican	Allamerican	C	2	0	HB	23,500	
Credit Winner	Allamerican	Allamerican	F	2	0	HB	21,500	
Credit Winner	Blue Chip	Bennett	C	1	0	LEX	60,000	
Credit Winner	Blue Chip	Blue Chip	C	12	1	HB	68,583	59,493
Credit Winner	Blue Chip	Blue Chip	F	5	1	HB	57,400	58,925
Credit Winner	Blue Chip	Blue Chip	C	4	0	LEX	94,750	
Credit Winner	Blue Chip	Blue Chip	F	5	2	LEX	96,400	131,684
Credit Winner	Blue Chip	Paradise	C	1	0	HB	9,000	

Sire	Consignor	Farm	Sex	Sold	$50,000 2 YOs	Sale	Avg Price	Avg $ Won
Credit Winner	Brittany	Brittany	C	2	0	LEX	12,500	
Credit Winner	Brittany	Brittany	F	2	0	LEX	16,500	
Credit Winner	Cameo Hills	Cameo Hills	C	3	2	LEX	64,000	241,490
Credit Winner	Cameo Hills	Cameo Hills	F	1	0	LEX	10,000	
Credit Winner	Cameo Hills	Zimpfer Stable	C	1	0	LEX	18,000	
Credit Winner	Cane Run	Cane Run	C	1	0	LEX	70,000	
Credit Winner	Cane Run	Cane Run	F	1	0	LEX	50,000	
Credit Winner	Concord	Concord	C	4	0	HB	78,750	
Credit Winner	Concord	Concord	F	5	0	HB	56,200	
Credit Winner	Concord	Hanover	F	1	0	HB	20,000	
Credit Winner	Concord	Marion	C	1	0	HB	6,000	
Credit Winner	Concord	Marion	F	3	1	HB	20,667	91,247
Credit Winner	Concord	Orchard Farm	C	1	0	HB	55,000	
Credit Winner	Diamond Creek	Diamond Creek	C	2	2	HB	75,000	118,944
Credit Winner	Diamond Creek	Diamond Creek	F	2	0	HB	58,500	
Credit Winner	Diamond Creek	Diamond Creek	C	1	0	LEX	55,000	
Credit Winner	Diamond Creek	Diamond Creek	F	4	1	LEX	74,750	81,656
Credit Winner	Dunroven	Dunroven	C	2	0	LEX	7,500	
Credit Winner	Dunroven	Dunroven	F	8	0	LEX	32,875	
Credit Winner	Fair Winds	Fair Winds	C	1	0	HB	65,000	
Credit Winner	Fair Winds	Fair Winds	F	2	1	HB	58,500	88,060
Credit Winner	Hanover	Hanover	C	6	0	HB	60,833	
Credit Winner	Hanover	Hanover	F	7	1	HB	46,714	83,862
Credit Winner	Hanover	Hanover	C	2	0	LEX	53,500	
Credit Winner	Hanover	Hanover	F	1	0	LEX	22,000	
Credit Winner	Hunterton	Crawford	C	2	0	LEX	77,500	
Credit Winner	Hunterton	Ernie Martinez	F	1	0	LEX	13,000	
Credit Winner	Hunterton	Hunterton	C	4	0	HB	35,500	
Credit Winner	Hunterton	Hunterton	F	2	0	HB	37,000	
Credit Winner	Hunterton	Hunterton	C	2	1	LEX	46,000	55,499
Credit Winner	Hunterton	Hunterton	F	1	0	LEX	130,000	
Credit Winner	Hunterton	Meadow Creek	F	1	0	HB	17,000	
Credit Winner	Hunterton	Walco	C	5	1	LEX	131,400	86,752
Credit Winner	Hunterton	Walco	F	3	0	LEX	18,667	
Credit Winner	Hunterton	Walnut Hall Ltd	C	1	0	LEX	80,000	
Credit Winner	Kentuckiana	Kentuckiana	F	1	0	LEX	13,000	
Credit Winner	Millstream	Millstream	F	2	0	HB	40,000	

Sire	Consignor	Farm	Sex	Sold	$50,000 2 YOs	Sale	Avg Price	Avg $ Won
Credit Winner	Northwood	Allerage	C	2	1	HB	56,000	71,817
Credit Winner	Northwood	Allerage	F	1	0	HB	15,000	
Credit Winner	Northwood	Allerage	C	1	0	LEX	35,000	
Credit Winner	Northwood	Allerage	F	2	1	LEX	55,000	263,138
Credit Winner	Northwood	Fox Valley	C	1	0	HB	77,000	
Credit Winner	Northwood	Stonehenge	C	1	0	HB	25,000	
Credit Winner	Northwood	White Hollow	F	1	0	HB	25,000	
Credit Winner	Peninsula	Deo Volente	F	1	0	HB	32,000	
Credit Winner	Peninsula	Deo Volente	C	1	0	LEX	20,000	
Credit Winner	Peninsula	Deo Volente	F	1	0	LEX	20,000	
Credit Winner	Peninsula	Peninsula	C	7	3	HB	106,286	106,002
Credit Winner	Peninsula	Peninsula	F	1	0	HB	28,000	
Credit Winner	Peninsula	Peninsula	C	4	0	LEX	64,250	
Credit Winner	Peninsula	Peninsula	F	2	0	LEX	100,000	
Credit Winner	Peninsula	Pheasant Hill	C	2	0	LEX	51,000	
Credit Winner	Peninsula	Silver Linden	C	2	0	HB	45,000	
Credit Winner	Peninsula	Silver Linden	F	1	1	HB	90,000	77,234
Credit Winner	Peninsula	Wizard Heights	C	1	0	LEX	165,000	
Credit Winner	Preferred	Bloodstock	C	1	0	LEX	22,000	
Credit Winner	Preferred	Brittany	C	1	0	HB	125,000	
Credit Winner	Preferred	Concord	F	1	0	LEX	4,000	
Credit Winner	Preferred	Dumain Haven	C	1	0	HB	60,000	
Credit Winner	Preferred	Fair Winds	C	1	0	LEX	23,000	
Credit Winner	Preferred	Joie De Vie	F	1	0	LEX	40,000	
Credit Winner	Preferred	Lindy	C	1	0	HB	30,000	
Credit Winner	Preferred	Lindy	F	2	0	HB	15,500	
Credit Winner	Preferred	Lindy	C	7	0	LEX	105,714	
Credit Winner	Preferred	Lindy	F	4	0	LEX	76,750	
Credit Winner	Preferred	Morrison	F	1	0	HB	42,000	
Credit Winner	Preferred	Northfields	C	1	0	HB	80,000	
Credit Winner	Preferred	Phil Hunt's	F	1	0	HB	28,000	
Credit Winner	Preferred	Southwind	C	1	0	LEX	5,000	
Credit Winner	Preferred	Southwind	F	2	0	LEX	75,500	
Credit Winner	Preferred	Stirling Brook	F	1	0	HB	20,000	
Credit Winner	Preferred	Stirling Brook	F	1	0	LEX	40,000	
Credit Winner	Preferred	White Birch	C	2	0	HB	50,000	
Credit Winner	Preferred	White Birch	F	6	0	HB	24,500	

Sire	Consignor	Farm	Sex	Sold	$50,000 2 YOs	Sale	Avg Price	Avg $ Won
Credit Winner	Saga	Saga	C	1	0	LEX	9,000	
Credit Winner	Saga	Saga	F	1	0	LEX	70,000	
Credit Winner	Spring Haven	Abby	C	1	0	LEX	35,000	
Credit Winner	Spring Haven	Jonas Schlabach's	C	1	0	HB	95,000	
Credit Winner	Spring Haven	Jonas Schlabach's	F	3	0	HB	22,333	
Credit Winner	Spring Haven	K.E.M. Standardbreds	C	1	0	LEX	25,000	
Credit Winner	Spring Haven	Wilbur Stoll Lang	F	1	0	LEX	80,000	
Credit Winner	Steiner Stock	Steiner Stock	F	1	1	LEX	70,000	156,680
Credit Winner	Stonegate	Stonegate	C	1	0	HB	24,000	
Credit Winner	Stonegate	Stonegate	F	1	0	HB	42,000	
Credit Winner	Vieux Carre	Vieux Carre	C	1	0	HB	150,000	
Credit Winner	Vieux Carre	Vieux Carre	F	2	0	HB	8,250	
Credit Winner	Walnridge	Walnridge	C	3	0	HB	48,333	
Credit Winner	Walnut Hall Stock	Walnut Hall Stock	C	1	0	LEX	90,000	
Credit Winner	Winterwood	Winterwood	F	1	0	HB	27,000	
Credit Winner				**209**	**21**			
Daguet Rapide	Preferred	D Farm	C	1	0	HB	40,000	
Daguet Rapide	Preferred	D Farm	F	1	0	HB	11,000	
Daguet Rapide	Preferred	D Farm	C	2	0	LEX	21,000	
Daguet Rapide	Preferred	D Farm	F	1	1	LEX	30,000	91,740
Daguet Rapide	Saga	Saga	F	1	0	LEX	45,000	
Daguet Rapide				**6**	**1**			
Donato Hanover	Allamerican	Allamerican	C	1	0	HB	7,000	
Donato Hanover	Brittany	Brittany	C	1	0	LEX	155,000	
Donato Hanover	Cameo Hills	Cameo Hills	C	2	0	LEX	18,000	
Donato Hanover	Cameo Hills	Cameo Hills	F	2	1	LEX	95,000	75,622
Donato Hanover	Concord	Concord	C	2	1	HB	137,500	290,206
Donato Hanover	Concord	Concord	F	1	0	HB	255,000	
Donato Hanover	Diamond Creek	Diamond Creek	C	1	0	LEX	55,000	
Donato Hanover	Diamond Creek	Diamond Creek	F	4	1	LEX	69,750	66,677
Donato Hanover	Fashion	Fashion	C	1	0	HB	35,000	
Donato Hanover	Fox Den	Hanover	C	1	0	HB	16,000	
Donato Hanover	Hanover	Hanover	C	11	1	HB	54,273	550,789
Donato Hanover	Hanover	Hanover	F	12	0	HB	36,417	
Donato Hanover	Hunterton	Hunterton	C	2	0	LEX	97,500	
Donato Hanover	Hunterton	Walco	C	3	1	LEX	108,333	84,300
Donato Hanover	Hunterton	Walco	F	1	0	LEX	62,000	

Sire	Consignor	Farm	Sex	Sold	$50,000 2 YOs	Sale	Avg Price	Avg $ Won
Donato Hanover	Kentuckiana	Kentuckiana	C	3	0	LEX	42,333	
Donato Hanover	Kentuckiana	Kentuckiana	F	1	0	LEX	70,000	
Donato Hanover	Northwood	Allerage	F	1	0	LEX	20,000	
Donato Hanover	Northwood	Fair Winds	C	1	0	LEX	25,000	
Donato Hanover	Northwood	Jonalee	F	1	0	HB	7,000	
Donato Hanover	Northwood	Kentuckiana	C	1	0	HB	23,000	
Donato Hanover	Northwood	White Hollow	F	1	1	HB	42,000	76,574
Donato Hanover	Peninsula	Peninsula	C	4	1	HB	111,750	168,425
Donato Hanover	Peninsula	Peninsula	F	1	0	HB	10,000	
Donato Hanover	Peninsula	Peninsula	F	1	0	LEX	50,000	
Donato Hanover	Peninsula	Quantum	C	1	0	HB	15,000	
Donato Hanover	Peninsula	Quantum	C	1	0	LEX	9,000	
Donato Hanover	Peninsula	Silver Linden	C	1	0	HB	33,000	
Donato Hanover	Perretti	Perretti	C	1	0	HB	65,000	
Donato Hanover	Perretti	Perretti	F	1	0	HB	37,000	
Donato Hanover	Preferred	D Farm	C	1	0	LEX	50,000	
Donato Hanover	Preferred	Lindy	C	2	0	LEX	165,000	
Donato Hanover	Preferred	Lindy	F	1	0	LEX	27,000	
Donato Hanover	Preferred	Southwind	C	1	0	LEX	7,000	
Donato Hanover	Preferred	White Birch	F	1	0	LEX	22,000	
Donato Hanover	Spring Haven	Spring Haven	C	1	0	LEX	90,000	
Donato Hanover	Spring Haven	Spring Haven	F	1	0	LEX	85,000	
Donato Hanover	Vieux Carre	Vieux Carre	F	3	0	HB	34,333	
Donato Hanover	Walnridge	Marion	C	1	0	HB	12,000	
Donato Hanover	Walnridge	Marion	F	1	0	HB	7,000	
Donato Hanover	Walnut Hall Ltd	Walnut Hall Ltd	C	1	0	HB	45,000	
Donato Hanover	Walnut Hall Ltd	Walnut Hall Ltd	F	1	0	HB	65,000	
Donato Hanover	Walnut Hall Stk	Walnut Hall Stock	C	1	0	LEX	80,000	
Donato Hanover				**81**	**7**			
Donerail	Dunroven	Dunroven	F	2	0	LEX	10,000	
Donerail	Hempt	Hempt	F	2	0	HB	5,250	
Donerail	Preferred	D Farm	F	1	0	HB	20,000	
Donerail	Spring Haven	Spring Haven	C	1	0	LEX	8,000	
Donerail	Vieux Carre	Vieux Carre	F	2	0	HB	15,500	
Donerail				**8**	**0**			
Dragon Again	Allamerican	Allamerican	C	3	1	HB	20,333	82,995
Dragon Again	Allamerican	Allamerican	F	2	0	HB	6,750	

Sire	Consignor	Farm	Sex	Sold	$50,000 2 YOs	Sale	Avg Price	Avg $ Won
Dragon Again	Blue Chip	Blue Chip	C	2	0	HB	16,750	
Dragon Again	Blue Chip	Blue Chip	F	1	0	HB	12,000	
Dragon Again	Concord	Concord	C	2	0	HB	27,000	
Dragon Again	Concord	Concord	F	1	0	HB	15,000	
Dragon Again	Concord	Ed Evans'	C	1	0	HB	22,000	
Dragon Again	Concord	Olive Branch	C	1	0	HB	45,000	
Dragon Again	Fair Winds	Bayberry	C	1	0	HB	45,000	
Dragon Again	Fair Winds	Fair Winds	C	2	0	HB	32,500	
Dragon Again	Fair Winds	Fair Winds	F	2	0	HB	31,000	
Dragon Again	Fair Winds	Stonehenge	C	1	0	HB	20,000	
Dragon Again	Fair Winds	Stonehenge	F	1	0	HB	11,000	
Dragon Again	Fox Den	Burnt Cabins	C	2	0	HB	23,000	
Dragon Again	Fox Den	Gregory Gehman's	C	1	0	HB	10,000	
Dragon Again	Fox Den	Hanover	C	1	0	HB	13,000	
Dragon Again	Fox Den	Misty Meadow	C.	1	0	HB	9,500	
Dragon Again	Fox Den	Shaffer Standardbreds	C	1	0	HB	10,000	
Dragon Again	Fox Den	Shaffer Standardbreds	F	6	0	HB	14,500	
Dragon Again	Fox Den	Stoltzfus	C	4	0	HB	5,250	
Dragon Again	Fox Den	Stoltzfus	F	1	0	HB	2,000	
Dragon Again	Hanover	Hanover	C	30	2	HB	43,433	109,461
Dragon Again	Hanover	Hanover	F	28	1	HB	36,750	81,443
Dragon Again	Hanover	Hanover	C	1	0	LEX	45,000	
Dragon Again	Hanover	Hanover	F	2	0	LEX	91,000	
Dragon Again	Hempt	Hempt	C	4	0	HB	11,875	
Dragon Again	Hempt	Hempt	F	3	0	HB	3,400	
Dragon Again	Hunterton	Hunterton	F	1	1	LEX	10,000	108,228
Dragon Again	Kentuckiana	Kentuckiana	C	3	0	LEX	34,000	
Dragon Again	Kentuckiana	Kentuckiana	F	2	0	LEX	30,000	
Dragon Again	Northwood	Andray	C	1	0	HB	8,000	
Dragon Again	Northwood	Andray	F	1	0	LEX	4,000	
Dragon Again	Northwood	Caviart	C	1	0	HB	25,000	
Dragon Again	Northwood	Century Spring	C	1	0	HB	17,000	
Dragon Again	Northwood	Fox Valley	C	1	0	HB	50,000	
Dragon Again	Northwood	Fox Valley	F	1	0	HB	42,000	
Dragon Again	Northwood	Kurt Hansen's	F	1	0	HB	4,500	
Dragon Again	Northwood	Maple Run	F	1	0	HB	11,000	
Dragon Again	Northwood	Marvin Raber	F	1	0	HB	15,000	

Sire	Consignor	Farm	Sex	Sold	$50,000 2 YOs	Sale	Avg Price	Avg $ Won
Dragon Again	Northwood	Marvin Raber	F	1	0	LEX	7,000	
Dragon Again	Northwood	Olive Branch	C	1	0	HB	41,000	
Dragon Again	Peninsula	Donna Perry	F	1	0	LEX	10,000	
Dragon Again	Peninsula	Green Creek	C	1	0	LEX	21,000	
Dragon Again	Peninsula	Green Creek	F	1	0	LEX	4,000	
Dragon Again	Peninsula	Odds On Acres	C	2	0	LEX	33,500	
Dragon Again	Peninsula	Odds On Acres	F	2	0	LEX	14,000	
Dragon Again	Peninsula	Odds On Racing	C	3	0	HB	48,333	
Dragon Again	Peninsula	Owen	F	1	0	HB	50,000	
Dragon Again	Peninsula	Peninsula	C	2	0	HB	64,000	
Dragon Again	Peninsula	Peninsula	C	1	0	LEX	50,000	
Dragon Again	Peninsula	Pheasant Hill	C	1	0	HB	55,000	
Dragon Again	Peninsula	Pheasant Hill	F	2	0	LEX	23,500	
Dragon Again	Peninsula	Shady Side	C	1	0	LEX	100,000	
Dragon Again	Peninsula	Shady Side	F	1	0	LEX	42,000	
Dragon Again	Peninsula	Shamrock	C	2	0	HB	62,500	
Dragon Again	Peninsula	Shamrock	F	1	0	HB	9,000	
Dragon Again	Peninsula	Walnridge	F	1	0	HB	20,000	
Dragon Again	Peninsula	Walstan	C	1	1	LEX	19,000	222,309
Dragon Again	Peninsula	Yankeeland	C	1	0	LEX	80,000	
Dragon Again	Pin Oak Lane	Pin Oak Lane	C	1	0	HB	50,000	
Dragon Again	Pin Oak Lane	Pin Oak Lane	F	1	0	HB	6,500	
Dragon Again	Preferred	Blue Chip	C	1	0	HB	84,000	
Dragon Again	Preferred	Oak Knoll	F	1	0	HB	45,000	
Dragon Again	Preferred	Southwind	C	1	0	HB	47,000	
Dragon Again	Preferred	Southwind	C	1	0	LEX	75,000	
Dragon Again	Preferred	Tara Hills	F	1	0	HB	40,000	
Dragon Again	Preferred	Twin Creeks	C	1	0	LEX	13,000	
Dragon Again	Preferred	Walnut Hall Ltd	F	2	0	LEX	53,000	
Dragon Again	Preferred	Warrawee	C	2	0	HB	29,000	
Dragon Again	Preferred	White Birch	C	3	1	HB	49,000	66,781
Dragon Again	Preferred	White Birch	F	3	0	HB	10,667	
Dragon Again	Saga	Bob Farmwald	F	1	0	LEX	30,000	
Dragon Again	Saga	Victory Hill	C	1	0	LEX	8,000	
Dragon Again	Saga	Victory Hill	F	1	0	LEX	2,000	
Dragon Again	Spring Haven	Bridgeview Acres	F	1	0	HB	30,000	
Dragon Again	Spring Haven	Hickory Lane	F	1	0	HB	9,000	

Sire	Consignor	Farm	Sex	Sold	$50,000 2 YOs	Sale	Avg Price	Avg $ Won
Dragon Again	Spring Haven	Lmn Bred	C	1	0	LEX	3,000	
Dragon Again	Spring Haven	Mindale	C	2	0	LEX	34,000	
Dragon Again	Spring Haven	Mindale	F	1	0	LEX	23,000	
Dragon Again	Spring Haven	Nathan Byler's	F	1	0	HB	11,000	
Dragon Again	Spring Haven	Sam Lambright Jr	F	1	0	LEX	16,000	
Dragon Again	Spring Haven	Spring Haven	F	1	0	HB	62,000	
Dragon Again	Spring Haven	Spring Haven	F	1	0	LEX	20,000	
Dragon Again	Steiner Stock	Steiner Stock	C	1	0	LEX	27,000	
Dragon Again	Steiner Stock	Steiner Stock	F	4	0	LEX	13,750	
Dragon Again	Stonegate	Stonegate	C	1	0	HB	9,500	
Dragon Again	Stonegate	Stonegate	F	1	0	HB	7,000	
Dragon Again	Vieux Carre	Vieux Carre	C	13	3	HB	28,923	142,746
Dragon Again	Vieux Carre	Vieux Carre	F	11	0	HB	12,591	
Dragon Again	Walnut Hall Ltd	Walnut Hall Ltd	C	2	0	HB	23,000	
Dragon Again	Walnut Hall Ltd	Walnut Hall Ltd	F	1	0	HB	35,000	
Dragon Again	Westwind	Westwind	F	2	0	HB	13,250	
Dragon Again	Winbak	Winbak	C	3	0	HB	69,000	
Dragon Again	Winbak	Winbak	F	1	0	HB	12,000	
Dragon Again	Winbak	Winbak	C	4	2	LEX	56,250	286,429
Dragon Again	Winbak	Winbak	F	1	0	LEX	57,000	
Dragon Again				**223**	**12**			
Dream Vacation	Cameo Hills	Crawford	F	1	0	LEX	7,000	
Dream Vacation	Hunterton	Crawford	C	2	0	LEX	16,000	
Dream Vacation	Hunterton	Crawford	F	2	0	LEX	14,000	
Dream Vacation	Midland Acres	Midland Acres	F	1	0	LEX	13,000	
Dream Vacation	Perretti	Perretti	C	2	0	LEX	14,000	
Dream Vacation	Perretti	Perretti	F	1	0	LEX	85,000	
Dream Vacation	Preferred	Lindy	C	2	0	HB	13,000	
Dream Vacation	Preferred	Lindy	F	2	1	LEX	47,500	97,334
Dream Vacation	Preferred	White Birch	C	1	0	HB	14,000	
Dream Vacation	Spring Haven	FJD	C	2	0	LEX	9,500	
Dream Vacation	Spring Haven	FJD	F	1	0	LEX	6,000	
Dream Vacation	Winbak	Winbak	C	2	0	LEX	5,500	
Dream Vacation	Winbak	Winbak	F	3	0	LEX	28,667	
Dream Vacation				**22**	**1**			
E Dee's Cam	Hanover	Hanover	C	3	0	HB	15,667	
E Dee's Cam	Hanover	Hanover	F	1	0	HB	4,000	

Sire	Consignor	Farm	Sex	Sold	$50,000 2 YOs	Sale	Avg Price	Avg $ Won
E Dee's Cam	Preferred	Blue Chip	F	1	1	HB	20,000	143,344
E Dee's Cam				5	1			
Equinox Bi	Blue Chip	Blue Chip	C	1	0	HB	65,000	
Equinox Bi	Brittany	Brittany	C	1	0	LEX	25,000	
Equinox Bi	Concord	Concord	C	1	0	HB	17,000	
Equinox Bi	Saga	Underdog	C	1	0	LEX	6,000	
Equinox Bi				4	0			
Four Starzzz Shark	Brittany	Brittany	C	8	1	LEX	34,375	61,170
Four Starzzz Shark	Brittany	Brittany	F	12	0	LEX	20,333	
Four Starzzz Shark	Concord	Concord	C	2	0	HB	17,000	
Four Starzzz Shark	Concord	Concord	F	1	0	HB	27,000	
Four Starzzz Shark	Fair Winds	Fair Winds	F	2	0	HB	10,000	
Four Starzzz Shark	Hanover	Hanover	C	2	0	HB	31,000	
Four Starzzz Shark	Hanover	Hanover	C	1	0	LEX	70,000	
Four Starzzz Shark	Hunterton	Hunterton	C	1	0	HB	15,000	
Four Starzzz Shark	Hunterton	Hunterton	F	3	0	HB	27,000	
Four Starzzz Shark	Hunterton	Hunterton	C	1	0	LEX	80,000	
Four Starzzz Shark	Hunterton	Hunterton	F	1	0	LEX	6,000	
Four Starzzz Shark	Hunterton	Meadow Creek	C	1	0	HB	11,000	
Four Starzzz Shark	Hunterton	Shady Lane Meadows	F	1	0	LEX	14,000	
Four Starzzz Shark	Midland Acres	Midland Acres	F	1	0	LEX	35,000	
Four Starzzz Shark	Northwood	Andray	F	1	0	HB	6,000	
Four Starzzz Shark	Northwood	Andray	F	1	0	LEX	15,000	
Four Starzzz Shark	Northwood	Valley View	F	1	0	LEX	15,000	
Four Starzzz Shark	Peninsula	Russ Beeman's	C	1	0	HB	13,000	
Four Starzzz Shark	Preferred	White Birch	C	5	1	HB	12,800	64,005
Four Starzzz Shark	Preferred	White Birch	F	1	0	HB	32,000	
Four Starzzz Shark	Spring Haven	Dale Decker	C	1	0	LEX	40,000	
Four Starzzz Shark	Spring Haven	Spring Haven	F	1	0	LEX	8,000	
Four Starzzz Shark	Vieux Carre	Brittany	C	2	1	HB	31,000	107,500
Four Starzzz Shark	Vieux Carre	Brittany	F	1	0	HB	1,500	
Four Starzzz Shark	Vieux Carre	Vieux Carre	C	1	0	HB	15,000	
Four Starzzz Shark	Walnridge	Walnridge	C	1	0	HB	20,000	
Four Starzzz Shark	Walnridge	Walnridge	F	5	2	HB	21,200	165,779
Four Starzzz Shark	Winbak	Winbak	F	1	0	HB	34,000	
Four Starzzz Shark	Winbak	Winbak	C	1	1	LEX	32,000	181,198
Four Starzzz Shark	Winbak	Winbak	F	1	0	LEX	42,000	

Sire	Consignor	Farm	Sex	Sold	$50,000 2 YOs	Sale	Avg Price	Avg $ Won
Four Starzzz Shark				62	6			
Glidemaster	Blue Chip	Blue Chip	C	1	0	HB	100,000	
Glidemaster	Brittany	Brittany	C	4	0	LEX	20,000	
Glidemaster	Brittany	Brittany	F	3	0	LEX	30,667	
Glidemaster	Cane Run	Cane Run	F	1	0	LEX	30,000	
Glidemaster	Concord	Marion	C	1	0	HB	22,000	
Glidemaster	Concord	Marion	F	1	0	HB	3,500	
Glidemaster	Hanover	Hanover	C	3	1	HB	28,333	194,028
Glidemaster	Hanover	Hanover	C	1	0	LEX	30,000	
Glidemaster	Hunterton	Hunterton	C	6	1	HB	30,250	402,568
Glidemaster	Hunterton	Hunterton	F	5	0	HB	28,800	
Glidemaster	Hunterton	Hunterton	C	4	0	LEX	116,000	
Glidemaster	Hunterton	Hunterton	F	9	0	LEX	35,556	
Glidemaster	Hunterton	Ideal	C	1	0	HB	37,000	
Glidemaster	Hunterton	Ideal	F	1	0	HB	27,000	
Glidemaster	Kentuckiana	Kentuckiana	C	2	0	LEX	24,500	
Glidemaster	Kentuckiana	Kentuckiana	F	2	1	LEX	46,000	155,594
Glidemaster	Northwood	Allerage	C	1	0	HB	20,000	
Glidemaster	Northwood	Allerage	C	1	0	LEX	50,000	
Glidemaster	Northwood	Andray	F	1	0	HB	13,000	
Glidemaster	Northwood	Bluestone	C	1	0	LEX	27,000	
Glidemaster	Peninsula	Andray	F	1	0	HB	14,000	
Glidemaster	Peninsula	Andray	F	1	0	LEX	40,000	
Glidemaster	Peninsula	Deo Volente	C	1	0	HB	20,000	
Glidemaster	Peninsula	Dottie Morone	C	1	0	LEX	30,000	
Glidemaster	Peninsula	In The Black	F	1	0	LEX	30,000	
Glidemaster	Peninsula	Oaklea	C	1	0	HB	80,000	
Glidemaster	Peninsula	Peninsula	F	1	0	HB	22,000	
Glidemaster	Peninsula	Peninsula	F	1	0	LEX	50,000	
Glidemaster	Peninsula	Quantum	C	1	0	LEX	17,000	
Glidemaster	Peninsula	Quantum	F	1	0	LEX	10,000	
Glidemaster	Peninsula	Richard W. Uhle	C	1	0	LEX	102,000	
Glidemaster	Preferred	Heritage Hill	F	1	0	HB	37,000	
Glidemaster	Preferred	Joie De Vie	F	1	0	LEX	140,000	
Glidemaster	Preferred	Lindy	C	1	0	LEX	6,000	
Glidemaster	Preferred	Northfields	C	1	0	HB	17,000	
Glidemaster	Preferred	Stirling Brook	C	1	0	HB	22,000	

Sire	Consignor	Farm	Sex	Sold	$50,000 2 YOs	Sale	Avg Price	Avg $ Won
Glidemaster	Preferred	Woodstock	F	1	0	LEX	70,000	
Glidemaster	Steiner Stock	Steiner Stock	F	1	0	LEX	65,000	
Glidemaster	Stonegate	Stonegate	F	1	0	HB	1,500	
Glidemaster	Vieux Carre	Vieux Carre	C	1	0	HB	65,000	
Glidemaster	Walnridge	Photo Mountain	F	1	0	HB	1,500	
Glidemaster	Walnridge	Torrey Ridge	C	1	0	HB	18,000	
Glidemaster	Walnridge	Torrey Ridge	F	1	0	HB	27,000	
Glidemaster	Walnridge	Walnridge	C	6	0	HB	48,500	
Glidemaster	Walnridge	Walnridge	F	4	0	HB	29,750	
Glidemaster	Winbak	Winbak	F	1	0	HB	22,000	
Glidemaster	Winbak	Winbak	F	1	0	LEX	35,000	
Glidemaster				84	3			
Grinfromeartoear	Dunroven	Dunroven	C	1	0	LEX	22,000	
Grinfromeartoear	Dunroven	Dunroven	F	1	0	LEX	11,000	
Grinfromeartoear	Peninsula	Linda & T.D. Van Kamp	C	1	0	LEX	11,000	
Grinfromeartoear	Spring Haven	Mindale	F	1	0	LEX	5,000	
Grinfromeartoear				4	0			
Here Comes Herbie	Fox Den	Fox Den	F	1	0	HB	17,000	
Here Comes Herbie	Hanover	Hanover	F	1	0	HB	7,000	
Here Comes Herbie	Hunterton	Ilazue	F	1	0	HB	25,000	
Here Comes Herbie	Preferred	Stonehenge	F	1	0	HB	190,000	
Here Comes Herbie	Preferred	Windsun	C	1	0	LEX	31,000	
Here Comes Herbie	Spring Haven	Jonas Schlabach's	C	1	0	HB	35,000	
Here Comes Herbie				6	0			
I Am A Fool	Blue Chip	Blue Chip	C	1	0	HB	17,000	
I Am A Fool	Blue Chip	Blue Chip	F	1	0	HB	13,000	
I Am A Fool	Concord	Stonebridge	C	1	0	HB	1,500	
I Am A Fool	Fair Winds	Fair Winds	C	1	0	HB	5,500	
I Am A Fool	Hanover	Hanover	C	1	0	HB	10,000	
I Am A Fool	Kentuckiana	Kentuckiana	C	24	0	LEX	13,083	
I Am A Fool	Kentuckiana	Kentuckiana	F	13	0	LEX	17,154	
I Am A Fool	Kentuckiana	Walstan	C	1	0	LEX	5,000	
I Am A Fool	Northwood	Andray	C	1	0	HB	15,000	
I Am A Fool	Northwood	Andray	F	1	0	HB	4,000	
I Am A Fool	Peninsula	Andray	F	1	0	HB	6,000	
I Am A Fool	Peninsula	Peninsula	C	1	0	LEX	8,000	
I Am A Fool	Preferred	Kentuckiana	F	2	0	HB	3,250	

Sire	Consignor	Farm	Sex	Sold	$50,000 2 YOs	Sale	Avg Price	Avg $ Won
I Am A Fool	Saga	Saga	F	1	0	LEX	6,000	
I Am A Fool	Saga	Victory Hill	C	1	0	LEX	13,000	
I Am A Fool	Spring Haven	Mindale	C	1	0	LEX	3,000	
I Am A Fool	Spring Haven	Mindale	F	2	0	LEX	5,000	
I Am A Fool	Spring Haven	Spring Haven	C	2	0	HB	23,500	
I Am A Fool	Spring Haven	Spring Haven	F	2	0	LEX	8,000	
I Am A Fool	Twinbrook	Killean Acres	C	1	1	HB	9,000	52,667
I Am A Fool	Vieux Carre	Mendez	F	1	0	HB	4,000	
I Am A Fool	Vieux Carre	Vieux Carre	C	5	0	HB	7,100	
I Am A Fool	Vieux Carre	Vieux Carre	F	1	0	HB	4,000	
I Am A Fool	Walnridge	Walnridge	F	1	0	HB	3,500	
I Am A Fool	Winterwood	Cashelmara	F	1	0	HB	1,500	
I Am A Fool				**68**	**1**			
Jate Lobell	Kentuckiana	Kentuckiana	C	2	0	LEX	12,000	
Jate Lobell	Kentuckiana	Kentuckiana	F	2	0	LEX	25,500	
Jate Lobell	Peninsula	Peninsula	C	1	0	LEX	38,000	
Jate Lobell	Saga	Wilbur Eash	F	1	0	LEX	12,000	
Jate Lobell	Spring Haven	Hickory Lane	C	1	0	LEX	11,000	
Jate Lobell	Spring Haven	Lmn Bred	C	1	0	LEX	5,000	
Jate Lobell	Spring Haven	Mindale	F	1	0	LEX	10,000	
Jate Lobell	Winbak	Winbak	C	1	0	LEX	40,000	
Jate Lobell				**10**	**0**			
Jenna's Beach Boy	Fox Den	Stoltzfus	F	1	0	HB	11,500	
Jenna's Beach Boy	Hunterton	Sunrise	F	1	0	LEX	20,000	
Jenna's Beach Boy	Peninsula	Donna Perry	F	1	0	LEX	20,000	
Jenna's Beach Boy	Peninsula	James Murphy	C	1	0	LEX	7,000	
Jenna's Beach Boy	Peninsula	Peninsula	C	1	0	LEX	27,000	
Jenna's Beach Boy	Peninsula	Peninsula	F	1	0	LEX	50,000	
Jenna's Beach Boy	Peninsula	Rockridge	F	2	0	LEX	5,500	
Jenna's Beach Boy	Peninsula	Walstan	F	1	0	LEX	15,000	
Jenna's Beach Boy	Preferred	Stonehenge	C	1	0	HB	20,000	
Jenna's Beach Boy	Spring Haven	Mindale	C	1	0	LEX	18,000	
Jenna's Beach Boy	Spring Haven	Sunrise	C	1	1	LEX	14,000	91,981
Jenna's Beach Boy	Winbak	Winbak	C	4	0	LEX	24,750	
Jenna's Beach Boy				**16**	**1**			
Jereme's Jet	Fair Winds	Charlotte Ranch	C	1	0	HB	30,000	
Jereme's Jet	Hanover	Hanover	F	2	1	HB	33,500	346,162

Sire	Consignor	Farm	Sex	Sold	$50,000 2 YOs	Sale	Avg Price	Avg $ Won
Jereme's Jet	Hempt	Hempt	C	1	0	HB	50,000	
Jereme's Jet	Hempt	Hempt	F	1	0	HB	11,000	
Jereme's Jet	Hunterton	Jeff S. Jones	F	1	0	LEX	92,000	
Jereme's Jet	Hunterton	Walco	F	1	0	LEX	9,000	
Jereme's Jet	Northwood	Andray	C	1	0	HB	8,000	
Jereme's Jet	Northwood	Andray	F	1	0	HB	45,000	
Jereme's Jet	Peninsula	Equine Center	F	1	0	LEX	7,000	
Jereme's Jet	Preferred	Pinestone	F	1	0	HB	65,000	
Jereme's Jet	Preferred	Tara Hills	C	2	0	HB	61,000	
Jereme's Jet	Preferred	Tara Hills	F	2	1	HB	72,500	63,879
Jereme's Jet	Spring Haven	Rails Edge	C	1	0	HB	90,000	
Jereme's Jet	Spring Haven	Spring Haven	C	2	0	HB	87,500	
Jereme's Jet	Twinbrook	Twinbrook	F	1	0	HB	80,000	
Jereme's Jet				**19**	**2**			
Justice Hall	Preferred	D Farm	C	1	0	LEX	1,000	
Justice Hall	Preferred	D Farm	F	1	0	LEX	1,000	
Justice Hall				**2**	**0**			
Kadabra	Blue Chip	Blue Chip	F	2	1	HB	48,000	63,392
Kadabra	Brittany	Brittany	F	1	0	LEX	7,000	
Kadabra	Concord	Concord	F	3	1	HB	69,333	1,037,099
Kadabra	Concord	Hanover	C	1	0	HB	35,000	
Kadabra	Concord	Hanover	F	1	0	HB	55,000	
Kadabra	Diamond Creek	Diamond Creek	F	1	0	HB	25,000	
Kadabra	Diamond Creek	Diamond Creek	F	1	0	LEX	27,000	
Kadabra	Dunroven	Dunroven	C	2	0	LEX	15,000	
Kadabra	Hanover	Hanover	C	3	0	HB	31,333	
Kadabra	Hanover	Hanover	F	1	0	HB	20,000	
Kadabra	Hunterton	Hunterton	C	2	0	HB	19,500	
Kadabra	Hunterton	Hunterton	F	2	0	HB	26,000	
Kadabra	Hunterton	Hunterton	C	3	0	LEX	42,667	
Kadabra	Hunterton	Hunterton	F	2	1	LEX	110,500	480,234
Kadabra	Hunterton	Ilazue	C	1	0	HB	17,000	
Kadabra	Hunterton	Martinez Equine	F	1	0	HB	27,000	
Kadabra	Hunterton	Raz Mackenzie	C	1	0	LEX	10,000	
Kadabra	Hunterton	Walco	F	1	0	LEX	65,000	
Kadabra	Millstream	Millstream	C	1	0	HB	50,000	
Kadabra	Northwood	Jonalee	F	1	0	HB	2,000	

Sire	Consignor	Farm	Sex	Sold	$50,000 2 YOs	Sale	Avg Price	Avg $ Won
Kadabra	Northwood	Shaffer Standardbreds	F	1	0	HB	17,000	
Kadabra	Peninsula	Birch Hollow	F	1	0	HB	16,000	
Kadabra	Peninsula	M. Smith And R. Uhle	C	1	1	HB	120,000	317,590
Kadabra	Peninsula	Oaklea	F	1	0	HB	35,000	
Kadabra	Peninsula	Peninsula	C	1	0	HB	30,000	
Kadabra	Peninsula	Peninsula	F	3	0	HB	34,833	
Kadabra	Peninsula	Quantum	F	1	0	HB	20,000	
Kadabra	Peninsula	Rupert	C	1	0	HB	42,000	
Kadabra	Preferred	Bennett	C	1	0	LEX	105,000	
Kadabra	Preferred	D Farm	F	1	0	HB	5,500	
Kadabra	Preferred	Green Gables	C	1	1	HB	7,000	182,153
Kadabra	Preferred	Hamstan	F	1	0	HB	18,000	
Kadabra	Preferred	Lindy	C	1	0	HB	25,000	
Kadabra	Preferred	Lindy	F	2	0	HB	17,500	
Kadabra	Preferred	Lindy	F	1	0	LEX	50,000	
Kadabra	Preferred	Morrison	C	1	0	HB	37,000	
Kadabra	Preferred	Paradox	F	1	0	HB	9,000	
Kadabra	Preferred	Pinestone	C	1	0	HB	31,000	
Kadabra	Preferred	Rolling Acres	F	1	0	HB	15,000	
Kadabra	Preferred	Seelster	F	1	0	HB	16,000	
Kadabra	Preferred	Southwind	C	1	1	HB	25,000	50,155
Kadabra	Preferred	Southwind	F	1	0	HB	17,000	
Kadabra	Preferred	Stirling Brook	F	1	0	HB	27,000	
Kadabra	Preferred	Stonehenge	F	1	0	HB	13,000	
Kadabra	Preferred	Talbot Creek	C	1	0	HB	24,000	
Kadabra	Preferred	White Birch	C	2	0	HB	5,500	
Kadabra	Preferred	White Birch	F	1	0	HB	20,000	
Kadabra	Preferred	Windsun	C	1	0	HB	22,000	
Kadabra	Preferred	Windsun	F	2	0	HB	18,500	
Kadabra	Spring Haven	FJD	C	1	0	LEX	17,000	
Kadabra	Spring Haven	Spring Haven	C	1	0	HB	30,000	
Kadabra	Walnridge	Walnridge	C	1	0	HB	25,000	
Kadabra	Walnut Hall Ltd	Walnut Hall Ltd	C	1	0	HB	38,000	
Kadabra	Walnut Hall Ltd	Walnut Hall Ltd	F	1	0	HB	42,000	
Kadabra	Walnut Hall Stock	Walnut Hall Stock	C	2	0	LEX	80,000	
Kadabra	Walnut Hall Stock	Walnut Hall Stock	F	1	0	LEX	40,000	
Kadabra				73	6			

Sire	Consignor	Farm	Sex	Sold	$50,000 2 YOs	Sale	Avg Price	Avg $ Won
Ken Warkentin	Cameo Hills	Fair Winds	C	1	0	LEX	28,000	
Ken Warkentin	Concord	Concord	F	1	0	HB	100,000	
Ken Warkentin	Concord	Farrow	C	1	0	HB	31,000	
Ken Warkentin	Fair Winds	Fair Winds	F	1	0	HB	25,000	
Ken Warkentin	Hanover	Hanover	C	2	0	HB	17,500	
Ken Warkentin	Hunterton	E and M Yoder	C	1	0	LEX	45,000	
Ken Warkentin	Hunterton	Ernie Martinez	F	1	0	LEX	5,000	
Ken Warkentin	Hunterton	Jean Cloutier	F	1	0	LEX	12,000	
Ken Warkentin	Hunterton	Little Moon Lake	C	1	1	LEX	19,000	83,858
Ken Warkentin	Kentuckiana	Kentuckiana	C	3	0	LEX	86,667	
Ken Warkentin	Kentuckiana	Wilbur Eash	C	1	0	LEX	35,000	
Ken Warkentin	Kentuckiana	Wilbur Eash	F	1	0	LEX	40,000	
Ken Warkentin	Northstar	Northstar	F	1	1	HB	21,000	124,183
Ken Warkentin	Northwood	Bluestone	F	1	0	LEX	25,000	
Ken Warkentin	Peninsula	Birch Creek	F	1	0	LEX	30,000	
Ken Warkentin	Peninsula	Marvin Raber	C	1	0	LEX	25,000	
Ken Warkentin	Peninsula	Robert Detweiler's	C	1	0	HB	20,000	
Ken Warkentin	Preferred	Hamstan	C	1	0	HB	40,000	
Ken Warkentin	Saga	Saga	F	1	0	LEX	14,000	
Ken Warkentin	Spring Haven	Spring Haven	F	1	0	HB	30,000	
Ken Warkentin	Twinbrook	Twinbrook	C	1	0	HB	22,000	
Ken Warkentin	Walnut Hall Stock	Walnut Hall Stock	F	1	0	LEX	15,000	
Ken Warkentin	Winterwood	Winterwood	F	1	1	HB	32,000	68,535
Ken Warkentin				**26**	**3**			
Like A Prayer	Concord	Concord	C	1	0	HB	22,000	
Like A Prayer	Diamond Creek	Diamond Creek	C	1	0	LEX	11,000	
Like A Prayer	Dunroven	Dunroven	C	3	0	LEX	9,000	
Like A Prayer	Dunroven	Dunroven	F	2	0	LEX	9,500	
Like A Prayer	Hunterton	Hunterton	C	4	1	LEX	19,250	127,438
Like A Prayer	Hunterton	Little Moon Lake	C	1	0	LEX	12,000	
Like A Prayer	Hunterton	Walnut Hall Ltd	C	1	1	LEX	13,000	136,600
Like A Prayer	Kentuckiana	Kentuckiana	C	1	0	LEX	10,000	
Like A Prayer	Kentuckiana	Kentuckiana	F	1	1	LEX	12,000	60,444
Like A Prayer	Midland Acres	Midland Acres	F	1	0	LEX	5,000	
Like A Prayer	Northwood	Bluestone	F	1	0	LEX	6,000	
Like A Prayer	Peninsula	Jonas Graber	F	1	0	LEX	4,000	
Like A Prayer	Preferred	Village Acres Ltd	F	1	0	LEX	62,000	

Sire	Consignor	Farm	Sex	Sold	$50,000 2 YOs	Sale	Avg Price	Avg $ Won
Like A Prayer	Saga	Oldfield	C	1	0	LEX	8,000	
Like A Prayer	Saga	Winterwood	C	1	1	LEX	9,000	137,181
Like A Prayer	Spring Haven	FJD	F	1	0	LEX	2,000	
Like A Prayer	Walnut Hall Ltd	Walnut Hall Ltd	F	1	0	HB	3,000	
Like A Prayer	Walnut Hall Stock	Walnut Hall Stock	C	1	0	LEX	15,000	
Like A Prayer	Winbak	Golden Cross	C	2	0	LEX	16,000	
Like A Prayer	Winbak	Winbak	C	3	0	LEX	11,000	
Like A Prayer	Winbak	Winbak	F	4	0	LEX	5,000	
Like A Prayer				**33**	**4**			
Lis Mara	Brittany	Brittany	F	1	0	LEX	6,000	
Lis Mara	Concord	Concord	C	1	0	HB	20,000	
Lis Mara	Concord	Smith Farmstead	F	1	0	HB	55,000	
Lis Mara	Hanover	Hanover	F	3	0	HB	6,167	
Lis Mara	Hunterton	Dan Kuhns'	F	1	0	HB	5,000	
Lis Mara	Hunterton	Hunterton	C	1	0	HB	10,000	
Lis Mara	Hunterton	Hunterton	C	1	0	LEX	6,000	
Lis Mara	Hunterton	Meadow Creek	C	1	0	HB	20,000	
Lis Mara	Kentuckiana	Kentuckiana	C	1	0	LEX	20,000	
Lis Mara	Kentuckiana	Wilt Standardbreds	F	1	0	LEX	18,000	
Lis Mara	Northwood	Caviart	C	1	0	LEX	12,000	
Lis Mara	Northwood	Caviart	F	1	0	LEX	5,000	
Lis Mara	Northwood	Deo Volente	F	3	0	HB	6,167	
Lis Mara	Peninsula	Holly Gate	C	1	0	HB	22,000	
Lis Mara	Perretti	Perretti	F	2	0	HB	6,000	
Lis Mara	Perretti	Perretti	C	1	0	LEX	13,000	
Lis Mara	Preferred	Deo Volente	C	2	0	LEX	8,500	
Lis Mara	Preferred	Deo Volente	F	1	0	LEX	8,000	
Lis Mara	Preferred	Emerald Heights	C	1	0	LEX	19,000	
Lis Mara	Preferred	Eternal	C	1	0	LEX	32,000	
Lis Mara	Spring Haven	Spring Haven	C	1	0	HB	20,000	
Lis Mara	Spring Haven	Spring Haven	F	2	0	HB	14,500	
Lis Mara	Spring Haven	Sunrise	F	1	0	LEX	15,000	
Lis Mara	Walnridge	Deo Volente	C	1	0	HB	7,000	
Lis Mara	Winterwood	Winterwood	C	1	0	HB	5,500	
Lis Mara				**32**	**0**			
Mach Three	Concord	Concord	F	1	1	HB	12,000	166,045
Mach Three	Fair Winds	Charlotte Ranch	C	1	0	HB	42,000	

Sire	Consignor	Farm	Sex	Sold	$50,000 2 YOs	Sale	Avg Price	Avg $ Won
Mach Three	Fair Winds	Fair Winds	F	1	0	HB	62,000	
Mach Three	Hanover	Hanover	C	3	1	HB	27,000	52,575
Mach Three	Hempt	Hempt	F	4	1	HB	16,750	134,195
Mach Three	Hunterton	Hunterton	C	5	0	HB	40,400	
Mach Three	Hunterton	Hunterton	F	2	0	HB	19,250	
Mach Three	Hunterton	Hunterton	C	1	0	LEX	15,000	
Mach Three	Hunterton	Morrowland	C	1	0	HB	14,000	
Mach Three	Hunterton	Pine Hill	F	1	0	LEX	35,000	
Mach Three	Hunterton	Walco	F	1	0	LEX	9,000	
Mach Three	Kentuckiana	Big Al's	C	1	1	LEX	50,000	124,365
Mach Three	Northwood	Kendal Hills	F	1	0	HB	27,000	
Mach Three	Preferred	Olive Branch	C	1	0	LEX	4,000	
Mach Three	Preferred	Village Acres Ltd	F	1	0	HB	13,000	
Mach Three	Preferred	Walnut Hall Ltd	C	1	0	LEX	22,000	
Mach Three	Saga	Saga	F	1	0	LEX	35,000	
Mach Three	Spring Haven	Rails Edge	F	1	0	LEX	210,000	
Mach Three	Spring Haven	Spring Haven	C	4	0	HB	51,250	
Mach Three	Spring Haven	Spring Haven	F	4	0	HB	30,000	
Mach Three	Walnridge	Walnridge	C	1	0	HB	5,000	
Mach Three	Walnut Hall Ltd	Walnut Hall Ltd	C	1	0	HB	9,000	
Mach Three	Winterwood	Morrowland	C	1	0	HB	15,000	
Mach Three	Winterwood	Morrowland	F	2	0	HB	7,500	
Mach Three				**41**	**4**			
Majestic Son	Concord	Concord	C	1	0	HB	37,000	
Majestic Son	Concord	Concord	F	1	0	HB	15,000	
Majestic Son	Concord	Hanover	C	1	0	HB	1,000	
Majestic Son	Hanover	Hanover	C	1	0	HB	22,000	
Majestic Son	Hanover	Hanover	F	1	0	HB	15,000	
Majestic Son	Hempt	Hempt	F	1	0	HB	4,000	
Majestic Son	Hunterton	Hunterton	C	1	0	HB	50,000	
Majestic Son	Hunterton	Hunterton	F	1	0	HB	13,000	
Majestic Son	Hunterton	Martinez Equine	F	2	0	HB	19,500	
Majestic Son	Northwood	Andray	F	1	0	HB	15,000	
Majestic Son	Northwood	Lindwood	C	1	0	HB	10,000	
Majestic Son	Peninsula	Deo Volente	F	1	0	HB	23,000	
Majestic Son	Peninsula	Rupert	F	1	0	HB	18,000	
Majestic Son	Preferred	Kurt Hansen's	F	2	0	HB	7,750	

Sire	Consignor	Farm	Sex	Sold	$50,000 2 YOs	Sale	Avg Price	Avg $ Won
Majestic Son	Preferred	Southwind	C	1	0	LEX	110,000	
Majestic Son	Spring Haven	Jonas Schlabach's	C	3	0	HB	18,667	
Majestic Son	Spring Haven	Leroy Keim's	C	1	0	HB	25,000	
Majestic Son	Spring Haven	Spring Run	C	1	0	HB	1,500	
Majestic Son				**22**	**0**			
Malabar Man	Cane Run	Cane Run	F	1	0	LEX	15,000	
Malabar Man	Dunroven	Dunroven	C	2	1	LEX	16,000	63,575
Malabar Man	Northwood	Allerage	C	1	0	LEX	25,000	
Malabar Man	Northwood	Cameo Hills	C	1	0	HB	25,000	
Malabar Man	Peninsula	Equine Center	C	1	0	LEX	21,000	
Malabar Man	Peninsula	Quantum	C	1	0	LEX	20,000	
Malabar Man	Spring Haven	Bluebird Meadows	F	1	0	HB	6,000	
Malabar Man	Walnut Hall Stock	Walnut Hall Stock	C	2	0	LEX	31,000	
Malabar Man	Winbak	Winbak	C	4	2	HB	33,750	78,279
Malabar Man	Winbak	Winbak	F	4	0	HB	29,500	
Malabar Man	Winbak	Winbak	C	3	0	LEX	18,000	
Malabar Man	Winbak	Winbak	F	2	0	LEX	8,500	
Malabar Man				**23**	**3**			
Malabar Maple	Walnut Hall Stock	Walnut Hall Stock	C	1	0	LEX	55,000	
Master Glide	Brittany	Brittany	C	4	0	LEX	9,500	
Master Glide	Brittany	Brittany	F	2	0	LEX	24,000	
Master Glide	Cameo Hills	Blue Ridge	C	1	0	LEX	2,000	
Master Glide	Cameo Hills	Blue Ridge	F	1	0	LEX	1,000	
Master Glide	Midland Acres	Midland Acres	F	2	0	LEX	6,000	
Master Glide	Spring Haven	Owen	C	1	0	LEX	3,000	
Master Glide				**11**	**0**			
Mcardle	Blue Chip	Blue Chip	C	1	0	HB	23,000	
Mcardle	Cameo Hills	Cameo Hills	C	1	0	LEX	50,000	
Mcardle	Fair Winds	Fair Winds	C	1	0	HB	15,000	
Mcardle	Fox Den	Stoltzfus	F	1	0	HB	2,500	
Mcardle	Hunterton	Hoosier	C	1	0	LEX	32,000	
Mcardle	Hunterton	Hunterton	C	1	0	HB	2,500	
Mcardle	Hunterton	Hunterton	F	4	0	HB	26,750	
Mcardle	Hunterton	Hunterton	F	1	0	LEX	28,000	
Mcardle	Hunterton	Oak Park	C	1	0	LEX	9,000	
Mcardle	Hunterton	Robert Kuhns'	F	1	0	HB	3,000	
Mcardle	Hunterton	Walco	C	1	0	LEX	8,000	

Sire	Consignor	Farm	Sex	Sold	$50,000 2 YOs	Sale	Avg Price	Avg $ Won
Mcardle	Hunterton	Walco	F	1	0	LEX	12,000	
Mcardle	Northwood	Allerage	F	1	0	LEX	20,000	
Mcardle	Northwood	Andray	C	4	1	HB	14,875	56,688
Mcardle	Northwood	Andray	F	6	0	HB	11,583	
Mcardle	Northwood	Andray	C	2	0	LEX	38,500	
Mcardle	Northwood	Andray	F	2	0	LEX	39,500	
Mcardle	Northwood	Lindwood	C	1	0	HB	10,000	
Mcardle	Northwood	Lindwood	F	2	0	HB	4,250	
Mcardle	Peninsula	Andray	C	1	0	HB	35,000	
Mcardle	Peninsula	Andray	C	2	0	LEX	19,000	
Mcardle	Peninsula	Andray	F	1	0	LEX	2,000	
Mcardle	Peninsula	Donna Perry	F	1	0	LEX	1,000	
Mcardle	Peninsula	Lindwood	F	1	0	HB	7,500	
Mcardle	Perretti	Perretti	C	13	1	HB	19,885	59,667
Mcardle	Perretti	Perretti	F	8	1	HB	13,688	240,904
Mcardle	Perretti	Perretti	C	3	1	LEX	32,000	69,967
Mcardle	Perretti	Perretti	F	4	2	LEX	38,000	200,861
Mcardle	Preferred	Copper Cap	C	1	0	LEX	14,000	
Mcardle	Preferred	Hayden Durham	C	1	0	LEX	10,000	
Mcardle	Spring Haven	Cool Winds	C	1	0	LEX	25,000	
Mcardle	Spring Haven	Spring Haven	C	1	0	LEX	37,000	
Mcardle	Spring Haven	Spring Haven	F	1	0	LEX	19,000	
Mcardle	Vieux Carre	Vieux Carre	F	1	0	HB	17,000	
Mcardle				**73**	**6**			
Metropolitan	Concord	Loconte	F	1	0	HB	9,000	
Metropolitan	Fox Den	Mervin Graber's	F	1	0	HB	3,000	
Metropolitan	Hunterton	Walco	C	2	0	LEX	13,500	
Metropolitan	Kentuckiana	Kentuckiana	C	1	0	LEX	5,000	
Metropolitan	Midland Acres	Midland Acres	C	2	0	LEX	11,500	
Metropolitan	Northwood	Nandi	C	1	0	HB	5,000	
Metropolitan	Spring Haven	Spring Haven	C	5	0	LEX	33,600	
Metropolitan	Vieux Carre	Dennis Dowd's	C	1	0	HB	7,000	
Metropolitan				**14**	**0**			
Modern Art	Brittany	Brittany	F	1	0	LEX	6,000	
Modern Art	Concord	Concord	C	1	0	HB	25,000	
Modern Art	Concord	Concord	F	1	0	HB	23,000	
Modern Art	Hanover	Hanover	C	7	1	HB	19,571	87,551

Sire	Consignor	Farm	Sex	Sold	$50,000 2 YOs	Sale	Avg Price	Avg $ Won
Modern Art	Hanover	Hanover	F	2	0	HB	17,500	
Modern Art	Hunterton	Hunterton	C	1	0	HB	7,000	
Modern Art	Hunterton	Hunterton	F	2	0	HB	11,000	
Modern Art	Hunterton	Walco	C	1	0	LEX	35,000	
Modern Art	Northstar	Northstar	F	1	0	HB	3,000	
Modern Art	Spring Haven	Concord	C	1	0	LEX	15,000	
Modern Art	Spring Haven	Mindale	F	1	0	LEX	15,000	
Modern Art	Spring Haven	Spring Haven	C	1	0	HB	20,000	
Modern Art	Spring Haven	Spring Haven	F	1	0	LEX	18,000	
Modern Art				**21**	**1**			
Mr Feelgood	Brittany	Brittany	F	2	0	LEX	4,000	
Mr Feelgood	Hunterton	Hickory Lane	C	1	0	LEX	10,000	
Mr Feelgood	Hunterton	Hunterton	C	1	0	LEX	50,000	
Mr Feelgood	Hunterton	Starmaker	C	1	0	LEX	16,000	
Mr Feelgood	Peninsula	Shady Side	F	1	0	LEX	6,000	
Mr Feelgood	Spring Haven	Ruddick Stables	F	1	0	LEX	7,000	
Mr Feelgood	Spring Haven	Scott Rudnick	C	1	0	LEX	7,000	
Mr Feelgood				**8**	**0**			
Mr Lavec	Hempt	Hempt	F	1	0	HB	4,500	
Mr Lavec	Spring Haven	Doug Millard	C	1	0	LEX	60,000	
Mr Lavec				**2**	**0**			
Muscles Yankee	Allamerican	Allamerican	C	1	0	HB	30,000	
Muscles Yankee	Allamerican	Allamerican	F	1	0	HB	29,000	
Muscles Yankee	Blue Chip	Blue Chip	C	1	0	HB	37,000	
Muscles Yankee	Blue Chip	Blue Chip	F	3	0	HB	36,000	
Muscles Yankee	Blue Chip	Blue Chip	C	2	0	LEX	82,500	
Muscles Yankee	Boxwood	Boxwood	C	1	0	HB	37,000	
Muscles Yankee	Brittany	Brittany	C	1	0	LEX	50,000	
Muscles Yankee	Cane Run	Cane Run	C	1	0	LEX	90,000	
Muscles Yankee	Concord	Blairwood	C	1	0	HB	12,000	
Muscles Yankee	Concord	Blairwood	F	1	0	HB	35,000	
Muscles Yankee	Concord	Concord	C	1	0	HB	25,000	
Muscles Yankee	Concord	Concord	F	3	0	HB	12,000	
Muscles Yankee	Concord	Perretti	C	1	0	HB	20,000	
Muscles Yankee	Diamond Creek	Diamond Creek	C	2	0	HB	68,500	
Muscles Yankee	Diamond Creek	Diamond Creek	F	3	0	HB	48,333	
Muscles Yankee	Diamond Creek	Diamond Creek	C	2	0	LEX	53,500	

Sire	Consignor	Farm	Sex	Sold	$50,000 2 YOs	Sale	Avg Price	Avg $ Won
Muscles Yankee	Diamond Creek	Diamond Creek	F	3	0	LEX	58,333	
Muscles Yankee	Dunroven	Dunroven	F	4	0	LEX	46,500	
Muscles Yankee	Fair Winds	Fair Winds	C	2	0	HB	47,500	
Muscles Yankee	Fair Winds	Fair Winds	F	2	0	HB	26,500	
Muscles Yankee	Fashion	Fashion	F	1	0	HB	42,000	
Muscles Yankee	Fox Den	Fox Den	C	1	0	HB	35,000	
Muscles Yankee	Fox Den	Fox Den	F	1	0	HB	47,000	
Muscles Yankee	Futurity Hill	Futurity Hill	C	1	0	LEX	13,000	
Muscles Yankee	Futurity Hill	Futurity Hill	F	1	0	LEX	70,000	
Muscles Yankee	Hanover	Hanover	C	4	0	HB	23,750	
Muscles Yankee	Hanover	Hanover	F	5	1	HB	30,300	163,099
Muscles Yankee	Hanover	Hanover	C	2	0	LEX	97,500	
Muscles Yankee	Hanover	Hanover	F	1	0	LEX	60,000	
Muscles Yankee	Hunterton	Hunterton	C	1	0	HB	32,000	
Muscles Yankee	Hunterton	Hunterton	F	2	0	HB	19,000	
Muscles Yankee	Hunterton	Hunterton	C	3	0	LEX	175,000	
Muscles Yankee	Hunterton	Hunterton	F	2	0	LEX	54,500	
Muscles Yankee	Hunterton	Walco	C	3	0	LEX	75,667	
Muscles Yankee	Hunterton	Walco	F	2	0	LEX	52,500	
Muscles Yankee	Kentuckiana	Kentuckiana	C	1	0	LEX	100,000	
Muscles Yankee	Kentuckiana	Kentuckiana	F	2	0	LEX	11,500	
Muscles Yankee	Kentuckiana	Wilt Standardbreds	C	1	0	LEX	42,000	
Muscles Yankee	Midland Acres	Midland Acres	C	1	0	LEX	50,000	
Muscles Yankee	Midland Acres	Midland Acres	F	1	0	LEX	17,000	
Muscles Yankee	Northwood	Allerage	F	2	0	HB	19,500	
Muscles Yankee	Northwood	Allerage	C	1	0	LEX	10,000	
Muscles Yankee	Northwood	Allerage	F	1	0	LEX	55,000	
Muscles Yankee	Northwood	Andray	F	1	0	HB	22,000	
Muscles Yankee	Northwood	Andray	C	1	0	LEX	22,000	
Muscles Yankee	Northwood	Bluestone	F	1	0	LEX	100,000	
Muscles Yankee	Northwood	Bos Stable	F	1	0	LEX	70,000	
Muscles Yankee	Northwood	Groulx's Gatineau	F	1	0	HB	7,000	
Muscles Yankee	Northwood	Jonalee	C	1	0	HB	35,000	
Muscles Yankee	Northwood	Kentuckiana	F	1	0	HB	57,000	
Muscles Yankee	Northwood	Lindwood	F	1	0	HB	47,000	
Muscles Yankee	Northwood	Percy Davis	C	1	0	LEX	57,000	
Muscles Yankee	Northwood	White Hollow	C	1	0	HB	135,000	

Sire	Consignor	Farm	Sex	Sold	$50,000 2 YOs	Sale	Avg Price	Avg $ Won
Muscles Yankee	Peninsula	Green Gables	F	1	0	HB	30,000	
Muscles Yankee	Peninsula	Peninsula	C	8	3	HB	82,500	168,103
Muscles Yankee	Peninsula	Peninsula	F	7	0	HB	36,000	
Muscles Yankee	Peninsula	Shawnee Run	F	1	0	LEX	15,000	
Muscles Yankee	Peninsula	Three Crow	C	1	1	HB	35,000	105,122
Muscles Yankee	Peninsula	Winterwood	C	1	0	LEX	135,000	
Muscles Yankee	Perretti	Perretti	C	16	1	HB	84,156	53,740
Muscles Yankee	Perretti	Perretti	F	24	2	HB	32,479	511,839
Muscles Yankee	Perretti	Perretti	C	7	0	LEX	51,429	
Muscles Yankee	Perretti	Perretti	F	5	0	LEX	14,800	
Muscles Yankee	Preferred	Beal	C	1	0	HB	9,000	
Muscles Yankee	Preferred	Birch Creek	C	1	0	LEX	47,000	
Muscles Yankee	Preferred	Deo Volente	F	1	0	LEX	17,000	
Muscles Yankee	Preferred	George Story's	C	1	0	HB	4,500	
Muscles Yankee	Preferred	Green Gables	C	1	1	HB	45,000	136,977
Muscles Yankee	Preferred	Heritage Hill	C	2	0	HB	9,500	
Muscles Yankee	Preferred	Heritage Hill	F	1	0	HB	35,000	
Muscles Yankee	Preferred	Lindy	F	3	1	HB	32,667	149,627
Muscles Yankee	Preferred	Lindy	F	2	0	LEX	66,000	
Muscles Yankee	Preferred	Mackenzie	F	1	1	HB	40,000	209,633
Muscles Yankee	Preferred	Pinestone	C	1	0	HB	35,000	
Muscles Yankee	Preferred	Southwind	C	1	0	LEX	35,000	
Muscles Yankee	Preferred	Southwind	F	2	0	LEX	97,500	
Muscles Yankee	Preferred	Stirling Brook	F	1	0	HB	3,000	
Muscles Yankee	Preferred	Stirling Brook	C	1	0	LEX	50,000	
Muscles Yankee	Preferred	Stonehenge	C	1	0	LEX	37,000	
Muscles Yankee	Preferred	Talbot Creek	F	1	0	HB	17,000	
Muscles Yankee	Preferred	Tymal	F	1	0	LEX	14,000	
Muscles Yankee	Preferred	White Birch	C	1	0	HB	50,000	
Muscles Yankee	Saga	Saga	F	1	0	LEX	50,000	
Muscles Yankee	Spring Haven	Spring Haven	C	1	0	LEX	65,000	
Muscles Yankee	Spring Haven	Talbot Creek	F	1	0	LEX	7,000	
Muscles Yankee	Vieux Carre	Vieux Carre	C	1	0	HB	50,000	
Muscles Yankee	Walnridge	Walnridge	C	1	0	HB	180,000	
Muscles Yankee	Winbak	Winbak	C	1	0	HB	25,000	
Muscles Yankee	Winbak	Winbak	F	6	1	HB	19,000	246,302
Muscles Yankee	Winbak	Winbak	F	5	1	LEX	38,400	115,449

Sire	Consignor	Farm	Sex	Sold	$50,000 2 YOs	Sale	Avg Price	Avg $ Won
Muscles Yankee				198	13			
No Pan Intended	Cameo Hills	Marvin Raber	C	4	1	LEX	6,500	53,178
No Pan Intended	Cameo Hills	Marvin Raber	F	3	0	LEX	6,000	
No Pan Intended	Fox Den	Shaffer Standardbreds	C	1	0	HB	8,000	
No Pan Intended	Fox Den	Three Cedars	C	1	0	HB	9,000	
No Pan Intended	Hanover	Hanover	F	4	0	HB	21,750	
No Pan Intended	Northwood	Andray	C	1	0	HB	14,000	
No Pan Intended	Vieux Carre	Vieux Carre	F	1	0	HB	5,500	
No Pan Intended	Walnridge	Cameo Hills	C	1	0	HB	23,000	
No Pan Intended	Walnridge	Marvin Raber	C	5	0	HB	11,900	
No Pan Intended	Walnridge	Marvin Raber	F	3	0	HB	5,167	
No Pan Intended				24	1			
Pacific Fella	Dunroven	Dunroven	C	1	0	LEX	13,000	
Peruvian Hanover	Hanover	Hanover	F	1	0	HB	3,000	
Plesac	Winbak	Winbak	C	1	0	HB	23,000	
Ponder	Allamerican	Allamerican	C	1	0	HB	5,000	
Ponder	Allamerican	Allamerican	F	1	0	HB	6,000	
Ponder	Diamond Creek	Diamond Creek	C	1	0	HB	6,000	
Ponder	Diamond Creek	Diamond Creek	F	1	0	HB	18,000	
Ponder	Diamond Creek	Diamond Creek	C	2	0	LEX	17,500	
Ponder	Diamond Creek	Diamond Creek	F	3	0	LEX	21,000	
Ponder	Dunroven	Dunroven	C	1	0	LEX	5,000	
Ponder	Fox Den	Mel Kauffman's	C	1	0	HB	18,000	
Ponder	Hunterton	Meadow Creek	C	1	0	LEX	20,000	
Ponder	Northwood	Caviart	C	1	1	LEX	12,000	191,073
Ponder	Peninsula	Glassford Equine	F	1	0	HB	20,000	
Ponder	Peninsula	Odds On Acres	C	2	0	LEX	27,500	
Ponder	Peninsula	Peninsula	C	3	1	HB	37,000	214,058
Ponder	Peninsula	Peninsula	F	1	0	HB	30,000	
Ponder	Peninsula	Peninsula	C	5	0	LEX	18,600	
Ponder	Peninsula	Peninsula	F	2	1	LEX	15,000	164,705
Ponder	Preferred	Considine	C	1	0	LEX	23,000	
Ponder	Preferred	Seelster	C	1	0	HB	35,000	
Ponder	Preferred	Twin Willows	F	1	0	LEX	7,000	
Ponder	Saga	Saga	C	1	0	LEX	20,000	
Ponder	Spring Haven	Spring Haven	C	2	0	LEX	15,000	
Ponder	Spring Haven	White Oak	C	1	0	LEX	13,000	

Sire	Consignor	Farm	Sex	Sold	$50,000 2 YOs	Sale	Avg Price	Avg $ Won
Ponder	Vieux Carre	Dennis Dowd's	C	1	0	HB	7,000	
Ponder	Vieux Carre	Vieux Carre	C	3	0	HB	16,833	
Ponder	Winterwood	Winterwood	C	1	0	HB	6,500	
Ponder	Winterwood	Winterwood	F	1	0	HB	6,000	
Ponder				**40**	**3**			
Pro Bono Best	Hunterton	Crawford	F	1	0	HB	1,500	
Pro Bono Best	Peninsula	Ivan Sugg's	F	1	0	HB	35,000	
Pro Bono Best				**2**	**0**			
Quik Pulse Mindale	Winbak	Winbak	C	6	0	HB	26,167	
Quik Pulse Mindale	Winbak	Winbak	F	4	1	HB	15,000	128,875
Quik Pulse Mindale	Winbak	Winbak	C	4	0	LEX	24,250	
Quik Pulse Mindale	Winbak	Winbak	F	2	0	LEX	15,000	
Quik Pulse Mindale				**16**	**1**			
Real Artist	Concord	Concord	C	1	0	HB	17,000	
Real Artist	Fashion	Fashion	C	9	1	HB	13,222	116,333
Real Artist	Fashion	Fashion	F	12	0	HB	22,167	
Real Artist	Fox Den	Leon King's	F	1	0	HB	1,500	
Real Artist	Hunterton	Dennison	C	1	0	LEX	15,000	
Real Artist	Hunterton	Ernie Martinez	C	1	0	LEX	5,000	
Real Artist	Hunterton	Hunterton	F	2	0	HB	26,000	
Real Artist	Hunterton	Shady Lane Meadows	C	1	0	LEX	19,000	
Real Artist	Kentuckiana	Paul Liles	C	1	0	LEX	21,000	
Real Artist	Kentuckiana	Paul Liles	F	1	0	LEX	35,000	
Real Artist	Midland Acres	Midland Acres	C	1	0	LEX	20,000	
Real Artist	Midland Acres	Midland Acres	F	1	0	LEX	28,000	
Real Artist	Midland Acres	Morrowland	C	1	0	LEX	24,000	
Real Artist	Northwood	Nandi	C	2	0	HB	16,500	
Real Artist	Peninsula	Green Creek	C	1	1	LEX	65,000	72,422
Real Artist	Peninsula	Peninsula	F	1	0	LEX	4,000	
Real Artist	Preferred	Emerald Highlands	F	1	0	LEX	6,000	
Real Artist	Spring Haven	Executive Standardbred	F	1	0	LEX	5,000	
Real Artist	Spring Haven	Mindale	F	1	0	LEX	3,000	
Real Artist	Steiner Stock	Steiner Stock	F	1	0	LEX	5,000	
Real Artist	Walnut Hall Stock	Walnut Hall Stock	C	1	0	LEX	30,000	
Real Artist	Winbak	Winbak	F	1	0	HB	7,000	
Real Artist	Winbak	Winbak	C	1	0	LEX	9,000	
Real Artist	Winterwood	Winterwood	C	1	0	HB	17,000	

Sire	Consignor	Farm	Sex	Sold	$50,000 2 YOs	Sale	Avg Price	Avg $ Won
Real Artist				45	2			
Real Desire	Allamerican	Allamerican	C	1	0	HB	25,000	
Real Desire	Allamerican	Allamerican	F	1	1	HB	18,000	148,433
Real Desire	Brittany	Brittany	C	6	0	LEX	37,000	
Real Desire	Brittany	Brittany	F	7	0	LEX	12,000	
Real Desire	Cameo Hills	Blue Ridge	C	1	1	LEX	9,000	71,852
Real Desire	Diamond Creek	Diamond Creek	C	1	0	LEX	35,000	
Real Desire	Fair Winds	Fair Winds	C	1	0	HB	10,000	
Real Desire	Futurity Hill	Futurity Hill	F	1	0	LEX	30,000	
Real Desire	Hanover	Hanover	C	1	0	HB	25,000	
Real Desire	Hunterton	Hickory Lane	F	1	0	LEX	5,000	
Real Desire	Hunterton	Hunterton	C	4	0	HB	10,125	
Real Desire	Hunterton	Hunterton	F	1	1	HB	5,500	59,398
Real Desire	Hunterton	Hunterton	C	3	0	LEX	20,333	
Real Desire	Hunterton	Hunterton	F	6	1	LEX	29,500	63,850
Real Desire	Hunterton	Mark Horner's	F	1	0	HB	25,000	
Real Desire	Hunterton	Northfields	F	1	0	LEX	8,000	
Real Desire	Hunterton	Poole	F	1	0	LEX	4,000	
Real Desire	Hunterton	Randy Wilt's	C	1	0	HB	40,000	
Real Desire	Hunterton	Randy Wilt's	F	1	0	HB	3,000	
Real Desire	Hunterton	Winterwood	C	1	1	LEX	15,000	329,235
Real Desire	Northwood	Andray	C	1	0	HB	8,500	
Real Desire	Northwood	Andray	F	1	0	HB	10,000	
Real Desire	Northwood	Andray	F	1	0	LEX	23,000	
Real Desire	Peninsula	Al Tomlinson	F	1	0	HB	8,000	
Real Desire	Peninsula	Maple Lane	C	2	0	LEX	44,000	
Real Desire	Peninsula	Maple Lane	F	1	0	LEX	35,000	
Real Desire	Peninsula	Peninsula	C	1	0	LEX	26,000	
Real Desire	Perretti	Perretti	C	2	0	HB	14,250	
Real Desire	Perretti	Perretti	F	4	0	HB	6,500	
Real Desire	Perretti	Perretti	C	8	1	LEX	34,750	248,764
Real Desire	Perretti	Perretti	F	2	1	LEX	45,000	50,609
Real Desire	Preferred	Concord	C	1	0	LEX	13,000	
Real Desire	Preferred	Hayden Durham	C	1	0	LEX	35,000	
Real Desire	Preferred	Hayden Durham	F	1	0	LEX	7,000	
Real Desire	Preferred	Southwind	F	1	0	HB	42,000	
Real Desire	Preferred	Walnut Hall Ltd	C	1	0	LEX	22,000	

Sire	Consignor	Farm	Sex	Sold	$50,000 2 YOs	Sale	Avg Price	Avg $ Won
Real Desire	Preferred	White Birch	C	1	0	HB	30,000	
Real Desire	Preferred	White Birch	F	2	0	HB	6,250	
Real Desire	Saga	Blue Ridge	C	1	0	LEX	15,000	
Real Desire	Spring Haven	Aquatic	C	1	0	LEX	17,000	
Real Desire	Spring Haven	Aquatic	F	1	0	LEX	15,000	
Real Desire	Spring Haven	Lmn Bred	C	1	0	HB	8,000	
Real Desire	Spring Haven	Lmn Bred	C	1	0	LEX	10,000	
Real Desire	Spring Haven	Rails Edge	F	1	0	LEX	65,000	
Real Desire	Steiner Stock	Steiner Stock	C	1	0	LEX	5,000	
Real Desire	Twinbrook	Emerald Ridge	C	1	0	HB	37,000	
Real Desire	Vieux Carre	Brittany	C	1	0	HB	6,500	
Real Desire	Vieux Carre	Brittany	F	1	0	HB	3,000	
Real Desire	Vieux Carre	Vieux Carre	C	2	0	HB	20,500	
Real Desire	Walnridge	Walnridge	C	1	0	HB	13,000	
Real Desire	Walnridge	Walnridge	F	3	0	HB	19,000	
Real Desire	Walnut Hall Ltd	Walnut Hall Ltd	F	1	0	HB	35,000	
Real Desire	Walnut Hall Stock	Walnut Hall Stock	F	1	0	LEX	22,000	
Real Desire	Westwind	Walnut Hall Ltd	C	1	0	HB	15,000	
Real Desire	Winbak	Winbak	F	1	0	LEX	14,000	
Real Desire	Winterwood	Cashelmara	C	1	0	HB	8,000	
Real Desire	Winterwood	Winterwood	C	5	0	HB	18,800	
Real Desire	Winterwood	Winterwood	F	1	0	HB	16,000	
Real Desire				**100**	**7**			
Red River Hanover	Hunterton	Hunterton	F	3	0	LEX	7,000	
Red River Hanover	Kentuckiana	Kentuckiana	C	1	0	LEX	3,000	
Red River Hanover	Peninsula	Odds On Acres	F	1	0	LEX	10,000	
Red River Hanover	Peninsula	Rockridge	F	1	0	LEX	10,000	
Red River Hanover	Perretti	Perretti	C	4	0	HB	11,000	
Red River Hanover	Perretti	Perretti	F	10	0	HB	6,050	
Red River Hanover	Perretti	Perretti	F	3	0	LEX	9,333	
Red River Hanover	Preferred	Copper Cap	F	1	0	LEX	9,000	
Red River Hanover	Preferred	Cottonwood	F	1	0	LEX	8,000	
Red River Hanover	Preferred	Heritage Hill	C	1	0	LEX	2,000	
Red River Hanover	Spring Haven	Spring Haven	F	1	0	HB	6,000	
Red River Hanover				**27**	**0**			
Revenue S	Concord	Concord	F	1	0	HB	37,000	
Revenue S	Concord	Hanover	F	2	0	HB	2,750	

Sire	Consignor	Farm	Sex	Sold	$50,000 2 YOs	Sale	Avg Price	Avg $ Won
Revenue S	Concord	Smith Farmstead	C	1	0	HB	5,500	
Revenue S	Dunroven	Dunroven	C	1	0	LEX	1,000	
Revenue S	Fair Winds	Oakwood Equine	C	1	0	HB	9,000	
Revenue S	Futurity Hill	Futurity Hill	F	1	0	LEX	20,000	
Revenue S	Hanover	Hanover	F	1	0	HB	4,000	
Revenue S	Kentuckiana	Kentuckiana	C	1	0	LEX	22,000	
Revenue S	Kentuckiana	Northfields	C	1	0	LEX	25,000	
Revenue S	Kentuckiana	Paul Liles	C	1	0	LEX	5,000	
Revenue S	Millstream	Millstream	C	1	0	HB	13,000	
Revenue S	Northwood	Allerage	C	3	1	HB	22,333	104,532
Revenue S	Northwood	Bluestone	F	1	0	HB	9,500	
Revenue S	Northwood	Lynn Acres	C	1	0	HB	18,000	
Revenue S	Northwood	Perretti	C	1	0	HB	6,000	
Revenue S	Peninsula	Equine Center	C	1	0	LEX	1,000	
Revenue S	Peninsula	Oaklea	C	1	0	HB	1,000	
Revenue S	Peninsula	Oaklea	F	1	0	HB	4,000	
Revenue S	Peninsula	Peninsula	C	1	0	HB	30,000	
Revenue S	Perretti	Perretti	C	4	0	HB	13,125	
Revenue S	Perretti	Perretti	F	10	0	HB	24,400	
Revenue S	Perretti	Perretti	C	3	0	LEX	14,667	
Revenue S	Perretti	Perretti	F	3	0	LEX	20,000	
Revenue S	Saga	New Pioneer	C	1	0	LEX	16,000	
Revenue S	Spring Haven	Jonas Schlabach's	C	1	0	HB	20,000	
Revenue S	Spring Haven	Spring Haven	C	1	0	LEX	3,000	
Revenue S	Westwind	Rich Thompson's	C	1	0	HB	9,000	
Revenue S	Winbak	Winbak	F	1	0	HB	8,000	
Revenue S	Winterwood	Winterwood	C	1	0	HB	5,000	
Revenue S				**48**	**1**			
Riverboat King	Winbak	Winbak	C	2	0	HB	15,500	
Riverboat King	Winbak	Winbak	F	2	0	HB	11,500	
Riverboat King	Winbak	Winbak	C	1	0	LEX	30,000	
Riverboat King				**5**	**0**			
Rocknroll Hanover	Allamerican	Allamerican	F	1	0	HB	4,500	
Rocknroll Hanover	Blue Chip	Blue Chip	C	4	0	HB	101,250	
Rocknroll Hanover	Blue Chip	Blue Chip	F	4	0	HB	50,500	
Rocknroll Hanover	Blue Chip	Blue Chip	F	1	1	LEX	75,000	112,984
Rocknroll Hanover	Boxwood	Boxwood	C	1	0	HB	14,000	

Sire	Consignor	Farm	Sex	Sold	$50,000 2 YOs	Sale	Avg Price	Avg $ Won
Rocknroll Hanover	Brittany	Brittany	C	2	1	LEX	75,000	123,751
Rocknroll Hanover	Cameo Hills	Cameo Hills	C	2	0	LEX	135,000	
Rocknroll Hanover	Concord	Bucks N A Doe	F	1	0	HB	32,000	
Rocknroll Hanover	Concord	Concord	C	5	0	HB	48,600	
Rocknroll Hanover	Concord	Concord	F	4	0	HB	12,750	
Rocknroll Hanover	Concord	Sunny View	C	1	0	HB	47,000	
Rocknroll Hanover	Diamond Creek	Diamond Creek	C	5	1	HB	67,800	65,840
Rocknroll Hanover	Diamond Creek	Diamond Creek	F	1	0	HB	40,000	
Rocknroll Hanover	Diamond Creek	Diamond Creek	C	3	0	LEX	36,000	
Rocknroll Hanover	Diamond Creek	Diamond Creek	F	3	0	LEX	46,667	
Rocknroll Hanover	Dunroven	Dunroven	C	1	0	LEX	42,000	
Rocknroll Hanover	Fair Winds	Fair Winds	C	3	0	HB	74,333	
Rocknroll Hanover	Fair Winds	Fair Winds	F	4	0	HB	116,250	
Rocknroll Hanover	Hanover	Hanover	C	10	2	HB	61,300	85,162
Rocknroll Hanover	Hanover	Hanover	F	9	0	HB	73,667	
Rocknroll Hanover	Hanover	Hanover	C	2	0	LEX	97,500	
Rocknroll Hanover	Hanover	Hanover	F	2	0	LEX	75,000	
Rocknroll Hanover	Hunterton	Hunterton	C	1	0	HB	30,000	
Rocknroll Hanover	Hunterton	Hunterton	F	2	0	HB	16,000	
Rocknroll Hanover	Hunterton	Hunterton	C	13	4	LEX	84,615	397,316
Rocknroll Hanover	Hunterton	Hunterton	F	5	0	LEX	38,400	
Rocknroll Hanover	Hunterton	Meadow Creek	F	1	0	HB	15,000	
Rocknroll Hanover	Hunterton	Meadow Creek	C	2	0	LEX	47,000	
Rocknroll Hanover	Hunterton	Meadow Creek	F	1	0	LEX	27,000	
Rocknroll Hanover	Hunterton	Starmaker	C	3	0	LEX	14,333	
Rocknroll Hanover	Hunterton	Walco	F	2	0	LEX	36,000	
Rocknroll Hanover	Kentuckiana	Big Al's	C	1	0	LEX	32,000	
Rocknroll Hanover	Kentuckiana	Kentuckiana	C	2	0	LEX	67,500	
Rocknroll Hanover	Kentuckiana	Kentuckiana	F	3	1	LEX	46,667	732,379
Rocknroll Hanover	Midland Acres	Midland Acres	C	1	0	LEX	32,000	
Rocknroll Hanover	Northwood	Andray	F	1	0	LEX	60,000	
Rocknroll Hanover	Northwood	Caviart	C	1	0	LEX	70,000	
Rocknroll Hanover	Northwood	Deo Volente	C	1	0	HB	20,000	
Rocknroll Hanover	Northwood	Nandi	F	1	0	HB	16,000	
Rocknroll Hanover	Northwood	Perretti	C	2	0	HB	38,000	
Rocknroll Hanover	Peninsula	Andray	C	1	0	LEX	42,000	
Rocknroll Hanover	Peninsula	Deo Volente	F	2	0	HB	31,000	

Sire	Consignor	Farm	Sex	Sold	$50,000 2 YOs	Sale	Avg Price	Avg $ Won
Rocknroll Hanover	Peninsula	Glassford Equine	F	1	0	HB	10,000	
Rocknroll Hanover	Peninsula	Glassford Equine	C	1	0	LEX	50,000	
Rocknroll Hanover	Peninsula	Holly Gate	C	1	0	HB	55,000	
Rocknroll Hanover	Peninsula	Holly Gate	F	1	0	HB	50,000	
Rocknroll Hanover	Peninsula	Peninsula	C	1	0	HB	110,000	
Rocknroll Hanover	Peninsula	Peninsula	F	1	0	HB	45,000	
Rocknroll Hanover	Peninsula	Peninsula	C	2	0	LEX	31,000	
Rocknroll Hanover	Peninsula	Peninsula	F	2	0	LEX	33,500	
Rocknroll Hanover	Peninsula	Wilt Standardbreds	F	1	0	LEX	40,000	
Rocknroll Hanover	Peninsula	Yankeeland	C	2	0	LEX	92,500	
Rocknroll Hanover	Perretti	Perretti	C	33	2	HB	51,818	100,818
Rocknroll Hanover	Perretti	Perretti	F	28	3	HB	51,946	185,668
Rocknroll Hanover	Perretti	Perretti	C	11	0	LEX	59,545	
Rocknroll Hanover	Perretti	Perretti	F	12	3	LEX	37,333	131,017
Rocknroll Hanover	Preferred	Anderson	C	1	0	LEX	72,000	
Rocknroll Hanover	Preferred	Anderson	F	4	0	LEX	76,750	
Rocknroll Hanover	Preferred	Birch Creek	C	1	0	LEX	20,000	
Rocknroll Hanover	Preferred	Deo Volente	C	1	0	LEX	180,000	
Rocknroll Hanover	Preferred	Dumain Haven	F	1	0	HB	8,500	
Rocknroll Hanover	Preferred	Emerald Heights	C	1	0	LEX	38,000	
Rocknroll Hanover	Preferred	Emerald Highlands	C	9	1	LEX	49,556	98,617
Rocknroll Hanover	Preferred	Emerald Highlands	F	1	0	LEX	9,000	
Rocknroll Hanover	Preferred	Green Gables	C	1	1	HB	110,000	196,201
Rocknroll Hanover	Preferred	Heritage Hill	C	12	1	HB	47,417	204,147
Rocknroll Hanover	Preferred	Heritage Hill	F	3	0	HB	22,667	
Rocknroll Hanover	Preferred	Heritage Hill	C	2	1	LEX	48,500	109,965
Rocknroll Hanover	Preferred	Heritage Hill	F	3	0	LEX	28,000	
Rocknroll Hanover	Preferred	Joie De Vie	F	2	0	HB	27,500	
Rocknroll Hanover	Preferred	Joie De Vie	C	2	0	LEX	37,500	
Rocknroll Hanover	Preferred	Joie De Vie	F	1	0	LEX	40,000	
Rocknroll Hanover	Preferred	Lindy	C	1	0	LEX	85,000	
Rocknroll Hanover	Preferred	Lindy	F	4	0	LEX	93,000	
Rocknroll Hanover	Preferred	Lothlorien	C	1	0	HB	22,000	
Rocknroll Hanover	Preferred	Mackenzie	C	1	0	HB	4,000	
Rocknroll Hanover	Preferred	Rolling Acres	F	1	0	HB	80,000	
Rocknroll Hanover	Preferred	Rolling Acres	C	1	0	LEX	41,000	
Rocknroll Hanover	Preferred	Rolling Acres	F	2	0	LEX	76,000	

Sire	Consignor	Farm	Sex	Sold	$50,000 2 YOs	Sale	Avg Price	Avg $ Won
Rocknroll Hanover	Preferred	Silver Willow	C	1	0	HB	13,000	
Rocknroll Hanover	Preferred	Southwind	C	1	0	HB	15,000	
Rocknroll Hanover	Preferred	Southwind	C	1	0	LEX	90,000	
Rocknroll Hanover	Preferred	Southwind	F	1	0	LEX	40,000	
Rocknroll Hanover	Preferred	Twinbrook	F	1	0	LEX	37,000	
Rocknroll Hanover	Preferred	Village Acres Ltd	C	2	0	LEX	32,500	
Rocknroll Hanover	Preferred	Village Acres Ltd	F	4	0	LEX	42,750	
Rocknroll Hanover	Preferred	White Birch	C	1	0	HB	10,000	
Rocknroll Hanover	Preferred	White Birch	F	1	0	HB	8,000	
Rocknroll Hanover	Preferred	White Birch	C	2	1	LEX	58,500	231,578
Rocknroll Hanover	Preferred	White Birch	F	4	1	LEX	51,250	64,805
Rocknroll Hanover	Preferred	Windsun	C	2	0	HB	45,000	
Rocknroll Hanover	Saga	Oldfield	C	1	0	LEX	65,000	
Rocknroll Hanover	Saga	Victory Hill	F	1	0	LEX	95,000	
Rocknroll Hanover	Spring Haven	Spring Haven	C	1	0	LEX	52,000	
Rocknroll Hanover	Spring Haven	Spring Run	C	1	0	LEX	31,000	
Rocknroll Hanover	Stonegate	Stonegate	C	3	0	HB	25,667	
Rocknroll Hanover	Stonegate	Stonegate	F	3	0	HB	18,667	
Rocknroll Hanover	Twinbrook	Twinbrook	C	4	0	HB	59,250	
Rocknroll Hanover	Twinbrook	Twinbrook	F	3	0	HB	31,667	
Rocknroll Hanover	Vieux Carre	Vieux Carre	C	6	0	HB	40,667	
Rocknroll Hanover	Vieux Carre	Vieux Carre	F	4	0	HB	24,625	
Rocknroll Hanover	Walnridge	Walnridge	C	4	1	HB	47,500	863,325
Rocknroll Hanover	Westwind	Westwind	C	1	0	HB	75,000	
Rocknroll Hanover	Winbak	Winbak	C	2	0	HB	115,000	
Rocknroll Hanover	Winbak	Winbak	F	2	0	HB	38,000	
Rocknroll Hanover	Winbak	Winbak	C	3	0	LEX	39,000	
Rocknroll Hanover	Winbak	Winbak	F	2	1	LEX	102,500	91,981
Rocknroll Hanover				**330**	**26**			
Royal Mattjesty	Perretti	Perretti	C	6	0	HB	36,500	
Royal Mattjesty	Perretti	Perretti	F	1	0	HB	14,000	
Royal Mattjesty	Winbak	Winbak	C	2	0	HB	24,500	
Royal Mattjesty	Winbak	Winbak	F	3	0	HB	25,000	
Royal Mattjesty	Winbak	Winbak	C	4	0	LEX	19,750	
Royal Mattjesty	Winbak	Winbak	F	2	0	LEX	21,500	
Royal Mattjesty				**18**	**0**			
Rustler Hanover	Preferred	Twin Creeks	C	1	0	LEX	17,000	

Sire	Consignor	Farm	Sex	Sold	$50,000 2 YOs	Sale	Avg Price	Avg $ Won
SJ's Photo	Brittany	Brittany	C	2	0	LEX	29,000	
SJ's Photo	Dunroven	Bill Cottongim	C	1	0	LEX	35,000	
SJ's Photo	Dunroven	Dunroven	C	1	0	LEX	17,000	
SJ's Photo	Hunterton	Outback	F	1	0	LEX	8,000	
SJ's Photo	Kentuckiana	Benaire	C	1	0	LEX	37,000	
SJ's Photo	Kentuckiana	Farrier's Acres	C	1	0	LEX	17,000	
SJ's Photo	Northwood	Allerage	C	2	0	LEX	10,000	
SJ's Photo	Northwood	Andray	C	1	0	LEX	17,000	
SJ's Photo	Northwood	Wollam	C	1	0	HB	30,000	
SJ's Photo	Spring Haven	C And V Spellmire	C	1	0	LEX	3,000	
SJ's Photo	Spring Haven	FJD	F	1	0	LEX	13,000	
SJ's Photo	Spring Haven	Jonas Schlabach's	C	1	0	HB	22,000	
SJ's Photo	Spring Haven	Jonas Schlabach's	F	1	0	HB	65,000	
SJ's Photo	Vieux Carre	Vieux Carre	C	1	0	HB	10,000	
SJ's Photo	Winbak	Winbak	F	1	0	HB	55,000	
SJ's Photo				**17**	**0**			
Sand Vic	Spring Haven	Sunrise	C	1	0	LEX	7,000	
Sand Vic	Winbak	Winbak	C	1	0	HB	11,000	
Sand Vic	Winbak	Winbak	F	2	0	HB	22,500	
Sand Vic	Winbak	Winbak	C	1	0	LEX	10,000	
Sand Vic	Winbak	Winbak	F	1	0	LEX	12,000	
Sand Vic				**6**	**0**			
Shark Gesture	Concord	Concord	C	1	0	HB	30,000	
Shark Gesture	Hanover	Hanover	C	2	0	HB	25,000	
Shark Gesture	Kentuckiana	Kentuckiana	C	2	1	LEX	61,000	78,029
Shark Gesture	Spring Haven	Spring Haven	C	1	0	HB	35,000	
Shark Gesture	Spring Haven	Sunrise	C	1	0	LEX	23,000	
Shark Gesture				**7**	**1**			
SJ's Caviar	Blue Chip	Blue Chip	C	1	0	HB	22,000	
SJ's Caviar	Boxwood	Torrey Ridge	C	2	0	HB	8,000	
SJ's Caviar	Brittany	Brittany	C	2	1	LEX	27,500	210,581
SJ's Caviar	Cane Run	Cane Run	C	1	0	LEX	5,000	
SJ's Caviar	Concord	Concord	C	1	0	HB	23,000	
SJ's Caviar	Concord	Concord	F	1	0	HB	55,000	
SJ's Caviar	Concord	Hanover	C	3	0	HB	10,667	
SJ's Caviar	Concord	Hanover	F	2	0	HB	16,500	
SJ's Caviar	Concord	Marion	C	1	0	HB	13,000	

Sire	Consignor	Farm	Sex	Sold	$50,000 2 YOs	Sale	Avg Price	Avg $ Won
SJ's Caviar	Dunroven	Dunroven	C	1	0	LEX	13,000	
SJ's Caviar	Dunroven	Dunroven	F	1	0	LEX	27,000	
SJ's Caviar	Fair Winds	Fair Winds	C	2	0	HB	10,500	
SJ's Caviar	Fair Winds	Fair Winds	F	1	0	HB	6,000	
SJ's Caviar	Fashion	Fashion	C	1	0	HB	22,000	
SJ's Caviar	Fox Den	Hanover	C	1	0	HB	25,000	
SJ's Caviar	Fox Den	Kurt Hansen's	C	1	0	HB	20,000	
SJ's Caviar	Fox Den	Shaffer Standardbreds	F	1	0	HB	10,000	
SJ's Caviar	Fox Den	Stoltzfus	F	2	0	HB	13,750	
SJ's Caviar	Hanover	Hanover	C	6	0	HB	22,833	
SJ's Caviar	Hanover	Hanover	F	12	0	HB	18,917	
SJ's Caviar	Hempt	Hempt	C	2	0	HB	12,250	
SJ's Caviar	Hempt	Hempt	F	1	0	HB	11,000	
SJ's Caviar	Hunterton	Hunterton	F	1	0	HB	20,000	
SJ's Caviar	Hunterton	Hunterton	C	1	0	LEX	1,000	
SJ's Caviar	Hunterton	Hunterton	F	2	0	LEX	8,000	
SJ's Caviar	Hunterton	Starmaker	C	1	0	LEX	11,000	
SJ's Caviar	Hunterton	Walco	C	1	0	LEX	40,000	
SJ's Caviar	Hunterton	Walco	F	1	0	LEX	17,000	
SJ's Caviar	Hunterton	Wayne T. Zollars	C	1	0	LEX	25,000	
SJ's Caviar	Kentuckiana	Kentuckiana	C	1	0	LEX	13,000	
SJ's Caviar	Kentuckiana	Kentuckiana	F	1	0	LEX	95,000	
SJ's Caviar	Millstream	Millstream	C	2	0	HB	10,000	
SJ's Caviar	Millstream	Millstream	F	1	0	HB	40,000	
SJ's Caviar	Northstar	Northstar	C	1	0	HB	13,500	
SJ's Caviar	Northwood	Allerage	C	1	0	HB	20,000	
SJ's Caviar	Northwood	Allerage	F	1	0	LEX	8,000	
SJ's Caviar	Northwood	Beal	C	1	0	HB	22,000	
SJ's Caviar	Northwood	Bluestone	C	1	0	LEX	22,000	
SJ's Caviar	Northwood	Bluestone	F	2	0	LEX	6,000	
SJ's Caviar	Northwood	Canon Hill Vet	F	1	0	HB	16,000	
SJ's Caviar	Northwood	Rocky Ridge	C	1	0	HB	10,000	
SJ's Caviar	Peninsula	Peninsula	C	3	1	HB	23,333	55,527
SJ's Caviar	Peninsula	Peninsula	F	1	0	HB	25,000	
SJ's Caviar	Peninsula	Peninsula	F	1	0	LEX	12,000	
SJ's Caviar	Pin Oak Lane	Hanover	C	3	0	HB	11,167	
SJ's Caviar	Pin Oak Lane	Pin Oak Lane	C	2	0	HB	16,250	

Sire	Consignor	Farm	Sex	Sold	$50,000 2 YOs	Sale	Avg Price	Avg $ Won
SJ's Caviar	Pin Oak Lane	Pin Oak Lane	F	2	0	HB	9,250	
SJ's Caviar	Preferred	Heritage Hill	F	1	0	HB	27,000	
SJ's Caviar	Preferred	Joie De Vie	C	1	0	LEX	37,000	
SJ's Caviar	Preferred	Joie De Vie	F	1	0	LEX	20,000	
SJ's Caviar	Preferred	Kurt Hansen's	C	1	0	HB	19,000	
SJ's Caviar	Preferred	Lindy	C	4	0	HB	24,250	
SJ's Caviar	Preferred	Lindy	F	1	0	HB	32,000	
SJ's Caviar	Preferred	Southwind	C	1	0	HB	7,500	
SJ's Caviar	Preferred	Southwind	F	1	0	HB	14,000	
SJ's Caviar	Preferred	Stirling Brook	F	1	0	LEX	37,000	
SJ's Caviar	Preferred	Walker	C	1	0	HB	15,000	
SJ's Caviar	Preferred	White Birch	C	1	0	HB	18,000	
SJ's Caviar	Saga	Oldfield	C	1	0	LEX	5,000	
SJ's Caviar	Saga	Saga	C	1	0	LEX	12,000	
SJ's Caviar	Spring Haven	Hickory Lane	C	1	0	LEX	40,000	
SJ's Caviar	Spring Haven	Sunrise	F	1	0	LEX	12,000	
SJ's Caviar	Spring Haven	Talbot Creek	C	1	0	LEX	40,000	
SJ's Caviar	Steiner Stock	Steiner Stock	C	1	0	LEX	35,000	
SJ's Caviar	Vieux Carre	Mendez	C	1	0	HB	10,000	
SJ's Caviar	Vieux Carre	Vieux Carre	C	3	0	HB	10,667	
SJ's Caviar	Vieux Carre	Vieux Carre	F	4	0	HB	31,500	
SJ's Caviar	Walnridge	Nandi	C	1	0	HB	8,000	
SJ's Caviar	Winbak	Winbak	C	1	0	HB	17,000	
SJ's Caviar	Winbak	Winbak	F	1	0	HB	23,000	
SJ's Caviar	Winterwood	Winterwood	C	3	0	HB	13,500	
SJ's Caviar	Winterwood	Winterwood	F	4	0	HB	6,750	
SJ's Caviar				**118**	**2**			
Stonebridge Regal	Cameo Hills	Blue Ridge	C	1	0	LEX	3,000	
Stonebridge Regal	Hunterton	Abby	C	1	0	LEX	3,000	
Stonebridge Regal	Hunterton	Abby	F	1	0	LEX	9,000	
Stonebridge Regal	Midland Acres	Morrowland	C	1	0	LEX	9,000	
Stonebridge Regal	Spring Haven	Aquatic	C	1	0	LEX	13,000	
Stonebridge Regal	Spring Haven	Rails Edge	C	1	0	HB	67,000	
Stonebridge Regal				**6**	**0**			
Striking Sahbra	Cane Run	Cane Run	C	3	0	LEX	8,667	
Striking Sahbra	Concord	Concord	C	1	0	HB	42,000	
Striking Sahbra	Diamond Creek	Diamond Creek	F	1	0	LEX	30,000	

Sire	Consignor	Farm	Sex	Sold	$50,000 2 YOs	Sale	Avg Price	Avg $ Won
Striking Sahbra	Dunroven	Dunroven	F	1	0	LEX	11,000	
Striking Sahbra	Hanover	Hanover	C	2	0	HB	45,000	
Striking Sahbra	Hunterton	Emma and Mary Yoder	C	2	1	LEX	77,500	155,106
Striking Sahbra	Hunterton	Hunterton	C	1	0	LEX	10,000	
Striking Sahbra	Hunterton	Tom Schmucker's	F	1	0	HB	35,000	
Striking Sahbra	Hunterton	Walco	C	1	0	LEX	25,000	
Striking Sahbra	Northwood	Allerage	C	1	0	LEX	35,000	
Striking Sahbra	Peninsula	Cool Creek	C	1	0	LEX	80,000	
Striking Sahbra	Peninsula	Peninsula	C	1	0	HB	35,000	
Striking Sahbra	Peninsula	Peninsula	F	1	0	HB	55,000	
Striking Sahbra	Preferred	Olive Branch	C	1	0	HB	20,000	
Striking Sahbra	Preferred	Village Acres Ltd	F	1	0	HB	55,000	
Striking Sahbra	Saga	Wilbur Eash	F	2	0	LEX	2,000	
Striking Sahbra	Spring Haven	Jonas Schlabach's	F	1	0	HB	27,000	
Striking Sahbra	Spring Haven	Mindale	F	1	0	LEX	32,000	
Striking Sahbra	Spring Haven	Spring Haven	C	1	0	LEX	15,000	
Striking Sahbra	Spring Haven	Spring Haven	F	1	0	LEX	15,000	
Striking Sahbra	Spring Haven	Spring Run	F	1	0	HB	42,000	
Striking Sahbra	Spring Haven	Spring Run	C	1	0	LEX	23,000	
Striking Sahbra	Spring Haven	Windswept Valley	C	1	0	LEX	45,000	
Striking Sahbra	Walnut Hall Ltd	Walnut Hall Ltd	C	2	0	HB	30,000	
Striking Sahbra	Walnut Hall Ltd	Walnut Hall Ltd	F	2	0	HB	18,000	
Striking Sahbra	Westwind	Walnut Hall Ltd	C	1	1	HB	40,000	63,379
Striking Sahbra	Westwind	Walnut Hall Ltd	F	1	0	HB	12,000	
Striking Sahbra	Westwind	Westwind	F	1	0	HB	13,000	
Striking Sahbra	Winbak	Winbak	C	1	0	HB	5,500	
Striking Sahbra	Winbak	Winbak	F	2	1	HB	35,000	289,068
Striking Sahbra	Winbak	Winbak	C	1	0	LEX	30,000	
Striking Sahbra				**39**	**3**			
Tagliabue	Fashion	Fashion	C	1	0	HB	12,000	
Tagliabue	Fashion	Fashion	F	2	0	HB	18,500	
Tagliabue	Hunterton	Hunterton	F	1	1	HB	16,000	114,436
Tagliabue				**4**	**1**			
Taurus Dream	Preferred	D Farm	F	**2**	**1**	HB	34,500	584,392
Tell All	Brittany	Brittany	C	3	1	LEX	12,000	50,132
Tell All	Brittany	Brittany	F	3	0	LEX	2,000	
Tell All	Cameo Hills	Cameo Hills	C	1	0	LEX	6,000	

Sire	Consignor	Farm	Sex	Sold	$50,000 2 YOs	Sale	Avg Price	Avg $ Won
Tell All	Concord	Concord	C	1	0	HB	9,000	
Tell All	Hanover	Hanover	C	1	0	HB	8,000	
Tell All	Hunterton	Brittany	F	2	0	HB	2,750	
Tell All	Hunterton	Glassford Equine	F	1	0	LEX	12,000	
Tell All	Hunterton	Hunterton	C	5	0	HB	23,500	
Tell All	Hunterton	Hunterton	F	2	0	HB	2,250	
Tell All	Hunterton	Hunterton	C	3	0	LEX	24,000	
Tell All	Hunterton	Hunterton	F	2	0	LEX	2,500	
Tell All	Hunterton	Martinez Equine	F	1	0	HB	1,500	
Tell All	Hunterton	Seelster	C	1	0	HB	4,500	
Tell All	Kentuckiana	Kentuckiana	C	4	0	LEX	30,750	
Tell All	Kentuckiana	Kentuckiana	F	7	0	LEX	6,143	
Tell All	Peninsula	Peninsula	C	1	0	LEX	2,000	
Tell All	Peninsula	Shady Side	C	1	0	LEX	10,000	
Tell All	Perretti	Perretti	F	1	0	HB	6,500	
Tell All	Perretti	Perretti	F	1	0	LEX	23,000	
Tell All	Preferred	BJ's	C	1	0	HB	2,500	
Tell All	Preferred	Deo Volente	F	1	0	LEX	10,000	
Tell All	Preferred	Joie De Vie	F	1	0	HB	9,000	
Tell All	Preferred	Tom Knight's	C	1	0	HB	7,000	
Tell All	Preferred	White Birch	C	1	0	HB	5,500	
Tell All	Preferred	White Birch	F	1	0	HB	3,000	
Tell All	Spring Haven	Spring Run	F	1	0	HB	6,500	
Tell All	Spring Haven	The Pink Racing	F	1	0	HB	1,500	
Tell All	Steiner Stock	Steiner Stock	F	1	0	LEX	6,000	
Tell All	Stonegate	Stonegate	C	2	0	HB	4,750	
Tell All	Vieux Carre	Brittany	C	1	0	HB	3,500	
Tell All	Winterwood	Winterwood	C	1	0	HB	12,000	
Tell All				**54**	**1**			
The Panderosa	Allamerican	Allamerican	C	4	0	HB	22,750	
The Panderosa	Allamerican	Allamerican	F	1	0	HB	8,000	
The Panderosa	Blue Chip	Blue Chip	C	3	0	HB	39,000	
The Panderosa	Blue Chip	Blue Chip	F	1	0	HB	7,000	
The Panderosa	Cameo Hills	Cameo Hills	F	3	0	LEX	25,000	
The Panderosa	Cameo Hills	Marvin Raber	F	1	0	LEX	11,000	
The Panderosa	Concord	Ed Evans'	C	1	0	HB	30,000	
The Panderosa	Dunroven	Dunroven	F	1	0	LEX	10,000	

Sire	Consignor	Farm	Sex	Sold	$50,000 2 YOs	Sale	Avg Price	Avg $ Won
The Panderosa	Fair Winds	Fair Winds	C	1	0	HB	13,000	
The Panderosa	Fox Den	Anne Mcdonald's	C	1	0	HB	30,000	
The Panderosa	Fox Den	Glen Rock	C	1	0	HB	20,000	
The Panderosa	Fox Den	Gregory Gehman's	F	1	0	HB	8,500	
The Panderosa	Fox Den	Shaffer Standardbreds	C	1	0	HB	7,000	
The Panderosa	Fox Den	Shaffer Standardbreds	F	3	0	HB	8,667	
The Panderosa	Fox Den	Stoltzfus	C	3	0	HB	23,000	
The Panderosa	Fox Den	Stoltzfus	F	4	0	HB	20,750	
The Panderosa	Hanover	Hanover	C	22	2	HB	29,545	119,940
The Panderosa	Hanover	Hanover	F	17	1	HB	22,235	76,384
The Panderosa	Hanover	Hanover	C	1	0	LEX	57,000	
The Panderosa	Hunterton	Hunterton	F	1	0	HB	5,000	
The Panderosa	Hunterton	Hunterton	C	1	0	LEX	30,000	
The Panderosa	Hunterton	Hunterton	F	2	0	LEX	20,500	
The Panderosa	Hunterton	Walco	C	3	1	LEX	47,667	84,962
The Panderosa	Hunterton	Walco	F	2	0	LEX	10,000	
The Panderosa	Kentuckiana	Big Al's	C	1	0	LEX	12,000	
The Panderosa	Kentuckiana	Emerald Ridge	C	1	0	LEX	45,000	
The Panderosa	Midland Acres	Midland Acres	C	1	0	LEX	16,000	
The Panderosa	Northwood	Allerage	F	1	0	HB	10,000	
The Panderosa	Northwood	Engelman	C	1	0	HB	20,000	
The Panderosa	Northwood	Fox Valley	C	1	0	HB	45,000	
The Panderosa	Northwood	Maple Run	C	1	0	HB	12,000	
The Panderosa	Northwood	Nandi	C	1	0	HB	13,500	
The Panderosa	Northwood	Nandi	F	1	0	HB	30,000	
The Panderosa	Northwood	Spring Run	C	1	0	HB	20,000	
The Panderosa	Peninsula	Equine Center	C	1	0	LEX	15,000	
The Panderosa	Peninsula	Peninsula	C	1	0	LEX	25,000	
The Panderosa	Peninsula	Peninsula	F	1	0	LEX	8,000	
The Panderosa	Peninsula	Richard Malone's	C	1	0	HB	55,000	
The Panderosa	Peninsula	Walstan	F	1	0	LEX	30,000	
The Panderosa	Preferred	Birch Creek	F	1	0	HB	5,500	
The Panderosa	Preferred	BJ's	C	1	0	HB	12,000	
The Panderosa	Preferred	BJ's	F	1	0	HB	10,000	
The Panderosa	Preferred	Deo Volente	C	1	0	LEX	37,000	
The Panderosa	Preferred	Heritage Hill	C	1	0	HB	25,000	
The Panderosa	Preferred	Majestic View	F	1	0	HB	20,000	

Sire	Consignor	Farm	Sex	Sold	$50,000 2 YOs	Sale	Avg Price	Avg $ Won
The Panderosa	Preferred	Seelster	F	1	0	HB	7,000	
The Panderosa	Preferred	White Birch	C	1	0	HB	12,000	
The Panderosa	Preferred	White Birch	F	1	0	HB	20,000	
The Panderosa	Saga	Saga	C	1	0	LEX	15,000	
The Panderosa	Spring Haven	Mindale	C	1	0	LEX	18,000	
The Panderosa	Spring Haven	Mindale	F	2	0	LEX	10,500	
The Panderosa	Spring Haven	Rails Edge	C	1	0	LEX	3,000	
The Panderosa	Spring Haven	Spring Haven	C	1	0	HB	30,000	
The Panderosa	Spring Haven	Spring Haven	F	1	0	LEX	12,000	
The Panderosa	Spring Haven	Viking Meadows	F	1	0	LEX	18,000	
The Panderosa	Steiner Stock	Steiner Stock	C	1	0	LEX	34,000	
The Panderosa	Steiner Stock	Steiner Stock	F	1	0	LEX	15,000	
The Panderosa	Twinbrook	Charles Lawrence's	F	1	0	HB	9,000	
The Panderosa	Twinbrook	Twinbrook	F	1	0	HB	47,000	
The Panderosa	Vieux Carre	Mendez	F	1	0	HB	2,500	
The Panderosa	Vieux Carre	Vieux Carre	C	6	0	HB	14,167	
The Panderosa	Vieux Carre	Vieux Carre	F	4	1	HB	24,875	51,496
The Panderosa	Walnridge	Cameo Hills	F	2	0	HB	3,500	
The Panderosa	Walnridge	Marvin Raber	C	3	0	HB	5,833	
The Panderosa	Walnridge	Marvin Raber	F	2	0	HB	5,750	
The Panderosa	Walnridge	Walnridge	C	1	0	HB	30,000	
The Panderosa	Walnridge	Walnridge	F	2	0	HB	6,500	
The Panderosa	Walnut Hall Stock	Walnut Hall Stock	C	1	0	LEX	15,000	
The Panderosa	Winbak	Winbak	C	1	0	HB	10,000	
The Panderosa	Winbak	Winbak	F	2	0	HB	37,500	
The Panderosa				**140**	**5**			
Tom Ridge	Brittany	Brittany	C	1	0	LEX	115,000	
Tom Ridge	Brittany	Brittany	F	2	0	LEX	20,000	
Tom Ridge	Concord	Concord	C	1	0	HB	28,000	
Tom Ridge	Concord	Concord	F	1	0	HB	10,000	
Tom Ridge	Concord	Hanover	C	4	0	HB	8,375	
Tom Ridge	Concord	Hanover	F	1	1	HB	23,000	95,391
Tom Ridge	Fair Winds	Fair Winds	F	1	0	HB	3,500	
Tom Ridge	Hanover	Hanover	F	1	0	HB	6,000	
Tom Ridge	Hunterton	Hunterton	C	2	0	HB	8,000	
Tom Ridge	Hunterton	Hunterton	C	1	1	LEX	26,000	74,960
Tom Ridge	Hunterton	Starmaker	C	1	0	LEX	6,000	

Sire	Consignor	Farm	Sex	Sold	$50,000 2 YOs	Sale	Avg Price	Avg $ Won
Tom Ridge	Hunterton	Walco	C	1	0	LEX	15,000	
Tom Ridge	Hunterton	Walco	F	1	0	LEX	9,000	
Tom Ridge	Kentuckiana	Kentuckiana	C	1	0	LEX	15,000	
Tom Ridge	Northwood	Allerage	C	1	0	HB	7,000	
Tom Ridge	Northwood	Allerage	C	1	0	LEX	27,000	
Tom Ridge	Northwood	Allerage	F	1	0	LEX	20,000	
Tom Ridge	Northwood	Nandi	F	1	1	LEX	4,000	82,656
Tom Ridge	Peninsula	Lindwood	C	1	0	HB	12,000	
Tom Ridge	Peninsula	Peninsula	C	1	0	LEX	25,000	
Tom Ridge	Peninsula	Silver Linden	C	1	0	HB	13,000	
Tom Ridge	Preferred	Bloodstock	C	2	1	LEX	7,000	150,570
Tom Ridge	Preferred	Bloodstock	F	1	0	LEX	3,000	
Tom Ridge	Preferred	Joie De Vie	C	1	0	LEX	20,000	
Tom Ridge	Preferred	Lindy	C	1	0	HB	10,000	
Tom Ridge	Preferred	Lindy	C	2	0	LEX	26,000	
Tom Ridge	Preferred	Stirling Brook	F	1	0	HB	3,500	
Tom Ridge	Preferred	Warrawee	C	2	0	HB	12,500	
Tom Ridge	Spring Haven	Jonas Schlabach's	C	1	0	HB	30,000	
Tom Ridge	Spring Haven	Ruddick Stables	C	1	1	LEX	3,000	105,354
Tom Ridge	Walnridge	Nandi	C	6	1	HB	9,833	133,682
Tom Ridge	Walnridge	Nandi	F	6	1	HB	10,333	58,135
Tom Ridge	Walnut Hall Ltd	Walnut Hall Ltd	C	6	1	HB	23,083	52,723
Tom Ridge	Walnut Hall Ltd	Walnut Hall Ltd	F	10	2	HB	19,250	74,000
Tom Ridge	Westwind	Walnut Hall Ltd	C	5	0	HB	35,000	
Tom Ridge	Westwind	Walnut Hall Ltd	F	4	0	HB	14,750	
Tom Ridge				**75**	**10**			
Totally Western	Winbak	Winbak	C	**1**	**0**	HB	4,000	
Valley Victor	Brittany	Brittany	F	1	0	LEX	2,000	
Valley Victor	Cameo Hills	Cameo Hills	F	1	0	LEX	2,000	
Valley Victor	Cameo Hills	Fair Winds	F	1	0	LEX	4,000	
Valley Victor	Cane Run	Brannon	F	1	0	LEX	9,000	
Valley Victor	Cane Run	Cane Run	C	2	0	LEX	3,000	
Valley Victor	Cane Run	Cane Run	F	1	0	LEX	10,000	
Valley Victor	Concord	Concord	C	1	0	HB	70,000	
Valley Victor	Fair Winds	Fair Winds	C	1	0	HB	6,500	
Valley Victor	Futurity Hill	Futurity Hill	C	1	0	LEX	15,000	
Valley Victor	Hunterton	Harvey Knepp	F	1	0	LEX	5,000	

Sire	Consignor	Farm	Sex	Sold	$50,000 2 YOs	Sale	Avg Price	Avg $ Won
Valley Victor	Hunterton	Hunterton	C	5	1	LEX	18,600	52,412
Valley Victor	Hunterton	Hunterton	F	6	0	LEX	13,500	
Valley Victor	Hunterton	Meadow Creek	C	3	0	LEX	17,000	
Valley Victor	Midland Acres	Midland Acres	C	2	0	LEX	16,000	
Valley Victor	Millstream	Millstream	C	2	0	HB	18,250	
Valley Victor	Northwood	Bluestone	F	1	0	LEX	13,000	
Valley Victor	Peninsula	Benaire	C	1	0	LEX	17,000	
Valley Victor	Peninsula	Farrier's Acres	C	1	0	LEX	20,000	
Valley Victor	Peninsula	Farrier's Acres	F	1	1	LEX	20,000	80,523
Valley Victor	Peninsula	Green Creek	C	1	1	LEX	15,000	54,824
Valley Victor	Peninsula	Kentland	C	1	0	LEX	15,000	
Valley Victor	Peninsula	Linda & T.D. Van Kamp	C	1	0	LEX	12,000	
Valley Victor	Peninsula	Oaklea	F	2	0	LEX	3,500	
Valley Victor	Peninsula	Peninsula	C	8	1	LEX	22,875	185,252
Valley Victor	Peninsula	Peninsula	F	9	1	LEX	27,778	79,088
Valley Victor	Peninsula	Quantum	F	1	0	LEX	2,000	
Valley Victor	Peninsula	Robert J. Fraher	C	1	0	LEX	7,000	
Valley Victor	Peninsula	Robert Rietveld	F	1	0	LEX	15,000	
Valley Victor	Peninsula	Shawnee Run	F	5	0	LEX	15,200	
Valley Victor	Peninsula	Walstan	C	7	2	LEX	23,000	60,042
Valley Victor	Peninsula	Walstan	F	4	1	LEX	26,750	66,834
Valley Victor	Peninsula	Wilt Standardbreds	C	2	0	LEX	22,500	
Valley Victor	Preferred	Ecuries Vandenplas	F	1	0	HB	8,000	
Valley Victor	Preferred	Lindy	F	2	0	LEX	2,500	
Valley Victor	Preferred	Twin Willows	F	2	0	LEX	9,000	
Valley Victor	Saga	Saga	F	1	0	LEX	15,000	
Valley Victor	Spring Haven	Hickory Lane	C	1	0	LEX	11,000	
Valley Victor	Spring Haven	Jonas Schlabach's	F	1	0	HB	10,000	
Valley Victor	Walnridge	Walnridge	F	1	0	HB	40,000	
Valley Victor	Walnut Hall Stock	Walnut Hall Stock	C	2	0	LEX	22,000	
Valley Victor	Walnut Hall Stock	Walnut Hall Stock	F	2	0	LEX	3,000	
Valley Victor				**89**	**8**			
Varenne	Preferred	Southwind	C	1	0	HB	2,500	
Varenne	Preferred	Southwind	C	1	0	LEX	29,000	
Varenne				**2**	**0**			
Village Jolt	Boxwood	Shadowbrook	F	2	0	HB	2,750	
Village Jolt	Concord	Concord	C	3	0	HB	25,667	

Sire	Consignor	Farm	Sex	Sold	$50,000 2 YOs	Sale	Avg Price	Avg $ Won
Village Jolt	Concord	Concord	F	2	0	HB	10,500	
Village Jolt	Fair Winds	Fair Winds	C	4	0	HB	23,000	
Village Jolt	Fair Winds	Fair Winds	F	2	0	HB	22,500	
Village Jolt	Fashion	Fashion	C	10	0	HB	19,100	
Village Jolt	Fashion	Fashion	F	9	0	HB	13,056	
Village Jolt	Fox Den	Shaffer Standardbreds	C	1	0	HB	7,000	
Village Jolt	Hanover	Hanover	C	2	0	HB	8,500	
Village Jolt	Hanover	Hanover	F	1	0	HB	7,000	
Village Jolt	Hunterton	Walco	C	1	0	LEX	30,000	
Village Jolt	Hunterton	Walco	F	1	0	LEX	27,000	
Village Jolt	Northstar	Northstar	C	1	0	HB	7,000	
Village Jolt	Northwood	Birch Creek	F	1	0	HB	30,000	
Village Jolt	Northwood	Concord	F	1	0	LEX	18,000	
Village Jolt	Northwood	Nandi	C	1	0	HB	10,000	
Village Jolt	Northwood	Nandi	F	1	0	LEX	2,000	
Village Jolt	Northwood	Oak Hill Manor	C	2	0	HB	23,500	
Village Jolt	Northwood	Snowball Hill	F	1	0	HB	4,000	
Village Jolt	Peninsula	Lindwood	C	1	0	LEX	8,000	
Village Jolt	Perretti	Perretti	C	3	0	HB	40,333	
Village Jolt	Perretti	Perretti	F	1	0	HB	3,500	
Village Jolt	Pin Oak Lane	Pin Oak Lane	C	1	0	HB	5,000	
Village Jolt	Preferred	Emerald Highlands	C	4	0	LEX	25,500	
Village Jolt	Preferred	Emerald Highlands	F	2	0	LEX	11,500	
Village Jolt	Preferred	Englewood	F	1	0	LEX	4,000	
Village Jolt	Preferred	Heritage Hill	C	3	0	HB	14,667	
Village Jolt	Preferred	Heritage Hill	F	3	0	HB	6,667	
Village Jolt	Preferred	Heritage Hill	C	1	0	LEX	20,000	
Village Jolt	Preferred	Joie De Vie	F	1	0	HB	2,500	
Village Jolt	Preferred	Lindy	C	1	0	LEX	23,000	
Village Jolt	Spring Haven	Spring Haven	C	1	0	LEX	5,000	
Village Jolt	Twinbrook	Twinbrook	C	1	0	HB	20,000	
Village Jolt	Twinbrook	Twinbrook	F	1	0	HB	42,000	
Village Jolt	Vieux Carre	Vieux Carre	C	1	0	HB	25,000	
Village Jolt	Walnridge	Deo Volente	C	1	0	HB	18,000	
Village Jolt	Walnridge	Nandi	C	1	0	HB	16,000	
Village Jolt	Winterwood	Winterwood	C	1	0	HB	32,000	
Village Jolt	Winterwood	Winterwood	F	1	0	HB	6,000	

Sire	Consignor	Farm	Sex	Sold	$50,000 2 YOs	Sale	Avg Price	Avg $ Won
Village Jolt				76	0			
Western Hanover	Allamerican	Allamerican	C	4	1	HB	53,250	107,965
Western Hanover	Allamerican	Allamerican	F	1	0	HB	23,000	
Western Hanover	Blue Chip	Blue Chip	C	2	0	HB	55,000	
Western Hanover	Brittany	Brittany	F	2	1	LEX	27,500	62,750
Western Hanover	Concord	Concord	C	2	1	HB	41,500	62,568
Western Hanover	Concord	Concord	F	2	0	HB	14,000	
Western Hanover	Concord	Crosscountry	F	1	0	HB	5,000	
Western Hanover	Diamond Creek	Diamond Creek	F	3	0	HB	75,000	
Western Hanover	Diamond Creek	Diamond Creek	C	1	0	LEX	50,000	
Western Hanover	Diamond Creek	Diamond Creek	F	2	0	LEX	38,500	
Western Hanover	Fair Winds	Bayberry	C	1	1	HB	39,000	63,962
Western Hanover	Fair Winds	Fair Winds	C	8	1	HB	41,750	51,470
Western Hanover	Fair Winds	Fair Winds	F	4	1	HB	23,000	52,189
Western Hanover	Fashion	Fashion	F	1	0	HB	13,000	
Western Hanover	Fox Den	Shaffer Standardbreds	F	3	0	HB	13,333	
Western Hanover	Hanover	Hanover	C	25	0	HB	42,200	
Western Hanover	Hanover	Hanover	F	21	2	HB	27,524	82,487
Western Hanover	Hanover	Hanover	C	6	0	LEX	63,667	
Western Hanover	Hanover	Hanover	F	2	0	LEX	55,000	
Western Hanover	Hempt	Hempt	C	3	1	HB	17,000	54,041
Western Hanover	Hempt	Hempt	F	8	0	HB	14,250	
Western Hanover	Hunterton	Hunterton	F	1	0	LEX	62,000	
Western Hanover	Hunterton	Meadow Creek	C	1	0	HB	32,000	
Western Hanover	Hunterton	Meadow Creek	C	1	0	LEX	97,000	
Western Hanover	Kentuckiana	Kentuckiana	C	7	2	LEX	76,857	139,216
Western Hanover	Kentuckiana	Kentuckiana	F	6	1	LEX	52,000	57,757
Western Hanover	Northwood	Bluestone	C	1	0	LEX	35,000	
Western Hanover	Northwood	Bonley	F	1	0	HB	9,000	
Western Hanover	Northwood	Caviart	F	1	0	LEX	10,000	
Western Hanover	Northwood	Deo Volente	F	1	0	HB	50,000	
Western Hanover	Peninsula	Equine Center	F	1	0	LEX	35,000	
Western Hanover	Peninsula	Odds On Acres	F	1	1	HB	15,000	145,279
Western Hanover	Peninsula	Odds On Acres	C	1	0	LEX	40,000	
Western Hanover	Peninsula	Peninsula	C	1	1	HB	30,000	69,201
Western Hanover	Peninsula	Two Creeks	F	1	0	LEX	6,000	
Western Hanover	Perretti	Perretti	C	1	0	HB	40,000	

Sire	Consignor	Farm	Sex	Sold	$50,000 2 YOs	Sale	Avg Price	Avg $ Won
Western Hanover	Preferred	Birch Creek	F	1	0	HB	6,500	
Western Hanover	Preferred	Emerald Highlands	C	1	0	LEX	40,000	
Western Hanover	Preferred	Emerald Highlands	F	1	1	LEX	15,000	817,655
Western Hanover	Preferred	Heritage Hill	F	1	0	HB	30,000	
Western Hanover	Preferred	Heritage Hill	F	1	0	LEX	40,000	
Western Hanover	Preferred	Joie De Vie	C	1	0	LEX	110,000	
Western Hanover	Preferred	Tara Hills	C	1	0	HB	25,000	
Western Hanover	Preferred	White Birch	C	4	0	HB	23,500	
Western Hanover	Preferred	White Birch	F	1	0	HB	4,000	
Western Hanover	Spring Haven	Spring Haven	F	1	0	LEX	30,000	
Western Hanover	Stonegate	Stonegate	C	2	0	HB	11,000	
Western Hanover	Stonegate	Stonegate	F	2	0	HB	16,250	
Western Hanover	Vieux Carre	Vieux Carre	C	7	0	HB	37,429	
Western Hanover	Vieux Carre	Vieux Carre	F	5	1	HB	28,300	329,089
Western Hanover	Walnridge	Walnridge	F	1	0	HB	20,000	
Western Hanover	Walnut Hall Stock	Walnut Hall Stock	C	2	0	LEX	33,500	
Western Hanover	Walnut Hall Stock	Walnut Hall Stock	F	1	1	LEX	25,000	54,869
Western Hanover	Westwind	Walnut Hall Ltd	C	1	0	HB	75,000	
Western Hanover	Winbak	Winbak	C	4	0	HB	33,000	
Western Hanover	Winbak	Winbak	F	2	0	HB	43,500	
Western Hanover	Winbak	Winbak	C	2	0	LEX	40,000	
Western Hanover	Winbak	Winbak	F	3	0	LEX	50,000	
Western Hanover	Winterwood	Winterwood	F	1	0	HB	27,000	
Western Hanover				**174**	**17**			
Western Ideal	Allamerican	Allamerican	C	6	0	HB	12,917	
Western Ideal	Allamerican	Allamerican	F	5	0	HB	22,100	
Western Ideal	Blue Chip	Blue Chip	C	1	0	HB	47,000	
Western Ideal	Blue Chip	Blue Chip	F	2	0	HB	96,000	
Western Ideal	Blue Chip	Blue Chip	C	1	0	LEX	50,000	
Western Ideal	Boxwood	Boxwood	C	1	0	HB	6,000	
Western Ideal	Brittany	Brittany	C	14	2	LEX	50,643	66,723
Western Ideal	Brittany	Brittany	F	8	0	LEX	18,375	
Western Ideal	Cameo Hills	Cameo Hills	F	1	0	LEX	42,000	
Western Ideal	Concord	Concord	C	2	0	HB	66,000	
Western Ideal	Concord	Concord	F	1	0	HB	10,000	
Western Ideal	Diamond Creek	Diamond Creek	C	4	0	HB	42,500	
Western Ideal	Diamond Creek	Diamond Creek	F	3	0	HB	25,667	

Sire	Consignor	Farm	Sex	Sold	$50,000 2 YOs	Sale	Avg Price	Avg $ Won
Western Ideal	Diamond Creek	Diamond Creek	C	2	0	LEX	9,500	
Western Ideal	Diamond Creek	Diamond Creek	F	5	1	LEX	50,400	263,467
Western Ideal	Fair Winds	Fair Winds	C	1	0	HB	22,000	
Western Ideal	Fair Winds	Fair Winds	F	3	0	HB	26,667	
Western Ideal	Hanover	Hanover	C	29	1	HB	40,483	827,204
Western Ideal	Hanover	Hanover	F	20	2	HB	39,475	320,659
Western Ideal	Hanover	Hanover	C	3	0	LEX	85,667	
Western Ideal	Hanover	Hanover	F	3	1	LEX	30,000	54,866
Western Ideal	Hunterton	Brittany	C	1	0	HB	25,000	
Western Ideal	Hunterton	Hickory Lane	F	1	0	HB	40,000	
Western Ideal	Hunterton	Hunterton	C	2	0	HB	20,500	
Western Ideal	Hunterton	Hunterton	F	1	0	HB	19,000	
Western Ideal	Hunterton	Hunterton	C	3	0	LEX	56,333	
Western Ideal	Hunterton	Pine Hill	C	1	0	LEX	30,000	
Western Ideal	Kentuckiana	Goldfinger	C	1	0	LEX	40,000	
Western Ideal	Kentuckiana	Kentuckiana	C	1	0	LEX	55,000	
Western Ideal	Kentuckiana	Kentuckiana	F	5	2	LEX	85,000	98,919
Western Ideal	Northwood	Bluestone	C	1	0	HB	5,000	
Western Ideal	Northwood	Bluestone	C	3	0	LEX	18,333	
Western Ideal	Northwood	Bluestone	F	1	0	LEX	4,000	
Western Ideal	Northwood	Caviart	F	1	0	LEX	15,000	
Western Ideal	Northwood	Deo Volente	C	1	0	HB	110,000	
Western Ideal	Northwood	Deo Volente	F	1	0	HB	75,000	
Western Ideal	Northwood	Perretti	F	1	0	HB	130,000	
Western Ideal	Peninsula	Odds On Acres	F	1	0	LEX	25,000	
Western Ideal	Peninsula	Odds On Racing	C	1	0	HB	30,000	
Western Ideal	Peninsula	Peninsula	C	1	0	LEX	62,000	
Western Ideal	Peninsula	Two Creeks	C	1	0	LEX	10,000	
Western Ideal	Perretti	Perretti	F	1	0	HB	7,000	
Western Ideal	Perretti	Perretti	C	1	0	LEX	85,000	
Western Ideal	Preferred	Birch Creek	C	1	0	LEX	62,000	
Western Ideal	Preferred	Birch Creek	F	2	0	LEX	10,000	
Western Ideal	Preferred	Deo Volente	F	2	1	LEX	22,000	69,011
Western Ideal	Preferred	Gardiner	C	1	0	LEX	70,000	
Western Ideal	Preferred	Heritage Hill	F	1	0	HB	25,000	
Western Ideal	Preferred	Lindy	F	1	0	LEX	80,000	
Western Ideal	Preferred	Rolling Acres	C	1	0	HB	40,000	

Sire	Consignor	Farm	Sex	Sold	$50,000 2 YOs	Sale	Avg Price	Avg $ Won
Western Ideal	Preferred	Tara Hills	F	1	0	HB	55,000	
Western Ideal	Preferred	White Birch	C	1	0	HB	27,000	
Western Ideal	Preferred	White Birch	F	5	1	HB	22,200	302,615
Western Ideal	Preferred	White Birch	C	4	2	LEX	61,750	131,823
Western Ideal	Preferred	White Birch	F	1	0	LEX	20,000	
Western Ideal	Spring Haven	Spring Haven	F	1	1	LEX	18,000	87,044
Western Ideal	Stonegate	Stonegate	C	1	0	HB	47,000	
Western Ideal	Stonegate	Stonegate	F	4	2	HB	47,500	91,907
Western Ideal	Twinbrook	Twinbrook	C	1	0	HB	50,000	
Western Ideal	Twinbrook	Twinbrook	F	1	0	HB	8,000	
Western Ideal	Vieux Carre	Brittany	C	1	0	HB	20,000	
Western Ideal	Vieux Carre	Vieux Carre	C	4	0	HB	12,875	
Western Ideal	Walnridge	Walnridge	C	2	0	HB	48,000	
Western Ideal	Walnridge	Walnridge	F	1	0	HB	9,000	
Western Ideal	Walnut Hall Stock	Walnut Hall Stock	F	1	0	LEX	13,000	
Western Ideal	Winbak	Winbak	F	1	0	HB	3,500	
Western Ideal				**185**	**16**			
Western Terror	Blue Chip	Blue Chip	C	1	0	HB	127,000	
Western Terror	Blue Chip	Blue Chip	F	1	0	HB	105,000	
Western Terror	Boxwood	Shadowbrook	F	1	1	HB	50,000	296,156
Western Terror	Concord	Concord	F	1	0	HB	6,000	
Western Terror	Concord	Hanover	F	1	0	HB	60,000	
Western Terror	Dunroven	Dunroven	C	1	0	LEX	20,000	
Western Terror	Fox Den	King	C	1	0	HB	14,000	
Western Terror	Hanover	Hanover	C	1	0	HB	19,000	
Western Terror	Hanover	Hanover	F	1	0	HB	57,000	
Western Terror	Hunterton	Grassy Branch	C	1	0	LEX	11,000	
Western Terror	Hunterton	Oak Park	C	1	0	LEX	57,000	
Western Terror	Hunterton	Starmaker	F	1	0	LEX	20,000	
Western Terror	Hunterton	Walco	F	1	0	LEX	75,000	
Western Terror	Kentuckiana	Bulletproof Ent	F	1	0	LEX	5,000	
Western Terror	Kentuckiana	Goldfinger	C	2	0	LEX	25,000	
Western Terror	Kentuckiana	Goldfinger	F	3	0	LEX	8,000	
Western Terror	Kentuckiana	Kentuckiana	C	32	1	LEX	44,844	66,723
Western Terror	Kentuckiana	Kentuckiana	F	30	1	LEX	23,033	58,530
Western Terror	Northwood	Andray	F	1	0	HB	16,000	
Western Terror	Northwood	Andray	F	1	0	LEX	9,000	

Sire	Consignor	Farm	Sex	Sold	$50,000 2 YOs	Sale	Avg Price	Avg $ Won
Western Terror	Northwood	Howard Stables	C	1	0	HB	12,000	
Western Terror	Peninsula	Al Tomlinson	F	1	0	HB	37,000	
Western Terror	Peninsula	Equine Center	F	1	0	LEX	60,000	
Western Terror	Peninsula	Skipalong	F	1	0	LEX	15,000	
Western Terror	Preferred	Cross Creek	F	1	0	HB	19,000	
Western Terror	Preferred	Green Gables	C	1	0	HB	23,000	
Western Terror	Preferred	Heritage Hill	F	1	0	HB	2,000	
Western Terror	Preferred	Morning Star	C	1	0	HB	11,000	
Western Terror	Preferred	Oak Knoll	C	1	0	HB	37,000	
Western Terror	Preferred	White Birch	F	1	0	HB	13,000	
Western Terror	Saga	Saga	F	1	0	LEX	18,000	
Western Terror	Saga	Victory Hill	C	1	0	LEX	9,000	
Western Terror	Saga	Victory Hill	F	1	0	LEX	1,000	
Western Terror	Spring Haven	Spring Haven	C	1	0	HB	120,000	
Western Terror	Spring Haven	Spring Haven	C	1	0	LEX	47,000	
Western Terror	Vieux Carre	Mendez	C	1	0	HB	52,000	
Western Terror	Walnridge	Walnridge	C	5	0	HB	13,700	
Western Terror	Walnridge	Walnridge	F	8	0	HB	13,688	
Western Terror	Walnut Hall Stock	Walnut Hall Stock	C	2	0	LEX	36,000	
Western Terror	Walnut Hall Stock	Walnut Hall Stock	F	2	1	LEX	15,000	68,593
Western Terror				116	4			
Windsong's Legacy	Allamerican	Allamerican	C	1	0	HB	13,000	
Windsong's Legacy	Allamerican	Allamerican	F	1	0	HB	9,000	
Windsong's Legacy	Blue Chip	Blue Chip	C	1	0	HB	42,000	
Windsong's Legacy	Blue Chip	Blue Chip	F	1	0	HB	24,000	
Windsong's Legacy	Cane Run	Cane Run	C	2	0	LEX	15,000	
Windsong's Legacy	Cane Run	Cane Run	F	1	0	LEX	4,000	
Windsong's Legacy	Concord	Concord	C	2	1	HB	36,000	211,549
Windsong's Legacy	Concord	Concord	F	2	0	HB	10,500	
Windsong's Legacy	Concord	Hanover	C	4	0	HB	38,750	
Windsong's Legacy	Concord	Hanover	F	1	0	HB	24,000	
Windsong's Legacy	Diamond Creek	Diamond Creek	F	1	0	HB	8,000	
Windsong's Legacy	Diamond Creek	Diamond Creek	C	1	0	LEX	25,000	
Windsong's Legacy	Diamond Creek	Diamond Creek	F	2	0	LEX	35,000	
Windsong's Legacy	Dunroven	Dunroven	C	2	0	LEX	8,000	
Windsong's Legacy	Dunroven	Dunroven	F	1	0	LEX	5,000	
Windsong's Legacy	Dunroven	Richard Keys	F	1	0	LEX	15,000	

Sire	Consignor	Farm	Sex	Sold	$50,000 2 YOs	Sale	Avg Price	Avg $ Won
Windsong's Legacy	Hanover	Hanover	C	3	0	HB	32,000	
Windsong's Legacy	Hanover	Hanover	F	2	0	HB	91,500	
Windsong's Legacy	Hunterton	Dottie Morone	C	1	0	HB	1,500	
Windsong's Legacy	Hunterton	Hunterton	C	2	0	HB	11,000	
Windsong's Legacy	Hunterton	Hunterton	F	3	0	HB	16,667	
Windsong's Legacy	Hunterton	Hunterton	C	3	0	LEX	26,000	
Windsong's Legacy	Hunterton	Hunterton	F	1	0	LEX	25,000	
Windsong's Legacy	Hunterton	Little Moon Lake	F	1	0	LEX	40,000	
Windsong's Legacy	Hunterton	Talbot Creek	C	1	0	LEX	31,000	
Windsong's Legacy	Hunterton	Walco	C	1	0	LEX	7,000	
Windsong's Legacy	Millstream	Millstream	C	1	0	HB	15,000	
Windsong's Legacy	Millstream	Millstream	F	1	0	HB	1,000	
Windsong's Legacy	Northstar	Northstar	F	1	0	HB	8,000	
Windsong's Legacy	Northwood	Albert Schmucker's	C	1	0	HB	18,000	
Windsong's Legacy	Northwood	Allerage	F	1	0	HB	15,000	
Windsong's Legacy	Northwood	Allerage	C	1	0	LEX	37,000	
Windsong's Legacy	Northwood	Bluestone	C	2	0	LEX	16,000	
Windsong's Legacy	Northwood	Bluestone	F	3	0	LEX	27,667	
Windsong's Legacy	Northwood	Olive Branch	C	1	0	HB	12,000	
Windsong's Legacy	Peninsula	Peninsula	C	1	0	HB	90,000	
Windsong's Legacy	Peninsula	Peninsula	F	2	0	HB	48,500	
Windsong's Legacy	Peninsula	Peninsula	F	1	0	LEX	32,000	
Windsong's Legacy	Perretti	Perretti	C	10	2	HB	24,650	373,948
Windsong's Legacy	Perretti	Perretti	F	13	1	HB	49,923	335,250
Windsong's Legacy	Perretti	Perretti	C	3	0	LEX	17,333	
Windsong's Legacy	Perretti	Perretti	F	2	0	LEX	32,000	
Windsong's Legacy	Preferred	Joie De Vie	F	2	0	LEX	38,500	
Windsong's Legacy	Preferred	Southwind	C	1	0	LEX	55,000	
Windsong's Legacy	Preferred	Stirling Brook	F	1	0	LEX	7,000	
Windsong's Legacy	Preferred	Sun Valley	C	1	0	HB	4,000	
Windsong's Legacy	Preferred	White Birch	F	1	0	LEX	37,000	
Windsong's Legacy	Preferred	Windsun	F	1	0	LEX	20,000	
Windsong's Legacy	Spring Haven	Talbot Creek	C	1	0	LEX	8,000	
Windsong's Legacy	Stonegate	Stonegate	C	1	0	HB	16,000	
Windsong's Legacy	Vieux Carre	Vieux Carre	C	1	0	HB	10,000	
Windsong's Legacy	Vieux Carre	Vieux Carre	F	2	0	HB	27,000	
Windsong's Legacy	Walnridge	Maple Hill	F	1	0	HB	6,500	

Sire	Consignor	Farm	Sex	Sold	$50,000 2 YOs	Sale	Avg Price	Avg $ Won
Windsong's Legacy	Walnridge	Nandi	C	1	0	HB	2,500	
Windsong's Legacy	Walnridge	Nandi	F	2	0	HB	12,750	
Windsong's Legacy	Walnridge	Walnridge	F	2	0	HB	11,250	
Windsong's Legacy	Winbak	Winbak	C	1	0	HB	5,000	
Windsong's Legacy	Winbak	Winbak	F	1	0	HB	7,500	
Windsong's Legacy				106	4			
Yankee Cruiser	Concord	Concord	C	1	1	HB	38,000	686,647
Yankee Cruiser	Fair Winds	Charlotte Ranch	C	1	0	HB	8,000	
Yankee Cruiser	Fair Winds	Fair Winds	C	1	0	HB	10,000	
Yankee Cruiser	Fair Winds	Fair Winds	F	1	0	HB	20,000	
Yankee Cruiser	Fox Den	Shaffer Standardbreds	F	1	0	HB	2,500	
Yankee Cruiser	Hanover	Hanover	C	5	0	HB	28,400	
Yankee Cruiser	Hanover	Hanover	F	1	1	HB	20,000	98,714
Yankee Cruiser	Hempt	Patterson's	C	1	0	HB	10,000	
Yankee Cruiser	Hunterton	Ernie Martinez	F	1	0	LEX	7,000	
Yankee Cruiser	Hunterton	Hunterton	F	1	1	HB	5,000	58,435
Yankee Cruiser	Hunterton	Walco	F	1	0	LEX	2,000	
Yankee Cruiser	Midland Acres	Midland Acres	C	1	0	LEX	3,000	
Yankee Cruiser	Midland Acres	Midland Acres	F	1	0	LEX	7,000	
Yankee Cruiser	Peninsula	Ravenswood	C	1	0	LEX	3,000	
Yankee Cruiser	Preferred	Emerald Heights	C	2	0	LEX	14,000	
Yankee Cruiser	Saga	Saga	F	1	1	LEX	35,000	164,122
Yankee Cruiser	Saga	Walnut Hall Ltd	F	1	1	LEX	10,000	58,891
Yankee Cruiser	Spring Haven	Daniel H. Hale	C	1	0	LEX	5,000	
Yankee Cruiser	Spring Haven	Daniel H. Hale	F	1	0	LEX	3,000	
Yankee Cruiser	Spring Haven	Hickory Lane	F	1	0	HB	20,000	
Yankee Cruiser	Spring Haven	Lyle Slabach's	F	1	0	HB	13,000	
Yankee Cruiser	Spring Haven	Rails Edge	C	1	0	LEX	27,000	
Yankee Cruiser	Spring Haven	Spring Haven	C	2	0	LEX	40,500	
Yankee Cruiser	Steiner Stock	Steiner Stock	F	3	0	LEX	7,667	
Yankee Cruiser	Stonegate	Stonegate	C	1	0	HB	3,500	
Yankee Cruiser	Vieux Carre	Vieux Carre	C	3	0	HB	20,000	
Yankee Cruiser	Vieux Carre	Vieux Carre	F	2	0	HB	3,750	
Yankee Cruiser	Walnridge	Torrey Ridge	C	1	0	HB	11,000	
Yankee Cruiser				39	5			
Yankee Glide	Allamerican	Allamerican	C	5	1	HB	20,200	185,081
Yankee Glide	Allamerican	Allamerican	F	3	1	HB	25,833	219,815

Sire	Consignor	Farm	Sex	Sold	$50,000 2 YOs	Sale	Avg Price	Avg $ Won
Yankee Glide	Blue Chip	Blue Chip	C	1	0	HB	53,000	
Yankee Glide	Blue Chip	Blue Chip	F	2	0	HB	18,500	
Yankee Glide	Blue Chip	Blue Chip	F	1	0	LEX	87,000	
Yankee Glide	Brittany	Brittany	C	5	0	LEX	36,200	
Yankee Glide	Brittany	Brittany	F	4	0	LEX	53,250	
Yankee Glide	Cane Run	Cane Run	C	2	0	LEX	95,000	
Yankee Glide	Cane Run	Cane Run	F	3	0	LEX	47,667	
Yankee Glide	Concord	Concord	C	1	0	HB	75,000	
Yankee Glide	Concord	Hanover	F	1	0	HB	13,000	
Yankee Glide	Concord	Marion	C	1	0	HB	17,000	
Yankee Glide	Diamond Creek	Diamond Creek	C	2	0	HB	48,500	
Yankee Glide	Diamond Creek	Diamond Creek	C	3	0	LEX	61,000	
Yankee Glide	Diamond Creek	Diamond Creek	F	1	0	LEX	62,000	
Yankee Glide	Dunroven	Dunroven	C	3	0	LEX	13,000	
Yankee Glide	Dunroven	Dunroven	F	2	0	LEX	32,500	
Yankee Glide	Fair Winds	Fair Winds	F	1	1	HB	37,000	79,442
Yankee Glide	Fashion	Fashion	C	1	0	HB	14,000	
Yankee Glide	Hanover	Hanover	C	3	0	HB	27,333	
Yankee Glide	Hanover	Hanover	F	9	3	HB	55,444	146,191
Yankee Glide	Hempt	Hempt	C	5	0	HB	7,500	
Yankee Glide	Hempt	Hempt	F	3	0	HB	15,667	
Yankee Glide	Hunterton	Brittany	C	1	0	HB	3,500	
Yankee Glide	Hunterton	Hunterton	C	2	0	LEX	42,000	
Yankee Glide	Hunterton	Hunterton	F	2	0	LEX	45,000	
Yankee Glide	Hunterton	Walco	C	4	0	LEX	56,750	
Yankee Glide	Hunterton	Walco	F	1	0	LEX	50,000	
Yankee Glide	Kentuckiana	Kentuckiana	C	50	6	LEX	43,620	211,742
Yankee Glide	Kentuckiana	Kentuckiana	F	37	2	LEX	58,703	63,619
Yankee Glide	Northwood	Allerage	C	3	0	HB	21,667	
Yankee Glide	Northwood	Allerage	F	1	0	HB	90,000	
Yankee Glide	Northwood	Allerage	C	1	0	LEX	15,000	
Yankee Glide	Northwood	Bluestone	C	1	0	LEX	9,000	
Yankee Glide	Northwood	Bluestone	F	2	0	LEX	53,500	
Yankee Glide	Northwood	Kentuckiana	F	1	0	HB	40,000	
Yankee Glide	Northwood	Two Gaits	C	1	0	LEX	13,000	
Yankee Glide	Peninsula	Cool Creek	C	2	1	LEX	65,000	464,521
Yankee Glide	Peninsula	Doug Mcintosh	F	1	0	HB	55,000	

Sire	Consignor	Farm	Sex	Sold	$50,000 2 YOs	Sale	Avg Price	Avg $ Won
Yankee Glide	Peninsula	Hatfield	C	1	0	LEX	30,000	
Yankee Glide	Peninsula	Peninsula	C	5	0	HB	60,000	
Yankee Glide	Peninsula	Peninsula	F	3	1	HB	51,333	51,261
Yankee Glide	Peninsula	Peninsula	C	2	0	LEX	60,000	
Yankee Glide	Peninsula	Peninsula	F	1	0	LEX	60,000	
Yankee Glide	Peninsula	Pin Oak Lane	F	1	0	LEX	3,000	
Yankee Glide	Peninsula	Quantum	F	1	0	HB	21,000	
Yankee Glide	Peninsula	Quantum	F	1	0	LEX	12,000	
Yankee Glide	Peninsula	Silver Linden	F	1	0	HB	40,000	
Yankee Glide	Preferred	Fair Winds	F	1	0	LEX	25,000	
Yankee Glide	Preferred	Joie De Vie	C	1	0	LEX	32,000	
Yankee Glide	Preferred	Meadowbranch	C	1	0	LEX	42,000	
Yankee Glide	Preferred	Rolling Acres	F	1	0	LEX	115,000	
Yankee Glide	Preferred	Schunk Stables	C	1	0	LEX	5,000	
Yankee Glide	Preferred	Seelster	C	2	0	HB	50,000	
Yankee Glide	Preferred	Stirling Brook	C	1	0	HB	1,500	
Yankee Glide	Preferred	Twin Willows	F	1	0	LEX	20,000	
Yankee Glide	Preferred	Village Acres Ltd	F	1	0	LEX	115,000	
Yankee Glide	Preferred	Warrawee	C	1	0	HB	9,000	
Yankee Glide	Preferred	Warrawee	F	2	0	LEX	47,500	
Yankee Glide	Saga	Benaire	C	1	0	LEX	13,000	
Yankee Glide	Saga	Saga	C	7	0	LEX	17,714	
Yankee Glide	Saga	Saga	F	7	0	LEX	34,714	
Yankee Glide	Spring Haven	Hickory Lane	F	1	0	LEX	35,000	
Yankee Glide	Spring Haven	Spring Haven	C	1	0	HB	25,000	
Yankee Glide	Spring Haven	Windswept Valley	F	2	0	LEX	60,000	
Yankee Glide	Steiner Stock	Steiner Stock	C	1	0	LEX	50,000	
Yankee Glide	Vieux Carre	Vieux Carre	C	2	0	HB	20,750	
Yankee Glide	Walnridge	Marion	C	1	0	HB	7,000	
Yankee Glide	Winbak	Winbak	C	1	0	HB	11,000	
Yankee Glide				**225**	**16**			

Chapter 5: Consignor and Farm Success Rates

Before we review the farm and consignor performance, let's explain the methodology. In the sale catalogs, the place where the yearling was raised is the farm. The entity selling the yearling is the consignor. If we look at Hip Number 115 in the 2010 Harrisburg (Black Book) catalog, we see a colt by *Andover Hall* that was consigned by Concord Stud Farms (Concord), agent for Windsong Stable, and raised at Hanover Shoe Farm (Hanover). Therefore, in this volume, the consignor is Concord and the farm is Hanover.

Let's begin with the consignors, since they're the most visible. Chart 1 reflects the consignor's Success Rates in total and by Sale Venue. Immediately we can see some significant disparities. Take a look at Hanover. Their home court, so to speak, is Harrisburg where they have had a 266% better Success Rate than at Lexington. Hunterton has had a 98% higher Success Rate at LEX than HB. In addition, Winbak has been 75% better at LEX.

Reviewing this chart you notice that there are some Consignors who have very low, or in some cases zero % Success Rates at either HB or LEX. If you are interested in two yearlings and one is being offered by a farm/consignor with a poor Success Rate and the other by a farm/consignor with a solid Success Rate, would that influence your decision?

Chart 1: Consignor Success Rates

Consignor	Sold	$50,000 2 Year Olds	Success Rate	Sale	Average Price	Average $ Won
Allamerican	79	5	6.3%	HB	$21,608	$148,858
Blue Chip	151	11	7.3%	HB	45,576	156,085
	28	6	21.4%	LEX	75,857	95,223
	179	17	9.5%	Total	50,313	134,604
Boxwood	24	3	12.5%	HB	24,583	159,597
Brittany	176	10	5.7%	LEX	33,847	169,106
Cameo Hills	72	10	13.9%	LEX	35,792	114,726

Consignor	Sold	$50,000 2 Year Olds	Success Rate	Sale	Average Price	Average $ Won
Cane Run	26	0	0%	LEX	29,808	
Concord	190	13	6.8%	HB	32,863	241,919
Diamond Creek	53	4	7.5%	HB	51,283	104,602
	65	5	7.7%	LEX	50,477	131,229
	118	9	7.6%	Total	50,839	119,395
Dunroven	82	4	4.9%	LEX	19,744	74,590
Fair Winds	130	14	10.8%	HB	34,477	104,415
Fashion	71	4	5.6%	HB	17,113	317,313
Fox Den	67	0	0%	HB	14,351	
Futurity Hill	8	0	0%	LEX	23,375	
Hanover	562	49	8.7%	HB	36,537	172,718
	42	1	2.4%	LEX	61,857	54,866
	604	50	8.3%	Total	38,298	170,361
Hempt	71	8	11.3%	HB	15,552	91,587
Hunterton	154	7	4.5%	HB	22,666	225,221
	288	26	9.0%	LEX	40,611	188,472
	442	33	7.5%	Total	34,359	196,267
Kentuckiana	409	30	7.3%	LEX	34,330	146,444
Majestic View	2	0	0%	HB	9,750	
Midland Acres	31	2	6.5%	LEX	21,258	186,621
Millstream	16	0	0%	HB	27,094	
Northstar	7	1	14.3%	HB	12,357	124,183
Northwood	153	9	5.9%	HB	22,729	93,976
	98	6	6.1%	LEX	26,847	145,653
	251	15	6.0%	Total	24,337	114,647
Peninsula	215	19	8.8%	HB	46,793	127,281
	215	15	7.0%	LEX	32,302	141,722
	430	34	7.9%	Total	39,548	133,652
Perretti	217	16	7.4%	HB	38,827	238,655
	80	9	11.3%	LEX	35,750	137,443
	297	25	8.4%	Total	37,998	202,219
Pin Oak Lane	15	0	0.0%	HB	16,600	
Preferred	347	23	6.6%	HB	25,883	149,570

Consignor	Sold	$50,000 2 Year Olds	Success Rate	Sale	Average Price	Average $ Won
	338	27	8.0%	LEX	44,550	148,690
	685	50	7.3%	Total	35,094	149,095
Saga	79	6	7.6%	LEX	20,241	90,518
Spring Haven	72	0	0%	HB	32,118	
	150	5	3.3%	LEX	26,033	81,329
	222	5	2.3%	Total	28,007	81,329
Steiner Stock	27	1	3.7%	LEX	21,185	156,680
Stonegate	52	3	5.8%	HB	22,981	98,904
Twinbrook	39	2	5.1%	HB	37,000	59,076
Vieux Carre	174	11	6.3%	HB	22,405	193,450
Walnridge	125	7	5.6%	HB	23,966	241,298
Walnut Hall Ltd	57	5	8.8%	HB	25,763	67,568
Walnut Hall Stock	39	3	7.7%	LEX	35,179	104,050
Westwind	27	2	7.4%	HB	26,611	76,411
Winbak	183	10	5.5%	HB	28,199	175,007
	136	13	9.6%	LEX	29,588	131,098
	319	23	7.2%	Total	28,792	150,188
Winterwood	43	1	2.3%	HB	12,942	68,535
TOTAL	**5685**	**406**	**7.1%**		**32,698**	**$154,323**

Our next chart, which is far more detailed, will illustrate the Success Rates of each farm by gait, gender, consignor and sale.

Here are a few observations. Firstly, there are many farms with very low Success Rates. One has to be wary of these low Success Rates. My opinion is that farms tend to sell many of their yearlings from the same mares or grand-dams. If they have been chronically unsuccessful, then one must be very brave to fly in the face of history. Yes, every horse is an individual that has the potential to break the mold. It's up to each buyer to weigh the odds.

Some Farms that have sold a small amount of yearlings have done very well. *Walstan, White Hollow, Shadowbrook,* and *Green Gables* have very high Success Rates from very small consignments. *Green Gables* has had 3 elite performers out of only 6 sold, while *Shadowbrook* has had 3 out of 9. The sampling is small. But, the production of *three elite performers* by each of these farms has eclipsed the performance of some farms that have sold double, triple, quadruple or more horses.

In reviewing the large Farms, take notice of disparities in Success Rates between the sale venues. For example, *White Birch* has sold 9 elite two-year olds out of only 33 at Lexington for an impressive 27.3% or 1 in 3.7. At Harrisburg White Birch has had 6 out of 83 for 7.23% Success Rate.

Take a look at Perretti's performance with filly pacers at Lexington. They've had 7 elite performers out of just 27 for a 25.9% Success Rate, or 1 in 3.9.

Chart 2: Farm Success Rates

Farm	Consignor	Sale	Sex	Gait	Sold	$50,000 2 Year Olds	Success Rate	Avg Price
Abby	Hunterton	LEX	C	P	1	0	0%	$3,000
	Spring Haven	LEX	C	T	1	0	0%	35,000
	Hunterton	LEX	F	P	1	0	0%	9,000
					3	0	0%	15,667
Al Tomlinson	Peninsula	HB	F	P	2	0	0%	22,500
	Peninsula	LEX	C	P	1	0	0%	12,000
					3	0	0%	19,000
Albert Schmucker's	Northwood	HB	C	T	1	0	0%	18,000
Allamerican	Allamerican	HB	C	P	30	2	6.7%	25,483
	Allamerican	HB	C	T	11	1	9.1%	20,727
	Allamerican	HB	F	P	27	1	3.7%	17,241
	Allamerican	HB	F	T	11	1	9.1%	22,636
					79	5	6.3%	21,608
Allerage	Northwood	HB	C	T	17	2	11.8%	25,265
	Northwood	HB	F	P	1	0	0%	10,000
	Northwood	HB	F	T	12	0	0%	26,167
	Northwood	LEX	C	T	16	0	0%	26,188
	Northwood	LEX	F	P	1	0	0%	20,000
	Northwood	LEX	F	T	12	2	16.7%	37,250
					59	4	6.8%	27,788
Anderson	Preferred	LEX	C	P	2	0	0%	71,000
	Preferred	LEX	C	T	2	0	0%	108,500
	Preferred	LEX	F	P	4	0	0%	76,750
	Preferred	LEX	F	T	3	1	33.3%	80,667
					11	1	9.1%	82,545
Andray	Northwood	HB	C	P	10	2	20.0%	15,500
	Peninsula	HB	C	P	1	0	0%	35,000
	Northwood	HB	F	P	11	0	0%	13,682
	Peninsula	HB	F	P	1	0	0%	6,000
	Northwood	HB	F	T	3	0	0%	16,667
	Peninsula	HB	F	T	1	0	0%	14,000

Farm	Consignor	Sale	Sex	Gait	Sold	$50,000 2 Year Olds	Success Rate	Avg Price
	Northwood	LEX	C	P	2	0	0%	38,500
	Peninsula	LEX	C	P	3	0	0%	26,667
	Northwood	LEX	C	T	2	0	0%	19,500
	Peninsula	LEX	C	T	1	0	0%	40,000
	Northwood	LEX	F	P	7	0	0%	27,143
	Peninsula	LEX	F	P	1	0	0%	2,000
	Northwood	LEX	F	T	1	0	0%	12,000
	Peninsula	LEX	F	T	1	0	0%	40,000
					45	2	4.4%	19,789
Anne McDonald's	Fox Den	HB	C	P	1	0	0%	30,000
Aquatic	Spring Haven	LEX	C	P	3	0	0%	16,667
	Spring Haven	LEX	F	P	1	0	0%	15,000
					4	0	0%	16,250
Archie Downey	Twinbrook	HB	C	P	1	0	0%	6,000
Avonlea	Fox Den	HB	F	T	3	0	0%	12,667
Barefoot	Hempt	HB	F	P	1	0	0%	14,000
Bayberry	Fair Winds	HB	C	P	2	1	50.0%	42,000
Beal	Northwood	HB	C	T	2	0	0%	13,750
	Preferred	HB	C	T	1	0	0%	9,000
	Northwood	HB	F	T	1	0	0%	25,000
					4	0	0%	15,375
Benaire	Kentuckiana	LEX	C	T	2	0	0%	24,500
	Peninsula	LEX	C	T	1	0	0%	17,000
	Saga	LEX	C	T	1	0	0%	13,000
	Kentuckiana	LEX	F	T	1	0	0%	6,000
					5	0		17,000
Bennett	Blue Chip	LEX	C	T	1	0	0%	60,000
	Preferred	LEX	C	T	2	0	0%	67,500
					3	0	0%	65,000
Big Al's	Kentuckiana	LEX	C	P	4	1	25.0%	28,500
Bill Cottongim	Dunroven	LEX	C	T	1	0	0%	35,000
Birch Creek	Preferred	HB	C	P	1	0	0%	13,000
	Northwood	HB	F	P	1	0	0%	30,000
	Preferred	HB	F	P	2	0	0%	6,000
	Preferred	LEX	C	P	2	0	0%	41,000
	Preferred	LEX	C	T	2	0	0%	58,500
	Preferred	LEX	F	P	2	0	0%	10,000
	Peninsula	LEX	F	T	1	0	0%	30,000
					11	0	0%	27,636
Birch Hollow	Peninsula	HB	F	T	1	0	0%	16,000
BJ's	Preferred	HB	C	P	2	0	0%	7,250

Farm	Consignor	Sale	Sex	Gait	Sold	$50,000 2 Year Olds	Success Rate	Avg Price
	Preferred	HB	F	P	3	0	0%	5,667
					5	0	0%	6,300
Blairwood	Concord	HB	C	T	1	0	0%	12,000
	Concord	HB	F	T	1	0	0%	35,000
					2	0	0%	23,500
Bloodstock	Preferred	LEX	C	T	5	1	20.0%	12,000
	Preferred	LEX	F	T	3	0	0%	32,667
					8	1	12.5%	19,750
Blue Chip	Blue Chip	HB	C	P	64	6	9.4%	43,336
	Preferred	HB	C	P	1	0	0.0%	84,000
	Blue Chip	HB	C	T	23	1	4.3%	59,913
	Blue Chip	HB	F	P	43	2	4.7%	42,105
	Preferred	HB	F	P	1	1	100.0%	20,000
	Blue Chip	HB	F	T	20	2	10.0%	45,550
	Blue Chip	LEX	C	P	5	0	0%	60,400
	Blue Chip	LEX	C	T	6	0	0%	90,667
	Blue Chip	LEX	F	P	7	3	42.9%	62,714
	Blue Chip	LEX	F	T	9	3	33.3%	86,556
					179	18	10.1%	50,508
Blue Ridge	Cameo Hills	LEX	C	P	4	1	25.0%	4,500
	Saga	LEX	C	P	2	0	0%	11,000
	Cameo Hills	LEX	C	T	2	0	0%	2,000
	Cameo Hills	LEX	F	T	2	0	0%	11,500
					10	1	10.0%	6,700
Bluebird Meadows	Spring Haven	HB	F	T	1	0	0%	6,000
Bluestone	Northwood	HB	C	P	1	0	0%	5,000
	Northwood	HB	C	T	1	0	0%	2,500
	Northwood	HB	F	T	2	0	0%	14,750
	Northwood	LEX	C	P	4	0	0%	22,500
	Northwood	LEX	C	T	13	0	0%	29,615
	Northwood	LEX	F	P	2	0	0%	7,000
	Northwood	LEX	F	T	20	2	10.0%	27,450
					43	2	4.7%	25,000
Bob Farmwald	Saga	LEX	F	P	1	0	0%	30,000
Bonley	Northwood	HB	C	P	2	0	0%	13,500
	Northwood	HB	F	P	1	0	0%	9,000
					3	0	0%	12,000
Bos Stable	Northwood	LEX	F	T	1	0	0%	70,000
Boxwood	Boxwood	HB	C	P	4	0	0%	19,500
	Boxwood	HB	C	T	2	0	0%	23,500
	Boxwood	HB	F	P	2	0	0%	26,000

Farm	Consignor	Sale	Sex	Gait	Sold	$50,000 2 Year Olds	Success Rate	Avg Price
	Boxwood	HB	F	T	2	0	0%	28,000
					10	0	0%	23,300
Boyce	Winterwood	HB	C	P	1	0	0%	8,000
Brannon	Cane Run	LEX	F	T	1	0	0%	9,000
Bridgeview Acres	Spring Haven	HB	F	P	1	0	0%	30,000
Brittany	Hunterton	HB	C	P	3	0	0%	22,333
	Preferred	HB	C	P	3	0	0%	16,833
	Vieux Carre	HB	C	P	5	1	20.0%	18,400
	Hunterton	HB	C	T	2	0	0%	26,750
	Preferred	HB	C	T	2	0	0%	87,500
	Hunterton	HB	F	P	2	0	0%	2,750
	Preferred	HB	F	P	2	0	0%	16,500
	Vieux Carre	HB	F	P	2	0	0%	2,250
	Brittany	LEX	C	P	55	6	10.9%	45,945
	Brittany	LEX	C	T	48	3	6.3%	37,896
	Brittany	LEX	F	P	45	1	2.2%	17,133
	Brittany	LEX	F	T	28	0	0%	30,000
					197	11	5.6%	32,680
Bucks N A Doe	Concord	HB	F	P	1	0	0%	32,000
Bulletproof Ent	Kentuckiana	LEX	F	P	1	0	0%	5,000
Burnt Cabins	Fox Den	HB	C	P	4	0	0%	25,250
C and V Spellmire	Spring Haven	LEX	C	T	1	0	0%	3,000
	Spring Haven	LEX	F	T	1	0	0%	8,000
					2	0	0%	5,500
C.M.T.	Kentuckiana	LEX	F	P	1	0	0%	7,000
Cameo Hills	Walnridge	HB	C	P	1	0	0%	23,000
	Northwood	HB	C	T	1	0	0%	25,000
	Northwood	HB	F	P	1	0	0%	19,000
	Walnridge	HB	F	P	2	0	0%	3,500
	Cameo Hills	LEX	C	P	14	2	14.3%	80,571
	Cameo Hills	LEX	C	T	8	2	25.0%	43,750
	Cameo Hills	LEX	F	P	13	1	7.7%	37,154
	Cameo Hills	LEX	F	T	11	2	18.2%	31,455
					51	7	13.7%	46,686
Cane Run	Cane Run	LEX	C	T	16	0	0%	31,188
	Cane Run	LEX	F	T	9	0	0%	29,667
					25	0	0%	30,640
Canon Hill Vet	Northwood	HB	F	T	1	0	0%	16,000
Cashelmara	Winterwood	HB	C	P	2	0	0%	14,000
	Winterwood	HB	F	P	4	0	0%	6,625
					6	0	0%	9,083

Farm	Consignor	Sale	Sex	Gait	Sold	$50,000 2 Year Olds	Success Rate	Avg Price
Caviart	Northwood	HB	C	P	1	0	0%	25,000
	Northwood	LEX	C	P	3	1	33.3%	31,333
	Northwood	LEX	F	P	3	0	0%	10,000
					7	1	14.3%	21,286
Cedar Creek	Peninsula	LEX	C	T	1	0	0%	97,000
Cedar Post	Peninsula	HB	F	T	2	0	0.0%	24,000
Century Spring	Northwood	HB	C	P	3	1	33.3%	14,000
Chad Yoder	Preferred	LEX	F	P	1	0	0%	17,000
Charles Lawrence's	Twinbrook	HB	F	P	1	0	0%	9,000
Charlotte Ranch	Fair Winds	HB	C	P	3	0	0%	26,667
	Fair Winds	HB	F	P	2	0	0%	3,750
	Preferred	HB	F	P	1	0	0%	51,000
					6	0	0%	23,083
Cinder Lane	Peninsula	HB	C	P	1	0	0%	50,000
Concord	Concord	HB	C	P	26	2	7.7%	34,654
	Concord	HB	C	T	28	2	7.1%	48,732
	Concord	HB	F	P	26	1	3.8%	22,269
	Concord	HB	F	T	32	2	6.3%	42,281
	Preferred	LEX	C	P	1	0	0%	13,000
	Spring Haven	LEX	C	P	1	0	0%	15,000
	Northwood	LEX	F	P	1	0	0%	18,000
	Preferred	LEX	F	P	1	0	0%	18,000
	Preferred	LEX	F	T	1	0	0%	4,000
					117	7	6.0%	36,457
Considine	Preferred	LEX	C	P	1	0	0%	23,000
Cool Creek	Peninsula	LEX	C	T	3	1	33.3%	70,000
	Peninsula	LEX	F	T	1	0	0%	70,000
	Spring Haven	LEX	F	T	1	0	0%	48,000
					5	1	20.0%	65,600
Cool Winds	Spring Haven	LEX	C	P	1	0	0%	25,000
	Spring Haven	LEX	F	P	1	0	0%	7,000
					2	0	0%	16,000
Copper Cap	Preferred	LEX	C	P	1	0	0%	14,000
	Preferred	LEX	F	P	1	0	0%	9,000
					2	0	0%	11,500
Cornerstone	Walnridge	HB	C	P	1	0	0%	42,000
Cottonwood	Preferred	LEX	F	P	1	0	0%	8,000
Crawford	Hunterton	HB	F	P	1	0	0%	1,500
	Hunterton	HB	F	T	1	0	0%	12,000
	Cameo Hills	LEX	C	P	2	0	0%	6,500
	Hunterton	LEX	C	T	6	0	0%	41,500

Farm	Consignor	Sale	Sex	Gait	Sold	$50,000 2 Year Olds	Success Rate	Avg Price
	Cameo Hills	LEX	F	T	2	0	0%	8,500
	Hunterton	LEX	F	T	2	0	0%	14,000
					14	0	0%	22,893
Cross Creek	Preferred	HB	F	P	1	0	0%	19,000
Crosscountry	Concord	HB	C	P	2	0	0%	30,000
	Concord	HB	F	P	3	0	0%	8,667
					5	0	0%	17,200
D C P M Racing Stable	Preferred	HB	C	P	1	0	0%	4,000
D Farm	Preferred	HB	C	T	1	0	0%	40,000
	Preferred	HB	F	T	5	1	20.0%	21,100
	Preferred	LEX	C	P	1	0	0%	60,000
	Preferred	LEX	C	T	6	0	0%	27,167
	Preferred	LEX	F	P	1	0	0%	7,000
	Preferred	LEX	F	T	6	1	16.7%	57,167
					20	2	10.0%	35,925
Dale Decker	Spring Haven	LEX	C	P	1	0	0%	40,000
Dan Kuhns'	Hunterton	HB	C	T	1	0	0%	3,500
	Hunterton	HB	F	P	1	0	0%	5,000
					2	0	0%	4,250
Daniel H. Hale	Spring Haven	LEX	C	P	1	0	0%	5,000
	Spring Haven	LEX	F	P	1	0	0%	3,000
					2	0	0%	4,000
David Miller's	Preferred	HB	C	T	1	0	0%	50,000
Dennis Dowd's	Vieux Carre	HB	C	P	2	0	0%	7,000
Dennison	Hunterton	LEX	C	P	1	0	0%	15,000
Deo Volente	Northwood	HB	C	P	2	0	0%	65,000
	Walnridge	HB	C	P	2	0	0%	12,500
	Peninsula	HB	C	T	6	0	0%	42,500
	Northwood	HB	F	P	5	0	0%	28,700
	Peninsula	HB	F	P	2	0	0%	31,000
	Northwood	HB	F	T	1	0	0%	9,500
	Peninsula	HB	F	T	2	0	0%	27,500
	Preferred	LEX	C	P	4	0	0%	58,500
	Peninsula	LEX	C	T	4	0	0%	68,750
	Preferred	LEX	F	P	4	1	25.0%	15,500
	Peninsula	LEX	F	P	2	1	50.0%	60,000
	Preferred	LEX	F	T	1	0	0%	17,000
					35	2	5.7%	39,657
Diamond Creek	Diamond Creek	HB	C	P	14	1	7.1%	51,714
	Diamond Creek	HB	C	T	13	3	23.1%	51,385
	Diamond Creek	HB	F	P	12	0	0%	45,917

Farm	Consignor	Sale	Sex	Gait	Sold	$50,000 2 Year Olds	Success Rate	Avg Price
	Diamond Creek	HB	F	T	14	0	0%	55,357
	Diamond Creek	LEX	C	P	14	0	0%	30,786
	Diamond Creek	LEX	C	T	14	2	14.3%	55,500
	Diamond Creek	LEX	F	P	16	1	6.3%	37,625
	Diamond Creek	LEX	F	T	21	2	9.5%	70,048
					118	9	7.6%	50,839
Don Lamontagne	Preferred	LEX	F	T	1	0	0%	67,000
Donna Perry	Peninsula	LEX	F	P	3	0	0%	10,333
Dottie Morone	Peninsula	LEX	C	T	2	1	50.0%	30,000
	Peninsula	LEX	F	T	1	0	0%	37,000
	Hunterton	HB	C	T	1	0	0%	1,500
					4	1	25.0%	24,625
Double Spring	Spring Haven	HB	C	T	1	0	0.0%	35,000
	Spring Haven	LEX	F	T	1	1	100.0%	15,000
					2	1	50.0%	25,000
Doug Mcintosh	Peninsula	HB	F	T	1	0	0%	55,000
Doug Millard	Spring Haven	LEX	C	P	1	0	0%	30,000
	Spring Haven	LEX	C	T	2	0	0%	37,500
					3	0	0%	35,000
Dr. Robert Milkey's	Preferred	LEX	C	P	1	0	0%	27,000
	Preferred	HB	C	P	1	0	0%	10,000
					2	0	0%	18,500
Dumain Haven	Preferred	HB	C	P	1	0	0%	5,000
	Preferred	HB	C	T	2	1	50.0%	58,500
	Preferred	HB	F	P	3	0	0%	26,833
					6	1	16.7%	33,750
Dunroven	Dunroven	LEX	C	P	14	1	7.1%	14,357
	Dunroven	LEX	C	T	27	2	7.4%	16,926
	Dunroven	LEX	F	P	13	0	0%	11,923
	Dunroven	LEX	F	T	26	1	3.8%	29,077
					80	4	5.0%	19,613
E and M Yoder	Hunterton	LEX	C	T	1	0	0%	45,000
Ecuries Vandenplas	Preferred	HB	C	T	1	0	0%	10,000
	Preferred	HB	F	T	1	0	0%	8,000
					2	0	0.0%	9,000
Ed Evans'	Concord	HB	C	P	2	0	0%	26,000
Elam Esh	Hunterton	LEX	F	T	1	0	0%	15,000
Emerald Heights	Preferred	LEX	C	P	4	0	0%	21,250
Emerald Highlands	Preferred	LEX	C	P	15	1	6.7%	39,667
	Preferred	LEX	F	P	6	1	16.7%	10,500
					21	2	9.5%	31,333

Farm	Consignor	Sale	Sex	Gait	Sold	$50,000 2 Year Olds	Success Rate	Avg Price
Emerald Ridge	Twinbrook	HB	C	P	1	0	0%	37,000
	Kentuckiana	LEX	C	P	1	0	0%	45,000
					2	0	0%	41,000
Emma & Mary Yoder	Hunterton	LEX	C	T	2	1	50.0%	77,500
Engelman	Northwood	HB	C	P	1	0	0%	20,000
Englewood	Preferred	LEX	F	P	1	0	0%	4,000
Equine Center	Peninsula	LEX	C	P	3	0	0%	37,667
	Peninsula	LEX	C	T	2	0	0%	11,000
	Peninsula	LEX	F	P	5	0	0%	23,600
					10	0	0%	25,300
Ernie Martinez	Hunterton	LEX	C	P	2	0	0%	7,000
	Hunterton	LEX	C	T	2	0	0%	24,500
	Hunterton	LEX	F	P	1	0	0%	7,000
	Hunterton	LEX	F	T	2	0	0%	9,000
					7	0	0%	12,571
Eternal	Preferred	HB	C	P	1	0	0%	9,000
	Preferred	HB	F	P	1	0	0%	4,000
	Preferred	LEX	C	P	1	0	0%	32,000
					3	0	0%	15,000
Executive Standardbred	Spring Haven	LEX	F	P	2	0	0%	5,000
Fair Winds	Fair Winds	HB	C	P	48	5	10.4%	37,365
	Fair Winds	HB	C	T	16	2	12.5%	34,844
	Fair Winds	HB	F	P	40	4	10.0%	37,325
	Fair Winds	HB	F	T	13	2	15.4%	26,346
	Cameo Hills	LEX	C	T	1	0	0%	28,000
	Northwood	LEX	C	T	1	0	0%	25,000
	Preferred	LEX	C	T	3	0	0%	47,333
	Cameo Hills	LEX	F	T	1	0	0%	4,000
	Preferred	LEX	F	T	1	0	0%	25,000
					124	13	10.5%	35,569
Farrier's Acres	Kentuckiana	LEX	C	T	1	0	0%	17,000
	Peninsula	LEX	C	T	1	0	0%	20,000
	Peninsula	LEX	F	T	1	1	100.0%	20,000
					3	1	33.3%	19,000
Farrow	Concord	HB	C	T	1	0	0%	31,000
Fashion	Fashion	HB	C	P	20	1	5.0%	18,000
	Fashion	HB	C	T	14	1	7.1%	16,786
	Fashion	HB	F	P	22	0	0%	18,023
	Fashion	HB	F	T	15	2	13.3%	14,900
					71	4	5.6%	17,113
FJD	Spring Haven	LEX	C	P	2	0	0%	82,500

Farm	Consignor	Sale	Sex	Gait	Sold	$50,000 2 Year Olds	Success Rate	Avg Price
	Spring Haven	LEX	C	T	7	0	0%	12,286
	Spring Haven	LEX	F	P	1	0	0%	13,000
	Spring Haven	LEX	F	T	5	0	0%	21,600
					15	0	0%	24,800
Forty Hill	Cameo Hills	LEX	C	P	2	1	50.0%	37,500
	Cameo Hills	LEX	F	P	1	0	0%	15,000
					3	1	33.3%	30,000
Fox Den	Fox Den	HB	C	T	1	0	0%	35,000
	Fox Den	HB	F	T	3	0	0%	23,333
					4	0	0%	26,250
Fox Valley	Northwood	HB	C	P	2	0	0%	47,500
	Northwood	HB	C	T	1	0	0%	77,000
	Northwood	HB	F	P	1	0	0%	42,000
					4	0	0%	53,500
Freedom Hill	Preferred	LEX	C	P	1	0	0%	26,000
	Preferred	LEX	F	P	2	0	0%	13,000
					3	0	0%	17,333
Futurity Hill	Futurity Hill	LEX	C	T	4	0	0%	8,750
	Futurity Hill	LEX	F	P	1	0	0%	30,000
	Futurity Hill	LEX	F	T	3	0	0%	40,667
					8	0	0%	23,375
Gardiner	Preferred	LEX	C	P	1	0	0%	70,000
George Story's	Preferred	HB	C	T	1	0	0%	4,500
Glassford Equine	Peninsula	HB	C	P	1	0	0%	25,000
	Peninsula	HB	F	P	3	0	0%	15,667
	Peninsula	LEX	C	P	1	0	0%	50,000
	Hunterton	LEX	F	P	1	0	0%	12,000
	Hunterton	LEX	F	T	1	0	0%	30,000
					7	0	0%	23,429
Glen Rock	Fox Den	HB	C	P	1	0	0%	20,000
Gold Star	Saga	LEX	F	P	1	1	100.0%	13,000
Golden Cross	Winbak	LEX	C	T	2	0	0.0%	16,000
Golden Gait	Walnridge	HB	C	T	2	1	50.0%	32,500
Goldfinger	Kentuckiana	LEX	C	P	3	0	0%	30,000
	Kentuckiana	LEX	F	P	3	0	0%	8,000
					6	0	0%	19,000
Grassy Branch	Hunterton	LEX	C	P	1	0	0%	11,000
Green Creek	Peninsula	LEX	C	P	2	1	50.0%	43,000
	Hunterton	LEX	C	T	1	0	0%	12,000
	Peninsula	LEX	C	T	1	1	100.0%	15,000
	Peninsula	LEX	F	P	1	0	0%	4,000

Farm	Consignor	Sale	Sex	Gait	Sold	$50,000 2 Year Olds	Success Rate	Avg Price
					5	2	40.0%	23,400
Green Gables	Preferred	HB	C	P	3	1	33.3%	51,000
	Preferred	HB	C	T	2	2	100.0%	26,000
	Peninsula	HB	F	T	1	0	0%	30,000
					6	3	50.0%	39,167
Gregory Gehman's	Fox Den	HB	C	P	1	0	0%	10,000
	Fox Den	HB	F	P	1	0	0%	8,500
					2	0	0%	9,250
Groulx's Gatineau	Northwood	HB	F	T	1	0	0%	7,000
Hada Dream	Preferred	LEX	C	P	1	0	0%	25,000
Hamstan	Preferred	HB	C	T	4	0	0%	52,500
	Preferred	HB	F	T	2	0	0%	27,500
					6	0	0%	44,167
Hanover	Fox Den	HB	C	P	1	0	0%	13,000
	Hanover	HB	C	P	193	16	8.3%	39,565
	Concord	HB	C	T	22	2	9.1%	34,977
	Fox Den	HB	C	T	3	0	0%	16,333
	Hanover	HB	C	T	100	6	6.0%	39,045
	Pin Oak Lane	HB	C	T	4	0	0%	13,125
	Concord	HB	F	P	1	0	0%	60,000
	Hanover	HB	F	P	158	15	9.5%	31,595
	Concord	HB	F	T	13	2	15.4%	21,038
	Hanover	HB	F	T	111	12	10.8%	36,050
	Hanover	LEX	C	P	16	0	0%	73,813
	Hanover	LEX	C	T	8	0	0%	65,125
	Hanover	LEX	F	P	12	1	8.3%	54,750
	Hanover	LEX	F	T	6	0	0%	39,833
					648	54	8.3%	37,576
Harvey Knepp	Hunterton	LEX	F	T	1	0	0%	5,000
Hatfield	Peninsula	LEX	C	T	1	0	0%	30,000
Hayden Durham	Preferred	LEX	C	P	2	0	0%	22,500
	Preferred	LEX	F	P	1	0	0%	7,000
					3	0	0%	17,333
Hempt	Hempt	HB	C	P	13	2	15.4%	17,269
	Hempt	HB	C	T	15	3	20.0%	17,233
	Hempt	HB	F	P	22	2	9.1%	13,191
	Hempt	HB	F	T	19	1	5.3%	16,158
					69	8	11.6%	15,655
Heritage Hill	Northwood	HB	C	P	1	0	0%	1,000
	Preferred	HB	C	P	23	2	8.7%	34,543
	Preferred	HB	C	T	4	0	0%	7,500

Farm	Consignor	Sale	Sex	Gait	Sold	$50,000 2 Year Olds	Success Rate	Avg Price
	Preferred	HB	F	P	17	0	0%	24,647
	Preferred	HB	F	T	4	0	0%	29,500
	Preferred	LEX	C	P	5	1	20.0%	32,800
	Preferred	LEX	F	P	5	0	0%	26,400
	Preferred	LEX	F	T	1	0	0%	4,000
					60	3	5.0%	27,708
Hickory Lane	Hunterton	HB	F	P	1	0	0%	40,000
	Spring Haven	HB	F	P	2	0	0%	14,500
	Hunterton	LEX	C	P	1	0	0%	10,000
	Spring Haven	LEX	C	P	2	0	0%	20,500
	Spring Haven	LEX	C	T	3	0	0%	21,000
	Hunterton	LEX	F	P	1	0	0%	5,000
	Spring Haven	LEX	F	P	1	0	0%	30,000
	Spring Haven	LEX	F	T	1	0	0%	35,000
					12	0	0%	21,083
High Stakes	Hunterton	HB	F	P	1	0	0%	40,000
Hillsborough Stable	Northwood	LEX	C	P	1	0	0%	17,000
Holly Gate	Peninsula	HB	C	P	3	0	0%	30,667
	Walnridge	HB	C	P	1	0	0%	110,000
	Peninsula	HB	F	P	5	0	0%	33,000
					9	0	0%	40,778
Hoosier	Hunterton	LEX	C	P	1	0	0%	32,000
Howard Stables	Northwood	HB	C	P	1	0	0%	12,000
	Northwood	HB	F	T	1	1	100.0%	20,000
					2	1	50.0%	16,000
Hucks Undercover	Boxwood	HB	C	T	3	0	0%	12,667
Hunterton	Hunterton	HB	C	P	26	1	3.8%	21,481
	Hunterton	HB	C	T	25	1	4.0%	24,740
	Hunterton	HB	F	P	32	2	6.3%	24,016
	Hunterton	HB	F	T	25	1	4.0%	23,280
	Hunterton	LEX	C	P	30	5	16.7%	56,500
	Hunterton	LEX	C	T	45	5	11.1%	49,711
	Hunterton	LEX	F	P	35	4	11.4%	29,971
	Hunterton	LEX	F	T	31	1	3.2%	41,839
					249	20	8.0%	35,363
Ideal	Hunterton	HB	C	T	1	0	0%	37,000
	Hunterton	HB	F	T	1	0	0%	27,000
					2	0	0%	32,000
Ilazue	Hunterton	HB	C	P	1	0	0%	34,000
	Hunterton	HB	C	T	1	0	0%	17,000
	Hunterton	HB	F	T	3	0	0%	16,667

Farm	Consignor	Sale	Sex	Gait	Sold	$50,000 2 Year Olds	Success Rate	Avg Price
					5	0	0%	20,200
In The Black	Peninsula	LEX	F	T	1	0	0%	30,000
Ironstone Spring	Peninsula	HB	F	T	1	0	0%	3,500
Ivan Sugg's	Peninsula	HB	C	T	1	0	0%	25,000
	Peninsula	HB	F	P	1	0	0%	35,000
					2	0	0%	30,000
James Murphy	Peninsula	LEX	C	P	1	0	0%	7,000
Jean Cloutier	Hunterton	LEX	F	T	1	0	0%	12,000
Jeff S. Jones	Hunterton	LEX	F	P	2	0	0%	59,500
JM Farm	Westwind	HB	F	P	1	0	0%	35,000
Joie De Vie	Preferred	HB	C	T	1	0	0%	40,000
	Preferred	HB	F	P	5	0	0%	16,300
	Preferred	HB	F	T	3	0	0%	22,333
	Preferred	LEX	C	P	3	0	0%	61,667
	Preferred	LEX	C	T	5	0	0%	30,800
	Preferred	LEX	F	P	1	0	0%	40,000
	Preferred	LEX	F	T	9	0	0%	48,778
					27	0	0%	37,278
Jonalee	Northwood	HB	C	T	3	0	0%	20,667
	Northwood	HB	F	T	3	0	0%	8,000
					6	0	0%	14,333
Jonas Graber	Peninsula	LEX	F	T	1	0	0%	4,000
Jonas Schlabach's	Spring Haven	HB	C	T	9	0	0%	30,889
	Spring Haven	HB	F	T	7	0	0%	30,571
					16	0	0%	30,750
K.E.M. Standardbreds	Spring Haven	LEX	C	T	1	0	0%	25,000
Ken and Joan Bryant's	Twinbrook	HB	C	P	1	0	0%	40,000
Kendal Hills	Northwood	HB	F	P	1	0	0%	27,000
Kentland	Peninsula	LEX	C	T	1	0	0%	15,000
Kentuckiana	Northwood	HB	C	T	1	0	0%	23,000
	Preferred	HB	F	P	2	0	0%	3,250
	Northwood	HB	F	T	3	0	0%	38,333
	Kentuckiana	LEX	C	P	112	10	8.9%	34,527
	Kentuckiana	LEX	C	T	96	7	7.3%	36,677
	Kentuckiana	LEX	F	P	90	6	6.7%	29,333
	Kentuckiana	LEX	F	T	78	5	6.4%	42,244
					382	28	7.3%	35,255
Killean Acres	Twinbrook	HB	C	P	4	1	25.0%	58,500
	Twinbrook	HB	F	P	2	0	0%	22,000
					6	1	16.7%	46,333
King	Fox Den	HB	C	P	1	0	0%	14,000

Farm	Consignor	Sale	Sex	Gait	Sold	$50,000 2 Year Olds	Success Rate	Avg Price
Kronos	Preferred	LEX	F	T	1	0	0%	30,000
Kurt Hansen's	Fox Den	HB	C	T	1	0	0%	20,000
	Northwood	HB	C	T	1	0	0%	37,000
	Preferred	HB	C	T	1	0	0%	19,000
	Northwood	HB	F	P	1	0	0%	4,500
	Northwood	HB	F	T	1	0	0%	37,000
	Preferred	HB	F	T	3	0	0%	7,500
					8	0	0%	17,500
Lebo	Hunterton	HB	C	P	1	0	0%	14,000
Lee Taylor's	Preferred	HB	F	P	1	0	0%	25,000
Leon King's	Fox Den	HB	F	P	1	0	0%	1,500
Leroy Keim's	Spring Haven	HB	C	T	2	0	0%	22,500
Leroy Kemp	Hunterton	LEX	C	T	1	0	0%	33,000
Linda & T.D. Van Kamp	Peninsula	LEX	C	P	1	0	0%	11,000
	Peninsula	LEX	C	T	1	0	0%	12,000
					2	0	0%	11,500
Lindwood	Northwood	HB	C	P	1	0	0%	10,000
	Northwood	HB	C	T	1	0	0%	10,000
	Peninsula	HB	C	T	1	0	0%	12,000
	Northwood	HB	F	P	2	0	0%	4,250
	Peninsula	HB	F	P	2	0	0%	8,250
	Northwood	HB	F	T	1	0	0%	47,000
	Peninsula	LEX	C	P	1	0	0%	8,000
					9	0	0%	12,444
Lindy	Preferred	HB	C	P	3	0	0%	32,000
	Preferred	HB	C	T	16	0	0%	17,719
	Preferred	HB	F	P	1	0	0%	11,000
	Preferred	HB	F	T	11	1	9.1%	21,727
	Preferred	LEX	C	P	7	0	0%	43,429
	Preferred	LEX	C	T	26	1	3.8%	92,692
	Preferred	LEX	F	P	9	1	11.1%	65,333
	Preferred	LEX	F	T	26	2	7.7%	40,808
					99	5	5.1%	50,429
Little Moon Lake	Hunterton	LEX	C	T	2	1	50.0%	15,500
	Hunterton	LEX	F	T	1	0	0%	40,000
					3	1	33.3%	23,667
LMN Bred	Spring Haven	HB	C	P	1	0	0%	8,000
	Spring Haven	HB	C	T	1	0	0%	10,000
	Spring Haven	LEX	C	P	4	0	0%	6,750
	Spring Haven	LEX	F	P	1	0	0%	2,000
					7	0	0%	6,714

Farm	Consignor	Sale	Sex	Gait	Sold	$50,000 2 Year Olds	Success Rate	Avg Price
Loconte	Concord	HB	F	P	2	0	0%	24,500
Lothlorien	Preferred	HB	C	P	1	0	0%	22,000
Lyle Slabach's	Spring Haven	HB	C	P	1	0	0%	12,000
	Spring Haven	HB	F	P	1	0	0%	13,000
					2	0	0%	12,500
Lynn Acres	Northwood	HB	C	T	1	0	0%	18,000
M. Smith and R. Uhle	Peninsula	HB	C	T	1	1	100.0%	120,000
Mackenzie	Preferred	HB	C	P	1	0	0%	4,000
	Preferred	HB	C	T	1	0	0%	9,000
	Preferred	HB	F	T	1	1	100.0%	40,000
					3	1	33.3%	17,667
Majestic View	Majestic View	HB	C	P	2	0	0%	9,750
	Preferred	HB	F	P	1	0	0%	20,000
					3	0	0%	13,167
Maple Hill	Northwood	HB	C	T	1	0	0%	7,000
	Walnridge	HB	F	T	2	0	0%	20,750
					3	0	0%	16,167
Maple Lane	Peninsula	HB	C	P	1	0	0%	17,000
	Peninsula	LEX	C	P	3	0	0%	32,667
	Peninsula	LEX	F	P	1	0	0%	35,000
					5	0	0%	30,000
Maple Run	Northwood	HB	C	P	1	0	0%	12,000
	Northwood	HB	F	P	1	0	0%	11,000
					2	0	0%	11,500
Marion	Concord	HB	C	T	9	0	0%	12,500
	Walnridge	HB	C	T	5	0	0%	10,800
	Concord	HB	F	T	8	1	12.5%	21,938
	Walnridge	HB	F	T	6	0	0%	10,867
					28	1	3.6%	14,543
Mark Horner's	Hunterton	HB	F	P	1	0	0%	25,000
Martin Miller's	Spring Haven	HB	F	T	1	0	0%	30,000
Martinez Equine	Hunterton	HB	C	P	2	0	0%	16,500
	Hunterton	HB	F	P	1	0	0%	1,500
	Hunterton	HB	F	T	3	0	0%	22,000
					6	0	0%	16,750
Marvin Kuhn's	Peninsula	HB	C	P	1	0	0%	35,000
Marvin Raber	Walnridge	HB	C	P	8	0	0%	9,625
	Northwood	HB	F	P	1	0	0%	15,000
	Walnridge	HB	F	P	5	0	0%	5,400
	Cameo Hills	LEX	C	P	4	1	25.0%	6,500
	Peninsula	LEX	C	T	1	0	0%	25,000

Farm	Consignor	Sale	Sex	Gait	Sold	$50,000 2 Year Olds	Success Rate	Avg Price
	Cameo Hills	LEX	F	P	4	0	0%	7,250
	Northwood	LEX	F	P	1	0	0%	7,000
					24	1	4.2%	8,583
Meadow Creek	Hunterton	HB	C	P	7	1	14.3%	34,643
	Hunterton	HB	F	P	2	1	50.0%	27,500
	Hunterton	HB	F	T	1	0	0%	17,000
	Hunterton	LEX	C	P	6	0	0%	60,333
	Hunterton	LEX	C	T	3	0	0%	17,000
	Hunterton	LEX	F	P	1	0	0%	27,000
	Hunterton	LEX	F	T	1	0	0%	35,000
					21	2	9.5%	37,595
Meadowbranch	Preferred	LEX	C	T	2	0	0%	27,000
Mel Kauffman's	Fox Den	HB	C	P	2	0	0%	11,500
Mendez	Vieux Carre	HB	C	P	1	0	0%	52,000
	Vieux Carre	HB	C	T	1	0	0%	10,000
	Vieux Carre	HB	F	P	2	0	0%	3,250
					4	0	0%	17,125
Mervin Graber's	Fox Den	HB	F	P	1	0	0%	3,000
Midland Acres	Midland Acres	LEX	C	P	8	0	0%	22,500
	Midland Acres	LEX	C	T	5	0	0%	24,200
	Midland Acres	LEX	F	P	8	2	25.0%	27,125
	Midland Acres	LEX	F	T	8	0	0%	13,500
					29	2	6.9%	21,586
Mike Clucas	Hunterton	LEX	C	P	1	0	0%	25,000
Millcreek	Preferred	HB	F	P	1	0	0%	6,000
Millstream	Millstream	HB	C	T	9	0	0%	26,944
	Millstream	HB	F	T	7	0	0%	27,286
					16	0	0%	27,094
Mindale	Spring Haven	LEX	C	P	10	0	0%	27,800
	Spring Haven	LEX	C	T	1	0	0%	17,000
	Spring Haven	LEX	F	P	11	0	0%	9,182
	Spring Haven	LEX	F	T	3	0	0%	24,667
					25	0	0%	18,800
Misty Meadow	Fox Den	HB	C	P	1	0	0%	9,500
Morning Star	Preferred	HB	C	P	1	0	0%	11,000
Morrison	Preferred	HB	C	P	1	0	0%	55,000
	Preferred	HB	C	T	3	0	0%	24,167
	Preferred	HB	F	T	1	0	0%	42,000
					5	0	0%	33,900
Morrowland	Hunterton	HB	C	P	1	0	0%	14,000
	Winterwood	HB	C	P	1	0	0%	15,000

Farm	Consignor	Sale	Sex	Gait	Sold	$50,000 2 Year Olds	Success Rate	Avg Price
	Winterwood	HB	F	P	3	0	0%	8,000
	Midland Acres	LEX	C	P	2	0	0%	16,500
					7	0	0%	12,286
Mulberry Meadows	Preferred	HB	C	P	2	0	0%	11,500
Nandi	Northwood	HB	C	P	8	0	0%	12,813
	Walnridge	HB	C	P	1	0	0%	16,000
	Walnridge	HB	C	T	10	1	10.0%	10,400
	Northwood	HB	F	P	2	0	0%	23,000
	Walnridge	HB	F	T	8	1	12.5%	10,938
	Northwood	LEX	F	P	2	0	0%	4,500
	Northwood	LEX	F	T	1	1	100.0%	4,000
					32	3	9.4%	11,531
Nathan Byler's	Spring Haven	HB	F	P	1	0	0%	11,000
New Pioneer	Saga	LEX	C	T	2	0	0%	28,000
	Saga	LEX	F	T	1	1	100.0%	12,000
					3	1	33.3%	22,667
Northfields	Preferred	HB	C	T	2	0	0%	48,500
	Kentuckiana	LEX	C	T	1	0	0%	25,000
	Hunterton	LEX	F	P	1	0	0%	8,000
					4	0	0%	32,500
Northstar	Northstar	HB	C	P	1	0	0%	7,000
	Northstar	HB	C	T	2	0	0%	20,250
	Preferred	HB	C	T	1	0	0%	70,000
	Northstar	HB	F	P	2	0	0%	5,000
	Northstar	HB	F	T	2	1	50.0%	14,500
	Preferred	HB	F	T	1	0	0%	25,000
					9	1	11.1%	20,167
Northway	Concord	HB	C	T	1	0	0%	20,000
	Concord	HB	F	T	1	0	0%	2,500
					2	0	0%	11,250
Oak Hill Manor	Northwood	HB	C	P	2	0	0%	23,500
Oak Knoll	Preferred	HB	C	P	3	1	33.3%	44,667
	Preferred	HB	F	P	2	0	0%	30,000
					5	1	20.0%	38,800
Oak Park	Hunterton	LEX	C	P	2	0	0%	33,000
	Hunterton	LEX	F	T	1	0	0%	12,000
					3	0	0%	26,000
Oaklea	Peninsula	HB	C	T	3	0	0%	33,667
	Peninsula	HB	F	T	3	0	0%	23,000
	Hunterton	LEX	F	T	1	0	0%	10,000
	Peninsula	LEX	F	T	2	0	0%	3,500

Farm	Consignor	Sale	Sex	Gait	Sold	$50,000 2 Year Olds	Success Rate	Avg Price
					9	0	0%	20,778
Oakwood Equine	Fair Winds	HB	C	T	1	0	0%	9,000
October Lane	Peninsula	LEX	C	P	1	0	0%	35,000
Odds On Acres	Peninsula	HB	F	P	1	1	100.0%	15,000
	Peninsula	LEX	C	P	5	0	0%	32,400
	Peninsula	LEX	F	P	4	0	0%	15,750
					10	1	10.0%	24,000
Odds On Racing	Peninsula	HB	C	P	5	0	0%	42,000
Oldfield	Saga	LEX	C	P	2	0	0%	49,500
	Saga	LEX	C	T	2	0	0%	6,500
					4	0	0%	28,000
Olive Branch	Concord	HB	C	P	2	0	0%	50,000
	Northwood	HB	C	P	2	0	0%	23,500
	Northwood	HB	C	T	1	0	0%	12,000
	Preferred	HB	C	T	1	0	0%	20,000
	Northwood	HB	F	P	2	1	50.0%	72,500
	Preferred	LEX	C	P	1	0	0%	4,000
	Northwood	LEX	F	T	1	0	0%	30,000
					10	1	10.0%	35,800
Omar Beiler	Preferred	LEX	C	P	1	0	0%	17,000
Orchard Farm	Concord	HB	C	T	2	1	50.0%	40,000
Outback	Hunterton	LEX	F	P	1	0	0%	5,000
	Hunterton	LEX	F	T	1	0	0%	8,000
					2	0	0%	6,500
Owen	Peninsula	HB	F	P	1	0	0%	50,000
	Spring Haven	LEX	C	T	1	0	0%	3,000
					2	0	0%	26,500
Paisley	Northwood	HB	C	T	1	0	0%	6,500
Paradise	Blue Chip	HB	C	T	1	0	0%	9,000
Paradox	Preferred	HB	F	T	1	0	0%	9,000
Patterson's	Hempt	HB	C	P	1	0	0%	10,000
Paul Liles	Kentuckiana	LEX	C	P	1	0	0%	21,000
	Kentuckiana	LEX	C	T	1	0	0%	5,000
	Kentuckiana	LEX	F	P	1	0	0%	35,000
					3	0	0%	20,333
Peninsula	Peninsula	HB	C	P	9	2	22.2%	48,778
	Peninsula	HB	C	T	59	10	16.9%	73,017
	Peninsula	HB	F	P	2	0	0%	37,500
	Peninsula	HB	F	T	36	3	8.3%	54,847
	Peninsula	LEX	C	P	18	0	0%	26,278
	Peninsula	LEX	C	T	27	2	7.4%	44,852

Farm	Consignor	Sale	Sex	Gait	Sold	$50,000 2 Year Olds	Success Rate	Avg Price
	Peninsula	LEX	F	P	8	1	12.5%	21,125
	Peninsula	LEX	F	T	20	1	5.0%	39,300
					179	19	10.6%	52,712
Percy Davis	Northwood	LEX	C	T	1	0	0%	57,000
Perretti	Northwood	HB	C	P	3	0	0%	29,333
	Perretti	HB	C	P	73	4	5.5%	41,233
	Concord	HB	C	T	2	0	0%	23,500
	Northwood	HB	C	T	1	0	0%	6,000
	Perretti	HB	C	T	33	4	12.1%	57,348
	Northwood	HB	F	P	1	0	0%	130,000
	Perretti	HB	F	P	62	4	6.5%	28,718
	Perretti	HB	F	T	49	4	8.2%	35,561
	Perretti	LEX	C	P	26	2	7.7%	44,885
	Perretti	LEX	C	T	16	0	0%	36,500
	Perretti	LEX	F	P	27	7	25.9%	30,593
	Perretti	LEX	F	T	11	0	0%	25,727
					304	25	8.2%	38,015
Pheasant Hill	Peninsula	HB	C	P	3	0	0%	37,333
	Peninsula	HB	F	P	4	0	0%	26,500
	Peninsula	HB	F	T	6	0	0%	23,833
	Peninsula	LEX	C	T	4	0	0%	48,000
	Peninsula	LEX	F	P	3	0	0%	29,000
	Peninsula	LEX	F	T	2	0	0%	8,000
					22	0	0%	29,818
Phil Hunt's	Preferred	HB	C	T	1	0	0%	11,000
	Preferred	HB	F	T	1	0	0%	28,000
					2	0	0%	19,500
Photo Mountain	Walnridge	HB	F	T	2	0	0%	45,750
Pin Oak Lane	Pin Oak Lane	HB	C	P	2	0	0%	27,500
	Pin Oak Lane	HB	C	T	5	0	0%	18,100
	Pin Oak Lane	HB	F	P	2	0	0%	16,250
	Pin Oak Lane	HB	F	T	2	0	0%	9,250
	Peninsula	LEX	F	T	2	0	0%	14,000
					13	0	0%	17,269
Pine Hill	Hunterton	LEX	C	P	1	0	0%	30,000
	Hunterton	LEX	C	T	1	1	100.0%	40,000
	Hunterton	LEX	F	P	1	0	0%	35,000
					3	1	33.3%	35,000
Pinestone	Preferred	HB	C	T	2	0	0%	33,000
	Preferred	HB	F	P	1	0	0%	65,000
					3	0	0%	43,667

Farm	Consignor	Sale	Sex	Gait	Sold	$50,000 2 Year Olds	Success Rate	Avg Price
Poole	Hunterton	LEX	F	P	1	0	0%	4,000
Quad	Peninsula	HB	C	P	1	0	0%	10,000
	Peninsula	HB	C	T	2	0	0%	52,000
					3	0	0%	38,000
Quantum	Peninsula	HB	C	T	5	0	0%	13,400
	Peninsula	HB	F	T	4	0	0%	20,000
	Peninsula	LEX	C	T	5	0	0%	15,200
	Peninsula	LEX	F	T	4	0	0%	7,250
					18	0	0%	14,000
Rails Edge	Spring Haven	HB	C	P	2	0	0%	78,500
	Spring Haven	LEX	C	P	3	0	0%	60,000
	Spring Haven	LEX	F	P	4	0	0%	74,750
					9	0	0%	70,667
Randy Wilt's	Hunterton	HB	C	P	1	0	0%	40,000
	Hunterton	HB	F	P	1	0	0%	3,000
					2	0	0%	21,500
Ravenswood	Peninsula	LEX	C	P	1	0	0%	3,000
Raz Mackenzie	Hunterton	LEX	C	T	1	0	0%	10,000
Rich Thompson's	Westwind	HB	C	T	1	0	0%	9,000
	Westwind	HB	F	T	1	0	0%	23,000
					2	0	0%	16,000
Richard Keys	Dunroven	LEX	F	T	1	0	0%	15,000
Richard Malone's	Peninsula	HB	C	P	1	0	0%	55,000
	Hunterton	HB	F	P	1	0	0%	15,000
					2	0	0%	35,000
Richard W. Uhle	Peninsula	LEX	C	T	1	0	0%	102,000
Rick Lewis	Spring Haven	HB	C	P	1	0	0%	10,000
Robert Detweiler's	Peninsula	HB	C	T	2	0	0%	17,500
Robert J. Fraher	Peninsula	LEX	C	T	1	0	0%	7,000
Robert Kuhns'	Hunterton	HB	F	P	1	0	0%	3,000
	Saga	LEX	F	T	1	0	0%	9,000
					2	0	0%	6,000
Robert Newman	Peninsula	LEX	C	P	1	0	0%	32,000
Robert Rietveld	Peninsula	LEX	F	T	1	0	0%	15,000
Rockridge	Peninsula	LEX	F	P	3	0	0%	7,000
Rocky Ridge	Northwood	HB	C	T	1	0	0%	10,000
Rolling Acres	Preferred	HB	C	P	3	0	0%	75,667
	Preferred	HB	F	P	1	0	0%	80,000
	Preferred	HB	F	T	1	0	0%	15,000
	Preferred	LEX	C	P	1	0	0%	41,000
	Preferred	LEX	F	P	4	0	0%	65,000

Farm	Consignor	Sale	Sex	Gait	Sold	$50,000 2 Year Olds	Success Rate	Avg Price
	Preferred	LEX	F	T	1	0	0%	115,000
					11	0	0%	67,091
Ruddick Stables	Spring Haven	LEX	F	P	1	0	0%	7,000
	Spring Haven	LEX	C	T	1	1	100.0%	3,000
					2	1	50.0%	5,000
Rupert	Peninsula	HB	C	T	1	0	0%	42,000
	Peninsula	HB	F	T	1	0	0%	18,000
	Hunterton	LEX	F	T	1	0	0%	37,000
	Peninsula	LEX	F	T	1	0	0%	65,000
					4	0	0%	40,500
Russ Beeman's	Peninsula	HB	C	P	1	0	0%	13,000
Saga	Saga	LEX	C	P	2	0	0%	17,500
	Saga	LEX	C	T	14	1	7.1%	22,214
	Saga	LEX	F	P	8	1	12.5%	16,875
	Saga	LEX	F	T	19	0	0%	30,947
					43	2	4.7%	24,860
Sam Lambright Jr	Spring Haven	LEX	F	P	1	0	0%	16,000
Samuel Zook's	Walnridge	HB	F	T	1	0	0%	12,000
Schunk Stables	Preferred	LEX	C	P	1	0	0%	82,000
	Preferred	LEX	C	T	2	0	0%	8,500
					3	0	0%	33,000
Schwartz Boarding	Preferred	LEX	C	P	1	0	0%	6,000
Scott Rudnick	Spring Haven	LEX	C	P	1	0	0%	7,000
Seelster	Hunterton	HB	C	P	1	0	0%	4,500
	Preferred	HB	C	P	2	0	0%	22,000
	Preferred	HB	C	T	3	0	0%	52,333
	Preferred	HB	F	P	2	0	0%	12,500
	Preferred	HB	F	T	1	0	0%	16,000
					9	0	0%	27,389
Seufert	Spring Haven	LEX	F	T	1	0	0%	10,000
Shadowbrook	Boxwood	HB	C	P	5	1	20.0%	40,500
	Boxwood	HB	F	P	4	2	50.0%	25,125
					9	3	33.3%	33,667
Shady Lane Meadows	Hunterton	LEX	C	P	2	0	0%	18,000
	Hunterton	LEX	F	P	1	0	0%	14,000
					3	0	0%	16,667
Shady Side	Peninsula	LEX	C	P	2	0	0%	55,000
	Peninsula	LEX	F	P	3	0	0%	22,667
					5	0	0%	35,600
Shaffer Standardbreds	Fox Den	HB	C	P	4	0	0%	8,000
	Fox Den	HB	C	T	1	0	0%	19,000

Farm	Consignor	Sale	Sex	Gait	Sold	$50,000 2 Year Olds	Success Rate	Avg Price
	Fox Den	HB	F	P	13	0	0%	11,962
	Fox Den	HB	F	T	2	0	0%	15,000
	Northwood	HB	F	T	1	0	0%	17,000
					21	0	0%	12,071
Shamrock	Peninsula	HB	C	P	4	0	0%	46,250
	Peninsula	HB	F	P	5	0	0%	19,400
					9	0	0%	31,333
Shawnee Run	Peninsula	LEX	C	T	1	0	0%	20,000
	Peninsula	LEX	F	T	6	0	0%	15,167
					7	0	0%	15,857
Sholty's Farm	Peninsula	HB	C	T	1	0	0%	62,000
Silver Linden	Peninsula	HB	C	T	6	0	0%	30,833
	Peninsula	HB	F	T	4	1	25.0%	44,250
	Peninsula	LEX	F	T	1	0	0%	13,000
					11	1	9.1%	34,091
Silver Willow	Preferred	HB	C	P	1	0	0%	13,000
Skipalong	Peninsula	LEX	F	P	1	0	0%	15,000
Skyhaven	Northwood	HB	F	T	1	0	0%	40,000
Slabach Bros	Spring Haven	HB	C	T	1	0	0%	31,000
Smith Farmstead	Concord	HB	C	T	1	0	0%	5,500
	Concord	HB	F	P	1	0	0%	55,000
					2	0	0%	30,250
Snowball Hill	Northwood	HB	F	P	2	0	0%	8,000
Something Special	Spring Haven	LEX	C	P	1	0	0%	10,000
Southwind	Preferred	HB	C	P	9	0	0%	28,056
	Preferred	HB	C	T	4	1	25.0%	11,250
	Preferred	HB	F	P	7	1	14.3%	20,429
	Preferred	HB	F	T	9	1	11.1%	19,278
	Preferred	LEX	C	P	4	0	0%	71,750
	Preferred	LEX	C	T	14	1	7.1%	35,571
	Preferred	LEX	F	P	10	4	40.0%	30,800
	Preferred	LEX	F	T	13	1	7.7%	60,385
					70	9	12.9%	35,600
Spring Haven	Spring Haven	HB	C	P	18	0	0%	48,389
	Spring Haven	HB	C	T	2	0	0%	27,500
	Spring Haven	HB	F	P	11	0	0%	28,182
	Spring Haven	HB	F	T	1	0	0%	30,000
	Spring Haven	LEX	C	P	18	1	5.6%	36,444
	Spring Haven	LEX	C	T	9	0	0%	29,556
	Spring Haven	LEX	F	P	12	1	8.3%	17,583
	Spring Haven	LEX	F	T	3	0	0%	39,333

Farm	Consignor	Sale	Sex	Gait	Sold	$50,000 2 Year Olds	Success Rate	Avg Price
					74	2	2.7%	34,014
Spring Run	Northwood	HB	C	P	1	0	0%	20,000
	Spring Haven	HB	C	P	1	0	0%	11,000
	Spring Haven	HB	C	T	2	0	0%	15,750
	Spring Haven	HB	F	P	2	0	0%	20,750
	Spring Haven	HB	F	T	1	0	0%	42,000
	Spring Haven	LEX	C	P	1	0	0%	31,000
	Spring Haven	LEX	C	T	1	0	0%	23,000
					9	0	0%	22,222
Spruce Run	Peninsula	HB	C	T	1	0	0%	9,000
Starmaker	Northwood	HB	C	T	2	0	0%	14,500
	Hunterton	LEX	C	P	4	0	0%	14,750
	Hunterton	LEX	C	T	2	0	0%	8,500
	Hunterton	LEX	F	P	2	0	0%	14,000
					10	0	0%	13,300
Steiner Stock	Spring Haven	LEX	C	P	1	0	0%	65,000
	Steiner Stock	LEX	C	P	5	0	0%	29,200
	Steiner Stock	LEX	C	T	4	0	0%	27,500
	Steiner Stock	LEX	F	P	13	0	0%	10,615
	Steiner Stock	LEX	F	T	5	1	20.0%	35,600
					28	1	3.6%	22,750
Stirling Brook	Preferred	HB	C	P	1	0	0%	15,000
	Preferred	HB	C	T	3	0	0%	10,833
	Preferred	HB	F	T	4	0	0%	13,375
	Preferred	LEX	C	P	1	0	0%	85,000
	Preferred	LEX	C	T	2	0	0%	50,000
	Preferred	LEX	F	T	5	0	0%	28,000
					16	0	0%	26,625
Stoltzfus	Fox Den	HB	C	P	8	0	0%	14,375
	Fox Den	HB	F	P	8	0	0%	13,313
	Fox Den	HB	F	T	3	0	0%	11,667
					19	0	0%	13,500
Stonebridge	Concord	HB	C	P	1	0	0%	1,500
Stonegate	Stonegate	HB	C	P	19	0	0%	19,684
	Stonegate	HB	C	T	9	0	0%	17,222
	Stonegate	HB	F	P	19	2	10.5%	28,868
	Stonegate	HB	F	T	5	1	20.0%	23,500
					52	3	5.8%	22,981
Stonehenge	Fair Winds	HB	C	P	3	0	0%	21,333
	Preferred	HB	C	P	1	0	0%	20,000
	Northwood	HB	C	T	1	0	0%	25,000

Farm	Consignor	Sale	Sex	Gait	Sold	$50,000 2 Year Olds	Success Rate	Avg Price
	Fair Winds	HB	F	P	2	0	0%	25,500
	Preferred	HB	F	T	2	0	0%	101,500
	Preferred	LEX	C	T	2	0	0%	27,000
	Preferred	LEX	F	T	1	0	0%	13,000
					12	0	0%	35,833
Sun Valley	Preferred	HB	C	T	1	0	0%	4,000
Sunny View	Concord	HB	C	P	1	0	0%	47,000
Sunrise	Spring Haven	LEX	C	P	2	1	50.0%	18,500
	Spring Haven	LEX	C	T	1	0	0%	7,000
	Hunterton	LEX	F	P	2	0	0%	17,500
	Spring Haven	LEX	F	P	1	0	0%	15,000
	Spring Haven	LEX	F	T	1	0	0%	12,000
					7	1	14.3%	15,143
Talbot Creek	Preferred	HB	C	T	2	0	0%	15,000
	Preferred	HB	F	P	1	0	0%	40,000
	Preferred	HB	F	T	1	0	0%	17,000
	Hunterton	LEX	C	T	1	0	0%	31,000
	Spring Haven	LEX	C	T	2	0	0%	24,000
	Spring Haven	LEX	F	T	1	0	0%	7,000
					8	0	0%	21,625
Tara Hills	Preferred	HB	C	P	5	0	0%	48,200
	Preferred	HB	F	P	4	1	25.0%	60,000
	Preferred	HB	F	T	1	0	0%	35,000
					10	1	10.0%	51,600
The Pink Racing	Spring Haven	HB	F	P	1	0	0%	1,500
Three Cedars	Fox Den	HB	C	P	1	0	0%	9,000
	Fox Den	HB	C	T	1	0	0%	14,000
					2	0	0%	11,500
Three Crow	Peninsula	HB	C	T	1	1	100.0%	35,000
Tom Knight's	Preferred	HB	C	P	1	0	0%	7,000
Tom Schmucker's	Hunterton	HB	F	T	1	0	0%	35,000
Torrey Ridge	Walnridge	HB	C	P	1	0	0%	11,000
	Boxwood	HB	C	T	2	0	0%	8,000
	Walnridge	HB	C	T	1	0	0%	18,000
	Walnridge	HB	F	T	1	0	0%	27,000
					5	0	0%	14,400
Twin Creeks	Preferred	LEX	C	P	2	0	0%	15,000
Twin Willows	Preferred	LEX	C	P	1	0	0%	30,000
	Preferred	LEX	F	P	2	0	0%	18,000
	Preferred	LEX	F	T	3	0	0%	12,667
					6	0	0%	17,333

Farm	Consignor	Sale	Sex	Gait	Sold	$50,000 2 Year Olds	Success Rate	Avg Price
Twinbrook	Twinbrook	HB	C	P	13	1	7.7%	45,462
	Twinbrook	HB	C	T	2	0	0%	15,500
	Twinbrook	HB	F	P	14	0	0%	32,214
	Preferred	LEX	F	P	1	0	0%	37,000
					30	1	3.3%	37,000
Two Creeks	Peninsula	LEX	C	P	2	0	0%	16,000
	Peninsula	LEX	F	P	1	0	0%	6,000
					3	0	0%	12,667
Two Gaits	Northwood	LEX	C	T	1	0	0%	13,000
Tymal	Preferred	LEX	F	T	1	0	0%	14,000
Underdog	Saga	LEX	C	T	1	0	0%	6,000
Valley View	Northwood	LEX	F	P	1	0	0%	15,000
Venture	Hunterton	LEX	C	T	1	0	0%	25,000
	Hunterton	LEX	F	T	1	0	0%	15,000
					2	0	0%	20,000
Victory Hill	Saga	LEX	C	P	8	0	0%	10,625
	Saga	LEX	F	P	9	0	0%	15,222
					17	0	0%	13,059
Vieux Carre	Vieux Carre	HB	C	P	66	5	7.6%	22,273
	Vieux Carre	HB	C	T	30	1	3.3%	29,433
	Vieux Carre	HB	F	P	41	3	7.3%	19,659
	Vieux Carre	HB	F	T	24	1	4.2%	23,354
					161	10	6.2%	23,102
Viking Meadows	Spring Haven	LEX	C	T	1	0	0%	4,000
	Spring Haven	LEX	F	P	1	0	0%	18,000
					2	0	0%	11,000
Village Acres Ltd	Preferred	HB	F	P	1	0	0%	13,000
	Preferred	HB	F	T	1	0	0%	55,000
	Preferred	LEX	C	P	2	0	0%	32,500
	Preferred	LEX	F	P	4	0	0%	42,750
	Preferred	LEX	F	T	2	0	0%	88,500
					10	0	0%	48,100
Walco	Hunterton	LEX	C	P	9	2	22.2%	33,667
	Hunterton	LEX	C	T	29	4	13.8%	73,724
	Hunterton	LEX	F	P	10	0	0%	22,600
	Hunterton	LEX	F	T	16	0	0%	37,750
					64	6	9.4%	51,109
Walker	Preferred	HB	C	T	1	0	0%	15,000
	Preferred	LEX	F	T	1	0	0%	15,000
					2	0	0%	15,000
Walnridge	Walnridge	HB	C	P	22	2	9.1%	29,750

Farm	Consignor	Sale	Sex	Gait	Sold	$50,000 2 Year Olds	Success Rate	Avg Price
	Walnridge	HB	C	T	14	0	0%	62,000
	Peninsula	HB	F	P	1	0	0%	20,000
	Walnridge	HB	F	P	21	2	9.5%	15,143
	Walnridge	HB	F	T	8	0	0%	31,438
					66	4	6.1%	32,000
Walnut Hall Ltd	Walnut Hall Ltd	HB	C	P	4	0	0%	20,750
	Westwind	HB	C	P	3	0	0%	41,667
	Walnut Hall Ltd	HB	C	T	25	2	8.0%	29,260
	Westwind	HB	C	T	7	1	14.3%	34,286
	Walnut Hall Ltd	HB	F	P	4	0	0%	20,624
	Westwind	HB	F	P	1	0	0%	9,000
	Walnut Hall Ltd	HB	F	T	24	3	12.5%	23,813
	Westwind	HB	F	T	8	0	0%	17,875
	Preferred	LEX	C	P	8	0	0%	14,625
	Hunterton	LEX	C	T	2	1	50.0%	46,500
	Preferred	LEX	F	P	10	1	10.0%	17,700
	Saga	LEX	F	P	1	1	100.0%	10,000
					97	9	9.3%	24,562
Walnut Hall Stock	Walnut Hall Stock	LEX	C	P	10	1	10.0%	34,500
	Walnut Hall Stock	LEX	C	T	17	0	0%	42,588
	Walnut Hall Stock	LEX	F	P	6	2	33.3%	23,667
	Walnut Hall Stock	LEX	F	T	6	0	0.0%	26,833
					39	3	7.7%	35,179
Walstan	Kentuckiana	LEX	C	P	1	0	0%	5,000
	Peninsula	LEX	C	P	2	1	50.0%	16,500
	Peninsula	LEX	C	T	7	2	28.6%	23,000
	Peninsula	LEX	F	P	2	0	0%	22,500
	Peninsula	LEX	F	T	4	1	25.0%	26,750
					16	4	25.0%	21,938
Warrawee	Preferred	HB	C	P	3	0	0%	36,000
	Preferred	HB	C	T	3	0	0%	11,333
	Preferred	HB	F	P	1	0	0%	9,000
	Preferred	LEX	F	T	2	0	0%	47,500
					9	0	0%	27,333
Wayne T. Zollars	Hunterton	LEX	C	T	1	0	0%	25,000
Westwind	Westwind	HB	C	P	1	0	0%	75,000
	Westwind	HB	F	P	3	1	33.3%	15,500

Farm	Consignor	Sale	Sex	Gait	Sold	$50,000 2 Year Olds	Success Rate	Avg Price
	Westwind	HB	F	T	1	0	0%	13,000
					5	1	20.0%	26,900
White Birch	Preferred	HB	C	P	30	3	10.0%	27,083
	Preferred	HB	C	T	13	0	0%	22,500
	Preferred	HB	F	P	29	2	6.9%	17,500
	Preferred	HB	F	T	11	1	9.1%	23,682
	Preferred	LEX	C	P	18	6	33.3%	68,056
	Preferred	LEX	C	T	2	0	0%	66,000
	Preferred	LEX	F	P	10	2	20.0%	41,100
	Preferred	LEX	F	T	3	1	33.3%	46,333
					116	15	12.9%	32,586
White Hollow	Northwood	HB	C	T	2	0	0%	69,750
	Northwood	HB	F	T	3	2	66.7%	28,333
					5	2	40.0%	44,900
White Oak	Spring Haven	LEX	C	P	1	0	0%	13,000
	Spring Haven	LEX	C	T	1	0	0%	30,000
					2	0	0%	21,500
Wilbur Eash	Kentuckiana	LEX	C	T	2	0	0%	22,000
	Saga	LEX	F	P	1	0	0%	12,000
	Kentuckiana	LEX	F	T	1	0	0%	40,000
	Saga	LEX	F	T	2	0	0%	2,000
					6	0	0%	16,667
Wilbur Stoll Lang	Spring Haven	LEX	F	T	2	0	0%	62,500
Wildewood	Preferred	HB	C	T	1	1	100.0%	10,000
	Preferred	HB	F	T	1	0	0%	24,000
					2	1	50.0%	17,000
Wilt Standardbreds	Kentuckiana	LEX	C	T	5	1	20.0%	25,400
	Peninsula	LEX	C	T	2	0	0%	22,500
	Kentuckiana	LEX	F	P	1	0	0%	18,000
	Peninsula	LEX	F	P	1	0	0%	40,000
	Hunterton	LEX	F	T	1	0	0%	30,000
	Kentuckiana	LEX	F	T	2	0	0%	20,500
					12	1	8.3%	25,083
Winbak	Winbak	HB	C	P	70	2	2.9%	30,736
	Winbak	HB	C	T	21	2	9.5%	27,500
	Winbak	HB	F	P	55	4	7.3%	24,264

Farm	Consignor	Sale	Sex	Gait	Sold	$50,000 2 Year Olds	Success Rate	Avg Price
	Winbak	HB	F	T	37	2	5.4%	29,649
	Winbak	LEX	C	P	55	7	12.7%	31,655
	Winbak	LEX	C	T	21	2	9.5%	22,571
	Winbak	LEX	F	P	34	3	8.8%	30,647
	Winbak	LEX	F	T	24	1	4.2%	30,625
					317	23	7.3%	28,872
Windsun	Preferred	HB	C	P	2	0	0%	45,000
	Preferred	HB	C	T	1	0	0%	22,000
	Preferred	HB	F	T	3	1	33.3%	14,000
	Preferred	LEX	C	T	1	0	0%	31,000
	Preferred	LEX	F	T	1	0	0%	20,000
					8	1	12.5%	25,625
Windswept Valley	Spring Haven	LEX	C	T	2	0	0%	67,500
	Spring Haven	LEX	F	T	2	0	0%	60,000
					4	0	0%	63,750
Winterwood	Winterwood	HB	C	P	13	0	0%	14,962
	Winterwood	HB	C	T	5	0	0%	14,500
	Winterwood	HB	F	P	7	0	0%	11,857
	Winterwood	HB	F	T	7	1	14.3%	15,000
	Hunterton	LEX	C	P	1	1	100.0%	15,000
	Peninsula	LEX	C	T	2	1	50.0%	97,500
	Saga	LEX	C	T	1	1	100.0%	9,000
					36	4	11.1%	18,722
Wizard Heights	Peninsula	LEX	C	T	3	0	0%	81,667
	Peninsula	LEX	F	P	1	0	0%	8,000
	Peninsula	LEX	F	T	1	0	0%	23,000
					5	0	0%	55,200
Wollam	Northwood	HB	C	T	1	0	0%	30,000
	Northwood	HB	F	T	1	0	0%	1,500
					2	0	0%	15,750
Woodstock	Preferred	LEX	F	T	1	0	0%	70,000
Yankeeland	Peninsula	LEX	C	P	3	0	0%	88,333
Zimpfer Stable	Cameo Hills	LEX	C	T	1	0	0%	18,000

Chapter 6: Broodmare Sire Success Rates

Knowing the Success Rates of individual broodmare sires within the scope of this criterion can be very helpful in the selection process. Noting the production differences by gender is especially important. The chart below details the broodmare sire performance by gender at each sale venue. By detailing this information in this manner, the reader can glean some interesting nuggets. Here are a few examples.

Muscles Yankee mares have produced 14 elite performers out of 146 sold for a 9.6% Success Rate. His colt producing mares were 7 out of 81 for 8.6%, while mares of fillies were 7 of 65 for 10.8%. Taking the data one step further, fillies offered at Lexington out of *Muscles Yankee* mares were 5 of 16 for a Success Rate of 31.3%, or 1 in 3.2.

American Winner mares have produced 6 elite performers from 52 sold. However, all 6 elites were fillies from only 23 offered. That's a Success Rate of 26.1% or 1 in 3.8.

Tagliabue mares have been the opposite. Their colt production of 4 elite performers out of 19 sold represents a 21.1% Success Rate. With fillies, his mares have been 0 out of 11.

Lindy Lane mares have been more productive with their colt offspring also. From 63 colts sold they have had 10 elite two-year olds for a 15.9% Success Rate. Even more impressive are his mares' colt output at Lexington. They produced 4 out of 21 for a 19.1% Success Rate. In addition, *Lindy Lane* mares have not been slackers at producing elite fillies either. They have had 4 out of 39 for a 10.3% Success Rate.

We're starting to see more *Western Ideal* broodmares. So far his mares have been 7 out of 67 for 10.5%, which is 46% above average. But, his mares have been far superior at producing elite fillies with a record of 6 out of 33 sold. That's a Success Rate of 18.2%, or 1 in 5.5.

SJ's Caviar mares have shown promise with 4 elite credits out of only 17 for a 23.5% Success Rate.

There are some studs that have not been very successful as broodmare sires at these sale venues. The babies of their mares are likely to keep reappearing at these sales.

Take a look at Ontario sire *Angus Hall*. His mares have been 1 for 55 (1.8% Success Rate). *Armbro Goal* mares have not been much better at 1 for 41 (2.4%). *Credit Winner* mares have been off to a slow start at 1 for 40 (2.5%). *Bettor's Delight* mares have yet to garner an elite performer credit for their sire. They've been 0 for 29. The same is true for *Die Laughing*. His mares are 0 for 35.

Chart 1: Broodmare Sire Success Rates

Broodmare Sire	Sale	Sex	Sold	$50,000 2 Year Olds	Success Rate
A Go Go Lauxmont	Lex	F	1	0	0.0%
Abercrombie	Hb	C	31	3	9.7%
	Lex	C	42	3	7.1%
		C	73	6	8.2%
	Hb	F	21	0	0.0%
	Lex	F	23	2	8.7%
		F	44	2	4.5%
	Total		117	8	6.8%
Admirals Galley	Hb	F	1	0	0.0%
Aggressive Way	Hb	F	1	0	0.0%
Albatross	Hb	C	5	0	0.0%
	Lex	C	7	0	0.0%
			12	0	0.0%
	Hb	F	4	1	25.0%
	Lex	F	4	0	0.0%
		F	8	1	12.5%
	Total		20	1	5.0%
Albert Albert	Hb	C	5	2	40.0%
	Lex	C	3	0	0.0%
		C	8	2	25.0%
	Hb	F	6	0	0.0%
	Lex	F	1	0	0.0%
		F	7	0	0.0%
	Total		15	2	13.3%
Allamerican Ingot	Lex	C	1	1	100.0%
	Lex	F	1	0	0.0%
	Total		2	1	50.0%
American Winner	Hb	C	11	0	0.0%
	Lex	C	18	0	0.0%
		C	29	0	0.0%
	Hb	F	9	3	33.3%
	Lex	F	14	3	21.4%
		F	23	6	26.1%
	Total		52	6	11.5%
Ameripan Gigolo	Lex	C	1	0	0.0%
Amigo Hall	Hb	C	1	0	0.0%
Amity Chef	Hb	F	1	0	0.0%
Andover Hall	Hb	C	8	1	12.5%
	Lex	C	1	0	0.0%
		C	9	1	11.1%
	Hb	F	3	1	33.3%
	Lex	F	11	1	9.1%
		F	14	2	14.3%
	Total		23	3	13.0%
Andrel	Lex	C	1	1	100.0%

Broodmare Sire	Sale	Sex	Sold	$50,000 2 Year Olds	Success Rate
Angus Hall	Hb	C	12	1	8.3%
	Lex	C	11	0	0.0%
		C	23	1	4.3%
	Hb	F	15	0	0.0%
	Lex	F	17	0	0.0%
		F	32	0	0.0%
	Total		**55**	**1**	**1.8%**
Apaches Fame	Hb	C	2	1	50.0%
	Lex	C	2	0	0.0%
		C	4	1	25.0%
	Lex	F	1	0	0.0%
	Total		**5**	**1**	**20.0%**
Armbro Agile	Lex	F	1	0	0.0%
Armbro Charger	Hb	C	2	0	0.0%
	Lex	C	1	0	0.0%
		C	3	0	0.0%
	Hb	F	1	0	0.0%
	Lex	F	1	0	0.0%
		F	2	0	0.0%
	Total		**5**	**0**	**0.0%**
Armbro Emerson	Hb	C	4	0	0.0%
	Lex	C	1	1	100.0%
		C	5	1	20.0%
	Hb	F	2	0	0.0%
	Total		**7**	**1**	**14.3%**
Armbro Goal	Hb	C	7	0	0.0%
	Lex	C	11	0	0.0%
		C	18	0	0.0%
	Hb	F	11	0	0.0%
	Lex	F	12	1	8.3%
		F	23	1	4.3%
	Total		**41**	**1**	**2.4%**
Armbro Iliad	Hb	C	3	0	0.0%
	Lex	C	3	1	33.3%
		C	6	1	16.7%
	Hb	F	1	0	0.0%
	Lex	F	1	0	0.0%
		F	2	0	0.0%
	Total		**8**	**1**	**12.5%**
Armbro Laser	Hb	C	1	0	0.0%
	Lex	F	2	1	50.0%
	Total		**3**	**1**	**33.3%**
Armbro Mackintosh	Hb	C	1	0	0.0%
	Lex	C	1	0	0.0%
		C	2	0	0.0%
	Hb	F	2	0	0.0%
	Lex	F	1	0	0.0%

Broodmare Sire	Sale	Sex	Sold	$50,000 2 Year Olds	Success Rate
		F	3	0	0.0%
	Total		5	0	0.0%
Armbro Operative	Hb	C	1	0	0.0%
	Lex	C	1	0	0.0%
		C	2	0	0.0%
	Hb	F	1	0	0.0%
	Total		3	0	0.0%
Armbro Wolf	Lex	C	1	0	0.0%
Arndon	Hb	C	2	0	0.0%
	Lex	F	1	0	0.0%
	Total		3	0	0.0%
Arnies Exchange	Hb	C	2	0	0.0%
	Lex	C	1	0	0.0%
	Total	C	3	0	0.0%
Art Major	Hb	C	4	2	50.0%
	Hb	F	3	1	33.3%
	Lex	F	1	0	0.0%
		F	4	1	25.0%
	Total		8	3	37.5%
Artiscape	Hb	C	25	1	4.0%
	Lex	C	14	2	14.3%
		C	39	3	7.7%
	Hb	F	13	1	7.7%
	Lex	F	14	1	7.1%
		F	27	2	7.4%
	Total		66	5	7.6%
Artsplace	Hb	C	131	8	6.1%
	Lex	C	93	8	8.6%
		C	224	16	7.1%
	Hb	F	122	9	7.4%
	Lex	F	79	9	11.4%
		F	201	18	9.0%
	Total		425	34	8.0%
Arturo	Hb	C	3	0	0.0%
	Lex	C	2	0	0.0%
		C	5	0	0.0%
	Hb	F	1	0	0.0%
	Lex	F	2	0	0.0%
		F	3	0	0.0%
	Total		8	0	0.0%
Astreos	Lex	F	1	0	0.0%
B.G's Bunny	Hb	C	1	0	0.0%
	Hb	F	1	0	0.0%
	Total		2	0	0.0%
Back Fin	Lex	C	1	0	0.0%
	Lex	F	1	0	0.0%
	Total		2	0	0.0%

Broodmare Sire	Sale	Sex	Sold	$50,000 2 Year Olds	Success Rate
Badlands Hanover	Hb	C	1	0	0.0%
Balanced Image	Hb	C	36	3	8.3%
	Lex	C	31	2	6.5%
		C	67	5	7.5%
	Hb	F	49	3	6.1%
	Lex	F	23	1	4.3%
		F	72	4	5.6%
	Total		139	9	6.5%
Ball And Chain	Hb	C	1	0	0.0%
	Lex	C	1	0	0.0%
	Total		2	0	0.0%
Baltic Speed	Hb	C	5	0	0.0%
	Lex	C	4	0	0.0%
		C	9	0	0.0%
	Hb	F	2	0	0.0%
	Lex	F	2	0	0.0%
		F	4	0	0.0%
	Total		13	0	0.0%
Banker Hall	Hb	C	1	0	0.0%
	Hb	F	1	0	0.0%
	Total		2	0	0.0%
Barberry Spur	Lex	C	1	0	0.0%
Beach Towel	Hb	C	11	2	18.2%
	Lex	C	5	1	20.0%
		C	16	3	18.8%
	Hb	F	9	0	0.0%
	Lex	F	3	0	0.0%
		F	12	0	0.0%
	Total		28	3	10.7%
Beastmaster	Hb	F	1	0	0.0%
Bettor's Delight	Hb	C	9	0	0.0%
	Lex	C	8	0	0.0%
		C	17	0	0.0%
	Hb	F	10	0	0.0%
	Lex	F	2	0	0.0%
		F	12	0	0.0%
	Total		29	0	0.0%
Big Rube	Hb	C	2	0	0.0%
	Hb	F	1	0	0.0%
	Total		3	0	0.0%
Big Towner	Hb	C	29	1	3.4%
	Lex	C	12	1	8.3%
		C	41	2	4.9%
	Hb	F	15	0	0.0%
	Lex	F	9	0	0.0%
		F	24	0	0.0%
	Total		65	2	3.1%

Broodmare Sire	Sale	Sex	Sold	$50,000 2 Year Olds	Success Rate
Billy Dart	Lex	C	1	0	0.0%
	Hb	F	1	0	0.0%
	Total		2	0	0.0%
BJ's Mac	Hb	C	1	0	0.0%
	Lex	C	1	0	0.0%
		C	2	0	0.0%
	Hb	F	3	0	0.0%
	Lex	F	2	0	0.0%
		F	5	0	0.0%
	Total		7	0	0.0%
Blissful Hall	Hb	C	10	0	0.0%
	Lex	C	1	0	0.0%
		C	11	0	0.0%
	Hb	F	4	0	0.0%
	Lex	F	5	0	0.0%
		F	9	0	0.0%
	Total		20	0	0.0%
Bo Knows Jate	Hb	C	3	0	0.0%
	Hb	F	1	0	0.0%
	Total		4	0	0.0%
Bonefish	Lex	C	3	0	0.0%
	Lex	F	1	0	0.0%
	Total		4	0	0.0%
Bostonian	Hb	C	1	0	0.0%
Bret Hanover	Hb	C	1	0	0.0%
Brisco Hanover	Hb	C	3	0	0.0%
	Hb	F	2	0	0.0%
	Total		5	0	0.0%
Brisco Herbert	Lex	C	2	0	0.0%
Broadway Hall	Hb	F	1	0	0.0%
	Lex	F	1	0	0.0%
	Total		2	0	0.0%
Broadway Jate	Hb	C	1	0	0.0%
	Hb	F	1	0	0.0%
	Lex	F	1	0	0.0%
		F	2	0	0.0%
	Total		3	0	0.0%
Call For Rain	Lex	C	1	0	0.0%
	Hb	F	2	0	0.0%
	Total		3	0	0.0%
Cam Cam Cameo	Lex	C	1	0	0.0%
Cam Fella	Hb	C	12	2	16.7%
	Lex	C	4	0	0.0%
		C	16	2	12.5%
	Hb	F	6	0	0.0%
	Lex	F	5	1	20.0%
		F	11	1	9.1%

Broodmare Sire	Sale	Sex	Sold	$50,000 2 Year Olds	Success Rate
	Total		**27**	**3**	**11.1%**
Cam's Magic Trick	**Lex**	**C**	**1**	**0**	**0.0%**
Cam Terrific	**Hb**	**C**	**1**	**0**	**0.0%**
Cambest	Hb	C	24	0	0.0%
	Lex	C	14	2	14.3%
		C	38	2	5.3%
	Hb	F	23	3	13.0%
	Lex	F	21	1	4.8%
		F	44	4	9.1%
	Total		**82**	**6**	**7.3%**
Camluck	Hb	C	39	2	5.1%
	Lex	C	18	1	5.6%
		C	57	3	5.3%
	Hb	F	27	2	7.4%
	Lex	F	19	2	10.5%
		F	46	4	8.7%
	Total		**103**	**7**	**6.8%**
Cam's Card Shark	Hb	C	49	6	12.2%
	Lex	C	25	3	12.0%
		C	74	9	12.2%
	Hb	F	26	1	3.8%
	Lex	F	20	3	15.0%
		F	46	4	8.7%
	Total		**120**	**13**	**10.8%**
Camtastic	Hb	C	5	0	0.0%
	Lex	C	3	0	0.0%
		C	8	0	0.0%
	Hb	F	5	0	0.0%
	Lex	F	1	0	0.0%
		F	6	0	0.0%
	Total		**14**	**0**	**0.0%**
Caprock	**Hb**	**C**	**2**	**0**	**0.0%**
Carlsbad Cam	Hb	C	1	0	0.0%
	Lex	F	1	0	0.0%
	Total		**2**	**0**	**0.0%**
Carry The Message	Hb	C	1	0	0.0%
	Lex	C	4	1	25.0%
		C	5	1	20.0%
	Hb	F	2	0	0.0%
	Lex	F	1	0	0.0%
		F	3	0	0.0%
	Total		**8**	**1**	**12.5%**
Castleton Success	**Hb**	**F**	**1**	**0**	**0.0%**
Catch A Thrill	**Hb**	**C**	**3**	**2**	**66.7%**
Cheyenne Spur	Hb	C	1	0	0.0%
	Lex	C	1	0	0.0%
		C	2	0	0.0%

Broodmare Sire	Sale	Sex	Sold	$50,000 2 Year Olds	Success Rate
	Hb	F	2	1	50.0%
	Total		4	1	25.0%
Chiola Hanover	**Lex**	**C**	**2**	**0**	**0.0%**
Coal Harbor	Hb	C	1	0	0.0%
	Hb	F	1	0	0.0%
	Total		2	0	0.0%
Coktail Jet	**Lex**	**F**	**1**	**0**	**0.0%**
Cole Muffler	Hb	C	8	0	0.0%
	Lex	C	2	0	0.0%
		C	10	0	0.0%
	Hb	F	7	1	14.3%
	Lex	F	1	0	0.0%
		F	8	1	12.5%
	Total		18	1	5.6%
Colt Fortysix	**Hb**	**F**	**2**	**0**	**0.0%**
Conway Hall	Hb	C	23	2	8.7%
	Lex	C	28	1	3.6%
		C	51	3	5.9%
	Hb	F	21	0	0.0%
	Lex	F	23	1	4.3%
		F	44	1	2.3%
	Total		95	4	4.2%
Cooper Lobell	Lex	C	1	0	0.0%
	Lex	F	2	0	0.0%
	Total		3	0	0.0%
Copter Lobell	**Hb**	**C**	**1**	**0**	**0.0%**
Covert Action	**Hb**	**C**	**1**	**0**	**0.0%**
CR Commando	Hb	C	1	0	0.0%
	Hb	F	1	1	100.0%
	Total		2	1	50.0%
Credit Winner	Hb	C	15	0	0.0%
	Lex	C	9	0	0.0%
		C	24	0	0.0%
	Hb	F	10	0	0.0%
	Lex	F	6	1	16.7%
		F	16	1	6.3%
	Total		40	1	2.5%
Crowning Point	Hb	C	5	1	20.0%
	Lex	C	7	0	0.0%
		C	12	1	8.3%
	Hb	F	1	0	0.0%
	Lex	F	6	0	0.0%
		F	7	0	0.0%
	Total		19	1	5.3%
Crysta's Crown	Lex	C	3	0	0.0%
	Hb	F	3	0	0.0%
	Lex	F	2	0	0.0%

Broodmare Sire	Sale	Sex	Sold	$50,000 2 Year Olds	Success Rate
		F	5	0	0.0%
	Total		8	0	0.0%
Cumin	Lex	C	5	0	0.0%
	Hb	F	3	0	0.0%
	Lex	F	3	0	0.0%
		F	6	0	0.0%
	Total		11	0	0.0%
Curragh	Lex	F	1	0	0.0%
D M Dilinger	Hb	C	1	0	0.0%
	Hb	F	1	0	0.0%
	Total		2	0	0.0%
Dancer's Victory	Hb	C	3	0	0.0%
	Lex	C	2	0	0.0%
		C	5	0	0.0%
	Hb	F	3	0	0.0%
	Lex	F	2	0	0.0%
		F	5	0	0.0%
	Total		10	0	0.0%
David's Pass	Hb	C	1	0	0.0%
	Hb	F	1	0	0.0%
	Lex	F	3	0	0.0%
		F	4	0	0.0%
	Total		5	0	0.0%
Defiant Yankee	Hb	F	1	1	100.0%
Deliberate Speed	Lex	F	1	1	100.0%
Denali	Hb	C	1	0	0.0%
Dexter Nukes	Hb	C	4	0	0.0%
	Lex	C	5	1	20.0%
		C	9	1	11.1%
	Hb	F	8	0	0.0%
	Lex	F	3	1	33.3%
		F	11	1	9.1%
	Total		20	2	10.0%
Die Laughing	Hb	C	10	0	0.0%
	Lex	C	6	0	0.0%
		C	16	0	0.0%
	Hb	F	13	0	0.0%
	Lex	F	6	0	0.0%
		F	19	0	0.0%
	Total		35	0	0.0%

Broodmare Sire	Sale	Sex	Sold	$50,000 2 Year Olds	Success Rate
Direct Flight	Hb	F	1	0	0.0%
Direct Scooter	Hb	C	7	0	0.0%
	Lex	C	4	0	0.0%
		C	11	0	0.0%
	Hb	F	4	1	25.0%
	Lex	F	3	1	33.3%
		F	7	2	28.6%
	Total		18	2	11.1%
Donerail	Hb	C	39	3	7.7%
	Lex	C	49	2	4.1%
		C	88	5	5.7%
	Hb	F	38	4	10.5%
	Lex	F	40	2	5.0%
		F	78	6	7.7%
	Total		166	11	6.6%
Dragon Again	Hb	C	12	1	8.3%
	Lex	C	9	0	0.0%
		C	21	1	4.8%
	Hb	F	8	0	0.0%
	Lex	F	3	1	33.3%
		F	11	1	9.1%
	Total		32	2	6.3%
Dragon's Lair	Hb	C	14	0	0.0%
	Lex	C	11	0	0.0%
		C	25	0	0.0%
	Hb	F	8	0	0.0%
	Lex	F	11	1	9.1%
		F	19	1	5.3%
	Total		44	1	2.3%
Dream Away	Hb	C	3	0	0.0%
	Lex	C	1	0	0.0%
		C	4	0	0.0%
	Hb	F	4	0	0.0%
	Lex	F	2	0	0.0%
		F	6	0	0.0%
	Total		10	0	0.0%
Dream Of Glory	Hb	C	2	1	50.0%
	Lex	C	1	0	0.0%

Broodmare Sire	Sale	Sex	Sold	$50,000 2 Year Olds	Success Rate
		C	3	1	33.3%
	Hb	F	6	1	16.7%
	Total		9	2	**22.2%**
Dream Vacation	Hb	C	8	2	25.0%
	Lex	C	9	1	11.1%
		C	17	3	17.6%
	Hb	F	5	0	0.0%
	Lex	F	2	0	0.0%
		F	7	0	0.0%
	Total		24	3	**12.5%**
Duke Of York	**Hb**	**F**	**1**	**0**	**0.0%**
Earl	Hb	C	2	1	50.0%
	Lex	C	1	0	0.0%
		C	3	1	33.3%
	Hb	F	2	0	0.0%
	Lex	F	2	0	0.0%
		F	4	0	0.0%
	Total		7	1	**14.3%**
El Paso Kash	Lex	C	1	0	0.0%
	Lex	F	1	0	0.0%
	Total		2	0	**0.0%**
Elegant Osborne	**Hb**	**C**	**1**	**1**	**100.0%**
Enjoy Lavec	Hb	C	7	0	0.0%
	Lex	C	12	2	16.7%
		C	19	2	10.5%
	Hb	F	3	1	33.3%
	Lex	F	5	0	0.0%
		F	8	1	12.5%
	Total		27	3	**11.1%**
Equitable	**Lex**	**F**	**1**	**1**	**100.0%**
Esquire Spur	**Lex**	**F**	**2**	**0**	**0.0%**
Expensive Scooter	Lex	C	2	0	0.0%
	Lex	F	1	0	0.0%
	Total		3	0	**0.0%**
Falcon Almahurst	Hb	C	1	0	0.0%
	Lex	C	4	0	0.0%
		C	5	0	0.0%
	Hb	F	2	0	0.0%

Broodmare Sire	Sale	Sex	Sold	$50,000 2 Year Olds	Success Rate
	Total		7	0	0.0%
Falcon Seelster	Hb	C	19	0	0.0%
	Lex	C	9	2	22.2%
		C	28	2	7.1%
	Hb	F	9	1	11.1%
	Lex	F	13	1	7.7%
		F	22	2	9.1%
	Total		50	4	8.0%
Falcons Future	Hb	C	4	1	25.0%
	Lex	C	2	0	0.0%
		C	6	1	16.7%
	Hb	F	2	0	0.0%
	Total		8	1	12.5%
Fill V	Hb	F	1	0	0.0%
Final Score	Hb	C	1	0	0.0%
	Lex	C	1	0	0.0%
		C	2	0	0.0%
	Hb	F	1	0	0.0%
	Lex	F	1	0	0.0%
		F	2	0	0.0%
	Total		4	0	0.0%
Flak Bait	Hb	C	2	0	0.0%
Flight Of Fire	Hb	C	1	0	0.0%
Florida Pro	Hb	C	2	0	0.0%
Forrest Skipper	Hb	C	2	0	0.0%
Fortune Richie	Lex	F	1	0	0.0%
Frugal Gormet	Hb	C	1	0	0.0%
Garland Lobell	Hb	C	26	1	3.8%
	Lex	C	23	3	13.0%
		C	49	4	8.2%
	Hb	F	28	4	14.3%
	Lex	F	12	1	8.3%
		F	40	5	12.5%
	Total		89	9	10.1%
Giant Hit	Hb	C	6	0	0.0%
	Hb	F	2	0	0.0%
	Lex	F	3	0	0.0%

Broodmare Sire	Sale	Sex	Sold	$50,000 2 Year Olds	Success Rate
		F	5	0	0.0%
	Total		11	0	0.0%
Giant Victory	Hb	C	3	0	0.0%
	Lex	C	1	0	0.0%
		C	4	0	0.0%
	Hb	F	6	1	16.7%
	Total		10	1	10.0%
Go Get Lost	Hb	F	2	0	0.0%
Goalie Jeff	Hb	C	3	1	33.3%
	Lex	C	2	0	0.0%
		C	5	1	20.0%
	Hb	F	4	0	0.0%
	Lex	F	4	0	0.0%
		F	8	0	0.0%
	Total		13	1	7.7%
Grinfromeartoear	Hb	C	5	0	0.0%
	Lex	C	16	0	0.0%
		C	21	0	0.0%
	Hb	F	7	0	0.0%
	Lex	F	16	1	6.3%
		F	23	1	4.3%
	Total		44	1	2.3%
Harmonious	Hb	C	1	0	0.0%
	Lex	C	1	0	0.0%
		C	2	0	0.0%
	Hb	F	1	0	0.0%
	Lex	F	1	0	0.0%
		F	2	0	0.0%
	All		4	0	0.0%
Hi Ho Silverheels	Hb	F	1	0	0.0%
Higher Power	Hb	C	1	0	0.0%
Historic	Lex	C	1	0	0.0%
Hit The Bid	Hb	C	2	0	0.0%
Hoist The Yankee	Lex	F	2	0	0.0%
Homesick	Hb	C	1	0	0.0%
	Hb	F	2	0	0.0%
	Total		3	0	0.0%
Ideal Society	Lex	F	1	0	0.0%

Broodmare Sire	Sale	Sex	Sold	$50,000 2 Year Olds	Success Rate
Imperial Victory	Lex	C	2	1	50.0%
In The Pocket	Hb	C	1	0	0.0%
	Lex	C	4	1	25.0%
		C	5	1	20.0%
	Lex	F	2	0	0.0%
	Total		7	1	14.3%
Incredible Abe	Lex	F	2	0	0.0%
Incredible Finale	Hb	C	2	1	50.0%
	Lex	C	1	0	0.0%
		C	3	1	33.3%
	Hb	F	2	1	50.0%
	Lex	F	2	0	0.0%
		F	4	1	25.0%
	Total		7	2	28.6%
Incredible Nevele	Hb	F	2	0	0.0%
	Lex	F	2	0	0.0%
	Total		4	0	0.0%
Inquirer	Hb	C	1	0	0.0%
	Hb	F	3	0	0.0%
	Total		4	0	0.0%
International Chip	Lex	F	1	0	0.0%
Island Fantasy	Hb	C	7	0	0.0%
	Lex	C	3	0	0.0%
		C	10	0	0.0%
	Hb	F	1	0	0.0%
	Total		11	0	0.0%
Jaguar Spur	Hb	C	1	0	0.0%
Jamuga	Hb	F	1	0	0.0%
Jate Lobell	Hb	C	56	5	8.9%
	Lex	C	46	5	10.9%
		C	102	10	9.8%
	Hb	F	34	0	0.0%
	Lex	F	42	7	16.7%
		F	76	7	9.2%
	Total		178	17	9.6%
Jazz Cosmos	Hb	C	1	0	0.0%
Jenna's Beach Boy	Hb	C	25	3	12.0%
	Lex	C	13	0	0.0%

Broodmare Sire	Sale	Sex	Sold	$50,000 2 Year Olds	Success Rate
		C	38	3	7.9%
	Hb	F	24	3	12.5%
	Lex	F	23	0	0.0%
		F	47	3	6.4%
	Total		85	6	7.1%
Jeremys Gambit	Hb	C	2	0	0.0%
	Lex	C	1	0	0.0%
		C	3	0	0.0%
	Hb	F	2	0	0.0%
	Total		5	0	0.0%
JK Outlaw	Hb	C	1	0	0.0%
	Lex	F	1	0	0.0%
	Total		2	0	0.0%
Jobie Tempest	Hb	C	1	0	0.0%
Joie De Vie	Hb	C	1	0	0.0%
	Hb	F	4	0	0.0%
	Total		5	0	0.0%
Kadabra	Lex	C	1	0	0.0%
	Lex	F	1	0	0.0%
	Total		2	0	0.0%
Kentucky Spur	Hb	C	1	0	0.0%
	Lex	F	2	0	0.0%
	Total		3	0	0.0%
Keystone Ore	Hb	F	1	0	0.0%
Keystone Raider	Lex	C	4	0	0.0%
	Hb	F	1	0	0.0%
	Total		5	0	0.0%
Kick Tail	Hb	F	1	0	0.0%
Kiev Hanover	Hb	C	2	1	50.0%
	Hb	F	2	0	0.0%
	Lex	F	3	0	0.0%
		F	5	0	0.0%
	Total		7	1	14.3%
King Conch	Hb	C	11	0	0.0%
	Lex	C	5	0	0.0%
		C	16	0	0.0%
	Hb	F	7	2	28.6%
	Lex	F	7	0	0.0%

Broodmare Sire	Sale	Sex	Sold	$50,000 2 Year Olds	Success Rate
		F	14	2	14.3%
	Total		30	2	6.7%
King Kong Ranger	Lex	C	1	0	0.0%
Kingston	Hb	C	1	0	0.0%
Laag	Hb	C	6	0	0.0%
	Lex	C	6	1	16.7%
		C	12	1	8.3%
	Hb	F	10	1	10.0%
	Lex	F	4	0	0.0%
		F	14	1	7.1%
	Total		26	2	7.7%
Landslide	Hb	C	1	0	0.0%
Lemon Dra	Lex	C	1	0	0.0%
	Lex	F	1	1	100.0%
	Total		2	1	50.0%
Life Sign	Hb	C	44	1	2.3%
	Lex	C	34	4	11.8%
		C	78	5	6.4%
	Hb	F	42	3	7.1%
	Lex	F	33	2	6.1%
		F	75	5	6.7%
	Total		153	10	6.5%
Like A Prayer	Hb	C	2	0	0.0%
	Lex	C	1	0	0.0%
		C	3	0	0.0%
	Hb	F	2	0	0.0%
	Lex	F	1	0	0.0%
		F	3	0	0.0%
	Total		6	0	0.0%
Lindy Lane	Hb	C	42	6	14.3%
	Lex	C	21	4	19.0%
		C	63	10	15.9%
	Hb	F	27	3	11.1%
	Lex	F	12	1	8.3%
		F	39	4	10.3%
	Total		102	14	13.7%
Lindy's Crown	Hb	F	1	0	0.0%
Lislea	Hb	F	1	0	0.0%

Broodmare Sire	Sale	Sex	Sold	$50,000 2 Year Olds	Success Rate
Look Sharp	Hb	F	1	0	0.0%
Lusty Leader	Hb	C	1	0	0.0%
LV Glory Bound	Lex	C	1	0	0.0%
Mack Lobell	Lex	C	4	0	0.0%
	Lex	F	2	0	0.0%
	Total		6	0	0.0%
Magical Mike	Hb	C	6	0	0.0%
	Lex	C	3	0	0.0%
		C	9	0	0.0%
	Hb	F	9	3	33.3%
	Lex	F	5	1	20.0%
		F	14	4	28.6%
	Total		23	4	17.4%
Magna Force	Hb	C	1	0	0.0%
Malabar Man	Hb	C	53	3	5.7%
	Lex	C	40	0	0.0%
		C	93	3	3.2%
	Hb	F	46	4	8.7%
	Lex	F	41	1	2.4%
		F	87	5	5.7%
	Total		180	8	4.4%
Marauder	Hb	C	1	0	0.0%
Masquerade	Lex	C	1	0	0.0%
	Lex	F	1	0	0.0%
	Total		2	0	0.0%
Master Lavec	Lex	C	1	0	0.0%
Matt's Scooter	Hb	C	33	1	3.0%
	Lex	C	15	2	13.3%
		C	48	3	6.3%
	Hb	F	34	0	0.0%
	Lex	F	10	1	10.0%
		F	44	1	2.3%
	Total		92	4	4.3%
Meadow Road	Hb	C	2	0	0.0%
	Hb	F	3	0	0.0%
	Lex	F	1	0	0.0%
		F	4	0	0.0%
	Total		6	0	0.0%

Broodmare Sire	Sale	Sex	Sold	$50,000 2 Year Olds	Success Rate
Meadowbranch Jerzy	Lex	C	2	0	0.0%
	Lex	F	1	0	0.0%
	Total		3	0	0.0%
Mighty Crown	Hb	C	1	0	0.0%
Moving Forward	Hb	C	1	0	0.0%
Mr Lavec	Hb	C	18	1	5.6%
	Lex	C	10	2	20.0%
		C	28	3	10.7%
	Hb	F	16	1	6.3%
	Lex	F	12	1	8.3%
		F	28	2	7.1%
	Total		56	5	8.9%
Mr Vic	Hb	C	5	0	0.0%
	Lex	C	16	1	6.3%
		C	21	1	4.8%
	Hb	F	8	0	0.0%
	Lex	F	15	1	6.7%
		F	23	1	4.3%
	Total		44	2	4.5%
Muscles Yankee	Hb	C	54	7	13.0%
	Lex	C	27	0	0.0%
		C	81	7	8.6%
	Hb	F	49	2	4.1%
	Lex	F	16	5	31.3%
		F	65	7	10.8%
	Total		146	14	9.6%
Nearly Perfect	Hb	C	1	0	0.0%
	Lex	F	1	0	0.0%
	Total		2	0	0.0%
New Victory	Hb	C	1	0	0.0%
Niatross	Hb	C	3	0	0.0%
	Hb	F	1	0	0.0%
	Total		4	0	0.0%
Nicholas Hanover	Hb	F	1	0	0.0%
Nihilator	Hb	C	3	0	0.0%
	Lex	C	4	0	0.0%
		C	7	0	0.0%
	Hb	F	4	0	0.0%

Broodmare Sire	Sale	Sex	Sold	$50,000 2 Year Olds	Success Rate
	Lex	F	3	0	0.0%
		F	7	0	0.0%
	Total		14	0	0.0%
No Nukes	Hb	C	51	6	11.8%
	Lex	C	29	1	3.4%
		C	80	7	8.8%
	Hb	F	46	3	6.5%
	Lex	F	24	0	0.0%
		F	70	3	4.3%
	Total		150	10	6.7%
No Pan Intended	Hb	C	1	0	0.0%
	Hb	F	1	0	0.0%
	Total		2	0	0.0%
Nobleland Sam	Hb	C	1	0	0.0%
	Lex	C	3	0	0.0%
		C	4	0	0.0%
	Hb	F	1	0	0.0%
	Lex	F	4	1	25.0%
		F	5	1	20.0%
	Total		9	1	11.1%
Northern Luck	Hb	C	3	1	33.3%
	Lex	C	10	1	10.0%
		C	13	2	15.4%
	Hb	F	3	0	0.0%
	Lex	F	8	1	12.5%
		F	11	1	9.1%
	Total		24	3	12.5%
Nuclear Siren	Hb	C	2	0	0.0%
	Hb	F	2	0	0.0%
	Lex	F	1	0	0.0%
		F	3	0	0.0%
	Total		5	0	0.0%
On The Road Again	Hb	C	7	0	0.0%
	Lex	C	6	0	0.0%
		C	13	0	0.0%
	Hb	F	4	0	0.0%
	Lex	F	1	0	0.0%
		F	5	0	0.0%

Broodmare Sire	Sale	Sex	Sold	$50,000 2 Year Olds	Success Rate
	Total		18	0	0.0%
Overcomer	Hb	C	1	0	0.0%
	Lex	C	1	0	0.0%
		C	2	0	0.0%
	Hb	F	1	0	0.0%
	Lex	F	1	0	0.0%
		F	2	0	0.0%
	Total		4	0	0.0%
Oxford Fella	Lex	F	1	0	0.0%
Pacific Fella	Hb	C	6	0	0.0%
	Lex	C	3	1	33.3%
		C	9	1	11.1%
	Hb	F	3	0	0.0%
	Lex	F	2	0	0.0%
		F	5	0	0.0%
	Total		14	1	7.1%
Pacific Rocket	Lex	C	4	0	0.0%
	Hb	F	2	0	0.0%
	Lex	F	3	0	0.0%
		F	5	0	0.0%
	Total		9	0	0.0%
Park Place	Lex	F	2	0	0.0%
Photo Maker	Lex	C	1	0	0.0%
	Lex	F	1	0	0.0%
	Total		2	0	0.0%
Pine Chip	Hb	C	27	1	3.7%
	Lex	C	36	2	5.6%
		C	63	3	4.8%
	Hb	F	38	1	2.6%
	Lex	F	41	2	4.9%
		F	79	3	3.8%
	Total		142	6	4.2%
Power Seat	Lex	C	1	0	0.0%
	Lex	F	1	0	0.0%
	Total		2	0	0.0%
Powerful Toy	Lex	F	1	0	0.0%
Prakas	Hb	C	4	0	0.0%
	Lex	C	1	0	0.0%

Broodmare Sire	Sale	Sex	Sold	$50,000 2 Year Olds	Success Rate
		C	5	0	0.0%
	Hb	F	2	0	0.0%
	Total		7	0	0.0%
Precious Bunny	Hb	C	10	1	10.0%
	Lex	C	3	0	0.0%
		C	13	1	7.7%
	Hb	F	12	0	0.0%
	Lex	F	1	0	0.0%
		F	13	0	0.0%
	Total		26	1	3.8%
Presidential Ball	Hb	C	17	1	5.9%
	Lex	C	6	1	16.7%
		C	23	2	8.7%
	Hb	F	18	1	5.6%
	Lex	F	5	0	0.0%
		F	23	1	4.3%
	Total		46	3	6.5%
Pro Bono Best	Hb	C	2	0	0.0%
	Hb	F	5	2	40.0%
	Total		7	2	28.6%
Program Speed	Hb	F	1	0	0.0%
	Lex	F	1	0	0.0%
	Total		2	0	0.0%
Promising Catch	Hb	C	1	0	0.0%
	Hb	F	3	0	0.0%
	Total		4	0	0.0%
Quick Work	Lex	F	1	0	0.0%
Raffaello Ambrosio	Lex	C	1	1	100.0%
	Lex	F	1	0	0.0%
	Total		2	1	50.0%
Raging Glory	Hb	C	1	0	0.0%
Ralph Hanover	Hb	F	1	0	0.0%
Raven Hanover	Lex	F	1	0	0.0%
Real Artist	Hb	C	10	0	0.0%
	Lex	C	4	0	0.0%
		C	14	0	0.0%
	Hb	F	8	0	0.0%
	Lex	F	1	0	0.0%

Broodmare Sire	Sale	Sex	Sold	$50,000 2 Year Olds	Success Rate
		F	9	0	0.0%
	Total		23	0	0.0%
Real Desire	Hb	C	2	0	0.0%
	Lex	C	2	0	0.0%
		C	4	0	0.0%
	Hb	F	5	0	0.0%
	Lex	F	1	1	100.0%
		F	6	1	16.7%
	Total		10	1	10.0%
Red River Hanover	Hb	C	3	0	0.0%
	Hb	F	1	0	0.0%
	Total		4	0	0.0%
Richess Hanover	Lex	C	1	0	0.0%
	Lex	F	1	0	0.0%
	Total		2	0	0.0%
Riyadh	Hb	F	2	0	0.0%
	Lex	F	1	0	0.0%
	Total		3	0	0.0%
Rowdy Yankee	Lex	F	1	0	0.0%
Royal Prestige	Hb	C	6	1	16.7%
	Lex	C	9	1	11.1%
		C	15	2	13.3%
	Hb	F	6	0	0.0%
	Lex	F	4	1	25.0%
		F	10	1	10.0%
	Total		25	3	12.0%
Royal Strength	Hb	C	2	0	0.0%
	Lex	C	2	1	50.0%
		C	4	1	25.0%
	Hb	F	1	0	0.0%
	Lex	F	2	1	50.0%
		F	3	1	33.3%
	Total		7	2	28.6%
Royal Troubador	Hb	C	5	0	0.0%
	Lex	C	3	1	33.3%
		C	8	1	12.5%
	Hb	F	2	0	0.0%
	Lex	F	2	0	0.0%

Broodmare Sire	Sale	Sex	Sold	$50,000 2 Year Olds	Success Rate
		F	4	0	0.0%
	Total		12	1	8.3%
Ruffstuff Baker	Lex	F	1	0	0.0%
Rule The Wind	Lex	C	3	0	0.0%
	Hb	F	2	0	0.0%
	Total		5	0	0.0%
Rumpus Hanover	Hb	C	1	0	0.0%
Run The Table	Hb	C	11	1	9.1%
	Lex	C	3	0	0.0%
		C	14	1	7.1%
	Hb	F	8	0	0.0%
	Lex	F	3	0	0.0%
		F	11	0	0.0%
	Total		25	1	4.0%
Rustler Hanover	Hb	C	5	1	20.0%
	Hb	F	4	0	0.0%
	Lex	F	2	0	0.0%
		F	6	0	0.0%
	Total		11	1	9.1%
SJ's Photo	Hb	C	22	0	0.0%
	Lex	C	13	2	15.4%
		C	35	2	5.7%
	Hb	F	26	1	3.8%
	Lex	F	16	1	6.3%
		F	42	2	4.8%
	Total		77	4	5.2%
Safe N Rich	Hb	F	1	0	0.0%
Samadhi	Lex	C	1	0	0.0%
San Pellegrino	Lex	F	1	0	0.0%
Schimitar	Lex	F	1	0	0.0%
Scoot Herb	Hb	F	1	0	0.0%
Seahawk Hanover	Lex	F	1	0	0.0%
Sealed N Delivered	Hb	C	5	1	20.0%
Self Possessed	Hb	C	13	2	15.4%
	Lex	C	20	2	10.0%
		C	33	4	12.1%
	Hb	F	15	3	20.0%
	Lex	F	20	1	5.0%

Broodmare Sire	Sale	Sex	Sold	$50,000 2 Year Olds	Success Rate
		F	35	4	11.4%
	Total		68	8	11.8%
Shady Character	Hb	C	2	0	0.0%
	Lex	C	2	0	0.0%
		C	4	0	0.0%
	Hb	F	1	0	0.0%
	Lex	F	1	0	0.0%
		F	2	0	0.0%
	Total		6	0	0.0%
Sierra Kosmos	Hb	C	26	0	0.0%
	Lex	C	11	3	27.3%
		C	37	3	8.1%
	Hb	F	28	2	7.1%
	Lex	F	11	0	0.0%
		F	39	2	5.1%
	Total		76	5	6.6%
Silent Majority	Lex	C	2	0	0.0%
	Lex	F	2	0	0.0%
	Total		4	0	0.0%
Silver Almahurst	**Lex**	**C**	**1**	**0**	**0.0%**
Sir Taurus	Hb	C	10	2	20.0%
	Lex	C	5	0	0.0%
		C	15	2	13.3%
	Hb	F	9	2	22.2%
	Lex	F	3	0	0.0%
		F	12	2	16.7%
	Total		27	4	14.8%
SJ's Caviar	Hb	C	5	2	40.0%
	Lex	C	4	1	25.0%
		C	9	3	33.3%
	Hb	F	6	1	16.7%
	Lex	F	2	0	0.0%
		F	8	1	12.5%
	Total		17	4	23.5%
Slapstick	**Hb**	**F**	**1**	**0**	**0.0%**
Sonsam	Hb	C	1	0	0.0%
	Hb	F	3	0	0.0%
	Total		4	0	0.0%

Broodmare Sire	Sale	Sex	Sold	$50,000 2 Year Olds	Success Rate
Speed Bowl	Hb	F	1	0	0.0%
Speed In Action	Hb	F	1	0	0.0%
Speedy Crown	Hb	C	9	1	11.1%
	Lex	C	20	0	0.0%
		C	29	1	3.4%
	Hb	F	11	0	0.0%
	Lex	F	10	0	0.0%
		F	21	0	0.0%
	Total		50	1	2.0%
Speedy Primo	Hb	F	1	0	0.0%
Speedy Somolli	Hb	C	1	0	0.0%
	Lex	C	1	0	0.0%
		C	2	0	0.0%
	Lex	F	1	0	0.0%
	Total		3	0	0.0%
Sportsmaster	Hb	C	3	0	0.0%
	Lex	C	2	1	50.0%
		C	5	1	20.0%
	Hb	F	3	0	0.0%
	Lex	F	1	0	0.0%
		F	4	0	0.0%
	Total		9	1	11.1%
Stand Forever	Lex	F	2	0	0.0%
Storm Compensation	Hb	F	2	0	0.0%
Storm Damage	Hb	C	3	0	0.0%
	Lex	C	1	0	0.0%
		C	4	0	0.0%
	Hb	F	2	0	0.0%
	Total		6	0	0.0%
Striking Sahbra	Hb	C	13	1	7.7%
	Lex	C	9	0	0.0%
		C	22	1	4.5%
	Hb	F	15	2	13.3%
	Lex	F	4	0	0.0%
		F	19	2	10.5%
	Total		41	3	7.3%
Sturdy Sahbra	Lex	F	2	0	0.0%
Super Ben Joe	Lex	F	2	0	0.0%

Broodmare Sire	Sale	Sex	Sold	$50,000 2 Year Olds	Success Rate
Super Bowl	Hb	C	20	2	10.0%
	Lex	C	13	0	0.0%
		C	33	2	6.1%
	Hb	F	17	1	5.9%
	Lex	F	12	0	0.0%
		F	29	1	3.4%
	Total		62	3	4.8%
Super Pleasure	Hb	C	5	0	0.0%
	Lex	C	1	0	0.0%
		C	6	0	0.0%
	Hb	F	3	0	0.0%
	Total		9	0	0.0%
Supergill	Hb	C	16	0	0.0%
	Lex	C	14	1	7.1%
		C	30	1	3.3%
	Hb	F	9	0	0.0%
	Lex	F	6	1	16.7%
		F	15	1	6.7%
	Total		45	2	4.4%
Survivor Gold	Hb	C	2	0	0.0%
Sydney Hill	Lex	C	1	0	0.0%
Tabor Lobell	Hb	C	1	0	0.0%
	Lex	C	1	0	0.0%
		C	2	0	0.0%
	Lex	F	1	0	0.0%
	Total		3	0	0.0%
Tagliabue	Hb	C	7	1	14.3%
	Lex	C	12	3	25.0%
		C	19	4	21.1%
	Hb	F	5	0	0.0%
	Lex	F	6	0	0.0%
		F	11	0	0.0%
	Total		30	4	13.3%
The Big Dog	Lex	C	2	0	0.0%
	Hb	F	1	0	0.0%
	Total		3	0	0.0%
The Panderosa	Hb	C	30	1	3.3%
	Lex	C	7	1	14.3%

Broodmare Sire	Sale	Sex	Sold	$50,000 2 Year Olds	Success Rate
		C	37	2	5.4%
	Hb	F	25	3	12.0%
	Lex	F	8	1	12.5%
		F	33	4	12.1%
	Total		70	6	**8.6%**
Thirty Two	Hb	C	3	1	33.3%
	Lex	C	1	0	0.0%
	Total		4	1	**25.0%**
Three Wizzards	**Hb**	**C**	**1**	**0**	**0.0%**
Threefold	Hb	C	1	0	0.0%
	Lex	C	2	0	0.0%
	Total		3	0	**0.0%**
Till We Meet Again	**Lex**	**C**	**1**	**0**	**0.0%**
Tom Ridge	Hb	C	1	0	0.0%
	Hb	F	1	0	0.0%
	Total		2	0	**0.0%**
Tooter Scooter	**Lex**	**F**	**1**	**0**	**0.0%**
Topnotcher	**Hb**	**C**	**2**	**0**	**0.0%**
Totally Ruthless	Hb	C	1	0	0.0%
	Lex	C	1	0	0.0%
	Total		2	0	**0.0%**
Town Escort	**Hb**	**C**	**2**	**0**	**0.0%**
Towner's Big Guy	Hb	C	2	0	0.0%
	Lex	C	3	0	0.0%
	Total		5	0	**0.0%**
Troublemaker	Hb	C	2	0	0.0%
	Lex	C	2	0	0.0%
		C	4	0	0.0%
	Hb	F	1	0	0.0%
	Lex	F	1	0	0.0%
		F	2	0	0.0%
	Total		6	0	**0.0%**
Tyler B	Hb	C	7	0	0.0%
	Hb	F	6	0	0.0%
	Lex	F	3	0	0.0%
		F	9	0	0.0%
	Total		16	0	**0.0%**
Tyler's Mark	Hb	C	2	0	0.0%

Broodmare Sire	Sale	Sex	Sold	$50,000 2 Year Olds	Success Rate
	Hb	F	3	0	0.0%
	Lex	F	2	1	50.0%
		F	5	1	20.0%
	Total		7	1	14.3%
Uno Atout	Hb	C	1	0	0.0%
	Hb	F	1	0	0.0%
	Total		2	0	0.0%
Valley Victor	Hb	C	2	0	0.0%
	Lex	C	1	0	0.0%
		C	3	0	0.0%
	Hb	F	2	0	0.0%
	Lex	F	1	1	100.0%
		F	3	1	33.3%
	Total		6	1	16.7%
Valley Victory	Hb	C	31	2	6.5%
	Lex	C	35	3	8.6%
		C	66	5	7.6%
	Hb	F	28	3	10.7%
	Lex	F	18	0	0.0%
		F	46	3	6.5%
	Total		112	8	7.1%
Valleymeister	Hb	F	1	0	0.0%
Vaporize	Lex	C	1	0	0.0%
Varenne	Lex	C	3	0	0.0%
Victory Dream	Hb	C	7	0	0.0%
	Lex	C	9	2	22.2%
		C	16	2	12.5%
	Hb	F	1	0	0.0%
	Lex	F	4	0	0.0%
		F	5	0	0.0%
	Total		21	2	9.5%
Village Connection	Lex	F	1	0	0.0%
Village Jasper	Hb	C	1	0	0.0%
	Lex	F	2	0	0.0%
	Total		3	0	0.0%
Village Jiffy	Hb	C	1	0	0.0%
	Lex	C	1	0	0.0%
		C	2	0	0.0%

Broodmare Sire	Sale	Sex	Sold	$50,000 2 Year Olds	Success Rate
	Hb	F	1	0	0.0%
	Lex	F	3	0	0.0%
		F	4	0	0.0%
	Total		6	0	0.0%
Village Jove	**Hb**	**C**	**1**	**0**	**0.0%**
Vision's Pride	Lex	C	1	0	0.0%
	Lex	F	4	0	0.0%
	Total		5	0	0.0%
Wall Street Banker	Lex	C	3	0	0.0%
	Hb	F	1	0	0.0%
	Total		4	0	0.0%
Walton Hanover	Hb	C	8	1	12.5%
	Hb	F	4	1	25.0%
	Total		12	2	16.7%
Wesgate Crown	Hb	C	4	0	0.0%
	Lex	C	1	0	0.0%
		C	5	0	0.0%
	Lex	F	2	0	0.0%
	Total		7	0	0.0%
Western Hanover	Hb	C	90	7	7.8%
	Lex	C	50	7	14.0%
		C	140	14	10.0%
	Hb	F	98	8	8.2%
	Lex	F	35	1	2.9%
		F	133	9	6.8%
	Total		273	23	8.4%
Western Ideal	Hb	C	18	0	0.0%
	Lex	C	16	1	6.3%
		C	34	1	2.9%
	Hb	F	22	3	13.6%
	Lex	F	11	3	27.3%
		F	33	6	18.2%
	Total		67	7	10.4%
Workaholic	Hb	C	1	0	0.0%
	Lex	F	1	0	0.0%
	Total		2	0	0.0%
Worthy Bowl	**Hb**	**F**	**2**	**0**	**0.0%**
Yankee Glide	**Hb**	**C**	**26**	**2**	**7.7%**

Broodmare Sire	Sale	Sex	Sold	$50,000 2 Year Olds	Success Rate
	Lex	C	28	1	3.6%
		C	54	3	5.6%
	Hb	F	23	4	17.4%
	Lex	F	29	2	6.9%
		F	52	6	11.5%
	Total		106	9	8.5%
Yankee Paco	Hb	C	4	1	25.0%
	Lex	C	3	1	33.3%
		C	7	2	28.6%
	Hb	F	3	0	0.0%
	Lex	F	3	0	0.0%
		F	6	0	0.0%
	Total		13	2	15.4%
Total			5685	406	7.1%

Chapter 7: Sire-Broodmare Sire Crosses

Once again, our data is confined to the 5,685 yearlings sold at HB and LEX from 2008 to 2010. Therefore, a sire and broodmare sire combination that has failed to produce an elite two-year old from HB or LEX may have a connection outside of these venues.

The examination of crosses is an interesting exercise. In most cases the numbers are small and the individual Success Rates must be taken with a grain of salt. Let's look at some highlights contained in the next chart.

Take a look at one of today's great trotting sires, *Andover Hall*. Overall *Andover Hall* has an 11.4% Success Rate with 24 elite two-year olds out of 210 sold. With colts he has had 12 out of 121 for 9.9%. Of his 12 elite colts, 6 of them were out of *Donerail* and *Lindy Lane* mares. He was 3 out 14 (21.4%) with Donerail mares and 3 out of 12 (25%) with *Lindy Lane* mares. Conversely, *Andover Hall* colts have been 0 for 13 with *Valley Victory* mares and 0 for 8 with *Muscles Yankee* mares. These may not be gigantic samplings, but they certainly warrant consideration.

Art Major has matched well with *Camluck* mares. He has 5 elite performers from 17 sold—a 29.4% Success rate. But, he has been batting zero with *Cam Card Shark* mares at 0 for 13.

Credit Winner has had 6 yearlings sold out of mares by each of the following broodmare sires: Andover Hall, Garland Lobell and Mr Lavec. With each of them he's had 2 elite two-year olds for a 33.3% Success Rate. He's done well with Muscles Yankee mares, producing 4 elite performers from 21 for 19%. But, with *Self Possessed*, *SJ's Photo* and *Pine Chip,* he has been 0 for 9, 0 for 8, and 0 for 9 respectively.

New sire *Donato Hanover* seems to fancy *Self Possessed* mares. He has three elite two-year olds out of only six sold.

Ontario Sire *Mach Three* has three of his four elite performers from *Western Hanover* mares. In fact, only four *Mach Three–Western Hanover* yearlings have been sold at HB and LEX. Three have been elite performers.

I think it's important to review the overall Success Rates of the sire, broodmare sire, and the farm, in addition to the particular cross when considering any youngster.

Chart 1: Sire Bm Sire Crosses

Sire	Bm Sire	Sold	$50,000 2 Year Olds	Sex	Sale	Average Price
Allamerican Ingot	Abercrombie	1	0	C	Lex	$4,000
Allamerican Ingot	Albatross	1	0	C	Lex	9,000
Allamerican Ingot	Albert Albert	1	0	C	Lex	7,000
Allamerican Ingot	Artsplace	2	0	C	Lex	5,000
Allamerican Ingot	Artsplace	1	0	F	Lex	12,000
Allamerican Ingot	Beach Towel	1	0	C	Lex	7,000
Allamerican Ingot	Beach Towel	1	0	F	Lex	10,000
Allamerican Ingot	Cambest	1	0	F	Lex	9,000
Allamerican Ingot	Camluck	1	0	C	Lex	12,000
Allamerican Ingot	Cam's Card Shark	1	0	C	Lex	7,000
Allamerican Ingot	Die Laughing	1	0	C	Lex	32,000
Allamerican Ingot	Falcon Seelster	1	0	F	Lex	11,000
Allamerican Ingot	Grinfromeartoear	1	0	C	Lex	8,000
Allamerican Ingot	Jate Lobell	4	0	C	Lex	8,250
Allamerican Ingot	Jate Lobell	3	0	F	Lex	7,333
Allamerican Ingot	Life Sign	2	0	C	Lex	7,500
Allamerican Ingot	Life Sign	1	0	F	Lex	6,000
Allamerican Ingot	Northern Luck	2	0	C	Lex	21,000
Allamerican Ingot	Northern Luck	1	0	F	Lex	15,000
Allamerican Ingot	Presidential Ball	1	0	F	Lex	2,000
Allamerican Native	Abercrombie	2	0	C	Hb	7,750
Allamerican Native	Abercrombie	2	0	F	Hb	12,500
Allamerican Native	Abercrombie	2	0	F	Lex	24,000
Allamerican Native	Allamerican Ingot	1	0	F	Lex	12,000
Allamerican Native	Artsplace	1	0	C	Hb	1,500
Allamerican Native	Artsplace	1	1	C	Lex	34,000
Allamerican Native	Artsplace	2	0	F	Hb	19,000
Allamerican Native	Bettor's Delight	1	0	F	Hb	20,000
Allamerican Native	Big Towner	1	0	C	Hb	20,000
Allamerican Native	Call For Rain	1	0	F	Hb	12,000
Allamerican Native	Cambest	1	0	C	Hb	10,000
Allamerican Native	Cambest	2	0	F	Hb	15,000
Allamerican Native	Cambest	1	0	F	Lex	47,000
Allamerican Native	Cam's Card Shark	3	0	C	Hb	16,000
Allamerican Native	Die Laughing	1	0	C	Hb	5,500
Allamerican Native	Falcon Seelster	2	0	C	Hb	22,500
Allamerican Native	Flight Of Fire	1	0	C	Hb	3,000
Allamerican Native	Forrest Skipper	1	0	C	Hb	1,000
Allamerican Native	Goalie Jeff	1	0	F	Hb	6,500

Sire	Bm Sire	Sold	$50,000 2 Year Olds	Sex	Sale	Average Price
Allamerican Native	Grinfromeartoear	1	0	C	Lex	2,000
Allamerican Native	Island Fantasy	1	0	C	Lex	2,000
Allamerican Native	Jaguar Spur	1	0	C	Hb	5,000
Allamerican Native	Jate Lobell	2	0	C	Hb	8,000
Allamerican Native	Jate Lobell	2	0	F	Lex	10,500
Allamerican Native	Life Sign	3	0	F	Hb	33,667
Allamerican Native	Life Sign	1	0	F	Lex	6,000
Allamerican Native	Marauder	1	0	C	Hb	8,000
Allamerican Native	Matt's Scooter	2	0	F	Hb	26,000
Allamerican Native	No Nukes	1	0	C	Hb	10,000
Allamerican Native	No Nukes	4	1	F	Hb	27,500
Allamerican Native	Northern Luck	2	0	C	Lex	15,000
Allamerican Native	Northern Luck	1	0	F	Lex	4,000
Allamerican Native	Precious Bunny	1	0	C	Lex	2,000
Allamerican Native	Run The Table	1	0	F	Hb	11,000
Allamerican Native	Rustler Hanover	1	0	C	Hb	14,000
Allamerican Native	Rustler Hanover	1	0	F	Hb	6,500
Allamerican Native	Sealed N Delivered	1	0	C	Hb	40,000
Allamerican Native	The Panderosa	1	0	C	Hb	4,500
Allamerican Native	The Panderosa	2	1	F	Hb	9,000
Allamerican Native	Troublemaker	1	0	F	Hb	9,000
Allamerican Native	Tyler B	1	0	C	Hb	9,000
Allamerican Native	Tyler B	1	0	F	Hb	6,500
Allamerican Native	Tyler's Mark	1	0	F	Hb	7,000
Allamerican Native	Walton Hanover	1	1	F	Hb	17,000
Allamerican Native	Western Hanover	2	0	C	Hb	17,750
Allamerican Native	Western Hanover	3	0	F	Hb	19,500
Allamerican Native	Western Hanover	3	0	F	Lex	12,333
Allamerican Native	Western Ideal	1	0	F	Hb	5,000
Allstar Hall	Donerail	1	0	C	Lex	8,000
American Ideal	Abercrombie	1	0	C	Hb	57,000
American Ideal	Abercrombie	2	0	F	Hb	16,500
American Ideal	Abercrombie	3	0	F	Lex	17,333
American Ideal	Albert Albert	1	0	C	Hb	15,000
American Ideal	Ameripan Gigolo	1	0	C	Lex	85,000
American Ideal	Art Major	2	1	C	Hb	53,500
American Ideal	Art Major	1	0	F	Hb	3,000
American Ideal	Artiscape	2	0	C	Hb	57,500
American Ideal	Artiscape	1	0	F	Lex	10,000
American Ideal	Artsplace	6	0	C	Hb	21,667
American Ideal	Artsplace	6	1	C	Lex	72,833

Sire	Bm Sire	Sold	$50,000 2 Year Olds	Sex	Sale	Average Price
American Ideal	Artsplace	4	0	F	Hb	9,625
American Ideal	Artsplace	5	0	F	Lex	23,400
American Ideal	Arturo	1	0	F	Lex	10,000
American Ideal	Beach Towel	1	0	C	Hb	27,000
American Ideal	Bettor's Delight	1	0	C	Hb	15,000
American Ideal	Bettor's Delight	1	0	F	Hb	32,000
American Ideal	Broadway Jate	1	0	C	Hb	10,000
American Ideal	Cam Fella	1	0	C	Hb	20,000
American Ideal	Cambest	2	0	C	Hb	30,000
American Ideal	Cambest	1	0	C	Lex	22,000
American Ideal	Cambest	2	0	F	Hb	21,250
American Ideal	Camluck	2	0	C	Hb	11,250
American Ideal	Camluck	1	0	C	Lex	9,000
American Ideal	Camluck	1	0	F	Hb	20,000
American Ideal	Cam's Card Shark	5	1	C	Hb	38,400
American Ideal	Cam's Card Shark	1	0	F	Hb	12,000
American Ideal	Cole Muffler	1	0	F	Hb	6,500
American Ideal	David's Pass	1	0	F	Lex	19,000
American Ideal	Dragon Again	1	0	C	Hb	45,000
American Ideal	Dragon's Lair	1	0	C	Lex	30,000
American Ideal	Falcon Seelster	1	0	C	Hb	37,000
American Ideal	Falcon Seelster	1	0	C	Lex	57,000
American Ideal	Falcon Seelster	2	1	F	Hb	60,000
American Ideal	Grinfromeartoear	1	0	C	Hb	4,000
American Ideal	Grinfromeartoear	1	0	C	Lex	32,000
American Ideal	Jate Lobell	1	0	C	Hb	35,000
American Ideal	Jate Lobell	1	1	F	Lex	75,000
American Ideal	Jenna's Beach Boy	2	1	C	Hb	57,500
American Ideal	Jeremys Gambit	1	0	C	Lex	9,000
American Ideal	Laag	1	0	F	Hb	11,000
American Ideal	Life Sign	4	1	C	Hb	10,000
American Ideal	Life Sign	3	0	F	Hb	33,333
American Ideal	Magical Mike	2	1	F	Lex	20,000
American Ideal	No Nukes	1	1	C	Hb	19,000
American Ideal	No Nukes	2	0	C	Lex	39,000
American Ideal	No Nukes	1	0	F	Hb	54,000
American Ideal	No Nukes	2	0	F	Lex	14,000
American Ideal	On The Road Again	1	0	F	Hb	7,000
American Ideal	Oxford Fella	1	0	F	Lex	7,000
American Ideal	Pacific Fella	1	0	F	Hb	40,000
American Ideal	Precious Bunny	1	0	F	Lex	10,000

Sire	Bm Sire	Sold	$50,000 2 Year Olds	Sex	Sale	Average Price
American Ideal	Presidential Ball	1	0	C	Lex	60,000
American Ideal	Presidential Ball	2	0	F	Hb	18,000
American Ideal	Pro Bono Best	1	0	C	Hb	60,000
American Ideal	Real Artist	1	0	C	Hb	35,000
American Ideal	Riyadh	1	0	F	Hb	27,000
American Ideal	Riyadh	1	0	F	Lex	10,000
American Ideal	Run The Table	1	0	C	Lex	4,000
American Ideal	Sealed N Delivered	3	1	C	Hb	29,000
American Ideal	Storm Damage	2	0	F	Hb	7,750
American Ideal	Three Wizzards	1	0	C	Hb	30,000
American Winner	Vision's Pride	1	0	F	Lex	26,000
Amigo Hall	American Winner	1	0	F	Lex	6,000
Amigo Hall	Angus Hall	1	0	F	Hb	35,000
Amigo Hall	Conway Hall	1	0	F	Hb	19,000
Amigo Hall	Crowning Point	1	0	C	Lex	12,000
Amigo Hall	Garland Lobell	1	0	C	Hb	30,000
Amigo Hall	SJ's Photo	1	0	C	Lex	22,000
Amigo Hall	Sir Taurus	1	0	F	Hb	12,000
Amigo Hall	Speedy Crown	1	0	C	Lex	12,000
Amigo Hall	Supergill	1	0	C	Lex	37,000
Amigo Hall	Yankee Paco	1	0	F	Hb	12,000
Andover Hall	American Winner	2	0	C	Lex	46,000
Andover Hall	American Winner	1	0	F	Hb	22,000
Andover Hall	Armbro Goal	1	0	F	Hb	43,000
Andover Hall	Armbro Goal	1	1	F	Lex	30,000
Andover Hall	Balanced Image	2	0	C	Hb	16,500
Andover Hall	Balanced Image	2	0	C	Lex	38,500
Andover Hall	Balanced Image	5	1	F	Hb	32,800
Andover Hall	Balanced Image	4	0	F	Lex	58,250
Andover Hall	Coktail Jet	1	0	F	Lex	110,000
Andover Hall	Credit Winner	2	0	C	Hb	62,500
Andover Hall	Credit Winner	1	0	C	Lex	110,000
Andover Hall	Credit Winner	2	1	F	Lex	61,000
Andover Hall	Crowning Point	1	0	C	Hb	20,000
Andover Hall	Crowning Point	1	0	F	Lex	50,000
Andover Hall	Cumin	1	0	C	Lex	17,000
Andover Hall	Dancer's Victory	1	0	F	Hb	9,500
Andover Hall	Defiant Yankee	1	1	F	Hb	40,000
Andover Hall	Donerail	6	1	C	Hb	36,667
Andover Hall	Donerail	8	2	C	Lex	62,750
Andover Hall	Donerail	13	2	F	Hb	83,154

Sire	Bm Sire	Sold	$50,000 2 Year Olds	Sex	Sale	Average Price
Andover Hall	Donerail	6	0	F	Lex	40,667
Andover Hall	Dream Of Glory	1	1	C	Hb	25,000
Andover Hall	Dream Vacation	1	0	C	Hb	85,000
Andover Hall	Dream Vacation	2	1	C	Lex	60,500
Andover Hall	Dream Vacation	2	0	F	Hb	31,500
Andover Hall	Final Score	1	0	C	Lex	24,000
Andover Hall	Giant Hit	2	0	C	Hb	21,000
Andover Hall	Giant Victory	1	0	F	Hb	25,000
Andover Hall	King Conch	1	0	F	Lex	30,000
Andover Hall	Lindy Lane	9	2	C	Hb	93,667
Andover Hall	Lindy Lane	3	1	C	Lex	90,000
Andover Hall	Lindy Lane	5	2	F	Hb	44,000
Andover Hall	Mack Lobell	1	0	F	Lex	50,000
Andover Hall	Malabar Man	5	1	C	Hb	33,600
Andover Hall	Malabar Man	5	0	C	Lex	54,800
Andover Hall	Malabar Man	7	1	F	Hb	45,214
Andover Hall	Malabar Man	3	0	F	Lex	70,000
Andover Hall	Mr Lavec	1	0	C	Hb	9,000
Andover Hall	Mr Vic	1	0	C	Hb	8,000
Andover Hall	Mr Vic	2	0	C	Lex	21,000
Andover Hall	Mr Vic	1	0	F	Lex	90,000
Andover Hall	Muscles Yankee	6	0	C	Hb	63,500
Andover Hall	Muscles Yankee	2	0	C	Lex	37,500
Andover Hall	Muscles Yankee	6	0	F	Hb	47,833
Andover Hall	Muscles Yankee	2	1	F	Lex	51,000
Andover Hall	Pine Chip	3	0	C	Hb	20,667
Andover Hall	Pine Chip	3	0	C	Lex	44,000
Andover Hall	Pine Chip	1	0	F	Hb	14,000
Andover Hall	Pine Chip	2	1	F	Lex	127,500
Andover Hall	SJ's Photo	3	0	C	Hb	65,000
Andover Hall	SJ's Photo	3	0	F	Hb	42,000
Andover Hall	SJ's Photo	1	0	F	Lex	45,000
Andover Hall	Self Possessed	4	1	C	Lex	79,250
Andover Hall	Self Possessed	1	0	F	Hb	100,000
Andover Hall	Sierra Kosmos	1	0	F	Lex	40,000
Andover Hall	Sir Taurus	3	0	C	Hb	71,000
Andover Hall	SJ's Caviar	1	1	C	Hb	85,000
Andover Hall	Speedy Crown	2	0	C	Hb	9,750
Andover Hall	Speedy Somolli	1	0	C	Hb	10,000
Andover Hall	Striking Sahbra	1	0	C	Hb	42,000
Andover Hall	Striking Sahbra	1	0	C	Lex	12,000

Sire	Bm Sire	Sold	$50,000 2 Year Olds	Sex	Sale	Average Price
Andover Hall	Striking Sahbra	1	0	F	Hb	11,000
Andover Hall	Sturdy Sahbra	1	0	F	Lex	45,000
Andover Hall	Super Bowl	1	0	C	Hb	14,000
Andover Hall	Supergill	2	0	C	Hb	32,000
Andover Hall	Supergill	2	0	F	Hb	36,000
Andover Hall	Valley Victor	1	0	C	Hb	14,000
Andover Hall	Valley Victory	7	0	C	Hb	36,000
Andover Hall	Valley Victory	6	0	C	Lex	51,667
Andover Hall	Valley Victory	1	0	F	Hb	15,000
Andover Hall	Valley Victory	3	0	F	Lex	158,333
Andover Hall	Victory Dream	2	0	C	Hb	52,000
Andover Hall	Wall Street Banker	1	0	C	Lex	30,000
Andover Hall	Yankee Glide	9	1	C	Hb	94,556
Andover Hall	Yankee Glide	4	0	C	Lex	22,500
Andover Hall	Yankee Glide	3	1	F	Hb	83,333
Andover Hall	Yankee Glide	3	0	F	Lex	29,333
Angus Hall	American Winner	1	0	F	Lex	25,000
Angus Hall	Armbro Charger	2	0	C	Hb	45,000
Angus Hall	Armbro Goal	1	0	C	Hb	37,000
Angus Hall	Armbro Goal	1	0	C	Lex	11,000
Angus Hall	Armbro Laser	1	0	F	Lex	10,000
Angus Hall	Balanced Image	3	0	C	Hb	25,000
Angus Hall	Balanced Image	2	0	C	Lex	60,000
Angus Hall	Balanced Image	2	0	F	Hb	28,500
Angus Hall	Balanced Image	1	0	F	Lex	10,000
Angus Hall	Baltic Speed	1	0	C	Hb	27,000
Angus Hall	Baltic Speed	1	0	C	Lex	12,000
Angus Hall	Baltic Speed	1	0	F	Lex	35,000
Angus Hall	Catch A Thrill	1	0	C	Hb	20,000
Angus Hall	Credit Winner	1	0	F	Hb	55,000
Angus Hall	Crowning Point	1	0	F	Hb	40,000
Angus Hall	Crysta's Crown	2	0	F	Hb	17,000
Angus Hall	Cumin	1	0	F	Hb	32,000
Angus Hall	Dancer's Victory	1	0	F	Hb	25,000
Angus Hall	Donerail	1	0	C	Hb	10,000
Angus Hall	Donerail	1	0	C	Lex	35,000
Angus Hall	Donerail	4	0	F	Lex	24,500
Angus Hall	Dream Of Glory	1	0	F	Hb	23,000
Angus Hall	Dream Vacation	1	0	C	Hb	30,000
Angus Hall	Enjoy Lavec	1	0	C	Lex	150,000
Angus Hall	Imperial Victory	1	1	C	Lex	37,000

Sire	Bm Sire	Sold	$50,000 2 Year Olds	Sex	Sale	Average Price
Angus Hall	Jazz Cosmos	1	0	C	Hb	17,000
Angus Hall	King Conch	1	0	C	Hb	9,000
Angus Hall	King Conch	1	0	F	Hb	6,500
Angus Hall	King Conch	1	0	F	Lex	72,000
Angus Hall	Lindy Lane	3	1	C	Hb	17,667
Angus Hall	Lindy Lane	1	0	C	Lex	4,000
Angus Hall	Lindy Lane	2	0	F	Hb	60,000
Angus Hall	Lindy Lane	1	0	F	Lex	45,000
Angus Hall	Malabar Man	1	0	C	Hb	50,000
Angus Hall	Malabar Man	3	0	C	Lex	16,333
Angus Hall	Malabar Man	3	0	F	Hb	26,000
Angus Hall	Meadow Road	1	0	F	Hb	25,000
Angus Hall	Mr Lavec	3	0	C	Hb	39,333
Angus Hall	Mr Vic	2	0	C	Hb	52,500
Angus Hall	Mr Vic	2	0	F	Hb	58,500
Angus Hall	Muscles Yankee	1	0	C	Hb	22,000
Angus Hall	Muscles Yankee	1	0	C	Lex	50,000
Angus Hall	Muscles Yankee	2	0	F	Hb	11,500
Angus Hall	Pine Chip	1	0	C	Lex	25,000
Angus Hall	Pine Chip	3	0	F	Hb	53,333
Angus Hall	Pine Chip	1	0	F	Lex	17,000
Angus Hall	Royal Prestige	1	0	F	Hb	32,000
Angus Hall	Royal Troubador	1	0	F	Lex	15,000
Angus Hall	SJ's Photo	1	0	C	Hb	65,000
Angus Hall	SJ's Photo	4	1	C	Lex	30,500
Angus Hall	SJ's Photo	1	0	F	Hb	52,000
Angus Hall	San Pellegrino	1	0	F	Lex	25,000
Angus Hall	Self Possessed	1	1	F	Hb	40,000
Angus Hall	Self Possessed	1	0	F	Lex	30,000
Angus Hall	Sierra Kosmos	1	0	C	Hb	10,000
Angus Hall	Sierra Kosmos	1	0	F	Hb	55,000
Angus Hall	Speed Bowl	1	0	F	Hb	18,000
Angus Hall	Speedy Crown	2	0	C	Lex	25,000
Angus Hall	Speedy Crown	3	0	F	Hb	37,667
Angus Hall	Speedy Crown	1	0	F	Lex	15,000
Angus Hall	Striking Sahbra	1	0	C	Hb	70,000
Angus Hall	Sturdy Sahbra	1	0	F	Lex	42,000
Angus Hall	Super Bowl	1	0	C	Hb	12,000
Angus Hall	Super Bowl	1	0	F	Hb	42,000
Angus Hall	Super Bowl	1	0	F	Lex	20,000
Angus Hall	Super Pleasure	1	0	F	Hb	67,000

Sire	Bm Sire	Sold	$50,000 2 Year Olds	Sex	Sale	Average Price
Angus Hall	Supergill	2	0	C	Hb	63,500
Angus Hall	Supergill	1	0	C	Lex	35,000
Angus Hall	Uno Atout	1	0	C	Hb	30,000
Angus Hall	Valley Victor	1	0	C	Hb	75,000
Angus Hall	Valley Victory	3	0	C	Hb	45,667
Angus Hall	Valley Victory	2	0	C	Lex	40,000
Angus Hall	Valley Victory	1	0	F	Hb	7,000
Angus Hall	Valley Victory	3	0	F	Lex	37,333
Angus Hall	Yankee Glide	5	0	C	Lex	9,400
Angus Hall	Yankee Glide	4	0	F	Lex	34,750
Armbro Deuce	In The Pocket	1	0	C	Hb	5,000
Armbro Deuce	Life Sign	1	0	F	Hb	15,000
Armbro Deuce	No Nukes	1	0	F	Hb	5,000
Armbro Deuce	Tyler B	1	0	F	Lex	12,000
Armbro Deuce	Tyler's Mark	1	1	F	Lex	13,000
Art Major	Abercrombie	1	0	F	Lex	6,000
Art Major	Albert Albert	1	1	C	Hb	72,000
Art Major	Albert Albert	1	0	F	Hb	51,000
Art Major	Allamerican Ingot	1	1	C	Lex	60,000
Art Major	Amity Chef	1	0	F	Hb	25,000
Art Major	Badlands Hanover	1	0	C	Hb	23,000
Art Major	Beach Towel	2	1	C	Hb	19,500
Art Major	Bettor's Delight	3	0	C	Hb	27,667
Art Major	Bettor's Delight	3	0	C	Lex	57,333
Art Major	Bettor's Delight	3	0	F	Hb	30,667
Art Major	Bettor's Delight	1	0	F	Lex	30,000
Art Major	Big Towner	1	0	C	Lex	85,000
Art Major	Big Towner	1	0	F	Hb	30,000
Art Major	Blissful Hall	1	0	F	Hb	50,000
Art Major	Cam Terrific	1	0	C	Hb	8,000
Art Major	Cambest	3	0	C	Hb	44,667
Art Major	Cambest	4	1	C	Lex	63,000
Art Major	Cambest	3	2	F	Hb	41,667
Art Major	Camluck	5	1	C	Hb	55,000
Art Major	Camluck	3	1	C	Lex	50,667
Art Major	Camluck	5	1	F	Hb	33,200
Art Major	Camluck	4	2	F	Lex	39,750
Art Major	Cam's Card Shark	5	0	C	Hb	25,800
Art Major	Cam's Card Shark	3	0	C	Lex	29,667
Art Major	Cam's Card Shark	5	0	F	Hb	37,200
Art Major	Camtastic	2	0	F	Hb	48,500

Sire	Bm Sire	Sold	$50,000 2 Year Olds	Sex	Sale	Average Price
Art Major	Cole Muffler	2	0	C	Hb	43,500
Art Major	Cole Muffler	1	1	F	Hb	30,000
Art Major	David's Pass	1	0	C	Hb	42,000
Art Major	Dexter Nukes	1	0	C	Hb	30,000
Art Major	Dexter Nukes	3	0	F	Hb	39,667
Art Major	Die Laughing	1	0	C	Hb	25,000
Art Major	Die Laughing	4	0	F	Hb	23,000
Art Major	Die Laughing	1	0	F	Lex	25,000
Art Major	Direct Flight	1	0	F	Hb	2,500
Art Major	Dragon Again	2	1	C	Hb	66,000
Art Major	Dragon Again	2	0	F	Hb	31,000
Art Major	Dragon Again	1	1	F	Lex	47,000
Art Major	Dragon's Lair	2	0	F	Lex	37,500
Art Major	Falcon Almahurst	1	0	C	Hb	10,000
Art Major	Falcon Seelster	2	0	C	Hb	12,000
Art Major	Falcon Seelster	1	0	F	Hb	14,000
Art Major	Falcon Seelster	2	0	F	Lex	12,500
Art Major	Goalie Jeff	2	1	C	Hb	41,000
Art Major	Goalie Jeff	1	0	C	Lex	70,000
Art Major	Goalie Jeff	1	0	F	Hb	13,000
Art Major	Grinfromeartoear	1	0	C	Lex	30,000
Art Major	In The Pocket	2	1	C	Lex	37,500
Art Major	Jate Lobell	7	1	C	Hb	24,786
Art Major	Jate Lobell	3	1	C	Lex	43,000
Art Major	Jate Lobell	1	0	F	Hb	33,000
Art Major	Jate Lobell	4	2	F	Lex	41,250
Art Major	Jenna's Beach Boy	4	1	C	Hb	39,000
Art Major	Jenna's Beach Boy	4	0	F	Hb	39,250
Art Major	Jenna's Beach Boy	4	0	F	Lex	19,000
Art Major	Jeremys Gambit	1	0	C	Hb	17,000
Art Major	Kiev Hanover	1	0	F	Hb	25,000
Art Major	Laag	1	0	F	Hb	67,000
Art Major	Life Sign	2	0	C	Hb	12,500
Art Major	Life Sign	1	0	F	Lex	29,000
Art Major	Look Sharp	1	0	F	Hb	4,000
Art Major	Magical Mike	1	0	F	Hb	16,000
Art Major	Matt's Scooter	4	0	C	Hb	35,750
Art Major	Matt's Scooter	2	0	C	Lex	85,000
Art Major	Matt's Scooter	1	0	F	Hb	27,000
Art Major	Matt's Scooter	1	1	F	Lex	42,000
Art Major	Nihilator	1	0	C	Lex	17,000

Sire	Bm Sire	Sold	$50,000 2 Year Olds	Sex	Sale	Average Price
Art Major	Nihilator	1	0	F	Hb	20,000
Art Major	No Nukes	3	2	C	Hb	56,333
Art Major	No Nukes	4	0	C	Lex	46,250
Art Major	No Nukes	1	0	F	Hb	27,000
Art Major	No Nukes	4	0	F	Lex	44,750
Art Major	No Pan Intended	1	0	C	Hb	85,000
Art Major	Nobleland Sam	1	0	F	Lex	15,000
Art Major	Northern Luck	1	1	C	Lex	22,000
Art Major	Nuclear Siren	1	0	F	Lex	22,000
Art Major	On The Road Again	1	0	C	Hb	18,000
Art Major	On The Road Again	1	0	C	Lex	30,000
Art Major	On The Road Again	1	0	F	Hb	25,000
Art Major	Pacific Fella	1	0	C	Hb	55,000
Art Major	Pacific Fella	1	1	C	Lex	52,000
Art Major	Precious Bunny	1	0	C	Hb	16,000
Art Major	Precious Bunny	1	0	C	Lex	82,000
Art Major	Precious Bunny	1	0	F	Hb	40,000
Art Major	Presidential Ball	2	0	C	Hb	35,000
Art Major	Presidential Ball	1	0	C	Lex	62,000
Art Major	Pro Bono Best	1	0	C	Hb	30,000
Art Major	Real Desire	2	0	F	Hb	42,500
Art Major	Real Desire	1	1	F	Lex	30,000
Art Major	Run The Table	1	0	C	Hb	10,000
Art Major	Rustler Hanover	1	0	F	Lex	17,000
Art Major	Sealed N Delivered	1	0	C	Hb	28,000
Art Major	Sonsam	1	0	F	Hb	80,000
Art Major	Storm Damage	1	0	C	Hb	20,000
Art Major	The Panderosa	5	1	C	Hb	44,800
Art Major	The Panderosa	1	0	C	Lex	32,000
Art Major	The Panderosa	5	0	F	Hb	23,000
Art Major	Tyler's Mark	1	0	F	Hb	26,000
Art Major	Tyler's Mark	1	0	F	Lex	15,000
Art Major	Village Jasper	1	0	C	Hb	145,000
Art Major	Western Hanover	12	1	C	Hb	37,750
Art Major	Western Hanover	10	3	C	Lex	53,000
Art Major	Western Hanover	14	2	F	Hb	23,357
Art Major	Western Hanover	4	1	F	Lex	42,500
Art Major	Western Ideal	3	0	C	Hb	54,000
Art Major	Western Ideal	5	1	F	Hb	50,300
Art Major	Western Ideal	2	1	F	Lex	51,000
Artiscape	Abercrombie	1	0	C	Hb	25,000

Sire	Bm Sire	Sold	$50,000 2 Year Olds	Sex	Sale	Average Price
Artiscape	Abercrombie	1	0	F	Hb	7,000
Artiscape	Armbro Mackintosh	1	0	C	Lex	16,000
Artiscape	Bettor's Delight	1	0	C	Lex	40,000
Artiscape	Billy Dart	1	0	F	Hb	20,000
Artiscape	Call For Rain	1	0	F	Hb	20,000
Artiscape	Cam Fella	2	0	C	Hb	24,000
Artiscape	Cam Fella	1	0	F	Hb	33,000
Artiscape	Cambest	2	0	F	Hb	17,500
Artiscape	Camluck	1	0	C	Hb	32,000
Artiscape	Camluck	2	0	C	Lex	17,000
Artiscape	Camluck	3	0	F	Lex	5,667
Artiscape	Cam's Card Shark	1	0	C	Hb	30,000
Artiscape	Cam's Card Shark	2	0	C	Lex	15,000
Artiscape	Cam's Card Shark	2	0	F	Hb	8,500
Artiscape	Dexter Nukes	1	0	C	Lex	35,000
Artiscape	Direct Scooter	1	1	F	Lex	25,000
Artiscape	Dragon Again	1	0	C	Lex	35,000
Artiscape	Falcon Seelster	1	0	C	Hb	70,000
Artiscape	Falcons Future	1	0	C	Lex	20,000
Artiscape	Fortune Richie	1	0	F	Lex	10,000
Artiscape	Incredible Finale	1	0	F	Hb	32,000
Artiscape	Island Fantasy	1	0	C	Lex	21,000
Artiscape	Jamuga	1	0	F	Hb	12,000
Artiscape	Jate Lobell	4	0	C	Hb	33,750
Artiscape	Jate Lobell	1	0	F	Hb	4,500
Artiscape	Jate Lobell	1	0	F	Lex	7,000
Artiscape	Jenna's Beach Boy	1	0	C	Hb	17,000
Artiscape	Jenna's Beach Boy	1	0	F	Hb	1,000
Artiscape	Jenna's Beach Boy	1	0	F	Lex	10,000
Artiscape	Magical Mike	1	0	C	Hb	27,000
Artiscape	Magical Mike	1	0	C	Lex	19,000
Artiscape	Magical Mike	1	0	F	Hb	22,000
Artiscape	Masquerade	1	0	C	Lex	40,000
Artiscape	Matt's Scooter	1	0	C	Hb	80,000
Artiscape	Matt's Scooter	1	0	F	Hb	20,000
Artiscape	Matt's Scooter	1	0	F	Lex	35,000
Artiscape	Niatross	1	0	F	Hb	7,000
Artiscape	Nihilator	1	0	C	Lex	32,000
Artiscape	Nihilator	1	0	F	Hb	30,000
Artiscape	No Nukes	2	0	C	Hb	15,500
Artiscape	No Nukes	3	1	C	Lex	32,333

Sire	Bm Sire	Sold	$50,000 2 Year Olds	Sex	Sale	Average Price
Artiscape	No Nukes	1	0	F	Hb	30,000
Artiscape	No Nukes	3	0	F	Lex	15,667
Artiscape	Northern Luck	1	0	F	Hb	9,500
Artiscape	On The Road Again	1	0	C	Hb	100,000
Artiscape	On The Road Again	3	0	C	Lex	31,667
Artiscape	On The Road Again	1	0	F	Hb	60,000
Artiscape	Pacific Fella	2	0	C	Hb	32,500
Artiscape	Precious Bunny	1	0	F	Hb	7,000
Artiscape	Presidential Ball	3	0	C	Hb	12,667
Artiscape	Presidential Ball	1	0	F	Hb	25,000
Artiscape	Pro Bono Best	2	0	F	Hb	12,000
Artiscape	Richess Hanover	1	0	C	Lex	27,000
Artiscape	Slapstick	1	0	F	Hb	2,000
Artiscape	Storm Damage	1	0	C	Hb	17,000
Artiscape	The Panderosa	1	0	C	Hb	7,000
Artiscape	Totally Ruthless	1	0	C	Hb	22,000
Artiscape	Towner's Big Guy	1	0	C	Hb	12,500
Artiscape	Towner's Big Guy	1	0	C	Lex	3,000
Artiscape	Troublemaker	2	0	C	Hb	16,000
Artiscape	Troublemaker	1	0	C	Lex	21,000
Artiscape	Tyler B	1	0	C	Hb	25,000
Artiscape	Tyler's Mark	1	0	F	Hb	10,000
Artiscape	Village Jiffy	1	0	F	Hb	7,000
Artiscape	Village Jiffy	1	0	F	Lex	20,000
Artiscape	Village Jove	1	0	C	Hb	16,000
Artiscape	Western Hanover	4	0	C	Hb	30,000
Artiscape	Western Hanover	2	0	C	Lex	85,000
Artiscape	Western Hanover	1	0	F	Hb	22,000
Artiscape	Western Hanover	2	0	F	Lex	12,000
Artiscape	Western Ideal	2	0	C	Hb	9,750
Artiscape	Western Ideal	3	0	C	Lex	23,667
Artiscape	Western Ideal	2	0	F	Hb	10,500
Artiscape	Western Ideal	2	1	F	Lex	15,500
Artsplace	Armbro Wolf	1	0	C	Lex	8,000
Artsplace	Beach Towel	1	0	F	Hb	26,000
Artsplace	Big Towner	2	0	C	Hb	19,000
Artsplace	Cam Fella	1	0	C	Hb	50,000
Artsplace	Cam Fella	1	0	F	Hb	70,000
Artsplace	Camluck	1	0	C	Lex	22,000
Artsplace	Camluck	2	0	F	Lex	16,500
Artsplace	Cam's Card Shark	2	0	C	Hb	12,500

Sire	Bm Sire	Sold	$50,000 2 Year Olds	Sex	Sale	Average Price
Artsplace	Cam's Card Shark	1	0	C	Lex	25,000
Artsplace	Cam's Card Shark	1	1	F	Hb	10,000
Artsplace	Cam's Card Shark	1	0	F	Lex	25,000
Artsplace	Camtastic	1	0	C	Hb	45,000
Artsplace	Castleton Success	1	0	F	Hb	7,000
Artsplace	Cole Muffler	1	0	F	Hb	19,000
Artsplace	Dexter Nukes	1	0	C	Hb	20,000
Artsplace	Dexter Nukes	1	0	C	Lex	32,000
Artsplace	Die Laughing	1	0	C	Lex	182,000
Artsplace	Die Laughing	1	0	F	Hb	12,000
Artsplace	Direct Scooter	1	0	C	Lex	30,000
Artsplace	Dragon Again	1	0	C	Lex	150,000
Artsplace	Dragon's Lair	2	0	C	Hb	17,500
Artsplace	Falcon Seelster	1	0	C	Hb	9,000
Artsplace	Jate Lobell	2	1	C	Hb	38,500
Artsplace	Jate Lobell	2	0	C	Lex	77,500
Artsplace	Jate Lobell	3	0	F	Hb	29,000
Artsplace	Jate Lobell	4	1	F	Lex	39,250
Artsplace	Jenna's Beach Boy	1	0	F	Hb	15,000
Artsplace	Life Sign	1	0	C	Hb	11,000
Artsplace	Matt's Scooter	3	1	C	Hb	60,000
Artsplace	Matt's Scooter	1	0	F	Hb	35,000
Artsplace	Nihilator	1	0	C	Hb	52,000
Artsplace	No Nukes	3	0	C	Hb	19,333
Artsplace	No Nukes	1	0	C	Lex	10,000
Artsplace	No Nukes	4	0	F	Hb	23,750
Artsplace	No Nukes	2	0	F	Lex	26,500
Artsplace	Nuclear Siren	1	0	C	Hb	65,000
Artsplace	On The Road Again	1	0	C	Hb	20,000
Artsplace	On The Road Again	1	0	C	Lex	44,000
Artsplace	Presidential Ball	3	0	F	Hb	11,667
Artsplace	Presidential Ball	1	0	F	Lex	7,000
Artsplace	Sportsmaster	1	0	C	Hb	9,500
Artsplace	The Panderosa	2	0	C	Hb	22,500
Artsplace	The Panderosa	1	0	C	Lex	65,000
Artsplace	The Panderosa	2	0	F	Lex	15,500
Artsplace	Village Jiffy	1	0	F	Lex	45,000
Artsplace	Western Hanover	6	0	C	Hb	23,333
Artsplace	Western Hanover	3	0	C	Lex	51,667
Artsplace	Western Hanover	4	1	F	Hb	18,250
Artsplace	Western Hanover	2	0	F	Lex	27,500

Sire	Bm Sire	Sold	$50,000 2 Year Olds	Sex	Sale	Average Price
Artsplace	Western Ideal	1	0	C	Hb	50,000
Artsplace	Western Ideal	1	0	C	Lex	25,000
Artsplace	Western Ideal	1	0	F	Hb	14,000
Artsplace	Western Ideal	1	0	F	Lex	8,000
Astreos	Beach Towel	1	0	C	Lex	150,000
Astreos	Cambest	1	0	F	Hb	5,000
Astreos	Falcon Seelster	1	0	C	Hb	3,500
Astreos	Jate Lobell	2	1	C	Hb	35,000
Astreos	Laag	1	1	F	Hb	20,000
Astreos	No Nukes	1	0	C	Hb	14,000
Astreos	No Nukes	1	0	F	Hb	40,000
Astreos	Pacific Rocket	1	0	F	Hb	25,000
Astreos	Western Hanover	1	0	F	Hb	10,000
Badlands Hanover	Camluck	1	1	C	Hb	62,000
Badlands Hanover	Cam's Card Shark	1	1	C	Hb	38,000
Badlands Hanover	Falcon Seelster	1	0	F	Lex	20,000
Badlands Hanover	Goalie Jeff	1	0	F	Lex	5,000
Badlands Hanover	Matt's Scooter	1	0	F	Hb	19,000
Badlands Hanover	Topnotcher	1	0	C	Hb	75,000
Bettor's Delight	Abercrombie	3	0	C	Hb	36,333
Bettor's Delight	Abercrombie	2	0	C	Lex	18,000
Bettor's Delight	Abercrombie	2	0	F	Hb	27,500
Bettor's Delight	Abercrombie	1	0	F	Lex	24,000
Bettor's Delight	Andrel	1	1	C	Lex	35,000
Bettor's Delight	Artiscape	2	0	C	Hb	29,500
Bettor's Delight	Artiscape	1	0	C	Lex	65,000
Bettor's Delight	Artiscape	2	1	F	Hb	14,000
Bettor's Delight	Artiscape	2	0	F	Lex	57,500
Bettor's Delight	Artsplace	9	1	C	Hb	32,500
Bettor's Delight	Artsplace	5	0	C	Lex	67,400
Bettor's Delight	Artsplace	18	2	F	Hb	29,639
Bettor's Delight	Artsplace	7	0	F	Lex	92,286
Bettor's Delight	Arturo	1	0	C	Lex	150,000
Bettor's Delight	Ball And Chain	1	0	C	Lex	90,000
Bettor's Delight	Beach Towel	2	0	C	Hb	36,000
Bettor's Delight	Big Rube	1	0	C	Hb	31,000
Bettor's Delight	Big Rube	1	0	F	Hb	75,000
Bettor's Delight	Camtastic	1	0	C	Lex	30,000
Bettor's Delight	Cole Muffler	1	0	F	Hb	15,000
Bettor's Delight	Dexter Nukes	1	0	C	Lex	85,000
Bettor's Delight	Dexter Nukes	1	1	F	Lex	70,000

Sire	Bm Sire	Sold	$50,000 2 Year Olds	Sex	Sale	Average Price
Bettor's Delight	Die Laughing	1	0	F	Lex	35,000
Bettor's Delight	Dragon Again	1	0	C	Hb	15,000
Bettor's Delight	Dragon's Lair	1	0	C	Hb	65,000
Bettor's Delight	Dragon's Lair	1	0	C	Lex	30,000
Bettor's Delight	Dragon's Lair	1	0	F	Hb	35,000
Bettor's Delight	Dream Away	1	0	C	Hb	27,000
Bettor's Delight	Dream Away	2	0	F	Hb	31,500
Bettor's Delight	Dream Away	1	0	F	Lex	5,000
Bettor's Delight	Equitable	1	1	F	Lex	30,000
Bettor's Delight	Falcon Seelster	2	0	C	Hb	26,000
Bettor's Delight	Falcon Seelster	1	1	C	Lex	35,000
Bettor's Delight	Falcon Seelster	1	0	F	Hb	22,000
Bettor's Delight	Falcon Seelster	2	0	F	Lex	7,000
Bettor's Delight	Goalie Jeff	1	0	C	Lex	60,000
Bettor's Delight	Grinfromeartoear	2	0	F	Lex	16,000
Bettor's Delight	Historic	1	0	C	Lex	25,000
Bettor's Delight	Jate Lobell	4	1	C	Hb	45,500
Bettor's Delight	Jate Lobell	1	0	C	Lex	65,000
Bettor's Delight	Jate Lobell	8	0	F	Hb	41,000
Bettor's Delight	Jate Lobell	3	1	F	Lex	46,333
Bettor's Delight	Jenna's Beach Boy	2	0	C	Hb	39,500
Bettor's Delight	Jenna's Beach Boy	2	0	C	Lex	5,000
Bettor's Delight	Jenna's Beach Boy	3	0	F	Hb	33,667
Bettor's Delight	Jenna's Beach Boy	2	0	F	Lex	44,000
Bettor's Delight	Jk Outlaw	1	0	C	Hb	42,000
Bettor's Delight	Keystone Ore	1	0	F	Hb	3,000
Bettor's Delight	Life Sign	5	0	C	Hb	51,400
Bettor's Delight	Life Sign	6	3	C	Lex	69,500
Bettor's Delight	Life Sign	3	0	F	Hb	59,333
Bettor's Delight	Life Sign	4	0	F	Lex	43,500
Bettor's Delight	Magical Mike	2	0	C	Hb	46,000
Bettor's Delight	Magical Mike	1	0	F	Lex	27,000
Bettor's Delight	Matt's Scooter	1	0	F	Hb	90,000
Bettor's Delight	No Nukes	5	0	C	Hb	18,000
Bettor's Delight	No Nukes	3	0	C	Lex	17,667
Bettor's Delight	No Nukes	5	1	F	Hb	30,000
Bettor's Delight	Northern Luck	1	1	C	Hb	20,000
Bettor's Delight	Northern Luck	1	0	F	Hb	57,000
Bettor's Delight	Precious Bunny	1	0	C	Hb	6,500
Bettor's Delight	Precious Bunny	1	0	F	Hb	6,000
Bettor's Delight	Presidential Ball	1	0	C	Hb	25,000

Sire	Bm Sire	Sold	$50,000 2 Year Olds	Sex	Sale	Average Price
Bettor's Delight	Real Artist	1	0	C	Hb	10,000
Bettor's Delight	Real Artist	2	0	F	Hb	65,000
Bettor's Delight	Run The Table	1	0	C	Hb	45,000
Bettor's Delight	Run The Table	1	0	F	Hb	38,000
Bettor's Delight	Rustler Hanover	1	1	C	Hb	75,000
Bettor's Delight	Silent Majority	1	0	C	Lex	92,000
Bettor's Delight	Sonsam	1	0	C	Hb	19,000
Bettor's Delight	The Panderosa	3	0	C	Hb	24,667
Bettor's Delight	The Panderosa	1	0	C	Lex	26,000
Bettor's Delight	The Panderosa	2	0	F	Lex	14,500
Bettor's Delight	Tyler B	1	0	F	Hb	2,500
Bettor's Delight	Walton Hanover	2	0	F	Hb	45,000
Bettor's Delight	Western Hanover	11	2	C	Hb	60,545
Bettor's Delight	Western Hanover	1	1	C	Lex	35,000
Bettor's Delight	Western Hanover	8	2	F	Hb	55,000
Bettor's Delight	Western Hanover	1	0	F	Lex	52,000
Bettor's Delight	Western Ideal	2	0	C	Hb	48,500
Bettor's Delight	Western Ideal	4	0	C	Lex	59,250
Bettor's Delight	Western Ideal	1	0	F	Lex	32,000
Blissful Hall	Armbro Operative	1	0	C	Lex	17,000
Blissful Hall	Direct Scooter	1	0	F	Hb	9,000
Blissful Hall	Direct Scooter	1	0	F	Lex	7,000
Blissful Hall	Falcon Seelster	1	0	C	Lex	32,000
Blissful Hall	Laag	1	0	C	Lex	9,000
Blissful Hall	Matt's Scooter	1	0	C	Hb	13,000
Blissful Hall	No Nukes	1	0	F	Hb	6,500
Blissful Hall	No Nukes	1	0	F	Lex	8,000
Broadway Hall	American Winner	1	0	C	Lex	43,000
Broadway Hall	American Winner	1	0	F	Hb	25,000
Broadway Hall	Andover Hall	1	0	F	Lex	10,000
Broadway Hall	Angus Hall	1	0	C	Hb	10,000
Broadway Hall	Armbro Iliad	1	0	C	Lex	30,000
Broadway Hall	Armbro Laser	1	1	F	Lex	15,000
Broadway Hall	Arnies Exchange	1	0	C	Hb	25,000
Broadway Hall	Balanced Image	1	0	C	Hb	24,000
Broadway Hall	Balanced Image	1	0	C	Lex	7,000
Broadway Hall	Balanced Image	1	0	F	Hb	11,000
Broadway Hall	Baltic Speed	2	0	C	Hb	9,000
Broadway Hall	Carry The Message	1	0	C	Hb	25,000
Broadway Hall	Credit Winner	1	0	C	Lex	22,000
Broadway Hall	Credit Winner	1	0	F	Hb	32,000

Sire	Bm Sire	Sold	$50,000 2 Year Olds	Sex	Sale	Average Price
Broadway Hall	Dancer's Victory	1	0	C	Hb	19,000
Broadway Hall	Donerail	4	1	C	Hb	14,000
Broadway Hall	Donerail	1	0	C	Lex	17,000
Broadway Hall	Donerail	3	0	F	Hb	10,333
Broadway Hall	Donerail	4	0	F	Lex	14,750
Broadway Hall	Enjoy Lavec	1	0	F	Hb	8,000
Broadway Hall	Final Score	1	0	F	Hb	1,500
Broadway Hall	Giant Victory	1	1	F	Hb	1,500
Broadway Hall	Harmonious	1	0	F	Hb	3,500
Broadway Hall	Lindy Lane	3	0	C	Hb	23,167
Broadway Hall	Lindy Lane	1	0	C	Lex	50,000
Broadway Hall	Lindy Lane	3	0	F	Hb	21,333
Broadway Hall	Lindy Lane	1	0	F	Lex	17,000
Broadway Hall	Lindy's Crown	1	0	F	Hb	12,000
Broadway Hall	Malabar Man	4	0	C	Hb	28,750
Broadway Hall	Malabar Man	2	0	F	Hb	38,000
Broadway Hall	Malabar Man	1	0	F	Lex	10,000
Broadway Hall	Meadow Road	1	0	C	Hb	7,000
Broadway Hall	Mighty Crown	1	0	C	Hb	20,000
Broadway Hall	Mr Lavec	1	0	F	Lex	30,000
Broadway Hall	Mr Vic	1	0	C	Hb	5,000
Broadway Hall	Mr Vic	1	0	C	Lex	13,000
Broadway Hall	Muscles Yankee	4	0	C	Hb	10,500
Broadway Hall	Muscles Yankee	2	0	C	Lex	36,000
Broadway Hall	Muscles Yankee	3	1	F	Hb	16,333
Broadway Hall	Muscles Yankee	1	0	F	Lex	37,000
Broadway Hall	Pine Chip	1	0	F	Hb	19,000
Broadway Hall	Promising Catch	1	0	C	Hb	9,000
Broadway Hall	Promising Catch	2	0	F	Hb	21,000
Broadway Hall	SJ's Photo	1	0	C	Hb	15,000
Broadway Hall	SJ's Photo	4	0	F	Hb	26,050
Broadway Hall	Self Possessed	1	0	C	Hb	45,000
Broadway Hall	Self Possessed	1	0	F	Hb	20,000
Broadway Hall	Self Possessed	1	0	F	Lex	12,000
Broadway Hall	Sierra Kosmos	3	0	C	Hb	23,333
Broadway Hall	Sierra Kosmos	2	0	F	Hb	16,750
Broadway Hall	Speedy Crown	1	0	C	Hb	10,000
Broadway Hall	Speedy Crown	1	0	C	Lex	120,000
Broadway Hall	Speedy Crown	1	0	F	Hb	15,000
Broadway Hall	Speedy Crown	1	0	F	Lex	40,000
Broadway Hall	Striking Sahbra	1	0	C	Lex	8,000

Sire	Bm Sire	Sold	$50,000 2 Year Olds	Sex	Sale	Average Price
Broadway Hall	Super Bowl	1	0	C	Hb	8,000
Broadway Hall	Super Bowl	1	0	C	Lex	7,000
Broadway Hall	Supergill	1	0	C	Hb	25,000
Broadway Hall	Tagliabue	4	1	C	Hb	18,375
Broadway Hall	Tagliabue	2	0	F	Hb	14,500
Broadway Hall	Valley Victory	1	0	C	Hb	20,000
Broadway Hall	Valley Victory	4	0	F	Hb	12,375
Broadway Hall	Victory Dream	1	0	F	Lex	20,000
Broadway Hall	Yankee Glide	1	0	C	Hb	27,000
Broadway Hall	Yankee Glide	1	0	C	Lex	40,000
Broadway Hall	Yankee Glide	1	1	F	Hb	9,000
Broadway Hall	Yankee Glide	2	0	F	Lex	30,000
Cambest	Abercrombie	3	0	C	Lex	13,000
Cambest	Abercrombie	1	0	F	Lex	5,000
Cambest	Artsplace	1	0	C	Hb	40,000
Cambest	Artsplace	2	0	C	Lex	8,000
Cambest	Artsplace	4	1	F	Lex	17,500
Cambest	Big Towner	1	0	C	Lex	27,000
Cambest	Direct Scooter	1	0	C	Lex	34,000
Cambest	Dragon's Lair	1	0	F	Lex	6,000
Cambest	Falcon Seelster	1	0	C	Lex	10,000
Cambest	Falcon Seelster	1	0	F	Hb	5,500
Cambest	Jate Lobell	1	0	C	Hb	10,000
Cambest	Jate Lobell	2	0	C	Lex	20,000
Cambest	Jate Lobell	1	0	F	Lex	13,000
Cambest	Keystone Raider	1	0	C	Lex	12,000
Cambest	Laag	1	0	F	Hb	9,000
Cambest	Life Sign	1	0	C	Hb	3,500
Cambest	Life Sign	1	0	C	Lex	5,000
Cambest	Life Sign	2	0	F	Lex	8,500
Cambest	Magical Mike	1	0	F	Lex	20,000
Cambest	Matt's Scooter	1	0	F	Lex	9,000
Cambest	No Nukes	2	0	C	Hb	24,000
Cambest	No Nukes	2	0	C	Lex	22,500
Cambest	No Nukes	2	0	F	Lex	10,000
Cambest	Raven Hanover	1	0	F	Lex	7,000
Cambest	Ruffstuff Baker	1	0	F	Lex	30,000
Cambest	Troublemaker	1	0	C	Lex	15,000
Cambest	Village Jiffy	1	0	F	Lex	3,000
Cambest	Western Hanover	2	0	C	Lex	33,500
Cambest	Western Hanover	1	0	F	Lex	7,000

Sire	Bm Sire	Sold	$50,000 2 Year Olds	Sex	Sale	Average Price
Camluck	Abercrombie	3	0	C	Hb	34,000
Camluck	Abercrombie	1	0	F	Hb	25,000
Camluck	Albatross	1	1	F	Hb	4,000
Camluck	Apaches Fame	1	0	C	Hb	55,000
Camluck	Apaches Fame	1	0	C	Lex	29,000
Camluck	Artsplace	3	0	C	Hb	52,667
Camluck	Artsplace	12	0	F	Hb	33,583
Camluck	Artsplace	2	0	F	Lex	11,000
Camluck	Barberry Spur	1	0	C	Lex	37,000
Camluck	Beach Towel	1	0	F	Hb	32,000
Camluck	Big Towner	2	0	C	Hb	66,000
Camluck	Big Towner	1	0	F	Hb	6,000
Camluck	Big Towner	1	0	F	Lex	40,000
Camluck	Dragon Again	1	0	C	Lex	15,000
Camluck	Dragon's Lair	1	0	F	Lex	15,000
Camluck	Grinfromeartoear	1	0	F	Hb	40,000
Camluck	Jate Lobell	1	0	C	Hb	40,000
Camluck	Jate Lobell	2	0	C	Lex	102,500
Camluck	Jate Lobell	1	0	F	Hb	35,000
Camluck	Jate Lobell	1	0	F	Lex	5,000
Camluck	Jenna's Beach Boy	1	0	C	Hb	15,000
Camluck	Laag	1	0	C	Hb	30,000
Camluck	Laag	1	0	F	Lex	13,000
Camluck	Life Sign	3	0	C	Hb	75,000
Camluck	Life Sign	1	0	C	Lex	17,000
Camluck	Matt's Scooter	1	0	F	Hb	35,000
Camluck	No Nukes	1	0	C	Hb	65,000
Camluck	No Nukes	1	0	C	Lex	32,000
Camluck	No Nukes	1	0	F	Hb	20,000
Camluck	Pacific Rocket	2	0	C	Lex	25,000
Camluck	Presidential Ball	1	0	F	Hb	17,000
Camluck	Ralph Hanover	1	0	F	Hb	30,000
Camluck	Real Desire	1	0	C	Lex	15,000
Camluck	Run The Table	2	0	C	Hb	26,000
Camluck	Rustler Hanover	1	0	C	Hb	17,000
Camluck	Rustler Hanover	1	0	F	Hb	32,000
Camluck	Silver Almahurst	1	0	C	Lex	17,000
Camluck	The Panderosa	1	0	C	Hb	50,000
Camluck	The Panderosa	1	0	F	Hb	5,000
Camluck	Towner's Big Guy	1	0	C	Lex	45,000
Camluck	Walton Hanover	1	1	C	Hb	45,000

Sire	Bm Sire	Sold	$50,000 2 Year Olds	Sex	Sale	Average Price
Camluck	Western Hanover	5	0	C	Hb	59,200
Camluck	Western Hanover	1	1	C	Lex	60,000
Camluck	Western Hanover	3	0	F	Hb	31,333
Camluck	Western Ideal	1	0	C	Hb	20,000
Camluck	Western Ideal	1	0	C	Lex	22,000
Cam's Card Shark	Abercrombie	4	0	C	Hb	21,250
Cam's Card Shark	Abercrombie	1	0	C	Lex	24,000
Cam's Card Shark	Abercrombie	1	0	F	Lex	1,000
Cam's Card Shark	Albatross	1	0	C	Hb	5,500
Cam's Card Shark	Albatross	1	0	F	Lex	13,000
Cam's Card Shark	Armbro Emerson	1	0	C	Hb	9,000
Cam's Card Shark	Armbro Emerson	1	1	C	Lex	100,000
Cam's Card Shark	Artiscape	1	0	C	Hb	12,000
Cam's Card Shark	Artsplace	4	0	C	Hb	43,000
Cam's Card Shark	Artsplace	1	0	C	Lex	17,000
Cam's Card Shark	Artsplace	1	0	F	Hb	47,000
Cam's Card Shark	Artsplace	1	0	F	Lex	21,000
Cam's Card Shark	B.G's Bunny	1	0	F	Hb	3,000
Cam's Card Shark	Beach Towel	1	0	F	Hb	12,000
Cam's Card Shark	Beach Towel	1	0	F	Lex	7,000
Cam's Card Shark	Big Towner	1	0	F	Lex	9,000
Cam's Card Shark	David's Pass	1	0	F	Hb	1,500
Cam's Card Shark	Die Laughing	2	0	C	Hb	16,000
Cam's Card Shark	Die Laughing	1	0	F	Hb	18,000
Cam's Card Shark	Dragon Again	1	0	C	Hb	30,000
Cam's Card Shark	Dragon's Lair	1	0	F	Hb	5,000
Cam's Card Shark	Dragon's Lair	1	0	F	Lex	30,000
Cam's Card Shark	Dream Away	1	0	C	Hb	27,000
Cam's Card Shark	Falcon Seelster	1	0	C	Hb	14,000
Cam's Card Shark	Falcon Seelster	1	0	C	Lex	5,000
Cam's Card Shark	Falcon Seelster	1	0	F	Lex	6,000
Cam's Card Shark	Goalie Jeff	2	0	F	Lex	55,000
Cam's Card Shark	Island Fantasy	1	0	C	Hb	15,000
Cam's Card Shark	Island Fantasy	1	0	F	Hb	4,000
Cam's Card Shark	Jate Lobell	1	0	C	Hb	8,500
Cam's Card Shark	Jate Lobell	1	0	C	Lex	52,000
Cam's Card Shark	Jenna's Beach Boy	2	0	C	Lex	4,000
Cam's Card Shark	Jenna's Beach Boy	1	1	F	Hb	22,000
Cam's Card Shark	Jenna's Beach Boy	2	0	F	Lex	6,500
Cam's Card Shark	Kentucky Spur	1	0	F	Lex	10,000
Cam's Card Shark	Keystone Raider	1	0	C	Lex	6,000

Sire	Bm Sire	Sold	$50,000 2 Year Olds	Sex	Sale	Average Price
Cam's Card Shark	Laag	1	0	C	Lex	5,000
Cam's Card Shark	Laag	1	0	F	Hb	5,000
Cam's Card Shark	Landslide	1	0	C	Hb	45,000
Cam's Card Shark	Life Sign	7	0	C	Hb	33,714
Cam's Card Shark	Life Sign	3	0	C	Lex	20,667
Cam's Card Shark	Life Sign	2	0	F	Hb	27,500
Cam's Card Shark	Life Sign	1	0	F	Lex	3,000
Cam's Card Shark	Magical Mike	1	0	C	Hb	13,000
Cam's Card Shark	Matt's Scooter	1	0	C	Hb	35,000
Cam's Card Shark	Matt's Scooter	1	0	F	Hb	20,000
Cam's Card Shark	Niatross	1	0	C	Hb	12,000
Cam's Card Shark	Nihilator	1	0	C	Hb	17,000
Cam's Card Shark	No Nukes	5	2	C	Hb	44,000
Cam's Card Shark	On The Road Again	1	0	C	Hb	5,000
Cam's Card Shark	Real Desire	1	0	C	Hb	25,000
Cam's Card Shark	Run The Table	1	0	C	Hb	8,000
Cam's Card Shark	Sonsam	1	0	F	Hb	4,000
Cam's Card Shark	Stand Forever	1	0	F	Lex	8,000
Cam's Card Shark	The Panderosa	2	0	C	Hb	81,000
Cam's Card Shark	The Panderosa	3	1	F	Hb	15,000
Cam's Card Shark	Topnotcher	1	0	C	Hb	35,000
Cam's Card Shark	Walton Hanover	1	0	C	Hb	25,000
Cam's Card Shark	Western Hanover	7	2	C	Hb	50,000
Cam's Card Shark	Western Hanover	3	1	C	Lex	40,667
Cam's Card Shark	Western Hanover	8	0	F	Hb	17,938
Cam's Card Shark	Western Ideal	4	0	C	Hb	15,750
Cantab Hall	American Winner	3	0	C	Hb	39,000
Cantab Hall	American Winner	2	0	F	Lex	22,500
Cantab Hall	Andover Hall	2	0	C	Hb	31,000
Cantab Hall	Andover Hall	1	0	F	Hb	70,000
Cantab Hall	Angus Hall	2	0	C	Hb	28,500
Cantab Hall	Angus Hall	2	0	C	Lex	85,000
Cantab Hall	Angus Hall	3	0	F	Lex	31,000
Cantab Hall	Back Fin	1	0	F	Lex	30,000
Cantab Hall	Balanced Image	3	1	C	Hb	45,500
Cantab Hall	Balanced Image	4	0	F	Hb	21,000
Cantab Hall	Baltic Speed	1	0	F	Hb	25,000
Cantab Hall	Banker Hall	1	0	F	Hb	31,000
Cantab Hall	BJ's Mac	1	0	F	Hb	9,000
Cantab Hall	BJ's Mac	1	0	F	Lex	15,000
Cantab Hall	Chiola Hanover	1	0	C	Lex	120,000

Sire	Bm Sire	Sold	$50,000 2 Year Olds	Sex	Sale	Average Price
Cantab Hall	Conway Hall	1	0	C	Lex	19,000
Cantab Hall	Credit Winner	1	0	C	Hb	9,000
Cantab Hall	Credit Winner	1	0	F	Hb	14,000
Cantab Hall	Credit Winner	2	0	F	Lex	11,000
Cantab Hall	Crowning Point	2	0	C	Hb	49,000
Cantab Hall	Cumin	1	0	C	Lex	12,000
Cantab Hall	Cumin	1	0	F	Lex	15,000
Cantab Hall	Donerail	3	0	C	Hb	13,333
Cantab Hall	Donerail	5	0	C	Lex	28,800
Cantab Hall	Donerail	4	0	F	Hb	18,500
Cantab Hall	Donerail	1	0	F	Lex	52,000
Cantab Hall	Dream Vacation	2	0	C	Hb	22,500
Cantab Hall	Earl	1	1	C	Hb	30,000
Cantab Hall	El Paso Kash	1	0	F	Lex	37,000
Cantab Hall	Enjoy Lavec	6	2	C	Lex	43,500
Cantab Hall	Enjoy Lavec	1	0	F	Lex	27,000
Cantab Hall	Garland Lobell	2	0	C	Hb	15,500
Cantab Hall	Garland Lobell	2	1	F	Hb	39,000
Cantab Hall	Garland Lobell	1	0	F	Lex	40,000
Cantab Hall	Giant Hit	1	0	F	Hb	20,000
Cantab Hall	Giant Victory	1	0	C	Hb	20,000
Cantab Hall	Joie De Vie	1	0	F	Hb	9,000
Cantab Hall	Kadabra	1	0	C	Lex	85,000
Cantab Hall	King Conch	1	0	C	Hb	30,000
Cantab Hall	King Conch	1	0	F	Lex	65,000
Cantab Hall	Lemon Dra	1	1	F	Lex	8,000
Cantab Hall	Lindy Lane	5	1	C	Hb	71,800
Cantab Hall	Lindy Lane	1	0	C	Lex	17,000
Cantab Hall	Lindy Lane	4	1	F	Hb	47,500
Cantab Hall	Lindy Lane	2	0	F	Lex	23,500
Cantab Hall	Mack Lobell	2	0	C	Lex	28,500
Cantab Hall	Malabar Man	4	1	C	Hb	16,250
Cantab Hall	Malabar Man	2	0	C	Lex	43,500
Cantab Hall	Malabar Man	7	1	F	Hb	30,929
Cantab Hall	Malabar Man	3	0	F	Lex	37,667
Cantab Hall	Mr Lavec	1	0	C	Hb	6,500
Cantab Hall	Mr Lavec	2	0	F	Hb	10,000
Cantab Hall	Mr Vic	2	0	C	Lex	20,000
Cantab Hall	Mr Vic	2	0	F	Lex	41,000
Cantab Hall	Muscles Yankee	3	1	C	Hb	45,667
Cantab Hall	Muscles Yankee	4	0	F	Hb	32,375

Sire	Bm Sire	Sold	$50,000 2 Year Olds	Sex	Sale	Average Price
Cantab Hall	New Victory	1	0	C	Hb	20,000
Cantab Hall	Overcomer	1	0	C	Hb	6,500
Cantab Hall	Pine Chip	2	0	C	Hb	19,500
Cantab Hall	Pine Chip	3	0	C	Lex	40,667
Cantab Hall	Pine Chip	2	0	F	Hb	46,000
Cantab Hall	Pine Chip	9	1	F	Lex	43,778
Cantab Hall	Prakas	1	0	F	Hb	25,000
Cantab Hall	Royal Prestige	1	0	F	Hb	22,000
Cantab Hall	Royal Strength	1	0	C	Hb	15,000
Cantab Hall	Royal Troubador	2	0	C	Hb	20,000
Cantab Hall	Royal Troubador	2	1	C	Lex	65,000
Cantab Hall	SJ's Photo	1	0	C	Hb	12,000
Cantab Hall	SJ's Photo	1	0	C	Lex	10,000
Cantab Hall	SJ's Photo	2	0	F	Hb	16,500
Cantab Hall	SJ's Photo	3	0	F	Lex	34,000
Cantab Hall	Sierra Kosmos	4	0	C	Hb	8,375
Cantab Hall	Sierra Kosmos	2	0	F	Hb	21,000
Cantab Hall	Sir Taurus	1	0	F	Hb	13,000
Cantab Hall	Sir Taurus	1	0	F	Lex	35,000
Cantab Hall	SJ's Caviar	1	0	C	Lex	20,000
Cantab Hall	Speedy Crown	1	0	C	Hb	19,000
Cantab Hall	Speedy Crown	1	0	F	Hb	6,500
Cantab Hall	Striking Sahbra	1	0	C	Hb	17,000
Cantab Hall	Striking Sahbra	1	0	F	Hb	95,000
Cantab Hall	Striking Sahbra	1	0	F	Lex	60,000
Cantab Hall	Super Bowl	2	1	C	Hb	13,000
Cantab Hall	Super Bowl	3	0	F	Hb	23,333
Cantab Hall	Supergill	2	0	C	Hb	22,500
Cantab Hall	Supergill	2	0	C	Lex	22,500
Cantab Hall	Supergill	1	1	F	Lex	100,000
Cantab Hall	Tagliabue	1	0	C	Hb	10,000
Cantab Hall	Valley Victor	1	0	C	Lex	16,000
Cantab Hall	Valley Victory	3	0	C	Hb	21,333
Cantab Hall	Valley Victory	4	0	C	Lex	120,000
Cantab Hall	Valley Victory	4	1	F	Hb	19,500
Cantab Hall	Valley Victory	2	0	F	Lex	28,500
Cantab Hall	Varenne	1	0	C	Lex	25,000
Cantab Hall	Workaholic	1	0	C	Hb	8,000
Cantab Hall	Workaholic	1	0	F	Lex	50,000
Cantab Hall	Worthy Bowl	1	0	F	Hb	6,000
Cantab Hall	Yankee Glide	3	0	C	Hb	36,667

Sire	Bm Sire	Sold	$50,000 2 Year Olds	Sex	Sale	Average Price
Cantab Hall	Yankee Glide	3	0	C	Lex	61,667
Cantab Hall	Yankee Glide	3	1	F	Hb	47,333
Cantab Hall	Yankee Glide	2	0	F	Lex	37,500
Cash Hall	Angus Hall	1	0	F	Hb	18,000
Cash Hall	Balanced Image	1	0	F	Hb	10,000
Cash Hall	Cheyenne Spur	1	0	F	Hb	25,000
Cash Hall	Conway Hall	1	0	C	Hb	12,000
Cash Hall	Conway Hall	2	0	F	Hb	15,000
Cash Hall	Credit Winner	1	0	C	Hb	37,000
Cash Hall	Cumin	1	0	F	Hb	20,000
Cash Hall	Donerail	2	0	F	Hb	7,750
Cash Hall	Garland Lobell	1	1	C	Lex	30,000
Cash Hall	Garland Lobell	2	1	F	Hb	37,500
Cash Hall	Giant Victory	1	0	C	Hb	9,000
Cash Hall	Inquirer	1	0	F	Hb	14,000
Cash Hall	King Conch	1	0	C	Hb	10,000
Cash Hall	Like A Prayer	1	0	C	Hb	18,000
Cash Hall	Lindy Lane	2	0	C	Hb	13,250
Cash Hall	Malabar Man	2	0	C	Hb	24,250
Cash Hall	Malabar Man	1	0	F	Hb	19,000
Cash Hall	Malabar Man	1	0	F	Lex	10,000
Cash Hall	Muscles Yankee	1	0	C	Hb	20,000
Cash Hall	Pine Chip	1	0	C	Hb	6,500
Cash Hall	Pine Chip	1	0	C	Lex	15,000
Cash Hall	Pine Chip	1	0	F	Hb	10,000
Cash Hall	Royal Troubador	1	0	C	Hb	10,000
Cash Hall	Royal Troubador	1	0	F	Hb	7,000
Cash Hall	SJ's Photo	1	0	C	Hb	5,000
Cash Hall	SJ's Caviar	1	0	C	Lex	30,000
Cash Hall	Striking Sahbra	3	0	C	Hb	25,167
Cash Hall	Super Bowl	1	0	F	Hb	15,000
Cash Hall	Super Pleasure	1	0	C	Hb	25,000
Cash Hall	Valley Victory	1	0	C	Hb	47,000
Cash Hall	Valley Victory	1	1	F	Hb	5,000
Chip Chip Hooray	Balanced Image	1	0	C	Lex	26,000
Chip Chip Hooray	Balanced Image	1	0	F	Lex	8,000
Chip Chip Hooray	Conway Hall	1	0	F	Lex	10,000
Chip Chip Hooray	Power Seat	1	0	C	Lex	13,000
Chip Chip Hooray	SJ's Photo	1	0	F	Lex	14,000
Chip Chip Hooray	Sierra Kosmos	1	0	F	Lex	8,000
Chip Chip Hooray	Sir Taurus	1	0	C	Lex	7,000

Sire	Bm Sire	Sold	$50,000 2 Year Olds	Sex	Sale	Average Price
Chip Chip Hooray	Supergill	1	0	C	Lex	8,000
Chip Chip Hooray	Tabor Lobell	1	0	F	Lex	23,000
Chocolatier	Andover Hall	2	0	F	Lex	63,500
Chocolatier	Armbro Charger	1	0	F	Hb	1,500
Chocolatier	Armbro Charger	1	0	F	Lex	22,000
Chocolatier	Armbro Goal	1	0	C	Lex	19,000
Chocolatier	Armbro Goal	1	0	F	Hb	12,000
Chocolatier	Armbro Goal	1	0	F	Lex	35,000
Chocolatier	Balanced Image	1	0	C	Lex	10,000
Chocolatier	Balanced Image	2	0	F	Lex	17,000
Chocolatier	Broadway Hall	1	0	F	Hb	38,000
Chocolatier	Conway Hall	4	0	C	Hb	71,375
Chocolatier	Conway Hall	2	0	C	Lex	42,500
Chocolatier	Conway Hall	1	0	F	Hb	16,000
Chocolatier	Conway Hall	5	0	F	Lex	24,400
Chocolatier	Dancer's Victory	1	0	C	Hb	10,000
Chocolatier	Donerail	1	0	C	Hb	8,000
Chocolatier	Donerail	3	0	F	Hb	31,000
Chocolatier	Donerail	1	0	F	Lex	52,000
Chocolatier	Dream Vacation	1	0	C	Hb	5,000
Chocolatier	Dream Vacation	4	0	C	Lex	86,250
Chocolatier	Dream Vacation	1	0	F	Hb	35,000
Chocolatier	Dream Vacation	1	0	F	Lex	20,000
Chocolatier	Garland Lobell	2	0	C	Hb	60,000
Chocolatier	Garland Lobell	1	0	C	Lex	50,000
Chocolatier	Garland Lobell	1	0	F	Hb	18,000
Chocolatier	Giant Hit	2	0	F	Lex	7,500
Chocolatier	International Chip	1	0	F	Lex	15,000
Chocolatier	Lindy Lane	1	0	F	Lex	60,000
Chocolatier	Malabar Man	2	0	C	Hb	77,500
Chocolatier	Malabar Man	3	0	C	Lex	60,000
Chocolatier	Malabar Man	1	0	F	Hb	40,000
Chocolatier	Malabar Man	3	0	F	Lex	93,333
Chocolatier	Mr Lavec	1	0	C	Hb	35,000
Chocolatier	Mr Lavec	1	0	F	Hb	20,000
Chocolatier	Muscles Yankee	3	0	C	Hb	19,667
Chocolatier	Muscles Yankee	1	0	C	Lex	75,000
Chocolatier	Pine Chip	1	0	C	Hb	10,000
Chocolatier	Pine Chip	3	0	C	Lex	65,667
Chocolatier	Pine Chip	1	0	F	Hb	30,000
Chocolatier	Pine Chip	2	0	F	Lex	30,000

Sire	Bm Sire	Sold	$50,000 2 Year Olds	Sex	Sale	Average Price
Chocolatier	SJ's Photo	1	0	C	Hb	13,000
Chocolatier	Self Possessed	1	0	C	Lex	47,000
Chocolatier	Self Possessed	1	0	F	Lex	27,000
Chocolatier	Sierra Kosmos	1	0	F	Hb	45,000
Chocolatier	Sir Taurus	1	0	F	Lex	50,000
Chocolatier	Speedy Crown	1	0	C	Lex	50,000
Chocolatier	Super Bowl	1	1	C	Hb	35,000
Chocolatier	Tagliabue	1	0	C	Lex	20,000
Chocolatier	Valley Victory	1	0	C	Lex	10,000
Chocolatier	Valley Victory	1	0	F	Hb	22,000
Chocolatier	Varenne	1	0	C	Lex	8,000
Chocolatier	Victory Dream	1	0	F	Lex	22,000
Chocolatier	Yankee Glide	1	0	C	Hb	24,000
Chocolatier	Yankee Glide	1	0	C	Lex	65,000
Chocolatier	Yankee Glide	3	0	F	Hb	38,000
Classic Photo	Andover Hall	1	0	C	Hb	9,000
Classic Photo	Angus Hall	2	0	C	Lex	3,500
Classic Photo	Angus Hall	1	0	F	Lex	27,000
Classic Photo	Armbro Goal	1	0	C	Lex	8,000
Classic Photo	Balanced Image	3	0	C	Hb	34,000
Classic Photo	Balanced Image	1	0	C	Lex	12,000
Classic Photo	Balanced Image	1	0	F	Hb	10,000
Classic Photo	Baltic Speed	1	0	C	Lex	25,000
Classic Photo	Bonefish	1	0	C	Lex	6,000
Classic Photo	Catch A Thrill	1	1	C	Hb	45,000
Classic Photo	Conway Hall	1	0	C	Lex	2,000
Classic Photo	Conway Hall	3	0	F	Lex	3,333
Classic Photo	Donerail	3	0	C	Lex	8,667
Classic Photo	Donerail	1	0	F	Hb	19,000
Classic Photo	Donerail	4	0	F	Lex	10,000
Classic Photo	Dream Of Glory	1	0	F	Hb	10,000
Classic Photo	Enjoy Lavec	1	0	C	Hb	25,000
Classic Photo	Giant Hit	1	0	F	Lex	45,000
Classic Photo	Harmonious	1	0	C	Hb	12,000
Classic Photo	Imperial Victory	1	0	C	Lex	24,000
Classic Photo	Kick Tail	1	0	F	Hb	4,000
Classic Photo	Lindy Lane	1	0	C	Hb	10,000
Classic Photo	Lindy Lane	3	1	C	Lex	21,000
Classic Photo	Lindy Lane	2	0	F	Hb	13,500
Classic Photo	Lindy Lane	2	0	F	Lex	33,500
Classic Photo	Malabar Man	1	0	C	Hb	17,000

Sire	Bm Sire	Sold	$50,000 2 Year Olds	Sex	Sale	Average Price
Classic Photo	Malabar Man	1	0	C	Lex	6,000
Classic Photo	Meadowbranch Jerzy	1	0	F	Lex	5,000
Classic Photo	Mr Vic	1	0	C	Hb	6,500
Classic Photo	Mr Vic	3	0	C	Lex	18,000
Classic Photo	Mr Vic	1	0	F	Hb	2,500
Classic Photo	Muscles Yankee	2	1	C	Hb	20,750
Classic Photo	Muscles Yankee	1	0	C	Lex	20,000
Classic Photo	Muscles Yankee	3	0	F	Hb	8,000
Classic Photo	Muscles Yankee	2	0	F	Lex	5,500
Classic Photo	Nearly Perfect	1	0	F	Lex	22,000
Classic Photo	Pine Chip	1	0	C	Hb	2,500
Classic Photo	Pine Chip	1	0	C	Lex	97,000
Classic Photo	Pine Chip	1	0	F	Hb	6,000
Classic Photo	Pine Chip	2	0	F	Lex	8,000
Classic Photo	Royal Prestige	1	0	C	Hb	15,000
Classic Photo	Royal Strength	1	1	C	Lex	10,000
Classic Photo	Royal Troubador	1	0	C	Lex	4,000
Classic Photo	Self Possessed	3	1	C	Lex	14,000
Classic Photo	Self Possessed	1	0	F	Lex	10,000
Classic Photo	Sierra Kosmos	1	0	C	Lex	12,000
Classic Photo	Sierra Kosmos	1	0	F	Hb	1,000
Classic Photo	Speedy Crown	1	0	C	Hb	6,000
Classic Photo	Speedy Crown	1	0	F	Lex	6,000
Classic Photo	Supergill	2	0	C	Lex	3,000
Classic Photo	Supergill	1	0	F	Hb	70,000
Classic Photo	Valley Victory	3	0	C	Hb	14,333
Classic Photo	Valley Victory	3	0	C	Lex	20,333
Classic Photo	Valley Victory	3	0	F	Lex	9,667
Classic Photo	Victory Dream	1	0	C	Hb	10,000
Classic Photo	Victory Dream	2	0	C	Lex	10,000
Classic Photo	Victory Dream	1	0	F	Lex	6,000
Classic Photo	Wall Street Banker	1	0	C	Lex	12,000
Classic Photo	Wesgate Crown	1	0	F	Lex	5,000
Classic Photo	Yankee Glide	3	0	C	Lex	14,333
Classic Photo	Yankee Glide	2	0	F	Hb	3,000
Classic Photo	Yankee Glide	4	1	F	Lex	21,500
Conway Hall	American Winner	1	0	C	Hb	80,000
Conway Hall	American Winner	1	0	C	Lex	77,000
Conway Hall	American Winner	2	1	F	Hb	19,500
Conway Hall	Armbro Goal	2	0	C	Hb	38,500
Conway Hall	Armbro Goal	1	0	F	Hb	35,000

Sire	Bm Sire	Sold	$50,000 2 Year Olds	Sex	Sale	Average Price
Conway Hall	Armbro Goal	2	0	F	Lex	29,000
Conway Hall	Balanced Image	1	1	C	Lex	22,000
Conway Hall	Balanced Image	4	0	F	Hb	26,250
Conway Hall	Balanced Image	2	0	F	Lex	42,000
Conway Hall	Baltic Speed	1	0	C	Lex	50,000
Conway Hall	BJ's Mac	1	0	F	Hb	30,000
Conway Hall	Credit Winner	5	0	C	Hb	34,800
Conway Hall	Credit Winner	1	0	C	Lex	60,000
Conway Hall	Credit Winner	1	0	F	Hb	12,000
Conway Hall	Cumin	1	0	C	Lex	25,000
Conway Hall	Cumin	1	0	F	Lex	27,000
Conway Hall	Dancer's Victory	1	0	F	Hb	30,000
Conway Hall	Donerail	2	0	C	Hb	12,500
Conway Hall	Donerail	5	0	C	Lex	32,800
Conway Hall	Donerail	2	0	F	Hb	20,500
Conway Hall	Donerail	2	1	F	Lex	8,000
Conway Hall	Dream Of Glory	1	0	C	Lex	33,000
Conway Hall	Dream Vacation	1	1	C	Hb	45,000
Conway Hall	Dream Vacation	1	0	F	Hb	55,000
Conway Hall	Garland Lobell	1	0	F	Hb	24,000
Conway Hall	Giant Victory	1	0	C	Hb	19,000
Conway Hall	King Conch	2	0	C	Hb	46,000
Conway Hall	King Conch	1	0	C	Lex	60,000
Conway Hall	King Conch	1	0	F	Hb	14,000
Conway Hall	Lindy Lane	2	0	C	Hb	25,000
Conway Hall	Lindy Lane	2	0	C	Lex	7,000
Conway Hall	Lindy Lane	2	0	F	Hb	30,500
Conway Hall	Lv Glory Bound	1	0	C	Lex	17,000
Conway Hall	Mack Lobell	1	0	C	Lex	30,000
Conway Hall	Malabar Man	4	0	C	Hb	46,000
Conway Hall	Malabar Man	2	0	C	Lex	40,000
Conway Hall	Malabar Man	4	0	F	Hb	30,000
Conway Hall	Malabar Man	1	1	F	Lex	100,000
Conway Hall	Mr Lavec	2	1	C	Hb	36,000
Conway Hall	Mr Lavec	3	0	F	Hb	40,667
Conway Hall	Mr Lavec	1	1	F	Lex	17,000
Conway Hall	Mr Vic	2	0	F	Hb	23,000
Conway Hall	Mr Vic	1	0	F	Lex	35,000
Conway Hall	Muscles Yankee	5	0	C	Hb	26,500
Conway Hall	Muscles Yankee	4	0	C	Lex	53,000
Conway Hall	Muscles Yankee	5	0	F	Hb	29,200

Sire	Bm Sire	Sold	$50,000 2 Year Olds	Sex	Sale	Average Price
Conway Hall	Nearly Perfect	1	0	C	Hb	12,000
Conway Hall	Pine Chip	3	0	C	Hb	55,667
Conway Hall	Pine Chip	2	0	C	Lex	97,500
Conway Hall	Pine Chip	1	0	F	Hb	40,000
Conway Hall	Pine Chip	5	0	F	Lex	27,000
Conway Hall	Royal Prestige	1	0	C	Hb	10,000
Conway Hall	Royal Prestige	1	1	C	Lex	17,000
Conway Hall	Royal Troubador	1	0	C	Hb	15,000
Conway Hall	SJ's Photo	1	0	C	Hb	110,000
Conway Hall	SJ's Photo	1	0	C	Lex	20,000
Conway Hall	Self Possessed	2	0	C	Hb	21,000
Conway Hall	Self Possessed	3	0	C	Lex	15,667
Conway Hall	Self Possessed	2	0	F	Hb	43,500
Conway Hall	Self Possessed	4	1	F	Lex	22,000
Conway Hall	Sierra Kosmos	1	0	C	Hb	35,000
Conway Hall	Sierra Kosmos	1	1	F	Hb	25,000
Conway Hall	Sir Taurus	1	0	C	Hb	22,000
Conway Hall	Sir Taurus	2	1	F	Hb	21,000
Conway Hall	SJ's Caviar	1	0	C	Lex	12,000
Conway Hall	SJ's Caviar	1	0	F	Hb	11,000
Conway Hall	Speedy Crown	1	0	C	Lex	37,000
Conway Hall	Speedy Crown	1	0	F	Hb	42,000
Conway Hall	Striking Sahbra	2	1	C	Hb	20,000
Conway Hall	Super Bowl	2	0	C	Hb	30,000
Conway Hall	Super Bowl	2	0	F	Hb	14,000
Conway Hall	Super Bowl	2	0	F	Lex	51,000
Conway Hall	Supergill	2	0	C	Hb	14,750
Conway Hall	Supergill	1	1	C	Lex	75,000
Conway Hall	Tagliabue	1	0	F	Lex	15,000
Conway Hall	Valley Victory	1	0	C	Hb	10,000
Conway Hall	Valley Victory	3	1	C	Lex	70,000
Conway Hall	Valley Victory	1	1	F	Hb	27,000
Conway Hall	Valley Victory	2	0	F	Lex	26,000
Conway Hall	Victory Dream	2	0	C	Hb	26,000
Conway Hall	Victory Dream	3	0	C	Lex	32,667
Conway Hall	Yankee Glide	4	0	C	Hb	32,250
Conway Hall	Yankee Glide	7	1	C	Lex	35,000
Conway Hall	Yankee Glide	1	0	F	Hb	25,000
Conway Hall	Yankee Glide	7	1	F	Lex	35,429
Conway Hall	Yankee Paco	1	0	C	Lex	32,000
CR Excalibur	Armbro Iliad	1	0	F	Hb	19,000

Sire	Bm Sire	Sold	$50,000 2 Year Olds	Sex	Sale	Average Price
Credit Winner	Andover Hall	4	1	C	Hb	87,500
Credit Winner	Andover Hall	1	0	C	Lex	112,000
Credit Winner	Andover Hall	1	1	F	Lex	70,000
Credit Winner	Angus Hall	3	0	C	Hb	80,000
Credit Winner	Angus Hall	1	0	C	Lex	8,000
Credit Winner	Angus Hall	3	0	F	Lex	24,333
Credit Winner	Armbro Goal	1	0	F	Hb	20,000
Credit Winner	Arnies Exchange	1	0	C	Lex	35,000
Credit Winner	Balanced Image	1	0	C	Hb	55,000
Credit Winner	Balanced Image	2	0	F	Hb	15,000
Credit Winner	Balanced Image	2	0	F	Lex	82,500
Credit Winner	Brisco Hanover	1	0	C	Hb	40,000
Credit Winner	Carry The Message	1	0	C	Lex	18,000
Credit Winner	Conway Hall	2	0	C	Hb	23,500
Credit Winner	Conway Hall	3	0	C	Lex	61,667
Credit Winner	Conway Hall	2	0	F	Hb	18,000
Credit Winner	Conway Hall	1	0	F	Lex	40,000
Credit Winner	Crowning Point	1	0	C	Lex	25,000
Credit Winner	Cumin	1	0	C	Lex	25,000
Credit Winner	Donerail	10	1	C	Hb	49,400
Credit Winner	Donerail	9	0	C	Lex	79,444
Credit Winner	Donerail	6	2	F	Hb	43,667
Credit Winner	Donerail	4	0	F	Lex	46,000
Credit Winner	Dream Vacation	1	0	C	Lex	40,000
Credit Winner	Enjoy Lavec	1	0	C	Hb	125,000
Credit Winner	Flak Bait	2	0	C	Hb	41,000
Credit Winner	Garland Lobell	1	0	C	Hb	23,000
Credit Winner	Garland Lobell	1	1	C	Lex	57,000
Credit Winner	Garland Lobell	2	0	F	Hb	31,000
Credit Winner	Garland Lobell	2	1	F	Lex	107,500
Credit Winner	Giant Hit	1	0	C	Hb	75,000
Credit Winner	Giant Victory	1	0	F	Hb	22,000
Credit Winner	King Conch	1	0	F	Hb	28,000
Credit Winner	Lindy Lane	3	1	C	Hb	82,333
Credit Winner	Lindy Lane	2	0	C	Lex	20,000
Credit Winner	Lindy Lane	2	0	F	Hb	17,000
Credit Winner	Lindy Lane	2	0	F	Lex	43,500
Credit Winner	Mack Lobell	1	0	F	Lex	27,000
Credit Winner	Malabar Man	2	0	C	Hb	50,000
Credit Winner	Malabar Man	4	0	C	Lex	91,250
Credit Winner	Malabar Man	1	0	F	Hb	25,000

Sire	Bm Sire	Sold	$50,000 2 Year Olds	Sex	Sale	Average Price
Credit Winner	Malabar Man	3	0	F	Lex	69,667
Credit Winner	Mr Lavec	1	0	C	Hb	9,000
Credit Winner	Mr Lavec	1	1	C	Lex	150,000
Credit Winner	Mr Lavec	2	1	F	Hb	26,000
Credit Winner	Mr Lavec	2	0	F	Lex	55,000
Credit Winner	Mr Vic	1	0	C	Lex	8,000
Credit Winner	Muscles Yankee	6	1	C	Hb	57,000
Credit Winner	Muscles Yankee	3	0	C	Lex	76,667
Credit Winner	Muscles Yankee	7	0	F	Hb	31,000
Credit Winner	Muscles Yankee	5	3	F	Lex	98,000
Credit Winner	Pine Chip	3	1	C	Hb	48,000
Credit Winner	Pine Chip	2	0	C	Lex	147,500
Credit Winner	Pine Chip	1	0	F	Hb	30,000
Credit Winner	Pine Chip	3	0	F	Lex	21,333
Credit Winner	Royal Prestige	1	0	F	Hb	27,000
Credit Winner	Royal Strength	1	0	F	Lex	42,000
Credit Winner	Royal Troubador	1	0	F	Lex	4,000
Credit Winner	SJ's Photo	2	0	C	Hb	18,000
Credit Winner	SJ's Photo	1	0	C	Lex	97,000
Credit Winner	SJ's Photo	2	0	F	Hb	38,500
Credit Winner	SJ's Photo	3	0	F	Lex	82,333
Credit Winner	Self Possessed	2	0	C	Hb	102,500
Credit Winner	Self Possessed	3	0	C	Lex	78,000
Credit Winner	Self Possessed	3	0	F	Hb	63,333
Credit Winner	Self Possessed	1	0	F	Lex	30,000
Credit Winner	Sierra Kosmos	1	0	C	Hb	150,000
Credit Winner	Sierra Kosmos	1	0	F	Hb	47,000
Credit Winner	Sierra Kosmos	1	0	F	Lex	42,000
Credit Winner	Sir Taurus	2	0	C	Hb	47,000
Credit Winner	Sir Taurus	2	1	F	Hb	76,000
Credit Winner	SJ's Caviar	1	0	F	Hb	27,000
Credit Winner	Speed In Action	1	0	F	Hb	17,000
Credit Winner	Speedy Crown	3	0	C	Lex	38,000
Credit Winner	Speedy Crown	1	0	F	Hb	32,000
Credit Winner	Speedy Crown	2	0	F	Lex	26,000
Credit Winner	Striking Sahbra	1	0	F	Hb	30,000
Credit Winner	Super Bowl	1	0	C	Hb	29,000
Credit Winner	Super Bowl	1	0	C	Lex	6,000
Credit Winner	Super Bowl	1	0	F	Lex	22,000
Credit Winner	Supergill	1	0	C	Hb	67,000
Credit Winner	Supergill	1	0	F	Hb	70,000

Sire	Bm Sire	Sold	$50,000 2 Year Olds	Sex	Sale	Average Price
Credit Winner	Tabor Lobell	1	0	C	Hb	25,000
Credit Winner	Tom Ridge	1	0	F	Hb	12,000
Credit Winner	Valley Victor	1	0	F	Hb	52,000
Credit Winner	Valley Victory	5	2	C	Hb	131,000
Credit Winner	Valley Victory	6	1	C	Lex	95,833
Credit Winner	Valley Victory	5	0	F	Hb	31,000
Credit Winner	Valley Victory	3	0	F	Lex	16,667
Credit Winner	Valleymeister	1	0	F	Hb	5,000
Credit Winner	Victory Dream	1	1	C	Lex	30,000
Credit Winner	Victory Dream	1	0	F	Lex	120,000
Credit Winner	Vision's Pride	1	0	C	Lex	9,000
Credit Winner	Vision's Pride	1	0	F	Lex	70,000
Credit Winner	Wall Street Banker	1	0	C	Lex	60,000
Credit Winner	Yankee Glide	3	0	C	Hb	66,667
Credit Winner	Yankee Glide	5	1	F	Hb	64,900
Credit Winner	Yankee Glide	1	0	F	Lex	50,000
Daguet Rapide	Garland Lobell	1	0	C	Lex	10,000
Daguet Rapide	Lindy Lane	1	0	C	Hb	40,000
Daguet Rapide	Lindy Lane	1	1	F	Lex	30,000
Daguet Rapide	Speedy Crown	1	0	C	Lex	32,000
Daguet Rapide	Supergill	1	0	F	Hb	11,000
Daguet Rapide	Vision's Pride	1	0	F	Lex	45,000
Donato Hanover	American Winner	1	0	C	Hb	35,000
Donato Hanover	Balanced Image	2	0	C	Hb	21,500
Donato Hanover	Balanced Image	1	0	F	Hb	57,000
Donato Hanover	Banker Hall	1	0	C	Hb	33,000
Donato Hanover	Brisco Hanover	1	0	C	Hb	20,000
Donato Hanover	Cr Commando	1	0	C	Hb	45,000
Donato Hanover	Credit Winner	1	0	F	Hb	45,000
Donato Hanover	Crowning Point	1	0	C	Hb	27,000
Donato Hanover	Donerail	2	0	F	Lex	78,500
Donato Hanover	Dream Vacation	1	0	C	Hb	30,000
Donato Hanover	Dream Vacation	1	0	C	Lex	14,000
Donato Hanover	Garland Lobell	1	0	C	Lex	27,000
Donato Hanover	King Conch	1	0	F	Lex	62,000
Donato Hanover	Lemon Dra	1	0	C	Lex	7,000
Donato Hanover	Like A Prayer	1	0	F	Hb	10,000
Donato Hanover	Like A Prayer	1	0	F	Lex	50,000
Donato Hanover	Lindy Lane	1	0	C	Hb	125,000
Donato Hanover	Lindy Lane	1	0	C	Lex	25,000
Donato Hanover	Lindy Lane	1	0	F	Hb	255,000

Sire	Bm Sire	Sold	$50,000 2 Year Olds	Sex	Sale	Average Price
Donato Hanover	Malabar Man	2	0	C	Hb	33,500
Donato Hanover	Malabar Man	4	0	F	Hb	37,000
Donato Hanover	Mr Lavec	1	0	F	Hb	28,000
Donato Hanover	Muscles Yankee	4	0	C	Hb	78,500
Donato Hanover	Muscles Yankee	3	0	C	Lex	73,333
Donato Hanover	Muscles Yankee	5	0	F	Hb	30,800
Donato Hanover	Muscles Yankee	4	1	F	Lex	73,750
Donato Hanover	Pine Chip	3	0	C	Lex	88,333
Donato Hanover	SJ's Photo	2	0	C	Hb	29,000
Donato Hanover	SJ's Photo	1	0	F	Hb	65,000
Donato Hanover	Self Possessed	4	2	C	Hb	101,250
Donato Hanover	Self Possessed	2	1	F	Hb	36,000
Donato Hanover	Sierra Kosmos	1	0	F	Hb	40,000
Donato Hanover	Sir Taurus	1	0	F	Hb	12,000
Donato Hanover	SJ's Caviar	1	0	F	Lex	100,000
Donato Hanover	Striking Sahbra	1	0	C	Hb	24,000
Donato Hanover	Supergill	1	0	C	Hb	140,000
Donato Hanover	Tagliabue	1	0	F	Lex	27,000
Donato Hanover	Valley Victor	1	0	F	Hb	10,000
Donato Hanover	Valley Victor	1	1	F	Lex	22,000
Donato Hanover	Valley Victory	5	1	C	Lex	107,800
Donato Hanover	Valley Victory	1	0	F	Hb	30,000
Donato Hanover	Varenne	1	0	C	Lex	120,000
Donato Hanover	Victory Dream	1	0	C	Lex	22,000
Donato Hanover	Yankee Glide	3	1	C	Hb	68,000
Donato Hanover	Yankee Glide	3	0	C	Lex	81,667
Donato Hanover	Yankee Glide	1	0	F	Hb	37,000
Donato Hanover	Yankee Glide	2	0	F	Lex	46,000
Donerail	Armbro Goal	1	0	F	Lex	5,000
Donerail	Balanced Image	1	0	F	Hb	4,500
Donerail	Fill V	1	0	F	Hb	20,000
Donerail	Pine Chip	1	0	F	Hb	22,000
Donerail	Rule The Wind	1	0	C	Lex	8,000
Donerail	Sierra Kosmos	1	0	F	Hb	6,000
Donerail	Sierra Kosmos	1	0	F	Lex	15,000
Donerail	Super Bowl	1	0	F	Hb	9,000
Dragon Again	Abercrombie	3	1	C	Hb	78,333
Dragon Again	Abercrombie	2	0	F	Hb	8,250
Dragon Again	Abercrombie	2	1	F	Lex	12,500
Dragon Again	Albatross	1	0	F	Hb	7,000
Dragon Again	Albert Albert	1	0	F	Hb	45,000

Sire	Bm Sire	Sold	$50,000 2 Year Olds	Sex	Sale	Average Price
Dragon Again	Armbro Operative	1	0	F	Hb	11,000
Dragon Again	Art Major	1	1	C	Hb	30,000
Dragon Again	Artsplace	9	2	C	Hb	42,778
Dragon Again	Artsplace	5	0	C	Lex	25,200
Dragon Again	Artsplace	7	0	F	Hb	19,500
Dragon Again	Artsplace	3	0	F	Lex	52,333
Dragon Again	Beach Towel	1	0	C	Hb	54,000
Dragon Again	Bettor's Delight	1	0	F	Hb	6,500
Dragon Again	Big Towner	3	0	C	Hb	16,833
Dragon Again	Big Towner	2	0	F	Lex	67,500
Dragon Again	Blissful Hall	1	0	F	Lex	30,000
Dragon Again	Bret Hanover	1	0	C	Hb	22,000
Dragon Again	Cam Fella	1	0	C	Hb	6,000
Dragon Again	Cambest	3	0	C	Hb	27,667
Dragon Again	Cambest	3	0	F	Hb	12,167
Dragon Again	Camluck	6	0	C	Hb	34,083
Dragon Again	Camluck	1	0	C	Lex	75,000
Dragon Again	Camluck	1	0	F	Hb	25,000
Dragon Again	Colt Fortysix	1	0	F	Hb	13,000
Dragon Again	Dexter Nukes	2	0	F	Hb	8,250
Dragon Again	Die Laughing	2	0	C	Hb	43,500
Dragon Again	Die Laughing	1	0	F	Hb	20,000
Dragon Again	Dream Away	1	0	C	Lex	45,000
Dragon Again	Falcon Seelster	2	0	C	Hb	13,000
Dragon Again	Falcon Seelster	1	0	F	Hb	30,000
Dragon Again	Goalie Jeff	1	0	C	Hb	35,000
Dragon Again	Grinfromeartoear	1	0	F	Hb	3,500
Dragon Again	Jate Lobell	7	1	C	Hb	35,000
Dragon Again	Jate Lobell	5	2	C	Lex	31,400
Dragon Again	Jate Lobell	2	0	F	Hb	18,500
Dragon Again	Jate Lobell	3	0	F	Lex	22,333
Dragon Again	Jenna's Beach Boy	3	0	C	Hb	38,333
Dragon Again	Jenna's Beach Boy	2	0	C	Lex	65,000
Dragon Again	Jenna's Beach Boy	3	0	F	Lex	18,667
Dragon Again	Keystone Raider	1	0	C	Lex	50,000
Dragon Again	Life Sign	4	0	C	Hb	14,000
Dragon Again	Life Sign	7	0	F	Hb	18,500
Dragon Again	Life Sign	1	0	F	Lex	6,000
Dragon Again	Matt's Scooter	3	0	C	Hb	61,667
Dragon Again	Matt's Scooter	1	1	C	Lex	82,000
Dragon Again	Matt's Scooter	2	0	F	Hb	33,500

Sire	Bm Sire	Sold	$50,000 2 Year Olds	Sex	Sale	Average Price
Dragon Again	No Nukes	7	1	C	Hb	43,857
Dragon Again	No Nukes	2	0	C	Lex	34,000
Dragon Again	No Nukes	5	0	F	Hb	30,200
Dragon Again	No Nukes	2	0	F	Lex	15,000
Dragon Again	Pacific Fella	1	0	F	Lex	12,000
Dragon Again	Precious Bunny	1	0	C	Hb	40,000
Dragon Again	Precious Bunny	3	0	F	Hb	67,833
Dragon Again	Presidential Ball	2	0	C	Hb	72,000
Dragon Again	Real Artist	2	0	C	Hb	37,000
Dragon Again	Real Desire	1	0	C	Hb	47,000
Dragon Again	Run The Table	1	0	C	Hb	22,000
Dragon Again	Run The Table	1	0	F	Hb	4,000
Dragon Again	Rustler Hanover	2	0	C	Hb	15,500
Dragon Again	Rustler Hanover	1	0	F	Hb	5,000
Dragon Again	The Panderosa	7	0	C	Hb	24,286
Dragon Again	The Panderosa	5	0	F	Hb	12,800
Dragon Again	The Panderosa	1	0	F	Lex	13,000
Dragon Again	Tyler's Mark	1	0	C	Hb	50,000
Dragon Again	Village Connection	1	0	F	Lex	20,000
Dragon Again	Walton Hanover	1	0	F	Hb	8,000
Dragon Again	Western Hanover	20	1	C	Hb	33,950
Dragon Again	Western Hanover	4	0	C	Lex	42,500
Dragon Again	Western Hanover	24	1	F	Hb	30,967
Dragon Again	Western Hanover	6	0	F	Lex	25,333
Dragon Again	Western Ideal	3	0	C	Hb	13,667
Dragon Again	Western Ideal	4	0	F	Hb	17,125
Dream Vacation	A Go Go Lauxmont	1	0	F	Lex	3,000
Dream Vacation	Angus Hall	1	0	F	Lex	45,000
Dream Vacation	Armbro Goal	1	0	F	Lex	7,000
Dream Vacation	Arndon	1	0	F	Lex	11,000
Dream Vacation	Balanced Image	1	0	C	Hb	14,000
Dream Vacation	BJ's Mac	1	0	F	Lex	60,000
Dream Vacation	Crowning Point	1	0	F	Lex	25,000
Dream Vacation	Donerail	3	0	C	Lex	9,333
Dream Vacation	El Paso Kash	1	0	C	Lex	2,000
Dream Vacation	Lindy Lane	1	0	F	Lex	6,000
Dream Vacation	Muscles Yankee	1	0	C	Lex	17,000
Dream Vacation	Program Speed	1	0	F	Lex	15,000
Dream Vacation	Royal Prestige	1	0	C	Lex	11,000
Dream Vacation	SJ's Photo	1	0	C	Hb	12,000
Dream Vacation	SJ's Photo	1	0	C	Lex	2,000

Sire	Bm Sire	Sold	$50,000 2 Year Olds	Sex	Sale	Average Price
Dream Vacation	SJ's Photo	1	1	F	Lex	50,000
Dream Vacation	Self Possessed	1	0	C	Hb	14,000
Dream Vacation	Sierra Kosmos	1	0	F	Lex	85,000
Dream Vacation	Sir Taurus	1	0	F	Lex	13,000
Dream Vacation	Speedy Crown	1	0	C	Lex	30,000
E Dee's Cam	Kentucky Spur	1	0	C	Hb	7,000
E Dee's Cam	No Nukes	1	0	C	Hb	30,000
E Dee's Cam	Tyler B	1	0	F	Hb	4,000
E Dee's Cam	Walton Hanover	1	0	C	Hb	10,000
E Dee's Cam	Western Ideal	1	1	F	Hb	20,000
Equinox Bi	Balanced Image	1	0	C	Hb	17,000
Equinox Bi	Muscles Yankee	1	0	C	Hb	65,000
Equinox Bi	Sir Taurus	1	0	C	Lex	6,000
Equinox Bi	Valley Victory	1	0	C	Lex	25,000
Four Starzzz Shark	Abercrombie	4	2	C	Lex	54,500
Four Starzzz Shark	Abercrombie	1	0	F	Hb	12,000
Four Starzzz Shark	Abercrombie	1	0	F	Lex	8,000
Four Starzzz Shark	Albert Albert	1	0	F	Hb	19,000
Four Starzzz Shark	Artiscape	2	1	C	Hb	21,000
Four Starzzz Shark	Artiscape	1	0	F	Hb	15,000
Four Starzzz Shark	Artiscape	2	0	F	Lex	6,000
Four Starzzz Shark	Artsplace	3	1	C	Hb	22,000
Four Starzzz Shark	Artsplace	5	0	C	Lex	31,200
Four Starzzz Shark	Artsplace	1	0	F	Hb	32,000
Four Starzzz Shark	Artsplace	4	0	F	Lex	13,250
Four Starzzz Shark	Beach Towel	1	0	F	Hb	26,000
Four Starzzz Shark	Ideal Society	1	0	F	Lex	14,000
Four Starzzz Shark	In The Pocket	1	0	F	Lex	42,000
Four Starzzz Shark	Incredible Finale	1	0	F	Lex	15,000
Four Starzzz Shark	Jate Lobell	1	0	C	Lex	3,000
Four Starzzz Shark	Jenna's Beach Boy	1	0	C	Hb	5,000
Four Starzzz Shark	Keystone Raider	1	0	C	Lex	40,000
Four Starzzz Shark	Life Sign	1	0	C	Hb	20,000
Four Starzzz Shark	Life Sign	3	1	F	Hb	17,833
Four Starzzz Shark	Life Sign	4	0	F	Lex	23,000
Four Starzzz Shark	Lusty Leader	1	0	C	Hb	13,000
Four Starzzz Shark	Matt's Scooter	1	0	C	Hb	15,000
Four Starzzz Shark	Matt's Scooter	1	0	F	Hb	18,000
Four Starzzz Shark	Matt's Scooter	1	0	F	Lex	15,000
Four Starzzz Shark	No Nukes	2	0	C	Hb	13,500
Four Starzzz Shark	No Nukes	1	0	F	Hb	6,000

Sire	Bm Sire	Sold	$50,000 2 Year Olds	Sex	Sale	Average Price
Four Starzzz Shark	No Nukes	1	0	F	Lex	23,000
Four Starzzz Shark	Nobleland Sam	1	0	F	Hb	5,000
Four Starzzz Shark	Nuclear Siren	1	0	C	Hb	6,000
Four Starzzz Shark	Nuclear Siren	1	0	F	Hb	27,000
Four Starzzz Shark	Presidential Ball	1	0	F	Hb	15,000
Four Starzzz Shark	Red River Hanover	1	0	C	Hb	12,000
Four Starzzz Shark	Riyadh	1	0	F	Hb	40,000
Four Starzzz Shark	Tyler B	1	0	C	Hb	20,000
Four Starzzz Shark	Western Hanover	2	0	C	Hb	35,000
Four Starzzz Shark	Western Hanover	1	1	F	Hb	39,000
Four Starzzz Shark	Western Hanover	3	0	F	Lex	35,000
Four Starzzz Shark	Western Ideal	1	0	C	Lex	80,000
Glidemaster	American Winner	1	0	C	Lex	102,000
Glidemaster	American Winner	2	1	F	Lex	33,500
Glidemaster	Amigo Hall	1	0	C	Hb	9,500
Glidemaster	Andover Hall	1	0	F	Hb	1,500
Glidemaster	Angus Hall	1	0	C	Hb	57,000
Glidemaster	Angus Hall	1	0	C	Lex	87,000
Glidemaster	Angus Hall	2	0	F	Lex	86,000
Glidemaster	Armbro Goal	2	0	C	Hb	98,500
Glidemaster	Armbro Goal	1	0	C	Lex	4,000
Glidemaster	Armbro Goal	1	0	F	Hb	42,000
Glidemaster	Balanced Image	1	0	C	Hb	20,000
Glidemaster	Balanced Image	1	0	F	Hb	1,500
Glidemaster	Conway Hall	2	0	C	Hb	38,500
Glidemaster	Conway Hall	2	0	C	Lex	153,500
Glidemaster	Conway Hall	3	0	F	Hb	29,667
Glidemaster	Credit Winner	2	0	C	Hb	61,000
Glidemaster	Donerail	1	0	C	Hb	15,000
Glidemaster	Donerail	5	0	F	Lex	26,800
Glidemaster	Garland Lobell	4	1	C	Hb	35,250
Glidemaster	Garland Lobell	3	0	C	Lex	24,667
Glidemaster	Garland Lobell	5	0	F	Hb	29,400
Glidemaster	Garland Lobell	2	0	F	Lex	40,000
Glidemaster	King Conch	1	0	F	Lex	50,000
Glidemaster	Malabar Man	4	0	C	Hb	35,500
Glidemaster	Malabar Man	2	0	C	Lex	25,500
Glidemaster	Malabar Man	1	0	F	Hb	22,000
Glidemaster	Malabar Man	3	0	F	Lex	78,333
Glidemaster	Mr Vic	1	0	F	Hb	27,000
Glidemaster	Muscles Yankee	1	0	C	Hb	8,000

Sire	Bm Sire	Sold	$50,000 2 Year Olds	Sex	Sale	Average Price
Glidemaster	Nicholas Hanover	1	0	F	Hb	22,000
Glidemaster	Pine Chip	1	0	C	Hb	22,000
Glidemaster	Pine Chip	2	0	F	Hb	9,500
Glidemaster	Pine Chip	1	0	F	Lex	10,000
Glidemaster	Royal Prestige	1	0	F	Hb	3,500
Glidemaster	SJ's Photo	2	0	F	Lex	52,500
Glidemaster	Self Possessed	1	0	C	Hb	60,000
Glidemaster	Self Possessed	3	0	C	Lex	24,667
Glidemaster	Self Possessed	2	0	F	Lex	26,000
Glidemaster	Sierra Kosmos	1	0	C	Hb	18,000
Glidemaster	Sierra Kosmos	2	0	F	Hb	28,500
Glidemaster	Sierra Kosmos	1	0	F	Lex	9,000
Glidemaster	Sir Taurus	1	0	C	Lex	6,000
Glidemaster	Speedy Crown	1	0	C	Lex	50,000
Glidemaster	Striking Sahbra	1	0	C	Lex	30,000
Glidemaster	Striking Sahbra	1	0	F	Lex	30,000
Glidemaster	Super Bowl	1	0	C	Hb	5,000
Glidemaster	Supergill	1	0	F	Lex	30,000
Glidemaster	Thirty Two	1	1	C	Hb	40,000
Glidemaster	Valley Victory	1	0	C	Lex	70,000
Glidemaster	Yankee Paco	1	0	C	Hb	25,000
Grinfromeartoear	Abercrombie	1	0	C	Lex	11,000
Grinfromeartoear	Cam Fella	1	0	C	Lex	22,000
Grinfromeartoear	Cam Fella	1	0	F	Lex	11,000
Grinfromeartoear	Jate Lobell	1	0	F	Lex	5,000
Here Comes Herbie	Armbro Iliad	1	0	C	Hb	35,000
Here Comes Herbie	Conway Hall	1	0	F	Hb	17,000
Here Comes Herbie	Earl	1	0	C	Lex	31,000
Here Comes Herbie	Mr Lavec	1	0	F	Hb	190,000
Here Comes Herbie	SJ's Photo	1	0	F	Hb	25,000
Here Comes Herbie	Sierra Kosmos	1	0	F	Hb	7,000
I Am A Fool	Abercrombie	1	0	C	Lex	13,000
I Am A Fool	Albatross	2	0	C	Lex	7,500
I Am A Fool	Albatross	1	0	F	Lex	2,000
I Am A Fool	Artiscape	2	0	C	Lex	22,500
I Am A Fool	Artsplace	5	0	C	Lex	14,400
I Am A Fool	Artsplace	1	0	F	Lex	2,000
I Am A Fool	Big Towner	1	0	C	Hb	10,000
I Am A Fool	Big Towner	1	0	C	Lex	8,000
I Am A Fool	Cambest	1	0	C	Hb	1,500
I Am A Fool	Cambest	1	0	F	Lex	6,000

Sire	Bm Sire	Sold	$50,000 2 Year Olds	Sex	Sale	Average Price
I Am A Fool	Cam's Card Shark	2	0	C	Lex	19,000
I Am A Fool	Cam's Card Shark	1	0	F	Lex	4,000
I Am A Fool	Cole Muffler	1	0	C	Hb	17,000
I Am A Fool	Dexter Nukes	1	0	C	Hb	5,000
I Am A Fool	Dexter Nukes	1	0	C	Lex	1,000
I Am A Fool	Dexter Nukes	2	0	F	Hb	3,250
I Am A Fool	Die Laughing	1	0	C	Lex	18,000
I Am A Fool	Dragon's Lair	1	0	C	Hb	15,000
I Am A Fool	Falcon Almahurst	1	0	F	Hb	1,500
I Am A Fool	Falcon Seelster	1	0	F	Lex	45,000
I Am A Fool	Grinfromeartoear	2	0	C	Lex	4,000
I Am A Fool	Grinfromeartoear	2	0	F	Lex	22,500
I Am A Fool	Jate Lobell	5	0	C	Lex	8,800
I Am A Fool	Jate Lobell	3	0	F	Lex	19,667
I Am A Fool	Jenna's Beach Boy	1	1	C	Hb	9,000
I Am A Fool	Laag	1	0	C	Hb	3,000
I Am A Fool	Nihilator	1	0	F	Lex	7,000
I Am A Fool	No Nukes	3	0	C	Hb	18,333
I Am A Fool	No Nukes	1	0	C	Lex	10,000
I Am A Fool	No Nukes	1	0	F	Hb	4,000
I Am A Fool	No Nukes	2	0	F	Lex	5,500
I Am A Fool	No Pan Intended	1	0	F	Hb	13,000
I Am A Fool	Nobleland Sam	1	0	F	Lex	7,000
I Am A Fool	Northern Luck	2	0	C	Lex	16,500
I Am A Fool	Northern Luck	1	0	F	Lex	10,000
I Am A Fool	Precious Bunny	1	0	C	Lex	23,000
I Am A Fool	Precious Bunny	1	0	F	Hb	3,500
I Am A Fool	Real Artist	1	0	F	Hb	4,000
I Am A Fool	The Panderosa	1	0	C	Hb	7,500
I Am A Fool	Tyler B	1	0	C	Hb	5,500
I Am A Fool	Western Hanover	1	0	C	Hb	12,000
I Am A Fool	Western Hanover	2	0	C	Lex	7,500
I Am A Fool	Western Hanover	1	0	F	Hb	4,000
I Am A Fool	Western Hanover	3	0	F	Lex	19,000
I Am A Fool	Western Ideal	1	0	F	Hb	6,000
Jate Lobell	Abercrombie	2	0	C	Lex	24,500
Jate Lobell	Abercrombie	2	0	F	Lex	11,000
Jate Lobell	Albatross	1	0	C	Lex	40,000
Jate Lobell	Cam Cam Cameo	1	0	C	Lex	5,000
Jate Lobell	Camtastic	1	0	C	Lex	17,000
Jate Lobell	Masquerade	1	0	F	Lex	34,000

Sire	Bm Sire	Sold	$50,000 2 Year Olds	Sex	Sale	Average Price
Jate Lobell	Nihilator	1	0	C	Lex	7,000
Jate Lobell	Tyler B	1	0	F	Lex	17,000
Jenna's Beach Boy	Abercrombie	2	0	C	Lex	22,500
Jenna's Beach Boy	Artsplace	1	0	C	Lex	25,000
Jenna's Beach Boy	Artsplace	1	0	F	Lex	50,000
Jenna's Beach Boy	Big Towner	1	0	F	Lex	6,000
Jenna's Beach Boy	Dexter Nukes	1	1	C	Lex	14,000
Jenna's Beach Boy	Dexter Nukes	1	0	F	Lex	20,000
Jenna's Beach Boy	Die Laughing	1	0	C	Lex	20,000
Jenna's Beach Boy	Falcon Seelster	1	0	F	Lex	5,000
Jenna's Beach Boy	Laag	1	0	C	Hb	20,000
Jenna's Beach Boy	Life Sign	1	0	C	Lex	12,000
Jenna's Beach Boy	Northern Luck	1	0	C	Lex	42,000
Jenna's Beach Boy	Pacific Rocket	1	0	F	Lex	15,000
Jenna's Beach Boy	Shady Character	1	0	F	Lex	20,000
Jenna's Beach Boy	Storm Damage	1	0	C	Lex	7,000
Jenna's Beach Boy	Western Hanover	1	0	F	Hb	11,500
Jereme's Jet	Admirals Galley	1	0	F	Hb	65,000
Jereme's Jet	Albatross	1	0	C	Hb	55,000
Jereme's Jet	Art Major	1	1	F	Hb	105,000
Jereme's Jet	Artsplace	1	0	C	Hb	8,000
Jereme's Jet	Artsplace	2	0	F	Hb	25,500
Jereme's Jet	Camluck	2	0	C	Hb	76,000
Jereme's Jet	Camluck	1	1	F	Hb	27,000
Jereme's Jet	Cam's Card Shark	1	0	C	Hb	30,000
Jereme's Jet	Cam's Card Shark	1	0	F	Hb	80,000
Jereme's Jet	Dream Away	1	0	F	Lex	9,000
Jereme's Jet	Goalie Jeff	1	0	F	Lex	7,000
Jereme's Jet	Incredible Finale	1	0	F	Lex	92,000
Jereme's Jet	Jate Lobell	1	0	C	Hb	50,000
Jereme's Jet	Matt's Scooter	1	0	C	Hb	120,000
Jereme's Jet	Matt's Scooter	1	0	F	Hb	45,000
Jereme's Jet	Nuclear Siren	1	0	F	Hb	40,000
Jereme's Jet	Precious Bunny	1	0	C	Hb	60,000
Justice Hall	Balanced Image	1	0	F	Lex	1,000
Justice Hall	Muscles Yankee	1	0	C	Lex	1,000
Kadabra	American Winner	1	0	C	Lex	80,000
Kadabra	American Winner	1	0	F	Hb	42,000
Kadabra	Angus Hall	1	0	C	Lex	105,000
Kadabra	Angus Hall	2	0	F	Hb	42,500
Kadabra	Angus Hall	1	0	F	Lex	65,000

Sire	Bm Sire	Sold	$50,000 2 Year Olds	Sex	Sale	Average Price
Kadabra	Balanced Image	4	1	C	Hb	25,750
Kadabra	Balanced Image	1	0	C	Lex	8,000
Kadabra	Balanced Image	6	0	F	Hb	14,583
Kadabra	Brisco Hanover	1	0	F	Hb	18,000
Kadabra	Carry The Message	1	0	F	Hb	55,000
Kadabra	Catch A Thrill	1	1	C	Hb	120,000
Kadabra	Conway Hall	2	0	C	Hb	26,000
Kadabra	Conway Hall	1	0	C	Lex	40,000
Kadabra	Conway Hall	3	1	F	Lex	92,333
Kadabra	Donerail	1	0	C	Hb	31,000
Kadabra	Donerail	1	0	F	Hb	20,000
Kadabra	Dream Vacation	1	0	F	Hb	15,000
Kadabra	Earl	1	0	C	Hb	35,000
Kadabra	Enjoy Lavec	1	0	F	Lex	50,000
Kadabra	Garland Lobell	1	0	C	Hb	50,000
Kadabra	Garland Lobell	1	0	C	Lex	10,000
Kadabra	Garland Lobell	2	1	F	Hb	102,500
Kadabra	King Conch	1	0	C	Hb	42,000
Kadabra	King Conch	1	1	F	Hb	26,000
Kadabra	Lindy Lane	2	1	C	Hb	21,000
Kadabra	Lindy Lane	1	0	F	Hb	13,000
Kadabra	Malabar Man	1	0	F	Hb	17,000
Kadabra	Mr Lavec	2	0	F	Hb	20,000
Kadabra	Muscles Yankee	3	0	C	Hb	24,333
Kadabra	Muscles Yankee	2	0	C	Lex	15,000
Kadabra	Muscles Yankee	3	0	F	Hb	15,167
Kadabra	Pine Chip	2	0	C	Hb	23,500
Kadabra	Pine Chip	1	0	C	Lex	25,000
Kadabra	Pine Chip	1	0	F	Hb	40,000
Kadabra	Promising Catch	1	0	F	Hb	8,000
Kadabra	SJ's Photo	2	0	F	Hb	34,500
Kadabra	Self Possessed	1	0	F	Hb	17,000
Kadabra	Sierra Kosmos	2	0	C	Hb	30,000
Kadabra	Sierra Kosmos	1	0	F	Hb	20,000
Kadabra	Striking Sahbra	1	0	C	Hb	38,000
Kadabra	Striking Sahbra	1	0	C	Lex	17,000
Kadabra	Striking Sahbra	1	0	F	Hb	20,000
Kadabra	Super Bowl	1	0	F	Hb	2,000
Kadabra	Valley Victory	1	0	C	Hb	4,000
Kadabra	Valley Victory	1	0	C	Lex	135,000
Kadabra	Valley Victory	2	0	F	Hb	43,500

Sire	Bm Sire	Sold	$50,000 2 Year Olds	Sex	Sale	Average Price
Kadabra	Valley Victory	1	0	F	Lex	11,000
Kadabra	Yankee Glide	1	0	F	Lex	7,000
Kadabra	Yankee Paco	1	0	C	Hb	5,000
Ken Warkentin	American Winner	1	1	F	Hb	32,000
Ken Warkentin	Armbro Goal	1	0	F	Lex	30,000
Ken Warkentin	Balanced Image	1	0	C	Hb	15,000
Ken Warkentin	Balanced Image	1	0	C	Lex	45,000
Ken Warkentin	Baltic Speed	1	0	C	Hb	20,000
Ken Warkentin	Brisco Hanover	1	0	C	Hb	40,000
Ken Warkentin	Cheyenne Spur	1	1	F	Hb	21,000
Ken Warkentin	Conway Hall	2	0	C	Lex	116,000
Ken Warkentin	Conway Hall	1	0	F	Hb	30,000
Ken Warkentin	Crowning Point	1	0	F	Lex	14,000
Ken Warkentin	Incredible Abe	1	0	F	Lex	12,000
Ken Warkentin	Joie De Vie	1	0	F	Hb	25,000
Ken Warkentin	Lindy Lane	1	0	C	Lex	35,000
Ken Warkentin	Malabar Man	1	0	C	Lex	28,000
Ken Warkentin	Mr Lavec	1	0	C	Hb	31,000
Ken Warkentin	Mr Lavec	1	1	C	Lex	19,000
Ken Warkentin	Mr Vic	1	0	F	Lex	40,000
Ken Warkentin	Pine Chip	1	0	F	Hb	100,000
Ken Warkentin	SJ's Photo	1	0	C	Lex	28,000
Ken Warkentin	Schimitar	1	0	F	Lex	15,000
Ken Warkentin	Self Possessed	1	0	F	Lex	25,000
Ken Warkentin	Sierra Kosmos	1	0	C	Hb	22,000
Ken Warkentin	Super Bowl	1	0	C	Hb	20,000
Ken Warkentin	Super Bowl	1	0	F	Lex	5,000
Ken Warkentin	Tabor Lobell	1	0	C	Lex	25,000
Like A Prayer	Armbro Goal	1	0	F	Hb	3,000
Like A Prayer	Balanced Image	1	0	C	Lex	20,000
Like A Prayer	Cheyenne Spur	1	0	C	Lex	17,000
Like A Prayer	Conway Hall	3	1	C	Lex	19,000
Like A Prayer	Crysta's Crown	2	0	C	Lex	16,000
Like A Prayer	Dancer's Victory	1	0	F	Lex	5,000
Like A Prayer	Donerail	1	1	F	Lex	12,000
Like A Prayer	Dream Vacation	1	0	C	Lex	8,000
Like A Prayer	Final Score	1	0	F	Lex	2,000
Like A Prayer	Garland Lobell	1	0	C	Lex	15,000
Like A Prayer	Garland Lobell	2	0	F	Lex	5,000
Like A Prayer	Giant Victory	1	0	C	Lex	6,000
Like A Prayer	Harmonious	1	0	F	Lex	6,000

Sire	Bm Sire	Sold	$50,000 2 Year Olds	Sex	Sale	Average Price
Like A Prayer	Malabar Man	1	0	F	Lex	62,000
Like A Prayer	Meadow Road	1	0	F	Lex	2,000
Like A Prayer	Mr Lavec	1	0	C	Hb	22,000
Like A Prayer	Pine Chip	2	0	C	Lex	8,000
Like A Prayer	SJ's Photo	3	1	C	Lex	14,000
Like A Prayer	SJ's Photo	1	0	F	Lex	6,000
Like A Prayer	Speedy Crown	1	0	F	Lex	6,000
Like A Prayer	Super Bowl	2	0	C	Lex	7,500
Like A Prayer	Tagliabue	1	1	C	Lex	9,000
Like A Prayer	Wesgate Crown	1	0	C	Lex	10,000
Like A Prayer	Wesgate Crown	1	0	F	Lex	6,000
Like A Prayer	Yankee Paco	1	0	F	Lex	13,000
Lis Mara	Artiscape	1	0	C	Lex	8,000
Lis Mara	Artsplace	1	0	C	Hb	10,000
Lis Mara	Artsplace	1	0	C	Lex	9,000
Lis Mara	Artsplace	2	0	F	Hb	31,000
Lis Mara	Artsplace	1	0	F	Lex	5,000
Lis Mara	Cole Muffler	1	0	F	Hb	6,500
Lis Mara	Dexter Nukes	1	0	F	Lex	15,000
Lis Mara	Dragon's Lair	2	0	C	Lex	9,500
Lis Mara	Falcon Seelster	1	0	C	Hb	20,000
Lis Mara	Falcon Seelster	1	0	C	Lex	32,000
Lis Mara	Falcons Future	1	0	C	Hb	20,000
Lis Mara	Island Fantasy	2	0	C	Hb	13,750
Lis Mara	Jenna's Beach Boy	1	0	F	Lex	8,000
Lis Mara	Life Sign	1	0	C	Lex	20,000
Lis Mara	Life Sign	1	0	F	Hb	9,000
Lis Mara	Matt's Scooter	1	0	C	Hb	7,000
Lis Mara	Matt's Scooter	1	0	F	Hb	5,000
Lis Mara	No Nukes	2	0	F	Hb	6,750
Lis Mara	Richess Hanover	1	0	F	Lex	18,000
Lis Mara	The Panderosa	1	0	F	Hb	5,500
Lis Mara	Western Hanover	1	0	C	Hb	20,000
Lis Mara	Western Hanover	2	0	C	Lex	15,500
Lis Mara	Western Hanover	4	0	F	Hb	9,125
Lis Mara	Western Hanover	1	0	F	Lex	6,000
Mach Three	Albatross	1	0	F	Hb	20,000
Mach Three	Apaches Fame	1	0	C	Lex	4,000
Mach Three	Artsplace	4	0	C	Hb	58,500
Mach Three	Artsplace	1	0	C	Lex	22,000
Mach Three	Artsplace	1	0	F	Hb	18,000

Sire	Bm Sire	Sold	$50,000 2 Year Olds	Sex	Sale	Average Price
Mach Three	Beach Towel	1	0	F	Lex	210,000
Mach Three	Big Towner	1	0	F	Hb	62,000
Mach Three	Cam Fella	1	0	F	Hb	25,000
Mach Three	Cambest	1	0	C	Hb	5,000
Mach Three	Cambest	1	0	F	Lex	35,000
Mach Three	Camluck	2	0	C	Hb	22,000
Mach Three	Camluck	1	0	F	Hb	27,000
Mach Three	Cam's Card Shark	1	0	C	Hb	19,000
Mach Three	Cam's Card Shark	1	0	F	Lex	35,000
Mach Three	Carlsbad Cam	1	0	C	Hb	40,000
Mach Three	Denali	1	0	C	Hb	25,000
Mach Three	Goalie Jeff	1	0	F	Hb	11,000
Mach Three	Jate Lobell	1	0	C	Hb	30,000
Mach Three	Jate Lobell	1	0	F	Hb	36,000
Mach Three	Jate Lobell	1	0	F	Lex	9,000
Mach Three	Jenna's Beach Boy	1	0	F	Hb	40,000
Mach Three	Laag	1	0	F	Hb	2,500
Mach Three	Nihilator	1	0	C	Hb	15,000
Mach Three	No Nukes	1	0	C	Hb	14,000
Mach Three	No Nukes	4	0	F	Hb	17,750
Mach Three	Pacific Fella	1	0	C	Lex	15,000
Mach Three	Precious Bunny	1	0	F	Hb	13,000
Mach Three	Presidential Ball	1	1	F	Hb	12,000
Mach Three	Red River Hanover	2	0	C	Hb	26,000
Mach Three	Western Hanover	2	1	C	Hb	47,500
Mach Three	Western Hanover	1	1	C	Lex	50,000
Mach Three	Western Hanover	1	1	F	Hb	17,000
Majestic Son	Armbro Laser	1	0	C	Hb	25,000
Majestic Son	Balanced Image	1	0	F	Hb	4,000
Majestic Son	Duke Of York	1	0	F	Hb	12,000
Majestic Son	Garland Lobell	1	0	C	Hb	1,500
Majestic Son	Inquirer	1	0	C	Hb	30,000
Majestic Son	Lindy Lane	1	0	C	Hb	22,000
Majestic Son	Pine Chip	1	0	F	Hb	23,000
Majestic Son	Royal Strength	1	0	F	Hb	18,000
Majestic Son	SJ's Photo	3	0	C	Hb	32,333
Majestic Son	SJ's Photo	1	0	F	Hb	15,000
Majestic Son	Self Possessed	1	0	F	Hb	34,000
Majestic Son	SJ's Caviar	1	0	F	Hb	13,000
Majestic Son	Striking Sahbra	1	0	C	Hb	14,000
Majestic Son	Striking Sahbra	1	0	F	Hb	15,000

Sire	Bm Sire	Sold	$50,000 2 Year Olds	Sex	Sale	Average Price
Majestic Son	Supergill	1	0	C	Hb	12,000
Majestic Son	Supergill	1	0	C	Lex	110,000
Majestic Son	Supergill	1	0	F	Hb	15,000
Majestic Son	Tagliabue	1	0	F	Hb	3,500
Majestic Son	Wesgate Crown	1	0	C	Hb	1,000
Majestic Son	Yankee Glide	1	0	F	Hb	5,000
Malabar Man	American Winner	1	0	F	Lex	2,000
Malabar Man	Balanced Image	2	0	C	Lex	21,500
Malabar Man	Conway Hall	1	0	C	Lex	42,000
Malabar Man	Crowning Point	1	1	C	Hb	35,000
Malabar Man	Cumin	1	0	C	Lex	12,000
Malabar Man	Donerail	1	0	C	Lex	20,000
Malabar Man	Dream Of Glory	1	0	F	Hb	32,000
Malabar Man	Garland Lobell	1	0	C	Hb	20,000
Malabar Man	Hoist The Yankee	1	0	F	Lex	15,000
Malabar Man	Like A Prayer	1	0	C	Lex	20,000
Malabar Man	Lindy Lane	1	1	C	Lex	24,000
Malabar Man	Muscles Yankee	1	0	F	Hb	22,000
Malabar Man	Royal Prestige	1	0	C	Hb	38,000
Malabar Man	Royal Strength	1	0	C	Lex	8,000
Malabar Man	SJ's Photo	1	0	C	Hb	25,000
Malabar Man	Sierra Kosmos	1	0	F	Hb	42,000
Malabar Man	Sierra Kosmos	1	0	F	Lex	15,000
Malabar Man	Speedy Crown	1	1	C	Hb	42,000
Malabar Man	Speedy Crown	1	0	C	Lex	20,000
Malabar Man	Speedy Primo	1	0	F	Hb	6,000
Malabar Man	Striking Sahbra	1	0	C	Lex	25,000
Malabar Man	Wall Street Banker	1	0	F	Hb	22,000
Malabar Maple	Lindy Lane	1	0	C	Lex	55,000
Master Glide	Chiola Hanover	1	0	C	Lex	25,000
Master Glide	Donerail	1	0	C	Lex	3,000
Master Glide	Enjoy Lavec	2	0	C	Lex	2,500
Master Glide	Enjoy Lavec	1	0	F	Lex	42,000
Master Glide	Harmonious	1	0	C	Lex	7,000
Master Glide	Malabar Man	1	0	F	Lex	10,000
Master Glide	Mr Lavec	1	0	F	Lex	1,000
Master Glide	Pine Chip	1	0	F	Lex	6,000
Master Glide	Royal Prestige	1	0	C	Lex	3,000
Master Glide	SJ's Photo	1	0	F	Lex	2,000
Mcardle	Abercrombie	1	0	C	Lex	32,000
Mcardle	Abercrombie	1	0	F	Lex	28,000

Sire	Bm Sire	Sold	$50,000 2 Year Olds	Sex	Sale	Average Price
Mcardle	Artiscape	1	0	C	Lex	10,000
Mcardle	Artsplace	6	0	C	Hb	22,250
Mcardle	Artsplace	2	0	F	Hb	9,750
Mcardle	Artsplace	3	1	F	Lex	24,667
Mcardle	Blissful Hall	3	0	C	Hb	22,667
Mcardle	Blissful Hall	1	0	F	Lex	2,000
Mcardle	Cambest	1	0	C	Lex	14,000
Mcardle	Cambest	1	0	F	Hb	8,000
Mcardle	Cam's Card Shark	1	1	C	Hb	20,000
Mcardle	Cam's Card Shark	1	0	F	Hb	1,500
Mcardle	Caprock	1	0	C	Hb	19,000
Mcardle	Die Laughing	1	0	F	Hb	12,000
Mcardle	Direct Scooter	1	0	C	Lex	9,000
Mcardle	Direct Scooter	1	0	F	Hb	3,500
Mcardle	Dragon's Lair	2	0	C	Hb	12,000
Mcardle	Dragon's Lair	3	0	F	Hb	10,167
Mcardle	Dream Away	1	0	F	Hb	20,000
Mcardle	Falcon Almahurst	1	0	C	Lex	25,000
Mcardle	Jate Lobell	1	0	C	Lex	37,000
Mcardle	Jate Lobell	1	0	F	Hb	15,000
Mcardle	Jate Lobell	1	0	F	Lex	20,000
Mcardle	Jeremys Gambit	1	0	C	Hb	30,000
Mcardle	Jeremys Gambit	2	0	F	Hb	24,500
Mcardle	Kiev Hanover	2	1	C	Hb	12,750
Mcardle	Kiev Hanover	1	0	F	Hb	10,000
Mcardle	Kiev Hanover	1	0	F	Lex	14,000
Mcardle	Life Sign	3	0	C	Lex	15,333
Mcardle	Life Sign	1	0	F	Hb	5,000
Mcardle	Life Sign	1	0	F	Lex	19,000
Mcardle	Lislea	1	0	F	Hb	30,000
Mcardle	Magical Mike	1	0	F	Lex	1,000
Mcardle	Matt's Scooter	1	0	C	Hb	6,000
Mcardle	Matt's Scooter	1	0	F	Lex	65,000
Mcardle	No Nukes	1	0	C	Lex	17,000
Mcardle	No Nukes	3	1	F	Hb	14,500
Mcardle	The Panderosa	2	0	C	Hb	16,500
Mcardle	The Panderosa	1	1	C	Lex	28,000
Mcardle	The Panderosa	1	0	F	Hb	40,000
Mcardle	Tyler B	1	0	F	Lex	20,000
Mcardle	Village Jiffy	1	0	C	Hb	4,500
Mcardle	Western Hanover	1	0	C	Hb	5,000

Sire	Bm Sire	Sold	$50,000 2 Year Olds	Sex	Sale	Average Price
Mcardle	Western Hanover	3	0	C	Lex	39,333
Mcardle	Western Hanover	3	0	F	Hb	11,167
Mcardle	Western Ideal	1	0	C	Hb	35,000
Mcardle	Western Ideal	1	0	C	Lex	60,000
Mcardle	Western Ideal	1	0	F	Hb	3,500
Mcardle	Western Ideal	1	1	F	Lex	70,000
Metropolitan	Arturo	1	0	F	Hb	9,000
Metropolitan	Cambest	1	0	C	Lex	15,000
Metropolitan	Cam's Card Shark	1	0	C	Lex	17,000
Metropolitan	Cam's Card Shark	1	0	F	Hb	3,000
Metropolitan	Direct Scooter	1	0	C	Hb	5,000
Metropolitan	Dragon's Lair	1	0	C	Lex	5,000
Metropolitan	Falcon Almahurst	3	0	C	Lex	24,667
Metropolitan	Laag	1	0	C	Lex	8,000
Metropolitan	Nobleland Sam	2	0	C	Lex	13,500
Metropolitan	Threefold	1	0	C	Lex	67,000
Metropolitan	Tyler B	1	0	C	Hb	7,000
Modern Art	Albatross	1	0	C	Hb	9,500
Modern Art	Beach Towel	1	0	F	Hb	15,000
Modern Art	Big Towner	2	0	C	Hb	16,000
Modern Art	Cam Fella	2	1	C	Hb	18,750
Modern Art	Camluck	1	0	C	Hb	33,000
Modern Art	Dragon's Lair	1	0	C	Lex	15,000
Modern Art	Falcons Future	1	0	C	Hb	25,000
Modern Art	Falcons Future	1	0	F	Hb	3,000
Modern Art	Jate Lobell	2	0	C	Hb	16,000
Modern Art	Jate Lobell	1	0	F	Hb	7,000
Modern Art	Jenna's Beach Boy	1	0	F	Lex	18,000
Modern Art	Matt's Scooter	1	0	F	Hb	20,000
Modern Art	Matt's Scooter	1	0	F	Lex	15,000
Modern Art	On The Road Again	1	0	F	Lex	6,000
Modern Art	Pacific Fella	1	0	F	Hb	23,000
Modern Art	Presidential Ball	1	0	C	Lex	35,000
Modern Art	Storm Damage	1	0	C	Hb	20,000
Modern Art	Western Hanover	1	0	F	Hb	15,000
Mr Feelgood	Abercrombie	1	0	C	Lex	50,000
Mr Feelgood	Cambest	1	0	C	Lex	7,000
Mr Feelgood	Camluck	1	0	F	Lex	2,000
Mr Feelgood	Dragon Again	1	0	F	Lex	6,000
Mr Feelgood	Falcon Seelster	1	0	F	Lex	6,000
Mr Feelgood	Pacific Fella	1	0	C	Lex	10,000

Sire	Bm Sire	Sold	$50,000 2 Year Olds	Sex	Sale	Average Price
Mr Feelgood	Till We Meet Again	1	0	C	Lex	16,000
Mr Feelgood	Western Hanover	1	0	F	Lex	7,000
Mr Lavec	Balanced Image	1	0	F	Hb	4,500
Mr Lavec	Garland Lobell	1	0	C	Lex	60,000
Muscles Yankee	American Winner	4	0	C	Hb	56,250
Muscles Yankee	American Winner	3	0	C	Lex	62,333
Muscles Yankee	American Winner	1	0	F	Hb	35,000
Muscles Yankee	Andover Hall	1	0	C	Hb	32,000
Muscles Yankee	Andover Hall	1	1	F	Hb	18,000
Muscles Yankee	Andover Hall	2	0	F	Lex	12,000
Muscles Yankee	Angus Hall	2	1	C	Hb	100,000
Muscles Yankee	Angus Hall	1	0	C	Lex	42,000
Muscles Yankee	Angus Hall	9	0	F	Hb	19,944
Muscles Yankee	Angus Hall	3	0	F	Lex	44,667
Muscles Yankee	Armbro Goal	1	0	C	Hb	50,000
Muscles Yankee	Armbro Goal	1	0	C	Lex	35,000
Muscles Yankee	Armbro Goal	1	0	F	Hb	47,000
Muscles Yankee	Armbro Goal	2	0	F	Lex	49,500
Muscles Yankee	Balanced Image	2	0	C	Lex	86,000
Muscles Yankee	Balanced Image	8	0	F	Hb	42,500
Muscles Yankee	Balanced Image	2	1	F	Lex	36,000
Muscles Yankee	BJ's Mac	1	0	C	Lex	57,000
Muscles Yankee	BJ's Mac	1	0	F	Hb	12,000
Muscles Yankee	Broadway Hall	1	0	F	Lex	10,000
Muscles Yankee	Conway Hall	5	2	C	Hb	46,000
Muscles Yankee	Conway Hall	4	0	C	Lex	148,000
Muscles Yankee	Conway Hall	3	0	F	Hb	37,167
Muscles Yankee	Conway Hall	4	0	F	Lex	35,000
Muscles Yankee	Credit Winner	2	0	C	Hb	62,250
Muscles Yankee	Credit Winner	2	0	C	Lex	82,500
Muscles Yankee	Credit Winner	4	0	F	Hb	36,000
Muscles Yankee	Crowning Point	1	0	F	Lex	50,000
Muscles Yankee	Cumin	1	0	F	Lex	20,000
Muscles Yankee	Donerail	1	0	C	Hb	72,000
Muscles Yankee	Donerail	2	0	F	Hb	40,000
Muscles Yankee	Donerail	1	0	F	Lex	30,000
Muscles Yankee	Dream Vacation	1	0	F	Lex	47,000
Muscles Yankee	Enjoy Lavec	3	0	C	Hb	43,333
Muscles Yankee	Enjoy Lavec	1	0	C	Lex	50,000
Muscles Yankee	Garland Lobell	3	0	C	Hb	92,333
Muscles Yankee	Garland Lobell	5	1	F	Hb	39,400

Sire	Bm Sire	Sold	$50,000 2 Year Olds	Sex	Sale	Average Price
Muscles Yankee	Garland Lobell	2	0	F	Lex	60,000
Muscles Yankee	Giant Hit	2	0	C	Hb	21,000
Muscles Yankee	Giant Hit	1	0	F	Hb	30,000
Muscles Yankee	Incredible Abe	1	0	F	Lex	15,000
Muscles Yankee	King Conch	1	0	C	Lex	22,000
Muscles Yankee	King Conch	1	0	F	Lex	7,000
Muscles Yankee	Like A Prayer	1	0	C	Hb	9,500
Muscles Yankee	Like A Prayer	1	0	F	Hb	12,000
Muscles Yankee	Malabar Man	11	1	C	Hb	48,455
Muscles Yankee	Malabar Man	6	0	C	Lex	44,667
Muscles Yankee	Malabar Man	6	1	F	Hb	20,167
Muscles Yankee	Malabar Man	4	0	F	Lex	47,250
Muscles Yankee	Mr Lavec	1	0	C	Hb	20,000
Muscles Yankee	Mr Lavec	2	0	C	Lex	56,000
Muscles Yankee	Mr Lavec	1	0	F	Lex	70,000
Muscles Yankee	Mr Vic	1	0	F	Lex	52,000
Muscles Yankee	Pine Chip	4	0	C	Hb	158,000
Muscles Yankee	Pine Chip	1	0	C	Lex	22,000
Muscles Yankee	Pine Chip	8	0	F	Hb	32,625
Muscles Yankee	Pine Chip	3	0	F	Lex	71,667
Muscles Yankee	Power Seat	1	0	F	Lex	32,000
Muscles Yankee	Rule The Wind	2	0	F	Hb	28,000
Muscles Yankee	SJ's Photo	3	0	C	Hb	16,000
Muscles Yankee	SJ's Photo	3	0	F	Hb	21,000
Muscles Yankee	Self Possessed	1	0	C	Lex	200,000
Muscles Yankee	Self Possessed	1	1	F	Hb	30,000
Muscles Yankee	Self Possessed	1	0	F	Lex	30,000
Muscles Yankee	Sierra Kosmos	2	0	C	Hb	10,000
Muscles Yankee	Sierra Kosmos	3	1	F	Hb	31,667
Muscles Yankee	Sierra Kosmos	1	0	F	Lex	50,000
Muscles Yankee	Sir Taurus	3	2	C	Hb	155,000
Muscles Yankee	Sir Taurus	1	0	C	Lex	50,000
Muscles Yankee	Sir Taurus	1	0	F	Hb	20,000
Muscles Yankee	SJ's Caviar	1	0	C	Hb	10,000
Muscles Yankee	SJ's Caviar	2	1	F	Hb	46,500
Muscles Yankee	Speedy Crown	1	0	C	Lex	35,000
Muscles Yankee	Speedy Crown	1	0	F	Hb	3,000
Muscles Yankee	Striking Sahbra	1	0	C	Lex	65,000
Muscles Yankee	Striking Sahbra	5	0	F	Hb	23,000
Muscles Yankee	Striking Sahbra	1	0	F	Lex	60,000
Muscles Yankee	Super Bowl	1	0	C	Hb	27,000

Sire	Bm Sire	Sold	$50,000 2 Year Olds	Sex	Sale	Average Price
Muscles Yankee	Super Bowl	1	0	C	Lex	10,000
Muscles Yankee	Super Bowl	1	0	F	Hb	45,000
Muscles Yankee	Super Bowl	1	0	F	Lex	55,000
Muscles Yankee	Supergill	1	0	C	Lex	75,000
Muscles Yankee	Supergill	1	0	F	Hb	60,000
Muscles Yankee	Supergill	2	0	F	Lex	72,500
Muscles Yankee	Tagliabue	2	0	C	Lex	105,000
Muscles Yankee	Thirty Two	1	0	C	Hb	25,000
Muscles Yankee	Thirty Two	1	0	C	Lex	13,000
Muscles Yankee	Wesgate Crown	1	0	C	Hb	12,000
Muscles Yankee	Yankee Glide	1	0	F	Hb	42,000
Muscles Yankee	Yankee Paco	1	0	F	Hb	15,000
No Pan Intended	Artsplace	1	0	C	Hb	14,000
No Pan Intended	Artsplace	2	1	C	Lex	6,000
No Pan Intended	Artsplace	1	0	F	Hb	5,500
No Pan Intended	Artsplace	1	0	F	Lex	9,000
No Pan Intended	B.G's Bunny	1	0	C	Hb	9,000
No Pan Intended	Beach Towel	1	0	F	Hb	22,000
No Pan Intended	Big Towner	1	0	C	Hb	10,000
No Pan Intended	Big Towner	1	0	C	Lex	8,000
No Pan Intended	Broadway Jate	1	0	F	Lex	2,000
No Pan Intended	Cam Fella	1	0	C	Hb	1,500
No Pan Intended	Coal Harbor	1	0	F	Hb	40,000
No Pan Intended	Life Sign	1	0	C	Hb	9,000
No Pan Intended	Magical Mike	1	0	F	Hb	5,500
No Pan Intended	Rustler Hanover	1	0	F	Hb	13,000
No Pan Intended	The Panderosa	1	0	C	Hb	22,000
No Pan Intended	The Panderosa	2	0	F	Hb	8,500
No Pan Intended	The Panderosa	1	0	F	Lex	7,000
No Pan Intended	Walton Hanover	1	0	C	Hb	8,000
No Pan Intended	Western Hanover	2	0	C	Hb	20,000
No Pan Intended	Western Hanover	1	0	C	Lex	6,000
No Pan Intended	Western Hanover	1	0	F	Hb	5,000
Pacific Fella	Abercrombie	1	0	C	Lex	13,000
Peruvian Hanover	Camluck	1	0	F	Hb	3,000
Plesac	Donerail	1	0	C	Hb	23,000
Ponder	Abercrombie	2	0	C	Hb	12,000
Ponder	Abercrombie	1	0	C	Lex	15,000
Ponder	Artsplace	1	1	C	Hb	70,000
Ponder	Artsplace	2	0	F	Hb	24,000
Ponder	Big Towner	1	0	C	Lex	20,000

Sire	Bm Sire	Sold	$50,000 2 Year Olds	Sex	Sale	Average Price
Ponder	Billy Dart	1	0	C	Lex	15,000
Ponder	Cam Fella	1	0	C	Lex	5,000
Ponder	Cambest	1	0	C	Hb	5,000
Ponder	Cambest	2	0	C	Lex	26,000
Ponder	Cambest	1	0	F	Hb	6,000
Ponder	Camluck	1	0	C	Hb	7,000
Ponder	Camluck	1	0	F	Hb	20,000
Ponder	Camluck	1	0	F	Lex	7,000
Ponder	Cam's Card Shark	2	0	C	Hb	16,250
Ponder	Cam's Card Shark	2	1	C	Lex	12,500
Ponder	Cam's Card Shark	1	0	F	Hb	6,000
Ponder	Cam's Card Shark	2	1	F	Lex	14,500
Ponder	Forrest Skipper	1	0	C	Hb	33,000
Ponder	Grinfromeartoear	1	0	C	Lex	33,000
Ponder	Jate Lobell	2	0	C	Lex	17,500
Ponder	Jenna's Beach Boy	1	0	C	Lex	6,000
Ponder	Life Sign	1	0	C	Lex	6,000
Ponder	Life Sign	1	0	F	Lex	17,000
Ponder	Nihilator	1	0	C	Lex	13,000
Ponder	No Nukes	1	0	C	Hb	15,000
Ponder	No Nukes	1	0	C	Lex	35,000
Ponder	No Nukes	1	0	F	Lex	10,000
Ponder	Real Artist	1	0	C	Hb	35,000
Ponder	Shady Character	1	0	C	Lex	23,000
Ponder	Threefold	1	0	C	Lex	23,000
Ponder	Walton Hanover	1	0	C	Hb	2,500
Ponder	Western Hanover	1	0	C	Hb	15,000
Ponder	Western Ideal	1	0	F	Lex	37,000
Pro Bono Best	Abercrombie	1	0	F	Hb	35,000
Pro Bono Best	Sonsam	1	0	F	Hb	1,500
Quik Pulse Mindale	Abercrombie	1	0	C	Lex	38,000
Quik Pulse Mindale	Albatross	1	0	C	Hb	10,000
Quik Pulse Mindale	Artsplace	1	0	C	Hb	30,000
Quik Pulse Mindale	Artsplace	1	0	C	Lex	18,000
Quik Pulse Mindale	Beach Towel	1	0	C	Hb	21,000
Quik Pulse Mindale	Big Towner	1	0	C	Lex	14,000
Quik Pulse Mindale	Cambest	1	0	C	Hb	16,000
Quik Pulse Mindale	Cambest	1	1	F	Hb	8,000
Quik Pulse Mindale	Camluck	1	0	F	Hb	11,000
Quik Pulse Mindale	Hit The Bid	2	0	C	Hb	40,000
Quik Pulse Mindale	In The Pocket	1	0	C	Lex	27,000

Sire	Bm Sire	Sold	$50,000 2 Year Olds	Sex	Sale	Average Price
Quik Pulse Mindale	Jate Lobell	1	0	F	Hb	25,000
Quik Pulse Mindale	Laag	1	0	F	Lex	13,000
Quik Pulse Mindale	Powerful Toy	1	0	F	Lex	17,000
Quik Pulse Mindale	Western Hanover	1	0	F	Hb	16,000
Real Artist	Apaches Fame	1	0	F	Lex	3,000
Real Artist	Armbro Emerson	1	0	F	Hb	18,000
Real Artist	Beach Towel	1	1	C	Lex	65,000
Real Artist	Bettor's Delight	1	0	C	Hb	15,000
Real Artist	Blissful Hall	2	0	C	Hb	16,500
Real Artist	Cam Fella	1	0	C	Hb	10,000
Real Artist	Cam Fella	1	0	F	Hb	95,000
Real Artist	Cam's Card Shark	2	0	C	Hb	15,500
Real Artist	Cam's Card Shark	2	0	F	Hb	13,250
Real Artist	Camtastic	1	0	F	Hb	32,000
Real Artist	Dragon's Lair	1	0	C	Lex	19,000
Real Artist	Elegant Osborne	1	1	C	Hb	35,000
Real Artist	Expensive Scooter	1	0	C	Lex	24,000
Real Artist	Falcon Seelster	1	0	F	Lex	4,000
Real Artist	Goalie Jeff	1	0	F	Hb	20,000
Real Artist	In The Pocket	1	0	C	Lex	21,000
Real Artist	In The Pocket	1	0	F	Lex	35,000
Real Artist	Jate Lobell	1	0	C	Hb	6,500
Real Artist	Jate Lobell	1	0	F	Hb	14,000
Real Artist	Jate Lobell	1	0	F	Lex	6,000
Real Artist	Matt's Scooter	2	0	C	Lex	17,500
Real Artist	No Nukes	1	0	C	Hb	17,000
Real Artist	No Nukes	1	0	C	Lex	20,000
Real Artist	No Nukes	2	0	F	Hb	10,500
Real Artist	The Panderosa	1	0	C	Hb	2,500
Real Artist	The Panderosa	1	0	F	Hb	17,000
Real Artist	Totally Ruthless	1	0	C	Lex	9,000
Real Artist	Western Hanover	3	0	C	Hb	12,000
Real Artist	Western Hanover	1	0	C	Lex	15,000
Real Artist	Western Hanover	5	0	F	Hb	14,800
Real Artist	Western Hanover	3	0	F	Lex	12,667
Real Artist	Western Ideal	1	0	F	Hb	9,000
Real Desire	Abercrombie	1	0	C	Hb	8,000
Real Desire	Abercrombie	1	0	C	Lex	35,000
Real Desire	Armbro Operative	1	0	C	Hb	5,000
Real Desire	Artiscape	2	0	C	Hb	30,000
Real Desire	Artiscape	2	2	C	Lex	23,500

Sire	Bm Sire	Sold	$50,000 2 Year Olds	Sex	Sale	Average Price
Real Desire	Artiscape	3	0	F	Hb	4,667
Real Desire	Artiscape	2	0	F	Lex	36,500
Real Desire	Artsplace	2	0	C	Hb	25,500
Real Desire	Artsplace	5	0	C	Lex	27,000
Real Desire	Artsplace	2	1	F	Hb	23,750
Real Desire	Artsplace	2	0	F	Lex	10,000
Real Desire	Bettor's Delight	1	0	F	Lex	9,000
Real Desire	Big Towner	1	0	C	Hb	28,000
Real Desire	Big Towner	2	1	C	Lex	20,500
Real Desire	Cambest	2	0	C	Hb	17,500
Real Desire	Cambest	1	0	C	Lex	50,000
Real Desire	Cambest	1	0	F	Lex	15,000
Real Desire	Camluck	2	0	C	Hb	16,500
Real Desire	Camluck	3	0	C	Lex	46,667
Real Desire	Camluck	2	0	F	Hb	27,500
Real Desire	Camluck	1	0	F	Lex	4,000
Real Desire	Cam's Card Shark	1	0	C	Hb	11,000
Real Desire	Cam's Card Shark	2	0	F	Hb	4,250
Real Desire	Die Laughing	1	0	F	Lex	4,000
Real Desire	Dragon's Lair	1	0	F	Lex	30,000
Real Desire	Falcon Almahurst	1	0	F	Hb	16,000
Real Desire	Falcon Seelster	1	0	C	Hb	8,000
Real Desire	Falcons Future	1	0	C	Lex	13,000
Real Desire	Jate Lobell	3	0	C	Hb	15,167
Real Desire	Jate Lobell	1	0	C	Lex	14,000
Real Desire	Jate Lobell	2	1	F	Lex	21,000
Real Desire	Jenna's Beach Boy	1	0	C	Hb	25,000
Real Desire	Jenna's Beach Boy	1	0	C	Lex	26,000
Real Desire	Jenna's Beach Boy	2	0	F	Lex	32,500
Real Desire	Kiev Hanover	2	0	F	Lex	49,500
Real Desire	Matt's Scooter	4	0	C	Hb	19,750
Real Desire	Matt's Scooter	1	0	F	Lex	22,000
Real Desire	No Nukes	3	0	C	Hb	11,667
Real Desire	No Nukes	2	0	C	Lex	26,000
Real Desire	No Nukes	3	0	F	Hb	17,667
Real Desire	No Nukes	3	0	F	Lex	18,000
Real Desire	Northern Luck	1	0	F	Lex	55,000
Real Desire	Pacific Fella	1	0	F	Lex	5,000
Real Desire	Real Artist	2	0	C	Lex	17,000
Real Desire	Real Artist	1	0	F	Hb	8,000
Real Desire	Run The Table	1	0	C	Lex	5,000

Sire	Bm Sire	Sold	$50,000 2 Year Olds	Sex	Sale	Average Price
Real Desire	The Panderosa	1	1	F	Hb	18,000
Real Desire	The Panderosa	1	1	F	Lex	40,000
Real Desire	Western Hanover	6	0	C	Lex	37,000
Real Desire	Western Hanover	3	0	F	Hb	9,667
Real Desire	Western Hanover	1	0	F	Lex	1,000
Real Desire	Western Ideal	1	0	C	Hb	6,500
Real Desire	Western Ideal	2	0	C	Lex	18,500
Real Desire	Western Ideal	1	0	F	Hb	12,000
Real Desire	Western Ideal	3	0	F	Lex	13,667
Red River Hanover	Abercrombie	2	0	F	Lex	7,500
Red River Hanover	Artiscape	1	0	F	Hb	6,000
Red River Hanover	Artsplace	3	0	F	Hb	6,000
Red River Hanover	Artsplace	1	0	F	Lex	10,000
Red River Hanover	Big Towner	1	0	C	Hb	10,000
Red River Hanover	Cambest	2	0	F	Lex	9,500
Red River Hanover	Cam's Card Shark	1	0	C	Lex	2,000
Red River Hanover	Cam's Card Shark	1	0	F	Hb	10,000
Red River Hanover	Carlsbad Cam	1	0	F	Lex	6,000
Red River Hanover	Cole Muffler	1	0	F	Lex	8,000
Red River Hanover	Die Laughing	1	0	F	Hb	5,000
Red River Hanover	Jenna's Beach Boy	1	0	C	Hb	5,000
Red River Hanover	Kingston	1	0	C	Hb	12,000
Red River Hanover	Laag	1	0	F	Hb	6,500
Red River Hanover	Matt's Scooter	1	0	C	Hb	17,000
Red River Hanover	Matt's Scooter	1	0	F	Hb	10,000
Red River Hanover	Presidential Ball	2	0	F	Hb	3,000
Red River Hanover	Presidential Ball	1	0	F	Lex	8,000
Red River Hanover	Pro Bono Best	1	0	F	Hb	5,000
Red River Hanover	Run The Table	1	0	F	Lex	10,000
Red River Hanover	Samadhi	1	0	C	Lex	3,000
Red River Hanover	Troublemaker	1	0	F	Lex	10,000
Revenue S	American Winner	1	0	C	Hb	15,000
Revenue S	Angus Hall	1	0	C	Hb	6,000
Revenue S	Armbro Iliad	1	0	C	Hb	20,000
Revenue S	Dancer's Victory	1	0	C	Hb	9,000
Revenue S	Donerail	1	0	C	Lex	3,000
Revenue S	Earl	1	0	F	Hb	4,000
Revenue S	Garland Lobell	1	0	C	Hb	13,000
Revenue S	Giant Victory	1	0	F	Hb	4,000
Revenue S	Incredible Nevele	1	0	F	Hb	5,500
Revenue S	Incredible Nevele	1	0	F	Lex	40,000

Sire	Bm Sire	Sold	$50,000 2 Year Olds	Sex	Sale	Average Price
Revenue S	Joie De Vie	1	0	F	Hb	100,000
Revenue S	King Conch	2	0	C	Hb	7,000
Revenue S	Lindy Lane	1	0	C	Hb	30,000
Revenue S	Malabar Man	1	0	F	Lex	20,000
Revenue S	Moving Forward	1	0	C	Hb	18,000
Revenue S	Mr Lavec	2	0	F	Hb	6,250
Revenue S	Mr Vic	1	0	C	Lex	22,000
Revenue S	Muscles Yankee	3	1	C	Hb	11,833
Revenue S	Muscles Yankee	1	0	C	Lex	1,000
Revenue S	Muscles Yankee	4	0	F	Hb	25,875
Revenue S	Pine Chip	2	0	F	Hb	5,250
Revenue S	Royal Prestige	1	0	C	Hb	20,000
Revenue S	Royal Prestige	1	0	C	Lex	1,000
Revenue S	SJ's Photo	1	0	F	Hb	37,000
Revenue S	Self Possessed	1	0	C	Hb	42,000
Revenue S	Sierra Kosmos	2	0	C	Lex	21,500
Revenue S	Sierra Kosmos	2	0	F	Hb	6,250
Revenue S	Speedy Crown	1	0	F	Lex	4,000
Revenue S	Super Bowl	2	0	C	Lex	3,000
Revenue S	Super Bowl	1	0	F	Hb	2,500
Revenue S	Supergill	2	0	C	Hb	4,000
Revenue S	Supergill	1	0	F	Hb	20,000
Revenue S	Valley Victory	1	0	C	Hb	5,500
Revenue S	Valley Victory	1	0	F	Lex	16,000
Revenue S	Victory Dream	1	0	C	Lex	25,000
Revenue S	Yankee Glide	1	0	C	Lex	16,000
Riverboat King	Big Towner	1	0	F	Hb	7,000
Riverboat King	Frugal Gormet	1	0	C	Hb	15,000
Riverboat King	Magical Mike	1	0	C	Hb	16,000
Riverboat King	On The Road Again	1	0	C	Lex	30,000
Riverboat King	Scoot Herb	1	0	F	Hb	16,000
Rocknroll Hanover	Abercrombie	5	0	C	Hb	50,000
Rocknroll Hanover	Abercrombie	7	1	C	Lex	74,571
Rocknroll Hanover	Abercrombie	2	0	F	Hb	22,500
Rocknroll Hanover	Abercrombie	2	0	F	Lex	49,000
Rocknroll Hanover	Albatross	2	0	C	Lex	43,500
Rocknroll Hanover	Albatross	2	0	F	Lex	67,500
Rocknroll Hanover	Albert Albert	1	0	C	Hb	55,000
Rocknroll Hanover	Albert Albert	1	0	C	Lex	32,000
Rocknroll Hanover	Albert Albert	1	0	F	Hb	50,000
Rocknroll Hanover	Armbro Emerson	2	0	C	Hb	127,500

Sire	Bm Sire	Sold	$50,000 2 Year Olds	Sex	Sale	Average Price
Rocknroll Hanover	Armbro Emerson	1	0	F	Hb	40,000
Rocknroll Hanover	Armbro Mackintosh	1	0	F	Lex	40,000
Rocknroll Hanover	Art Major	1	0	C	Hb	25,000
Rocknroll Hanover	Artiscape	5	0	C	Hb	20,200
Rocknroll Hanover	Artiscape	2	0	C	Lex	46,000
Rocknroll Hanover	Artiscape	3	0	F	Hb	37,333
Rocknroll Hanover	Artsplace	28	2	C	Hb	55,714
Rocknroll Hanover	Artsplace	17	2	C	Lex	70,765
Rocknroll Hanover	Artsplace	20	1	F	Hb	58,100
Rocknroll Hanover	Artsplace	16	4	F	Lex	48,188
Rocknroll Hanover	Astreos	1	0	F	Lex	120,000
Rocknroll Hanover	Beach Towel	1	0	C	Lex	52,000
Rocknroll Hanover	Beach Towel	1	0	F	Hb	20,000
Rocknroll Hanover	Bettor's Delight	1	0	C	Hb	75,000
Rocknroll Hanover	Bettor's Delight	3	0	C	Lex	82,333
Rocknroll Hanover	Bettor's Delight	3	0	F	Hb	20,333
Rocknroll Hanover	Big Rube	1	0	C	Hb	80,000
Rocknroll Hanover	Big Towner	1	0	C	Hb	48,000
Rocknroll Hanover	Big Towner	1	0	C	Lex	32,000
Rocknroll Hanover	Big Towner	2	0	F	Hb	13,500
Rocknroll Hanover	Big Towner	1	0	F	Lex	27,000
Rocknroll Hanover	Blissful Hall	2	0	C	Hb	21,500
Rocknroll Hanover	Blissful Hall	3	0	F	Hb	15,333
Rocknroll Hanover	Call For Rain	1	0	C	Lex	65,000
Rocknroll Hanover	Cam Fella	2	1	C	Hb	77,500
Rocknroll Hanover	Cam Fella	2	0	C	Lex	61,500
Rocknroll Hanover	Cam Fella	1	0	F	Lex	45,000
Rocknroll Hanover	Cambest	2	0	C	Hb	61,000
Rocknroll Hanover	Cambest	1	0	C	Lex	57,000
Rocknroll Hanover	Cambest	3	0	F	Hb	25,333
Rocknroll Hanover	Cambest	5	0	F	Lex	58,000
Rocknroll Hanover	Camluck	6	0	C	Hb	103,667
Rocknroll Hanover	Camluck	1	0	C	Lex	35,000
Rocknroll Hanover	Camluck	4	0	F	Hb	61,250
Rocknroll Hanover	Camluck	3	0	F	Lex	31,333
Rocknroll Hanover	Cam's Card Shark	5	2	C	Hb	44,400
Rocknroll Hanover	Cam's Card Shark	3	0	C	Lex	49,333
Rocknroll Hanover	Cam's Card Shark	2	0	F	Hb	16,500
Rocknroll Hanover	Cam's Card Shark	7	2	F	Lex	62,286
Rocknroll Hanover	Camtastic	1	0	C	Hb	55,000
Rocknroll Hanover	Camtastic	1	0	C	Lex	45,000

Sire	Bm Sire	Sold	$50,000 2 Year Olds	Sex	Sale	Average Price
Rocknroll Hanover	Camtastic	1	0	F	Hb	12,000
Rocknroll Hanover	Cole Muffler	1	0	C	Hb	17,000
Rocknroll Hanover	Die Laughing	2	0	C	Hb	35,000
Rocknroll Hanover	Die Laughing	1	0	C	Lex	20,000
Rocknroll Hanover	Die Laughing	1	0	F	Hb	40,000
Rocknroll Hanover	Die Laughing	1	0	F	Lex	20,000
Rocknroll Hanover	Dragon Again	1	0	C	Hb	60,000
Rocknroll Hanover	Dragon Again	3	0	C	Lex	90,000
Rocknroll Hanover	Dragon Again	1	0	F	Hb	95,000
Rocknroll Hanover	Dragon's Lair	3	0	C	Hb	35,667
Rocknroll Hanover	Dragon's Lair	3	0	C	Lex	26,000
Rocknroll Hanover	Dragon's Lair	1	0	F	Hb	47,000
Rocknroll Hanover	Dragon's Lair	1	0	F	Lex	40,000
Rocknroll Hanover	Dream Away	1	0	F	Hb	8,000
Rocknroll Hanover	Falcon Seelster	3	0	C	Hb	57,333
Rocknroll Hanover	Falcon Seelster	2	1	C	Lex	33,500
Rocknroll Hanover	Grinfromeartoear	1	0	C	Lex	22,000
Rocknroll Hanover	Grinfromeartoear	1	0	F	Hb	17,000
Rocknroll Hanover	Incredible Finale	2	1	C	Hb	19,500
Rocknroll Hanover	Incredible Finale	1	1	F	Hb	120,000
Rocknroll Hanover	Island Fantasy	2	0	C	Hb	14,000
Rocknroll Hanover	Jate Lobell	3	0	C	Hb	30,333
Rocknroll Hanover	Jate Lobell	7	1	C	Lex	77,000
Rocknroll Hanover	Jate Lobell	7	0	F	Hb	51,286
Rocknroll Hanover	Jate Lobell	1	0	F	Lex	15,000
Rocknroll Hanover	Jenna's Beach Boy	1	0	C	Hb	97,000
Rocknroll Hanover	Jenna's Beach Boy	2	0	F	Hb	120,000
Rocknroll Hanover	Jenna's Beach Boy	2	0	F	Lex	40,000
Rocknroll Hanover	Laag	1	1	C	Lex	25,000
Rocknroll Hanover	Life Sign	4	0	C	Lex	28,500
Rocknroll Hanover	Life Sign	4	0	F	Hb	25,750
Rocknroll Hanover	Life Sign	7	1	F	Lex	47,571
Rocknroll Hanover	Magical Mike	1	0	C	Hb	8,000
Rocknroll Hanover	Matt's Scooter	2	0	C	Hb	118,500
Rocknroll Hanover	Matt's Scooter	1	0	C	Lex	100,000
Rocknroll Hanover	Matt's Scooter	2	0	F	Hb	30,000
Rocknroll Hanover	Matt's Scooter	1	0	F	Lex	45,000
Rocknroll Hanover	Niatross	1	0	C	Hb	4,000
Rocknroll Hanover	Nihilator	1	0	F	Lex	50,000
Rocknroll Hanover	No Nukes	2	0	C	Hb	42,500
Rocknroll Hanover	No Nukes	2	0	C	Lex	69,000

Sire	Bm Sire	Sold	$50,000 2 Year Olds	Sex	Sale	Average Price
Rocknroll Hanover	No Nukes	3	0	F	Hb	84,833
Rocknroll Hanover	No Nukes	1	0	F	Lex	70,000
Rocknroll Hanover	Northern Luck	1	0	C	Hb	14,000
Rocknroll Hanover	On The Road Again	2	0	C	Hb	45,000
Rocknroll Hanover	Pacific Fella	2	0	C	Hb	29,500
Rocknroll Hanover	Pacific Rocket	1	0	C	Lex	40,000
Rocknroll Hanover	Park Place	1	0	F	Lex	42,000
Rocknroll Hanover	Precious Bunny	1	1	C	Hb	45,000
Rocknroll Hanover	Presidential Ball	4	1	C	Hb	39,000
Rocknroll Hanover	Presidential Ball	2	1	C	Lex	196,000
Rocknroll Hanover	Presidential Ball	3	0	F	Hb	12,000
Rocknroll Hanover	Presidential Ball	1	0	F	Lex	37,000
Rocknroll Hanover	Pro Bono Best	1	1	F	Hb	22,000
Rocknroll Hanover	Real Artist	1	0	C	Lex	25,000
Rocknroll Hanover	Real Artist	1	0	F	Lex	9,000
Rocknroll Hanover	Real Desire	1	0	C	Lex	35,000
Rocknroll Hanover	Real Desire	1	0	F	Hb	14,000
Rocknroll Hanover	Run The Table	3	0	C	Hb	57,333
Rocknroll Hanover	Run The Table	1	0	C	Lex	25,000
Rocknroll Hanover	Run The Table	2	0	F	Hb	143,500
Rocknroll Hanover	Sportsmaster	1	0	C	Hb	110,000
Rocknroll Hanover	Sportsmaster	1	1	C	Lex	36,000
Rocknroll Hanover	Sportsmaster	1	0	F	Hb	20,000
Rocknroll Hanover	Survivor Gold	2	0	C	Hb	30,000
Rocknroll Hanover	The Big Dog	1	0	C	Lex	10,000
Rocknroll Hanover	The Big Dog	1	0	F	Hb	11,000
Rocknroll Hanover	The Panderosa	1	0	C	Hb	20,000
Rocknroll Hanover	The Panderosa	2	0	C	Lex	50,000
Rocknroll Hanover	The Panderosa	1	0	F	Hb	5,500
Rocknroll Hanover	The Panderosa	1	0	F	Lex	29,000
Rocknroll Hanover	Towner's Big Guy	1	0	C	Hb	85,000
Rocknroll Hanover	Village Jasper	2	0	F	Lex	76,000
Rocknroll Hanover	Walton Hanover	2	0	C	Hb	56,000
Rocknroll Hanover	Western Hanover	1	0	C	Hb	165,000
Rocknroll Hanover	Western Hanover	2	0	C	Lex	40,000
Rocknroll Hanover	Western Hanover	1	0	F	Hb	19,000
Rocknroll Hanover	Western Hanover	1	0	F	Lex	150,000
Royal Mattjesty	Abercrombie	1	0	C	Lex	13,000
Royal Mattjesty	Armbro Emerson	1	0	C	Hb	37,000
Royal Mattjesty	Artiscape	1	0	C	Hb	53,000
Royal Mattjesty	Artsplace	1	0	F	Lex	35,000

Sire	Bm Sire	Sold	$50,000 2 Year Olds	Sex	Sale	Average Price
Royal Mattjesty	Big Towner	1	0	C	Hb	30,000
Royal Mattjesty	Blissful Hall	1	0	C	Lex	40,000
Royal Mattjesty	Cambest	1	0	F	Lex	8,000
Royal Mattjesty	Camluck	1	0	C	Hb	32,000
Royal Mattjesty	Cam's Card Shark	1	0	C	Lex	11,000
Royal Mattjesty	Cam's Card Shark	1	0	F	Hb	20,000
Royal Mattjesty	Camtastic	1	0	C	Hb	15,000
Royal Mattjesty	Caprock	1	0	C	Hb	42,000
Royal Mattjesty	Incredible Finale	1	0	C	Lex	15,000
Royal Mattjesty	Jate Lobell	1	0	C	Hb	25,000
Royal Mattjesty	Jate Lobell	1	0	F	Hb	22,000
Royal Mattjesty	Life Sign	1	0	F	Hb	33,000
Royal Mattjesty	Presidential Ball	1	0	C	Hb	34,000
Royal Mattjesty	Presidential Ball	1	0	F	Hb	14,000
Rustler Hanover	Shady Character	1	0	C	Lex	17,000
SJ's Photo	Armbro Iliad	1	0	C	Hb	22,000
SJ's Photo	Balanced Image	1	0	C	Lex	17,000
SJ's Photo	Donerail	1	0	C	Lex	17,000
SJ's Photo	Final Score	1	0	C	Hb	30,000
SJ's Photo	Garland Lobell	1	0	C	Lex	35,000
SJ's Photo	Garland Lobell	1	0	F	Hb	55,000
SJ's Photo	Inquirer	1	0	F	Hb	65,000
SJ's Photo	Lindy Lane	1	0	C	Lex	10,000
SJ's Photo	Malabar Man	1	0	C	Lex	10,000
SJ's Photo	Meadowbranch Jerzy	1	0	C	Lex	17,000
SJ's Photo	Overcomer	1	0	F	Lex	13,000
SJ's Photo	Pine Chip	1	0	F	Lex	8,000
SJ's Photo	Sierra Kosmos	2	0	C	Lex	20,000
SJ's Photo	Super Bowl	1	0	C	Hb	10,000
SJ's Photo	Valley Victory	2	0	C	Lex	29,000
Sand Vic	Balanced Image	1	0	C	Lex	7,000
Sand Vic	BJ's Mac	1	0	C	Hb	11,000
Sand Vic	Hoist The Yankee	1	0	F	Lex	12,000
Sand Vic	Pine Chip	1	0	F	Hb	35,000
Sand Vic	Striking Sahbra	1	0	C	Lex	10,000
Sand Vic	Worthy Bowl	1	0	F	Hb	10,000
Shark Gesture	Artsplace	1	0	C	Hb	30,000
Shark Gesture	Arturo	1	0	C	Hb	30,000
Shark Gesture	Jate Lobell	1	0	C	Hb	20,000
Shark Gesture	Jate Lobell	1	1	C	Lex	82,000
Shark Gesture	Northern Luck	1	0	C	Lex	40,000

Sire	Bm Sire	Sold	$50,000 2 Year Olds	Sex	Sale	Average Price
Shark Gesture	Sportsmaster	1	0	C	Lex	23,000
Shark Gesture	Threefold	1	0	C	Hb	35,000
SJ's Caviar	Aggressive Way	1	0	F	Hb	10,000
SJ's Caviar	American Winner	1	0	C	Hb	20,000
SJ's Caviar	American Winner	1	0	C	Lex	40,000
SJ's Caviar	American Winner	1	0	F	Hb	6,000
SJ's Caviar	American Winner	1	0	F	Lex	95,000
SJ's Caviar	Armbro Goal	1	0	F	Hb	4,000
SJ's Caviar	Balanced Image	3	0	C	Hb	11,667
SJ's Caviar	Balanced Image	1	0	F	Hb	13,000
SJ's Caviar	Balanced Image	1	0	F	Lex	8,000
SJ's Caviar	Baltic Speed	1	0	C	Hb	20,000
SJ's Caviar	Bostonian	1	0	C	Hb	13,500
SJ's Caviar	Brisco Hanover	1	0	F	Hb	20,000
SJ's Caviar	Carry The Message	1	0	F	Hb	29,000
SJ's Caviar	Conway Hall	1	0	C	Hb	25,000
SJ's Caviar	Conway Hall	1	0	F	Hb	27,000
SJ's Caviar	Credit Winner	2	0	C	Hb	17,000
SJ's Caviar	Credit Winner	1	0	C	Lex	35,000
SJ's Caviar	Dancer's Victory	1	0	C	Lex	40,000
SJ's Caviar	Donerail	2	0	C	Hb	24,000
SJ's Caviar	Donerail	2	0	C	Lex	8,500
SJ's Caviar	Donerail	1	0	F	Lex	12,000
SJ's Caviar	Florida Pro	1	0	C	Hb	20,000
SJ's Caviar	Garland Lobell	3	0	C	Hb	10,000
SJ's Caviar	Garland Lobell	4	0	F	Hb	40,250
SJ's Caviar	Giant Victory	2	0	F	Hb	29,000
SJ's Caviar	Go Get Lost	2	0	F	Hb	5,500
SJ's Caviar	Jobie Tempest	1	0	C	Hb	10,000
SJ's Caviar	Joie De Vie	1	0	F	Hb	23,000
SJ's Caviar	Lindy Lane	4	0	C	Hb	12,250
SJ's Caviar	Lindy Lane	1	0	C	Lex	22,000
SJ's Caviar	Lindy Lane	1	0	F	Hb	17,000
SJ's Caviar	Lindy Lane	1	0	F	Lex	27,000
SJ's Caviar	Malabar Man	3	0	C	Hb	17,667
SJ's Caviar	Malabar Man	2	0	F	Hb	15,500
SJ's Caviar	Meadow Road	1	0	C	Hb	7,500
SJ's Caviar	Meadowbranch Jerzy	1	0	C	Lex	13,000
SJ's Caviar	Mr Lavec	1	0	C	Lex	5,000
SJ's Caviar	Muscles Yankee	5	1	C	Hb	20,800
SJ's Caviar	Muscles Yankee	1	0	F	Hb	25,000

Sire	Bm Sire	Sold	$50,000 2 Year Olds	Sex	Sale	Average Price
SJ's Caviar	Muscles Yankee	1	0	F	Lex	37,000
SJ's Caviar	Overcomer	1	0	C	Lex	25,000
SJ's Caviar	Pine Chip	2	0	C	Hb	15,500
SJ's Caviar	Pine Chip	3	0	C	Lex	26,000
SJ's Caviar	Pine Chip	4	0	F	Hb	29,750
SJ's Caviar	Pine Chip	3	0	F	Lex	12,333
SJ's Caviar	Prakas	2	0	C	Hb	17,000
SJ's Caviar	Prakas	1	0	F	Hb	22,000
SJ's Caviar	Program Speed	1	0	F	Hb	14,000
SJ's Caviar	Quick Work	1	0	F	Lex	5,000
SJ's Caviar	Rule The Wind	1	0	C	Lex	11,000
SJ's Caviar	Self Possessed	1	0	C	Lex	30,000
SJ's Caviar	Self Possessed	2	0	F	Hb	16,000
SJ's Caviar	Self Possessed	1	0	F	Lex	6,000
SJ's Caviar	Sierra Kosmos	3	0	C	Hb	7,500
SJ's Caviar	Sierra Kosmos	4	0	F	Hb	13,375
SJ's Caviar	Speedy Crown	1	0	C	Hb	25,000
SJ's Caviar	Speedy Crown	1	0	F	Hb	6,000
SJ's Caviar	Speedy Crown	1	0	F	Lex	12,000
SJ's Caviar	Super Bowl	4	0	C	Hb	18,750
SJ's Caviar	Super Bowl	3	0	F	Hb	8,833
SJ's Caviar	Super Pleasure	1	0	C	Hb	13,000
SJ's Caviar	Supergill	1	0	C	Lex	13,000
SJ's Caviar	Tagliabue	2	0	C	Hb	19,000
SJ's Caviar	Tagliabue	1	0	F	Hb	10,000
SJ's Caviar	Town Escort	2	0	C	Hb	10,250
SJ's Caviar	Valley Victory	1	0	C	Hb	15,000
SJ's Caviar	Victory Dream	2	0	C	Hb	27,500
SJ's Caviar	Victory Dream	1	1	C	Lex	25,000
SJ's Caviar	Wesgate Crown	1	0	C	Hb	8,000
SJ's Caviar	Yankee Glide	2	0	C	Hb	17,500
SJ's Caviar	Yankee Glide	1	0	F	Hb	20,000
SJ's Caviar	Yankee Glide	1	0	F	Lex	17,000
Stonebridge Regal	Camluck	1	0	C	Lex	3,000
Stonebridge Regal	Cam's Card Shark	1	0	C	Lex	13,000
Stonebridge Regal	Expensive Scooter	1	0	C	Lex	9,000
Stonebridge Regal	Nobleland Sam	1	0	F	Lex	9,000
Stonebridge Regal	Towner's Big Guy	1	0	C	Lex	3,000
Stonebridge Regal	Western Hanover	1	0	C	Hb	67,000
Striking Sahbra	Angus Hall	1	0	C	Hb	5,500
Striking Sahbra	Angus Hall	1	0	F	Lex	15,000

Sire	Bm Sire	Sold	$50,000 2 Year Olds	Sex	Sale	Average Price
Striking Sahbra	Balanced Image	3	1	C	Hb	43,333
Striking Sahbra	Balanced Image	2	0	C	Lex	62,500
Striking Sahbra	Balanced Image	1	0	F	Hb	24,000
Striking Sahbra	Balanced Image	1	0	F	Lex	30,000
Striking Sahbra	Carry The Message	2	1	C	Lex	77,500
Striking Sahbra	Conway Hall	1	0	F	Hb	55,000
Striking Sahbra	Crysta's Crown	1	0	F	Hb	45,000
Striking Sahbra	Dancer's Victory	1	0	C	Lex	10,000
Striking Sahbra	Dancer's Victory	1	0	F	Lex	11,000
Striking Sahbra	Donerail	2	0	C	Lex	6,500
Striking Sahbra	Dream Of Glory	1	1	F	Hb	25,000
Striking Sahbra	Garland Lobell	1	0	C	Lex	15,000
Striking Sahbra	Inquirer	1	0	F	Hb	27,000
Striking Sahbra	King Conch	1	0	C	Hb	30,000
Striking Sahbra	King Conch	1	0	C	Lex	23,000
Striking Sahbra	Lindy Lane	1	0	F	Hb	12,000
Striking Sahbra	Malabar Man	1	0	F	Lex	32,000
Striking Sahbra	Master Lavec	1	0	C	Lex	25,000
Striking Sahbra	Mr Lavec	1	0	F	Hb	13,000
Striking Sahbra	Mr Vic	1	0	F	Lex	3,000
Striking Sahbra	Muscles Yankee	1	0	C	Hb	42,000
Striking Sahbra	Muscles Yankee	1	0	C	Lex	35,000
Striking Sahbra	Muscles Yankee	1	0	F	Hb	55,000
Striking Sahbra	Pine Chip	1	0	C	Lex	13,000
Striking Sahbra	SJ's Photo	1	0	F	Hb	35,000
Striking Sahbra	Speedy Crown	1	0	C	Lex	30,000
Striking Sahbra	Tom Ridge	1	0	C	Hb	30,000
Striking Sahbra	Valley Victory	1	0	C	Hb	35,000
Striking Sahbra	Valley Victory	1	0	F	Hb	42,000
Striking Sahbra	Wesgate Crown	1	0	C	Hb	20,000
Striking Sahbra	Yankee Glide	1	0	F	Hb	12,000
Striking Sahbra	Yankee Glide	1	0	F	Lex	1,000
Tagliabue	Angus Hall	1	0	F	Hb	9,000
Tagliabue	Mr Vic	1	0	F	Hb	28,000
Tagliabue	Muscles Yankee	1	1	F	Hb	16,000
Tagliabue	Pine Chip	1	0	C	Hb	12,000
Taurus Dream	Balanced Image	1	1	F	Hb	45,000
Taurus Dream	Valley Victory	1	0	F	Hb	24,000
Tell All	Albert Albert	1	0	F	Lex	6,000
Tell All	Artiscape	1	0	C	Hb	7,000
Tell All	Artiscape	3	0	F	Lex	2,000

Sire	Bm Sire	Sold	$50,000 2 Year Olds	Sex	Sale	Average Price
Tell All	Artsplace	2	0	C	Hb	38,500
Tell All	Artsplace	2	0	C	Lex	2,500
Tell All	Artsplace	4	0	F	Hb	5,000
Tell All	Artsplace	1	0	F	Lex	3,000
Tell All	Bettor's Delight	1	0	C	Hb	4,000
Tell All	Blissful Hall	1	0	F	Lex	10,000
Tell All	Cambest	1	0	C	Hb	8,500
Tell All	Camluck	1	0	C	Hb	4,500
Tell All	Camluck	1	0	C	Lex	70,000
Tell All	Camluck	2	0	F	Lex	7,000
Tell All	Cam's Card Shark	1	0	C	Hb	7,000
Tell All	Cam's Card Shark	1	0	C	Lex	20,000
Tell All	Cam's Card Shark	1	0	F	Lex	10,000
Tell All	Die Laughing	1	0	C	Hb	5,500
Tell All	Dragon Again	1	0	C	Hb	5,500
Tell All	Falcon Seelster	1	0	C	Hb	8,000
Tell All	Falcon Seelster	1	0	F	Hb	1,500
Tell All	Grinfromeartoear	1	0	C	Lex	30,000
Tell All	Jate Lobell	2	0	C	Hb	10,500
Tell All	Jate Lobell	4	0	F	Lex	6,500
Tell All	Jenna's Beach Boy	1	0	C	Lex	20,000
Tell All	Kentucky Spur	1	0	F	Lex	2,000
Tell All	Northern Luck	1	0	F	Lex	5,000
Tell All	Precious Bunny	1	0	C	Hb	2,500
Tell All	Precious Bunny	1	0	F	Hb	1,500
Tell All	Red River Hanover	1	0	F	Hb	2,500
Tell All	Sydney Hill	1	0	C	Lex	10,000
Tell All	The Panderosa	1	0	C	Hb	25,000
Tell All	Western Hanover	1	0	C	Hb	3,500
Tell All	Western Hanover	3	0	C	Lex	12,333
Tell All	Western Hanover	1	0	F	Hb	6,500
Tell All	Western Hanover	1	0	F	Lex	23,000
Tell All	Western Ideal	3	1	C	Lex	19,000
Tell All	Western Ideal	2	0	F	Hb	3,000
The Panderosa	Abercrombie	1	0	C	Lex	15,000
The Panderosa	Abercrombie	2	0	F	Hb	18,500
The Panderosa	Albert Albert	1	1	C	Hb	52,000
The Panderosa	Albert Albert	1	0	F	Hb	20,000
The Panderosa	Armbro Mackintosh	1	0	F	Hb	25,000
The Panderosa	Artiscape	1	0	F	Hb	6,000
The Panderosa	Artsplace	21	1	C	Hb	25,500

Sire	Bm Sire	Sold	$50,000 2 Year Olds	Sex	Sale	Average Price
The Panderosa	Artsplace	9	1	C	Lex	32,444
The Panderosa	Artsplace	10	2	F	Hb	20,200
The Panderosa	Artsplace	3	0	F	Lex	27,000
The Panderosa	Ball And Chain	1	0	C	Hb	55,000
The Panderosa	Beach Towel	2	0	C	Hb	22,000
The Panderosa	Beach Towel	1	0	F	Hb	4,500
The Panderosa	Big Towner	3	0	C	Hb	35,167
The Panderosa	Big Towner	1	0	F	Hb	30,000
The Panderosa	Blissful Hall	1	0	F	Lex	8,000
The Panderosa	Bo Knows Jate	1	0	C	Hb	20,000
The Panderosa	Broadway Jate	1	0	F	Hb	2,500
The Panderosa	Cam' S Magic Trick	1	0	C	Lex	16,000
The Panderosa	Cambest	1	0	C	Hb	9,000
The Panderosa	Cambest	2	0	F	Hb	4,500
The Panderosa	Cambest	2	0	F	Lex	11,000
The Panderosa	Camluck	1	0	C	Hb	30,000
The Panderosa	Camluck	4	0	F	Hb	10,375
The Panderosa	Cam's Card Shark	1	0	C	Hb	15,000
The Panderosa	Cam's Card Shark	1	0	F	Hb	2,500
The Panderosa	Cam's Card Shark	1	0	F	Lex	30,000
The Panderosa	Camtastic	1	0	C	Hb	7,000
The Panderosa	Camtastic	1	0	F	Hb	20,000
The Panderosa	Cole Muffler	1	0	C	Hb	20,000
The Panderosa	Covert Action	1	0	C	Hb	12,000
The Panderosa	Curragh	1	0	F	Lex	5,000
The Panderosa	Die Laughing	1	0	F	Hb	27,000
The Panderosa	Direct Scooter	1	0	C	Hb	20,000
The Panderosa	Dragon Again	1	0	C	Hb	8,000
The Panderosa	Grinfromeartoear	1	0	C	Lex	25,000
The Panderosa	Grinfromeartoear	2	0	F	Hb	23,000
The Panderosa	Island Fantasy	1	0	C	Hb	10,000
The Panderosa	Jate Lobell	3	0	C	Hb	20,333
The Panderosa	Jate Lobell	1	0	C	Lex	50,000
The Panderosa	Jate Lobell	1	0	F	Hb	20,000
The Panderosa	Jenna's Beach Boy	2	0	C	Hb	17,000
The Panderosa	Jenna's Beach Boy	1	0	C	Lex	15,000
The Panderosa	Jenna's Beach Boy	3	0	F	Hb	25,167
The Panderosa	Jenna's Beach Boy	1	0	F	Lex	10,000
The Panderosa	Laag	1	0	C	Hb	30,000
The Panderosa	Laag	1	0	C	Lex	18,000
The Panderosa	Laag	2	0	F	Lex	7,500

Sire	Bm Sire	Sold	$50,000 2 Year Olds	Sex	Sale	Average Price
The Panderosa	Life Sign	4	0	C	Hb	17,000
The Panderosa	Life Sign	2	0	F	Hb	30,000
The Panderosa	Magical Mike	1	0	F	Hb	5,000
The Panderosa	Matt's Scooter	3	0	C	Hb	28,000
The Panderosa	Matt's Scooter	7	0	F	Hb	22,286
The Panderosa	Matt's Scooter	2	0	F	Lex	15,000
The Panderosa	Nihilator	1	0	F	Hb	50,000
The Panderosa	Nobleland Sam	1	0	C	Lex	34,000
The Panderosa	Northern Luck	1	0	F	Lex	15,000
The Panderosa	Pacific Fella	1	0	C	Hb	13,000
The Panderosa	Pacific Rocket	1	0	F	Hb	8,500
The Panderosa	Precious Bunny	1	0	F	Hb	5,000
The Panderosa	Presidential Ball	2	0	C	Hb	17,500
The Panderosa	Presidential Ball	1	0	F	Hb	8,000
The Panderosa	Presidential Ball	1	0	F	Lex	30,000
The Panderosa	Raging Glory	1	0	C	Hb	30,000
The Panderosa	Rumpus Hanover	1	0	C	Hb	57,000
The Panderosa	Safe N Rich	1	0	F	Hb	6,000
The Panderosa	Sportsmaster	1	0	C	Hb	45,000
The Panderosa	Stand Forever	1	0	F	Lex	15,000
The Panderosa	Tyler B	1	0	C	Hb	14,000
The Panderosa	Tyler B	2	0	F	Hb	7,750
Tom Ridge	American Winner	2	0	C	Lex	10,500
Tom Ridge	American Winner	1	1	F	Hb	23,000
Tom Ridge	Armbro Goal	1	0	C	Hb	13,000
Tom Ridge	Armbro Goal	1	0	F	Hb	8,000
Tom Ridge	Arnies Exchange	1	0	C	Hb	13,000
Tom Ridge	Balanced Image	2	0	C	Hb	24,500
Tom Ridge	Balanced Image	3	0	F	Hb	13,000
Tom Ridge	Balanced Image	1	0	F	Lex	25,000
Tom Ridge	Conway Hall	3	0	C	Hb	8,000
Tom Ridge	Conway Hall	2	0	F	Hb	8,000
Tom Ridge	Cr Commando	1	1	F	Hb	33,000
Tom Ridge	Deliberate Speed	1	1	F	Lex	4,000
Tom Ridge	Donerail	2	0	C	Hb	11,000
Tom Ridge	Donerail	1	0	C	Lex	15,000
Tom Ridge	Dream Of Glory	1	0	C	Hb	25,000
Tom Ridge	Dream Of Glory	1	0	F	Hb	7,000
Tom Ridge	Garland Lobell	3	0	C	Hb	40,333
Tom Ridge	Garland Lobell	2	0	C	Lex	14,000
Tom Ridge	Garland Lobell	3	0	F	Hb	14,833

Sire	Bm Sire	Sold	$50,000 2 Year Olds	Sex	Sale	Average Price
Tom Ridge	Homesick	1	0	C	Hb	15,000
Tom Ridge	Homesick	2	0	F	Hb	20,000
Tom Ridge	Incredible Nevele	1	0	F	Hb	7,000
Tom Ridge	King Conch	1	0	C	Hb	15,000
Tom Ridge	King Conch	2	1	F	Hb	12,500
Tom Ridge	Lindy Lane	1	0	C	Hb	35,000
Tom Ridge	Lindy Lane	1	1	C	Lex	11,000
Tom Ridge	Magna Force	1	0	C	Hb	37,000
Tom Ridge	Malabar Man	1	0	C	Lex	32,000
Tom Ridge	Meadow Road	2	0	F	Hb	21,750
Tom Ridge	Mr Lavec	1	0	C	Lex	115,000
Tom Ridge	Pine Chip	2	0	C	Hb	17,000
Tom Ridge	Pine Chip	2	1	C	Lex	23,000
Tom Ridge	Royal Prestige	1	1	C	Hb	22,000
Tom Ridge	Royal Prestige	1	0	F	Hb	6,000
Tom Ridge	Royal Strength	1	0	C	Hb	10,000
Tom Ridge	Royal Troubador	1	0	F	Hb	30,000
Tom Ridge	SJ's Photo	1	0	F	Hb	10,000
Tom Ridge	Self Possessed	1	0	F	Lex	3,000
Tom Ridge	Sierra Kosmos	2	0	C	Hb	15,000
Tom Ridge	Sierra Kosmos	2	1	C	Lex	11,500
Tom Ridge	Sir Taurus	1	0	C	Hb	7,000
Tom Ridge	SJ's Caviar	1	1	C	Hb	11,000
Tom Ridge	SJ's Caviar	1	0	F	Hb	14,000
Tom Ridge	Speedy Crown	1	0	C	Hb	6,000
Tom Ridge	Speedy Crown	1	0	F	Hb	3,500
Tom Ridge	Striking Sahbra	2	0	C	Hb	6,750
Tom Ridge	Striking Sahbra	1	0	F	Lex	9,000
Tom Ridge	Super Bowl	1	0	C	Lex	27,000
Tom Ridge	Super Bowl	1	1	F	Hb	10,000
Tom Ridge	Super Bowl	2	0	F	Lex	17,500
Tom Ridge	Super Pleasure	1	0	C	Hb	4,500
Tom Ridge	Supergill	1	0	C	Hb	30,000
Tom Ridge	Yankee Paco	1	0	C	Hb	10,000
Totally Western	Laag	1	0	C	Hb	4,000
Valley Victor	American Winner	2	0	C	Lex	33,500
Valley Victor	American Winner	2	1	F	Lex	42,000
Valley Victor	Andover Hall	1	0	F	Lex	2,000
Valley Victor	Armbro Agile	1	0	F	Lex	9,000
Valley Victor	Armbro Charger	1	0	C	Lex	4,000
Valley Victor	Armbro Goal	1	0	C	Lex	5,000

Sire	Bm Sire	Sold	$50,000 2 Year Olds	Sex	Sale	Average Price
Valley Victor	Armbro Goal	1	0	F	Hb	40,000
Valley Victor	Armbro Goal	1	0	F	Lex	9,000
Valley Victor	Armbro Iliad	2	1	C	Lex	12,500
Valley Victor	Back Fin	1	0	C	Lex	10,000
Valley Victor	Balanced Image	2	0	C	Lex	10,500
Valley Victor	Balanced Image	1	0	F	Lex	2,000
Valley Victor	Baltic Speed	1	0	C	Lex	28,000
Valley Victor	Baltic Speed	1	0	F	Lex	9,000
Valley Victor	Conway Hall	3	0	C	Lex	12,333
Valley Victor	Conway Hall	3	0	F	Lex	3,000
Valley Victor	Crowning Point	1	0	C	Lex	20,000
Valley Victor	Crowning Point	1	0	F	Lex	15,000
Valley Victor	Crysta's Crown	1	0	C	Lex	15,000
Valley Victor	Crysta's Crown	2	0	F	Lex	17,000
Valley Victor	Donerail	1	0	C	Lex	3,000
Valley Victor	Donerail	1	0	F	Lex	5,000
Valley Victor	Earl	1	0	F	Lex	4,000
Valley Victor	Esquire Spur	2	0	F	Lex	11,500
Valley Victor	Garland Lobell	1	0	C	Hb	27,000
Valley Victor	Garland Lobell	1	0	C	Lex	20,000
Valley Victor	Garland Lobell	2	0	F	Lex	8,000
Valley Victor	Joie De Vie	1	0	C	Hb	6,500
Valley Victor	King Kong Ranger	1	0	C	Lex	7,000
Valley Victor	Malabar Man	2	0	C	Hb	39,750
Valley Victor	Malabar Man	3	0	C	Lex	20,000
Valley Victor	Malabar Man	3	0	F	Lex	36,667
Valley Victor	Mr Lavec	1	0	F	Lex	15,000
Valley Victor	Muscles Yankee	1	0	C	Lex	37,000
Valley Victor	Pine Chip	3	1	C	Lex	23,333
Valley Victor	Pine Chip	5	0	F	Lex	13,400
Valley Victor	Prakas	1	0	C	Lex	17,000
Valley Victor	Raffaello Ambrosio	1	1	C	Lex	26,000
Valley Victor	Raffaello Ambrosio	1	0	F	Lex	25,000
Valley Victor	Rowdy Yankee	1	0	F	Lex	14,000
Valley Victor	Royal Prestige	1	0	C	Lex	15,000
Valley Victor	Royal Prestige	1	1	F	Lex	20,000
Valley Victor	Royal Strength	1	1	F	Lex	15,000
Valley Victor	Rule The Wind	1	0	C	Lex	14,000
Valley Victor	SJ's Photo	1	0	F	Lex	4,000
Valley Victor	Self Possessed	1	0	F	Lex	2,000
Valley Victor	Sierra Kosmos	1	1	C	Lex	8,000

Sire	Bm Sire	Sold	$50,000 2 Year Olds	Sex	Sale	Average Price
Valley Victor	Sierra Kosmos	3	0	F	Lex	16,333
Valley Victor	SJ's Caviar	1	1	C	Lex	15,000
Valley Victor	SJ's Caviar	1	0	F	Lex	3,000
Valley Victor	Speedy Crown	3	0	C	Lex	22,667
Valley Victor	Speedy Crown	1	0	F	Lex	5,000
Valley Victor	Striking Sahbra	1	0	C	Lex	23,000
Valley Victor	Striking Sahbra	2	0	F	Hb	9,000
Valley Victor	Super Ben Joe	2	0	F	Lex	18,500
Valley Victor	Super Bowl	2	0	C	Lex	21,000
Valley Victor	Super Bowl	1	0	F	Lex	45,000
Valley Victor	Supergill	1	0	C	Lex	35,000
Valley Victor	Vaporize	1	0	C	Lex	35,000
Valley Victor	Vision's Pride	1	0	F	Lex	15,000
Varenne	Malabar Man	1	0	C	Hb	2,500
Varenne	Malabar Man	1	0	C	Lex	29,000
Village Jolt	Abercrombie	1	0	F	Hb	2,500
Village Jolt	Albert Albert	1	0	F	Hb	30,000
Village Jolt	Artiscape	1	0	C	Hb	20,000
Village Jolt	Artiscape	1	0	F	Lex	2,000
Village Jolt	Artsplace	4	0	C	Hb	24,500
Village Jolt	Artsplace	2	0	F	Hb	3,250
Village Jolt	Artsplace	1	0	F	Lex	18,000
Village Jolt	Beastmaster	1	0	F	Hb	5,000
Village Jolt	Big Towner	1	0	C	Lex	40,000
Village Jolt	Bo Knows Jate	2	0	C	Hb	12,000
Village Jolt	Cole Muffler	1	0	C	Lex	20,000
Village Jolt	Die Laughing	1	0	F	Hb	2,500
Village Jolt	Direct Scooter	3	0	C	Hb	26,333
Village Jolt	Dragon's Lair	1	0	F	Lex	4,000
Village Jolt	Expensive Scooter	1	0	F	Lex	27,000
Village Jolt	Falcon Seelster	1	0	C	Lex	5,000
Village Jolt	Falcon Seelster	1	0	F	Hb	10,000
Village Jolt	Falcons Future	1	0	C	Hb	11,000
Village Jolt	Falcons Future	1	0	F	Hb	16,000
Village Jolt	Jate Lobell	3	0	C	Hb	25,667
Village Jolt	Jate Lobell	2	0	F	Hb	17,500
Village Jolt	Jenna's Beach Boy	1	0	F	Hb	5,500
Village Jolt	Laag	1	0	C	Lex	30,000
Village Jolt	Laag	1	0	F	Hb	6,000
Village Jolt	Matt's Scooter	3	0	C	Hb	14,667
Village Jolt	No Nukes	5	0	C	Hb	14,400

Sire	Bm Sire	Sold	$50,000 2 Year Olds	Sex	Sale	Average Price
Village Jolt	No Nukes	2	0	F	Hb	17,000
Village Jolt	Nobleland Sam	1	0	C	Hb	17,000
Village Jolt	Presidential Ball	1	0	C	Hb	7,000
Village Jolt	Real Artist	4	0	C	Hb	24,625
Village Jolt	Real Artist	1	0	C	Lex	8,000
Village Jolt	Real Artist	2	0	F	Hb	19,250
Village Jolt	Rustler Hanover	1	0	F	Lex	13,000
Village Jolt	The Panderosa	1	0	C	Lex	32,000
Village Jolt	The Panderosa	2	0	F	Hb	3,500
Village Jolt	Tyler's Mark	1	0	C	Hb	5,000
Village Jolt	Western Hanover	7	0	C	Hb	25,214
Village Jolt	Western Hanover	3	0	C	Lex	17,667
Village Jolt	Western Hanover	6	0	F	Hb	17,000
Village Jolt	Western Hanover	1	0	F	Lex	10,000
Village Jolt	Western Ideal	1	0	F	Hb	3,500
Western Hanover	Abercrombie	4	2	C	Hb	32,500
Western Hanover	Abercrombie	2	0	C	Lex	65,000
Western Hanover	Abercrombie	3	0	F	Hb	20,000
Western Hanover	Abercrombie	2	1	F	Lex	42,500
Western Hanover	Albatross	1	0	C	Hb	22,000
Western Hanover	Albatross	1	0	F	Hb	42,000
Western Hanover	Apaches Fame	1	1	C	Hb	75,000
Western Hanover	Armbro Mackintosh	1	0	C	Hb	28,000
Western Hanover	Artiscape	5	0	C	Hb	80,000
Western Hanover	Artiscape	1	0	C	Lex	35,000
Western Hanover	Artiscape	1	0	F	Hb	80,000
Western Hanover	Artsplace	12	0	C	Hb	28,083
Western Hanover	Artsplace	6	1	C	Lex	53,333
Western Hanover	Artsplace	13	1	F	Hb	16,731
Western Hanover	Artsplace	8	2	F	Lex	40,750
Western Hanover	Arturo	1	0	C	Hb	25,000
Western Hanover	Arturo	1	0	C	Lex	42,000
Western Hanover	Beach Towel	1	1	C	Hb	75,000
Western Hanover	Bettor's Delight	2	0	C	Hb	20,500
Western Hanover	Bettor's Delight	1	0	C	Lex	40,000
Western Hanover	Bettor's Delight	1	0	F	Hb	4,000
Western Hanover	Big Towner	2	0	C	Hb	26,000
Western Hanover	Big Towner	1	0	C	Lex	97,000
Western Hanover	Big Towner	2	0	F	Hb	12,000
Western Hanover	Big Towner	1	0	F	Lex	35,000
Western Hanover	Blissful Hall	1	0	C	Hb	35,000

Sire	Bm Sire	Sold	$50,000 2 Year Olds	Sex	Sale	Average Price
Western Hanover	Cam Fella	1	0	F	Hb	20,000
Western Hanover	Cambest	2	0	C	Hb	76,000
Western Hanover	Cambest	1	0	F	Hb	28,000
Western Hanover	Camluck	2	0	C	Hb	41,000
Western Hanover	Camluck	2	0	F	Hb	31,500
Western Hanover	Cam's Card Shark	9	1	C	Hb	38,111
Western Hanover	Cam's Card Shark	3	1	C	Lex	91,667
Western Hanover	Cam's Card Shark	2	0	F	Hb	8,500
Western Hanover	Cam's Card Shark	1	0	F	Lex	10,000
Western Hanover	Cole Muffler	1	0	C	Hb	13,000
Western Hanover	Cole Muffler	2	0	F	Hb	74,500
Western Hanover	Colt Fortysix	1	0	F	Hb	30,000
Western Hanover	D M Dilinger	1	0	C	Hb	60,000
Western Hanover	Dexter Nukes	1	0	F	Hb	25,000
Western Hanover	Dragon Again	2	0	C	Lex	95,000
Western Hanover	Dragon Again	2	0	F	Hb	25,000
Western Hanover	Dragon's Lair	2	0	C	Hb	22,500
Western Hanover	Dragon's Lair	1	0	C	Lex	47,000
Western Hanover	Dragon's Lair	1	0	F	Hb	70,000
Western Hanover	Dragon's Lair	1	0	F	Lex	60,000
Western Hanover	Dream Away	1	0	C	Hb	62,000
Western Hanover	Falcon Seelster	1	0	F	Hb	25,000
Western Hanover	Grinfromeartoear	1	0	C	Lex	75,000
Western Hanover	Grinfromeartoear	1	0	F	Hb	3,000
Western Hanover	Hi Ho Silverheels	1	0	F	Hb	23,000
Western Hanover	Higher Power	1	0	C	Hb	25,000
Western Hanover	Jate Lobell	1	0	C	Lex	5,000
Western Hanover	Jate Lobell	3	1	F	Lex	44,000
Western Hanover	Jenna's Beach Boy	1	0	C	Hb	40,000
Western Hanover	Jenna's Beach Boy	2	1	F	Hb	32,500
Western Hanover	Jenna's Beach Boy	1	0	F	Lex	20,000
Western Hanover	Jk Outlaw	1	0	F	Lex	55,000
Western Hanover	Laag	1	0	F	Hb	4,000
Western Hanover	Life Sign	6	0	C	Hb	37,333
Western Hanover	Life Sign	3	0	C	Lex	61,000
Western Hanover	Life Sign	4	1	F	Hb	17,875
Western Hanover	Magical Mike	3	2	F	Hb	12,333
Western Hanover	Matt's Scooter	2	0	C	Hb	46,000
Western Hanover	Matt's Scooter	4	0	F	Hb	30,125
Western Hanover	Niatross	1	0	C	Hb	14,000
Western Hanover	Nihilator	1	0	F	Lex	17,000

Sire	Bm Sire	Sold	$50,000 2 Year Olds	Sex	Sale	Average Price
Western Hanover	Northern Luck	1	0	F	Hb	52,000
Western Hanover	Northern Luck	1	0	F	Lex	40,000
Western Hanover	Park Place	1	0	F	Lex	62,000
Western Hanover	Precious Bunny	2	0	C	Hb	27,000
Western Hanover	Precious Bunny	1	0	F	Hb	30,000
Western Hanover	Presidential Ball	1	0	F	Hb	31,000
Western Hanover	Real Artist	1	0	C	Hb	87,000
Western Hanover	Real Artist	1	0	F	Hb	30,000
Western Hanover	Run The Table	1	1	C	Hb	3,000
Western Hanover	Run The Table	3	0	F	Hb	11,333
Western Hanover	Run The Table	1	0	F	Lex	50,000
Western Hanover	Shady Character	2	0	C	Hb	24,000
Western Hanover	Shady Character	1	0	F	Hb	25,000
Western Hanover	Sportsmaster	1	0	F	Hb	80,000
Western Hanover	Sportsmaster	1	0	F	Lex	35,000
Western Hanover	Storm Compensation	1	0	F	Hb	30,000
Western Hanover	Walton Hanover	1	0	C	Hb	33,000
Western Ideal	Abercrombie	1	0	C	Hb	20,000
Western Ideal	Abercrombie	1	0	C	Lex	15,000
Western Ideal	Albatross	1	0	C	Lex	87,000
Western Ideal	Albert Albert	1	0	C	Hb	7,000
Western Ideal	Art Major	1	0	F	Hb	2,500
Western Ideal	Artiscape	2	0	C	Hb	60,000
Western Ideal	Artiscape	2	0	C	Lex	15,000
Western Ideal	Artiscape	1	0	F	Hb	19,000
Western Ideal	Artiscape	3	1	F	Lex	15,667
Western Ideal	Artsplace	9	0	C	Hb	33,778
Western Ideal	Artsplace	13	1	C	Lex	59,308
Western Ideal	Artsplace	13	2	F	Hb	52,769
Western Ideal	Artsplace	9	1	F	Lex	40,000
Western Ideal	Arturo	1	0	C	Hb	5,000
Western Ideal	Big Towner	7	1	C	Hb	25,929
Western Ideal	Big Towner	5	0	F	Hb	51,000
Western Ideal	Blissful Hall	2	0	C	Hb	13,000
Western Ideal	Blissful Hall	1	0	F	Lex	7,000
Western Ideal	Bo Knows Jate	1	0	F	Hb	13,000
Western Ideal	Cam Fella	1	0	C	Hb	15,000
Western Ideal	Cam Fella	1	1	F	Lex	75,000
Western Ideal	Cambest	1	0	C	Hb	13,000
Western Ideal	Cambest	1	0	F	Hb	3,500
Western Ideal	Cambest	3	0	F	Lex	68,333

Sire	Bm Sire	Sold	$50,000 2 Year Olds	Sex	Sale	Average Price
Western Ideal	Camluck	4	0	C	Hb	44,500
Western Ideal	Camluck	2	0	C	Lex	27,000
Western Ideal	Camluck	2	0	F	Hb	54,500
Western Ideal	Camluck	1	0	F	Lex	25,000
Western Ideal	Cam's Card Shark	7	0	C	Hb	45,571
Western Ideal	Cam's Card Shark	2	1	C	Lex	22,500
Western Ideal	Cam's Card Shark	1	0	F	Hb	60,000
Western Ideal	Cam's Card Shark	4	0	F	Lex	31,750
Western Ideal	Cole Muffler	2	0	C	Hb	18,000
Western Ideal	Cole Muffler	1	0	C	Lex	10,000
Western Ideal	David's Pass	1	0	F	Lex	10,000
Western Ideal	Dexter Nukes	1	0	C	Hb	20,000
Western Ideal	Die Laughing	1	0	C	Lex	50,000
Western Ideal	Die Laughing	1	0	F	Hb	10,000
Western Ideal	Die Laughing	1	0	F	Lex	10,000
Western Ideal	Direct Scooter	1	0	C	Hb	70,000
Western Ideal	Direct Scooter	1	1	F	Hb	95,000
Western Ideal	Dm Dilinger	1	0	F	Hb	15,000
Western Ideal	Dragon Again	4	0	C	Hb	11,375
Western Ideal	Dragon Again	1	0	F	Hb	6,000
Western Ideal	Dragon Again	1	0	F	Lex	9,000
Western Ideal	Dragon's Lair	2	0	C	Hb	97,500
Western Ideal	Dragon's Lair	1	0	F	Hb	14,000
Western Ideal	Dragon's Lair	2	1	F	Lex	26,500
Western Ideal	Grinfromeartoear	1	0	C	Hb	21,000
Western Ideal	Grinfromeartoear	1	1	F	Lex	65,000
Western Ideal	Island Fantasy	1	0	C	Lex	135,000
Western Ideal	Jate Lobell	3	0	C	Hb	22,000
Western Ideal	Jate Lobell	2	0	F	Hb	10,250
Western Ideal	Jate Lobell	1	0	F	Lex	85,000
Western Ideal	Jenna's Beach Boy	3	0	C	Hb	34,000
Western Ideal	Jenna's Beach Boy	2	0	C	Lex	45,000
Western Ideal	Jenna's Beach Boy	2	0	F	Hb	45,000
Western Ideal	Jenna's Beach Boy	1	0	F	Lex	25,000
Western Ideal	Laag	1	0	F	Hb	5,000
Western Ideal	Life Sign	3	0	C	Hb	65,667
Western Ideal	Life Sign	4	1	C	Lex	35,500
Western Ideal	Life Sign	6	1	F	Hb	31,000
Western Ideal	Life Sign	2	1	F	Lex	23,500
Western Ideal	Matt's Scooter	5	1	C	Lex	76,400
Western Ideal	Matt's Scooter	3	0	F	Hb	15,333

Sire	Bm Sire	Sold	$50,000 2 Year Olds	Sex	Sale	Average Price
Western Ideal	Nihilator	1	0	F	Hb	10,000
Western Ideal	No Nukes	1	0	C	Lex	25,000
Western Ideal	Northern Luck	1	0	C	Hb	60,000
Western Ideal	Northern Luck	1	0	C	Lex	57,000
Western Ideal	On The Road Again	1	0	F	Hb	10,000
Western Ideal	Pacific Rocket	1	0	F	Lex	45,000
Western Ideal	Precious Bunny	1	0	C	Hb	27,000
Western Ideal	Presidential Ball	1	0	C	Hb	6,000
Western Ideal	Presidential Ball	1	0	F	Hb	30,000
Western Ideal	Pro Bono Best	1	1	F	Hb	135,000
Western Ideal	Real Artist	1	0	F	Hb	31,000
Western Ideal	Real Desire	2	0	F	Hb	19,000
Western Ideal	Run The Table	1	0	C	Hb	120,000
Western Ideal	Sportsmaster	1	0	F	Hb	17,000
Western Ideal	Storm Compensation	1	0	F	Hb	25,000
Western Ideal	Tyler B	1	0	C	Hb	17,000
Western Ideal	Village Jiffy	1	0	C	Lex	27,000
Western Terror	Abercrombie	1	0	C	Hb	19,000
Western Terror	Abercrombie	5	0	C	Lex	18,000
Western Terror	Abercrombie	1	0	F	Hb	9,000
Western Terror	Abercrombie	2	0	F	Lex	15,500
Western Terror	Albert Albert	1	0	C	Lex	12,000
Western Terror	Art Major	1	0	F	Lex	18,000
Western Terror	Artiscape	1	0	C	Hb	37,000
Western Terror	Artiscape	2	0	C	Lex	40,000
Western Terror	Artsplace	1	0	C	Hb	127,000
Western Terror	Artsplace	3	0	C	Lex	27,000
Western Terror	Artsplace	3	0	F	Lex	35,000
Western Terror	Arturo	1	0	F	Lex	3,000
Western Terror	Beach Towel	1	0	C	Lex	45,000
Western Terror	Beach Towel	1	0	F	Hb	19,000
Western Terror	Big Towner	1	0	C	Hb	23,000
Western Terror	Big Towner	1	0	C	Lex	25,000
Western Terror	Big Towner	1	0	F	Hb	35,000
Western Terror	Big Towner	2	0	F	Lex	21,000
Western Terror	Cam Fella	1	0	F	Hb	6,000
Western Terror	Cam Fella	1	0	F	Lex	11,000
Western Terror	Cambest	1	0	C	Hb	17,000
Western Terror	Cambest	2	1	C	Lex	97,500
Western Terror	Cambest	2	0	F	Lex	24,000
Western Terror	Camluck	1	0	C	Hb	52,000

Sire	Bm Sire	Sold	$50,000 2 Year Olds	Sex	Sale	Average Price
Western Terror	Camluck	1	0	C	Lex	120,000
Western Terror	Camluck	1	0	F	Hb	5,000
Western Terror	Camluck	1	0	F	Lex	17,000
Western Terror	Cam's Card Shark	1	0	C	Lex	20,000
Western Terror	Cam's Card Shark	1	0	F	Hb	2,000
Western Terror	Camtastic	1	0	F	Lex	15,000
Western Terror	David's Pass	1	0	F	Lex	80,000
Western Terror	Die Laughing	1	0	F	Lex	15,000
Western Terror	Direct Scooter	1	0	C	Hb	14,000
Western Terror	Direct Scooter	1	0	C	Lex	57,000
Western Terror	Direct Scooter	1	0	F	Hb	6,000
Western Terror	Direct Scooter	1	0	F	Lex	28,000
Western Terror	Dragon Again	2	0	F	Hb	10,250
Western Terror	Falcon Seelster	2	1	F	Lex	10,000
Western Terror	Grinfromeartoear	3	0	C	Hb	4,500
Western Terror	Grinfromeartoear	5	0	C	Lex	22,600
Western Terror	Grinfromeartoear	1	0	F	Hb	5,000
Western Terror	Grinfromeartoear	11	0	F	Lex	21,000
Western Terror	Island Fantasy	1	0	C	Hb	11,000
Western Terror	Jate Lobell	6	0	C	Lex	41,833
Western Terror	Jate Lobell	1	0	F	Lex	4,000
Western Terror	Jenna's Beach Boy	1	0	C	Lex	20,000
Western Terror	Jenna's Beach Boy	3	1	F	Hb	34,333
Western Terror	Jenna's Beach Boy	1	0	F	Lex	6,000
Western Terror	Keystone Raider	1	0	F	Hb	37,000
Western Terror	Life Sign	1	0	C	Hb	38,000
Western Terror	Life Sign	3	0	C	Lex	51,000
Western Terror	Life Sign	5	0	F	Lex	25,200
Western Terror	Magical Mike	2	0	C	Lex	37,500
Western Terror	Magical Mike	1	0	F	Hb	105,000
Western Terror	Matt's Scooter	1	0	C	Hb	120,000
Western Terror	Matt's Scooter	3	0	C	Lex	92,667
Western Terror	Matt's Scooter	2	0	F	Hb	32,500
Western Terror	Northern Luck	1	1	F	Lex	52,000
Western Terror	Pacific Rocket	1	0	C	Lex	72,000
Western Terror	Pacific Rocket	1	0	F	Lex	60,000
Western Terror	Precious Bunny	1	0	C	Hb	12,000
Western Terror	Presidential Ball	1	0	C	Lex	10,000
Western Terror	Run The Table	1	0	F	Lex	4,000
Western Terror	Silent Majority	1	0	C	Lex	4,000
Western Terror	Silent Majority	2	0	F	Lex	12,500

Sire	Bm Sire	Sold	$50,000 2 Year Olds	Sex	Sale	Average Price
Western Terror	Tooter Scooter	1	0	F	Lex	7,000
Western Terror	Tyler B	1	0	F	Hb	57,000
Windsong's Legacy	American Winner	1	0	F	Lex	5,000
Windsong's Legacy	Andover Hall	1	0	F	Lex	35,000
Windsong's Legacy	Armbro Goal	1	0	C	Lex	3,000
Windsong's Legacy	Armbro Goal	1	0	F	Hb	16,000
Windsong's Legacy	Armbro Goal	1	0	F	Lex	32,000
Windsong's Legacy	Arndon	2	0	C	Hb	5,250
Windsong's Legacy	Balanced Image	2	0	C	Lex	16,000
Windsong's Legacy	Baltic Speed	1	0	F	Hb	7,500
Windsong's Legacy	Brisco Herbert	2	0	C	Lex	19,500
Windsong's Legacy	Cheyenne Spur	1	0	C	Hb	18,000
Windsong's Legacy	Copter Lobell	1	0	C	Hb	4,000
Windsong's Legacy	Donerail	2	0	C	Hb	32,000
Windsong's Legacy	Donerail	1	0	F	Hb	18,000
Windsong's Legacy	Dream Of Glory	1	0	F	Hb	32,000
Windsong's Legacy	Dream Vacation	1	1	C	Hb	42,000
Windsong's Legacy	Earl	1	0	F	Hb	24,000
Windsong's Legacy	Earl	1	0	F	Lex	20,000
Windsong's Legacy	Enjoy Lavec	1	0	C	Lex	11,000
Windsong's Legacy	Enjoy Lavec	1	0	F	Hb	140,000
Windsong's Legacy	Incredible Nevele	1	0	F	Lex	60,000
Windsong's Legacy	King Conch	1	0	C	Hb	1,500
Windsong's Legacy	King Conch	1	0	F	Hb	9,000
Windsong's Legacy	Lindy Lane	2	0	C	Hb	53,000
Windsong's Legacy	Lindy Lane	1	0	F	Hb	4,500
Windsong's Legacy	Mack Lobell	1	0	C	Lex	25,000
Windsong's Legacy	Malabar Man	1	0	C	Hb	5,000
Windsong's Legacy	Malabar Man	1	0	C	Lex	37,000
Windsong's Legacy	Malabar Man	4	0	F	Hb	4,750
Windsong's Legacy	Malabar Man	1	0	F	Lex	40,000
Windsong's Legacy	Mr Lavec	2	0	C	Hb	7,250
Windsong's Legacy	Mr Lavec	1	0	F	Lex	7,000
Windsong's Legacy	Mr Vic	1	0	F	Hb	37,000
Windsong's Legacy	Mr Vic	1	0	F	Lex	4,000
Windsong's Legacy	Muscles Yankee	5	2	C	Hb	40,800
Windsong's Legacy	Muscles Yankee	2	0	C	Lex	16,000
Windsong's Legacy	Muscles Yankee	3	0	F	Hb	88,833
Windsong's Legacy	Muscles Yankee	1	0	F	Lex	37,000
Windsong's Legacy	Pine Chip	1	0	C	Hb	30,000
Windsong's Legacy	Pine Chip	1	0	C	Lex	10,000

Sire	Bm Sire	Sold	$50,000 2 Year Olds	Sex	Sale	Average Price
Windsong's Legacy	Pine Chip	5	1	F	Hb	76,200
Windsong's Legacy	Pine Chip	2	0	F	Lex	12,000
Windsong's Legacy	Prakas	2	0	C	Hb	52,500
Windsong's Legacy	Royal Prestige	1	0	C	Hb	6,000
Windsong's Legacy	Royal Prestige	1	0	F	Hb	21,000
Windsong's Legacy	SJ's Photo	1	0	F	Hb	3,000
Windsong's Legacy	SJ's Photo	1	0	F	Lex	40,000
Windsong's Legacy	Self Possessed	3	0	F	Lex	36,667
Windsong's Legacy	Sierra Kosmos	2	0	C	Hb	11,000
Windsong's Legacy	Sierra Kosmos	1	0	F	Hb	8,000
Windsong's Legacy	SJ's Caviar	2	0	C	Hb	27,500
Windsong's Legacy	Speedy Crown	1	0	C	Hb	12,000
Windsong's Legacy	Speedy Crown	2	0	C	Lex	37,500
Windsong's Legacy	Speedy Crown	1	0	F	Hb	5,000
Windsong's Legacy	Speedy Crown	1	0	F	Lex	25,000
Windsong's Legacy	Super Bowl	1	0	C	Hb	25,000
Windsong's Legacy	Super Bowl	2	0	C	Lex	14,500
Windsong's Legacy	Super Bowl	2	0	F	Hb	8,000
Windsong's Legacy	Super Pleasure	1	0	C	Hb	25,000
Windsong's Legacy	Super Pleasure	1	0	C	Lex	4,000
Windsong's Legacy	Super Pleasure	1	0	F	Hb	6,000
Windsong's Legacy	Supergill	1	0	C	Lex	19,000
Windsong's Legacy	Supergill	1	0	F	Hb	15,000
Windsong's Legacy	Tagliabue	1	0	C	Lex	55,000
Windsong's Legacy	Tagliabue	1	0	F	Hb	8,000
Windsong's Legacy	Thirty Two	1	0	C	Hb	25,000
Windsong's Legacy	Uno Atout	1	0	F	Hb	17,000
Windsong's Legacy	Valley Victory	3	0	C	Hb	15,333
Windsong's Legacy	Valley Victory	5	0	F	Hb	26,900
Windsong's Legacy	Victory Dream	1	0	F	Hb	17,000
Windsong's Legacy	Yankee Glide	1	0	F	Lex	10,000
Windsong's Legacy	Yankee Paco	1	0	F	Lex	30,000
Yankee Cruiser	Abercrombie	2	0	C	Lex	8,500
Yankee Cruiser	Armbro Mackintosh	1	0	F	Hb	13,000
Yankee Cruiser	Beach Towel	1	0	C	Hb	22,000
Yankee Cruiser	Cam Fella	1	0	F	Lex	7,000
Yankee Cruiser	Cambest	1	0	C	Hb	37,000
Yankee Cruiser	Cambest	1	1	F	Lex	10,000
Yankee Cruiser	Cam's Card Shark	1	0	C	Hb	8,000
Yankee Cruiser	Cam's Card Shark	1	0	F	Lex	14,000
Yankee Cruiser	Camtastic	1	0	C	Hb	22,000

Sire	Bm Sire	Sold	$50,000 2 Year Olds	Sex	Sale	Average Price
Yankee Cruiser	Coal Harbor	1	0	C	Hb	15,000
Yankee Cruiser	Die Laughing	1	0	C	Hb	47,000
Yankee Cruiser	Dragon Again	1	0	C	Lex	3,000
Yankee Cruiser	Dragon's Lair	1	0	C	Hb	21,000
Yankee Cruiser	Falcons Future	1	1	C	Hb	38,000
Yankee Cruiser	Jenna's Beach Boy	1	0	C	Hb	16,000
Yankee Cruiser	Jenna's Beach Boy	1	0	F	Lex	3,000
Yankee Cruiser	Laag	1	0	C	Hb	10,000
Yankee Cruiser	Life Sign	1	0	C	Hb	3,500
Yankee Cruiser	Life Sign	1	0	C	Lex	27,000
Yankee Cruiser	Life Sign	1	0	F	Hb	2,500
Yankee Cruiser	Life Sign	2	0	F	Lex	2,500
Yankee Cruiser	Magical Mike	1	1	F	Hb	5,000
Yankee Cruiser	Matt's Scooter	1	0	C	Lex	14,000
Yankee Cruiser	No Nukes	1	0	C	Hb	10,000
Yankee Cruiser	No Nukes	2	0	C	Lex	40,500
Yankee Cruiser	Nobleland Sam	1	1	F	Lex	35,000
Yankee Cruiser	On The Road Again	1	0	C	Hb	11,000
Yankee Cruiser	Pacific Fella	1	0	F	Hb	20,000
Yankee Cruiser	Precious Bunny	1	0	F	Hb	5,000
Yankee Cruiser	Seahawk Hanover	1	0	F	Lex	6,000
Yankee Cruiser	The Big Dog	1	0	C	Lex	5,000
Yankee Cruiser	The Panderosa	1	0	C	Hb	22,000
Yankee Cruiser	Western Hanover	2	0	F	Hb	11,250
Yankee Cruiser	Western Hanover	1	0	F	Lex	7,000
Yankee Cruiser	Western Ideal	1	1	F	Hb	20,000
Yankee Glide	American Winner	4	0	C	Lex	51,250
Yankee Glide	American Winner	3	1	F	Lex	82,333
Yankee Glide	Andover Hall	3	0	F	Lex	41,333
Yankee Glide	Angus Hall	1	0	C	Hb	15,000
Yankee Glide	Angus Hall	3	0	C	Lex	29,000
Yankee Glide	Angus Hall	1	0	F	Hb	90,000
Yankee Glide	Angus Hall	2	0	F	Lex	92,500
Yankee Glide	Armbro Goal	4	0	C	Lex	36,750
Yankee Glide	Armbro Goal	1	0	F	Lex	105,000
Yankee Glide	Armbro Iliad	1	0	F	Lex	35,000
Yankee Glide	Balanced Image	5	0	C	Hb	19,400
Yankee Glide	Balanced Image	7	1	C	Lex	71,286
Yankee Glide	Balanced Image	4	1	F	Hb	39,000
Yankee Glide	Balanced Image	4	0	F	Lex	41,250
Yankee Glide	Bonefish	2	0	C	Lex	30,000

Sire	Bm Sire	Sold	$50,000 2 Year Olds	Sex	Sale	Average Price
Yankee Glide	Bonefish	1	0	F	Lex	50,000
Yankee Glide	Carry The Message	1	0	C	Lex	2,000
Yankee Glide	Carry The Message	1	0	F	Lex	37,000
Yankee Glide	Conway Hall	3	0	C	Hb	17,667
Yankee Glide	Conway Hall	5	0	C	Lex	46,800
Yankee Glide	Conway Hall	3	0	F	Hb	48,000
Yankee Glide	Conway Hall	3	0	F	Lex	63,333
Yankee Glide	Cooper Lobell	1	0	C	Lex	15,000
Yankee Glide	Cooper Lobell	2	0	F	Lex	51,000
Yankee Glide	Credit Winner	3	0	C	Lex	61,667
Yankee Glide	Credit Winner	1	0	F	Hb	27,000
Yankee Glide	Credit Winner	2	0	F	Lex	49,500
Yankee Glide	Crowning Point	4	0	C	Lex	13,250
Yankee Glide	Crowning Point	1	0	F	Lex	17,000
Yankee Glide	Cumin	1	0	F	Hb	3,000
Yankee Glide	Donerail	2	0	C	Hb	42,000
Yankee Glide	Donerail	3	0	C	Lex	44,667
Yankee Glide	Donerail	3	0	F	Lex	37,667
Yankee Glide	Enjoy Lavec	2	0	C	Hb	56,750
Yankee Glide	Enjoy Lavec	1	0	C	Lex	20,000
Yankee Glide	Enjoy Lavec	1	1	F	Hb	50,000
Yankee Glide	Enjoy Lavec	2	0	F	Lex	40,000
Yankee Glide	Florida Pro	1	0	C	Hb	3,000
Yankee Glide	Garland Lobell	2	0	C	Hb	43,500
Yankee Glide	Garland Lobell	7	1	C	Lex	95,143
Yankee Glide	Garland Lobell	1	0	F	Lex	180,000
Yankee Glide	Giant Hit	1	0	C	Hb	37,000
Yankee Glide	Kadabra	1	0	F	Lex	30,000
Yankee Glide	King Conch	2	0	C	Lex	21,000
Yankee Glide	King Conch	1	0	F	Lex	35,000
Yankee Glide	Lindy Lane	1	0	C	Hb	8,000
Yankee Glide	Lindy Lane	1	0	C	Lex	22,000
Yankee Glide	Lindy Lane	2	0	F	Hb	50,000
Yankee Glide	Malabar Man	4	0	C	Hb	41,000
Yankee Glide	Malabar Man	4	0	C	Lex	31,000
Yankee Glide	Malabar Man	2	1	F	Hb	38,500
Yankee Glide	Malabar Man	11	0	F	Lex	43,545
Yankee Glide	Mr Lavec	4	0	C	Hb	24,125
Yankee Glide	Mr Lavec	4	0	C	Lex	24,000
Yankee Glide	Mr Lavec	1	0	F	Hb	35,000
Yankee Glide	Mr Lavec	4	0	F	Lex	15,250

Sire	Bm Sire	Sold	$50,000 2 Year Olds	Sex	Sale	Average Price
Yankee Glide	Mr Vic	6	1	C	Lex	27,833
Yankee Glide	Mr Vic	7	1	F	Lex	41,857
Yankee Glide	Muscles Yankee	1	0	C	Lex	10,000
Yankee Glide	Overcomer	1	0	F	Hb	37,000
Yankee Glide	Photo Maker	1	0	C	Lex	15,000
Yankee Glide	Photo Maker	1	0	F	Lex	30,000
Yankee Glide	Pine Chip	3	0	C	Lex	13,333
Yankee Glide	Pine Chip	1	0	F	Lex	50,000
Yankee Glide	Royal Prestige	4	0	C	Lex	39,000
Yankee Glide	Royal Prestige	3	0	F	Lex	64,333
Yankee Glide	Royal Troubador	1	0	C	Hb	11,000
Yankee Glide	SJ's Photo	1	0	C	Hb	45,000
Yankee Glide	SJ's Photo	2	1	F	Hb	50,000
Yankee Glide	SJ's Photo	1	0	F	Lex	55,000
Yankee Glide	Self Possessed	1	0	C	Hb	3,500
Yankee Glide	Self Possessed	1	0	C	Lex	30,000
Yankee Glide	Self Possessed	1	0	F	Lex	45,000
Yankee Glide	Sierra Kosmos	3	0	C	Hb	12,167
Yankee Glide	Sierra Kosmos	3	1	C	Lex	20,000
Yankee Glide	Sierra Kosmos	2	0	F	Hb	10,500
Yankee Glide	Sir Taurus	1	0	C	Lex	15,000
Yankee Glide	Sir Taurus	1	0	F	Hb	20,000
Yankee Glide	Speedy Somolli	1	0	C	Lex	15,000
Yankee Glide	Speedy Somolli	1	0	F	Lex	80,000
Yankee Glide	Striking Sahbra	1	0	C	Lex	42,000
Yankee Glide	Striking Sahbra	3	2	F	Hb	72,667
Yankee Glide	Super Bowl	2	0	C	Hb	30,000
Yankee Glide	Super Bowl	1	0	C	Lex	50,000
Yankee Glide	Super Bowl	3	0	F	Lex	63,333
Yankee Glide	Super Pleasure	1	0	C	Hb	6,000
Yankee Glide	Super Pleasure	1	0	F	Hb	4,500
Yankee Glide	Supergill	1	0	C	Hb	85,000
Yankee Glide	Supergill	1	0	C	Lex	35,000
Yankee Glide	Supergill	2	0	F	Lex	47,500
Yankee Glide	Tagliabue	7	2	C	Lex	55,143
Yankee Glide	Tagliabue	4	0	F	Lex	111,750
Yankee Glide	Yankee Paco	1	1	C	Hb	35,000
Yankee Glide	Yankee Paco	2	1	C	Lex	28,000
Yankee Glide	Yankee Paco	1	0	F	Hb	28,000
Yankee Glide	Yankee Paco	1	0	F	Lex	20,000

Chapter 8: Success Rates of Raced versus Unraced Dam

Conventional wisdom is split on this issue. Some people feel that raced mares are better broodmares because of the racing experience they pass on to their progeny. Certainly the farms breed many more raced mares than unraced ones. Others argue that unraced mares probably have more pedigree; otherwise the farms wouldn't breed them. Both arguments make sense. Within the scope of our study we can see a difference.

Chart 1: Success Rates of Raced vs Unraced Dams by Gait and Gender

Gait/Sex	Dam	Sale	Sold	$50,000 2 Year Olds	Success Rate	Average Price
Pacing Colts	Unraced Dam	HB/LEX	237	11	4.6%	$28,236
Pacing Colts	Raced Dam	HB/LEX	1437	110	7.7%	35,516
Pacing Colts	TOTAL	HB/LEX	1674	121	7.2%	34,486
Pacing Fillies	Unraced Dam	HB/LEX	191	11	5.8%	20,385
Pacing Fillies	Raced Dam	HB/LEX	1229	88	7.2%	26,599
Pacing Fillies	TOTAL	HB/LEX	1420	99	7.0%	25,763
Total Pacers		**HB/LEX**	**3094**	**220**	**7.1%**	**30,482**
Trot Colts	Unraced Dam	HB/LEX	269	24	8.9%	32,840
Trot Colts	Raced Dam	HB/LEX	1102	76	6.9%	38,652
Trot Colts	TOTAL	HB/LEX	1371	100	7.3%	37,512
Trot Fillies	Unraced Dam	HB/LEX	263	12	4.6%	29,472
Trot Fillies	Raced Dam	HB/LEX	957	74	7.7%	33,853
Trot Fillies	TOTAL	HB/LEX	1220	86	7.0%	32,909
Total Trots		**HB/LEX**	**2591**	**186**	**7.2%**	**35,344**
Grand Total	**All Dams**	**HB/LEX**	**5685**	**406**	**7.1%**	**$32,698**

Looking at all 5,685 yearlings sold by gait and gender, we find that raced mares out-performed un-raced mares except for trotting colts. Overall, raced mares had a *22%* better Success Rate than unraced mares (7.4% to 6.0%). Raced mares were 64.9% better with pacing colts, 24.3 % better with pacing fillies, and 69.5 % better with trotting fillies. But, with trotting colts raced mares were 22.6% worse. The following chart will separate the sale venues.

Chart 2: Success Rates of Raced vs Unraced Dams by Gait and Gender

LEXINGTON

Gait/Sex	Dam	Sale	Sold	$50,000 2 Year Olds	Success Rate	Average Price
Pacing Colts	Unraced Dam	LEX	92	3	3.3%	$26,272
Pacing Colts	Raced Dam	LEX	552	51	9.2%	39,554
Pacing Colts	TOTAL	LEX	644	54	8.4%	37,657
Pacing Fillies	Unraced Dam	LEX	84	4	4.8%	20,405
Pacing Fillies	Raced Dam	LEX	471	42	8.9%	27,497
Pacing Fillies	TOTAL	LEX	555	46	8.3%	26,423
Total Pacers		**LEX**	**1199**	**100**	**8.3%**	**32,457**
Trot Colts	Unraced Dam	LEX	135	12	8.9%	33,726
Trot Colts	Raced Dam	LEX	515	34	6.6%	41,190
Trot Colts	TOTAL	LEX	650	46	7.1%	39,640
Trot Fillies	Unraced Dam	LEX	123	6	4.9%	33,675
Trot Fillies	Raced Dam	LEX	417	27	6.5%	37,544
Trot Fillies	TOTAL	LEX	540	33	6.1%	36,663
Total Trotters		**LEX**	**1190**	**79**	**6.6%**	**38,289**
Grand Total	**All Dams**	**LEX**	**2389**	**179**	**7.5%**	**$35,362**

HARRISBURG

Gait/Sex	DAM	Sale	Sold	$50,000 2 Year Old	Success Rate	Average Price
Pacing Colts	Unraced Dam	HB	145	8	5.5%	$29,483
Pacing Colts	Raced Dam	HB	885	59	6.7%	32,998
Pacing Colts	TOTAL	HB	1030	67	6.5%	32,503
Pacing Fillies	Unraced Dam	HB	107	7	6.5%	20,369
Pacing Fillies	Raced Dam	HB	758	46	6.1%	26,041
Pacing Fillies	TOTAL	HB	865	53	6.1%	25,340
Total Pacers		**HB**	**1895**	**120**	**6.3%**	**29,233**
Trot Colts	Unraced Dam	HB	134	12	9.0%	31,948
Trot Colts	Raced Dam	HB	587	42	7.2%	36,426
Trot Colts	TOTAL	HB	721	54	7.5%	35,594
Trot Fillies	Unraced Dam	HB	140	6	4.3%	25,779
Trot Fillies	Raced Dam	HB	540	47	8.7%	31,003
Trot Fillies	TOTAL	HB	680	53	7.8%	29,927
Total Trotters		**HB**	**1401**	**107**	**7.6%**	**32,843**
Grand Total		**HB**	**3296**	**227**	**6.9%**	**$30,768**

Even after separating the two sale venues, unraced mares had better Success Rates with colt trotters at both Harrisburg and Lexington. Colt trotters from unraced mares sold for 18% less than those of their raced mare counterparts at Lexington, and 12% less at HB.

At HB, excluding trotting fillies, the differences in output between the raced and unraced mares was not as large as LEX. In fact, notice that among HB pacing fillies, unraced mares had a higher Success Rate (6.5%) than raced mares (6.0%). However, both are below the average.

At LEX, the production of raced and unraced mares was very disparate with pacers. The colts from raced mares had a 183% better Success Rate (9.2%) than colts from unraced mares (3.3%). For LEX filly pacers, the Success Rates were 8.9% for raced mares to 4.8% for unraced, or 87% better.

At this point the reader may ask why we have not detailed any information regarding the race marks of raced mares. The explanation is that it's complicated and amorphous. Is a mare that took a three-year old mark of 1:55 on a mile track considered faster than one that went in 1:57 on a half? Is a mare with a two-year old mark of 1:56m better than a mare with a four-year old mark of 1:52m or 1:54h? We don't know. Another quandary is mares with multiple marks. If a mare has marks at two, three, and four, which one is most influential, most prescient in terms of production?

Chapter 9: Success Rate by Age of Dam

Another aspect of mares that we researched was their ages at the time of foaling. We were curious about a correlation between a mare's age and its Success Rate. The significance of this correlation will be determined by the reader. But there are some disparities worth noting. For example, offspring of four-year old mares had a 31.5% lower Success Rate than average: 4.9 % versus 7.1%. Dividing the data by gait and gender reveals the following:

Progeny of 4-Year Old Mares at LEX and HB, 2008-2010

Gate	Sex	Sold	$50,000 2 Year Olds	Success Rate	Percent to Average of 7.14%
P	C	78	6	7.7%	+ 7.7%
P	F	56	2	3.6%	- 50.0%
T	C	76	4	5.3%	- 26.3%
T	F	56	1	1.8%	- 74.9%

Fillies out of four-year old mares have had very low Success Rates.

The following five charts will show the Success Rates of mares by age. Chart 1 will illustrate the total population, while charts 2 through 5 will detail the data by gait, gender and sale venue.

Chart 1: Success Rate by Age of Dams

Dam's Age	HARRISBURG			LEXINGTON			TOTAL		
	Sold	$50,000 2 Year Olds	Success Rate	Sold	$50,000 2 Year Olds	Success Rate	Sold	$50,000 2 Year Olds	Success Rate
3	18	2	11.1%	10	1	10.0%	28	3	10.7%
4	152	9	5.9%	114	4	3.5%	266	13	4.9%
5	363	28	7.7%	238	18	7.6%	601	46	7.7%
6	365	27	7.4%	291	15	5.2%	656	42	6.4%
7	369	31	8.4%	284	28	9.9%	653	59	9.0%
8	308	19	6.2%	258	24	9.3%	566	43	7.6%
9	302	27	8.9%	207	21	10.1%	509	48	9.4%
10	251	11	4.4%	186	13	7.0%	437	24	5.5%
11	226	21	9.3%	151	13	8.6%	377	34	9.0%
12	191	12	6.3%	138	9	6.5%	329	21	6.4%
13	166	10	6.0%	103	8	7.8%	269	18	6.7%
14	130	4	3.1%	111	4	3.6%	241	8	3.3%
15	99	7	7.1%	81	5	6.2%	180	12	6.7%
16	100	8	8.0%	66	7	10.6%	166	15	9.0%
17	84	6	7.1%	40	1	2.5%	124	7	5.6%
18	52	2	3.8%	37	3	8.1%	89	5	5.6%
19	42	2	4.8%	30	3	10.0%	72	5	6.9%
20	31	0	0.0%	15	2	13.3%	46	2	4.3%
21	21	0	0.0%	10	0	0.0%	31	0	0.0%
22	9	0	0.0%	6	0	0.0%	15	0	0.0%
23	6	0	0.0%	8	0	0.0%	14	0	0.0%
24	8	1	12.5%	4	0	0.0%	12	1	8.3%
25	3	0	0.0%	1	0	0.0%	4	0	0.0%
TOTAL	3296	227	6.9%	2389	179	7.5%	5685	406	7.1%

Chart 2: Success Rate by Age of Dams for Pacing Colts

	HARRISBURG			LEXINGTON			TOTAL		
Dam's Age	Sold	$50,000 2 Year Olds	Success Rate	Sold	$50,000 2 Year Olds	Success Rate	Sold	$50,000 2 Year Olds	Success Rate
3	3	1	33.3%	1	0	0.0%	4	1	25.0%
4	47	5	10.6%	31	1	3.2%	78	6	7.7%
5	110	4	3.6%	62	5	8.1%	172	9	5.2%
6	112	4	3.6%	72	2	2.8%	184	6	3.3%
7	110	7	6.4%	78	5	6.4%	188	12	6.4%
8	89	4	4.5%	77	11	14.3%	166	15	9.0%
9	97	11	11.3%	42	5	11.9%	139	16	11.5%
10	66	3	4.5%	52	6	11.5%	118	9	7.6%
11	65	6	9.2%	34	4	11.8%	99	10	10.1%
12	70	6	8.6%	44	3	6.8%	114	9	7.9%
13	60	3	5.0%	36	4	11.1%	96	7	7.3%
14	50	2	4.0%	24	1	4.2%	74	3	4.1%
15	31	4	12.9%	22	2	9.1%	53	6	11.3%
16	35	4	11.4%	22	1	4.5%	57	5	8.8%
17	20	2	10.0%	12	0	0.0%	32	2	6.3%
18	18	0	0.0%	12	1	8.3%	30	1	3.3%
19	14	1	7.1%	7	1	14.3%	21	2	9.5%
20	12	0	0.0%	5	2	40.0%	17	2	11.8%
21	9	0	0.0%	6	0	0.0%	15	0	0.0%
22	3	0	0.0%	3	0	0.0%	6	0	0.0%
23	5	0	0.0%	0	0	0.0%	5	0	0.0%
24	2	0	0.0%	2	0	0.0%	4	0	0.0%
25	2	0	0.0%	0	0	0.0%	2	0	0.0%
TOTAL	1030	67	6.5%	644	54	8.4%	1674	121	7.2%

Chart 3: Success Rate by Age of Dams for Pacing Fillies

	HARRISBURG			LEXINGTON			TOTAL		
Dam's Age	Sold	$50,000 2 Year Olds	Success Rate	Sold	$50,000 2 Year Olds	Success Rate	Sold	$50,000 2 Year Olds	Success Rate
3	2	0	0.0%	3	1	33.3%	5	1	20.0%
4	36	1	2.8%	20	1	5.0%	56	2	3.6%
5	76	7	9.2%	52	4	7.7%	128	11	8.6%
6	88	8	9.1%	74	5	6.8%	162	13	8.0%
7	88	8	9.1%	65	8	12.3%	153	16	10.5%
8	86	4	4.7%	54	3	5.6%	140	7	5.0%
9	80	7	8.8%	44	5	11.4%	124	12	9.7%
10	73	4	5.5%	42	2	4.8%	115	6	5.2%
11	64	2	3.1%	42	5	11.9%	106	7	6.6%
12	45	1	2.2%	32	1	3.1%	77	2	2.6%
13	51	4	7.8%	24	3	12.5%	75	7	9.3%
14	39	1	2.6%	30	2	6.7%	69	3	4.3%
15	36	2	5.6%	24	1	4.2%	60	3	5.0%
16	23	1	4.3%	14	2	14.3%	37	3	8.1%
17	28	2	7.1%	11	1	9.1%	39	3	7.7%
18	13	0	0.0%	8	1	12.5%	21	1	4.8%
19	16	1	6.3%	8	1	12.5%	24	2	8.3%
20	10	0	0.0%	3	0	0.0%	13	0	0.0%
21	7	0	0.0%	2	0	0.0%	9	0	0.0%
22	3	0	0.0%	1	0	0.0%	4	0	0.0%
23	0	0	0.0%	2	0	0.0%	2	0	0.0%
24	1	0	0.0%	0	0	0.0%	1	0	0.0%
25	0	0	0.0%	0	0	0.0%	0	0	0.0%
TOTAL	865	53	6.1%	555	46	8.3%	1420	99	7.0%

Chart 4: Success Rate by Age of Dams for Trotting Colts

	HARRISBURG			LEXINGTON			TOTAL		
Dam's Age	Sold	$50,000 2 Year Olds	Success Rate	Sold	$50,000 2 Year Olds	Success Rate	Sold	$50,000 2 Year Olds	Success Rate
3	8	1	12.5%	3	0	0.0%	11	1	9.1%
4	45	2	4.4%	31	2	6.5%	76	4	5.3%
5	81	7	8.6%	68	5	7.4%	149	12	8.1%
6	85	8	9.4%	77	5	6.5%	162	13	8.0%
7	85	7	8.2%	81	8	9.9%	166	15	9.0%
8	65	5	7.7%	70	5	7.1%	135	10	7.4%
9	59	5	8.5%	62	7	11.3%	121	12	9.9%
10	56	3	5.4%	50	4	8.0%	106	7	6.6%
11	55	7	12.7%	38	0	0.0%	93	7	7.5%
12	40	2	5.0%	36	4	11.1%	76	6	7.9%
13	31	0	0.0%	26	1	3.8%	57	1	1.8%
14	24	1	4.2%	32	0	0.0%	56	1	1.8%
15	18	1	5.6%	22	2	9.1%	40	3	7.5%
16	18	2	11.1%	14	2	14.3%	32	4	12.5%
17	22	1	4.5%	8	0	0.0%	30	1	3.3%
18	11	1	9.1%	10	0	0.0%	21	1	4.8%
19	7	0	0.0%	8	1	12.5%	15	1	6.7%
20	3	0	0.0%	5	0	0.0%	8	0	0.0%
21	2	0	0.0%	1	0	0.0%	3	0	0.0%
22	1	0	0.0%	1	0	0.0%	2	0	0.0%
23	1	0	0.0%	4	0	0.0%	5	0	0.0%
24	4	1	25.0%	2	0	0.0%	6	1	16.7%
25	0	0	0.0%	1	0	0.0%	1	0	0.0%
TOTAL	721	54	7.5%	650	46	7.1%	1371	100	7.3%

Chart 5: Success Rate by Age of Dams for Trotting Fillies

	HARRISBURG			LEXINGTON			TOTAL		
Dam's Age	Sold	$50,000 2 Year Olds	Success Rate	Sold	$50,000 2 Year Olds	Success Rate	Sold	$50,000 2 Year Olds	Success Rate
3	5	0	0.0%	3	0	0.0%	8	0	0.0%
4	24	1	4.2%	32	0	0.0%	56	1	1.8%
5	96	10	10.4%	56	4	7.1%	152	14	9.2%
6	80	7	8.8%	68	3	4.4%	148	10	6.8%
7	86	9	10.5%	60	7	11.7%	146	16	11.0%
8	68	6	8.8%	57	5	8.8%	125	11	8.8%
9	66	4	6.1%	59	4	6.8%	125	8	6.4%
10	56	1	1.8%	42	1	2.4%	98	2	2.0%
11	42	6	14.3%	37	4	10.8%	79	10	12.7%
12	36	3	8.3%	26	1	3.8%	62	4	6.5%
13	24	3	12.5%	17	0	0.0%	41	3	7.3%
14	17	0	0.0%	25	1	4.0%	42	1	2.4%
15	14	0	0.0%	13	0	0.0%	27	0	0.0%
16	24	1	4.2%	16	2	12.5%	40	3	7.5%
17	14	1	7.1%	9	0	0.0%	23	1	4.3%
18	10	1	10.0%	7	1	14.3%	17	2	11.8%
19	5	0	0.0%	7	0	0.0%	12	0	0.0%
20	6	0	0.0%	2	0	0.0%	8	0	0.0%
21	3	0	0.0%	1	0	0.0%	4	0	0.0%
22	2	0	0.0%	1	0	0.0%	3	0	0.0%
23	0	0	0.0%	2	0	0.0%	2	0	0.0%
24	1	0	0.0%	0	0	0.0%	1	0	0.0%
25	1	0	0.0%	0	0	0.0%	1	0	0.0%
TOTAL	680	53	7.8%	540	33	6.1%	1220	86	7.0%

There are some surprising figures by gait, gender and venue. For example, 11 year-old mares of trotting colts are 0 for 38 at Lexington. At Harrisburg, 13 year-old mares of trotting colts are 0 for 31. Ten year-old mares of trotting fillies are 2 for 98 at both sale venues combined. Yet, 11 year old mares of trotting fillies are a remarkable 10 out of 79, for a 12.7% Success Rate. Eight year-old mares of pacing colts at Lexington are 11 out of 77, for a 14.3% Success Rate. Yet, incredibly, eight year-old mares of colt pacers at Harrisburg are only 4 out of 89, for a 4.5% Success Rate.

In reviewing the last two chapters regarding raced and unraced mares and the ages of mares, one might question the relevance of this information. The importance one places on these statistics is up to the individual. However, since many of the mares appear repeatedly at these sale venues, we think racing status and, to a lesser extent age, are factors in their production.

Chapter 10: Grand-dams Production

In studying pedigrees, we have been examining the performance of grand-dams more closely. We believe knowing the recent production record of the grand-dams can be helpful. Even though our records are confined to the 2008–2010 sales at Harrisburg and Lexington, this data gives us a good representation of current performance.

There are 2,652 grand-dams who have sent grandchildren through the sale rings at HB and LEX, and *367* of them have produced the 406 elite two-year olds. It's fairly gender specific also. Only 17 of the 367 grand-dams have both a colt and filly credit. Those 17 are: *Almost An Angel, B Cor Tamgo, Charlotte Newton, Country Kay Sue, Dominique Semalu, Forbidden Past, Lady Longlegs, Loving Proof, Mib Hanover, Midnight Stage, Panned Out, Rodine Hanover, Shake 'Em Up Suzy, Silksndiamonds, Sonspree, Sweet Affection,* and *Yankee Tomboy.*

Chart 1: Top Producing Grand-dams

COLTS

Grand-dam	Sold	$50,000 2 Year Olds
Abbeycrombie	2	1
Al Dente	3	1
Albaquel	3	1
Allamerican Cool	2	1
Allamerican Mocha	1	1
Almost An Angel	3	1
Always An Art	1	1
Amanda T Collins	2	1
American Splendor	1	1
American Wish	2	1
Anamosa Hanover	6	3
Annabel Lee	1	1

FILLIES

Grand-dam	Sold	$50,000 2 Year Olds
A Yankee Classic	4	1
Act Of Grace	1	1
Action Delight	2	1
Adored Yankee	1	1
Ain't No Stopn Me	1	1
Aldyth Hanover	3	1
All My Pleasure	1	1
Almost An Angel	3	1
Amour Angus	5	1
Armbro Glossy	2	1
Armbro Marilyn	2	1
Armbro Purse	3	1

COLTS

Grand-dam	Sold	$50,000 2 Year Olds
Armbro Éclair	5	1
Armbro Ophelia	3	1
Armbro Pantomime	1	1
Armbro Stacy	1	1
Armbro Whirl	2	1
Astoria Lobell	6	1
Athens Blue Chip	1	1
Aura Of Glory	1	1
Autumn Mindale	2	2
B Cor Tamgo	1	1
Bambi Windswept	2	1
Bassing	2	1
Bathonia	4	1
Beat The Wheel	3	1
Because I Said So	3	1
Beh Shert	2	1
Bequest Hanover	2	1
Best Of The Best	4	1
Betrayed By A Kiss	1	1
Bunch Hanover	7	1
Camden Dee	1	1
Cams Exotic	3	1
Cascadia	2	1
Casual Brilliance	1	1
Cathedra	3	1
CC's Saleofthecentury	1	1
Charlotte Newton	1	1
Cheryl Hanover	2	1
Cindys Action	1	1
Classic Casette	3	1
Come Unwound	2	1
Concert Goer	2	1
Cool Pink	2	1
Cool World	2	1
Countess Camae	1	1
Country Kay Sue	5	1
Darling Clementine	1	1
Decent Exposure	2	1
Décor	2	1
Devil's Dream	2	1
Disarmed	2	1
Dominique Semalu	3	2
Dr Mom	1	1
Dreamlands Oasis	1	1

FILLIES

Grand-dam	Sold	$50,000 2 Year Olds
Armbro Vanquish	1	1
Artful Mystique	1	1
Aurora Hanover	2	1
B Cor Tamgo	2	1
Beat The Band	1	1
Bedeviled	2	1
Bee Valiant	1	1
Before Sunrise	3	2
Blue Diamond	3	1
Broadway Creation	2	1
Campaign Leader	2	1
Casino Evil	1	1
CD's Girl	1	1
Charlotte Newton	2	1
Child Star	1	1
Classic Beauty	2	1
Classic Wish	1	1
Completely Sweet	2	1
Consuela Lobell	2	1
Cookout	5	1
Cool Elegance	2	1
Coquette Hanover	1	1
Country Kay Sue	4	1
Cream Puff	2	1
Crew Angel	1	1
Crown Crysta	1	1
Cursty For Me	1	1
Daisy Hanover	4	1
Dawn Q	3	1
Dawnmarie Seelster	2	1
Diana Lynn Lobell	2	1
Doc's Girl	2	1
Dominique Semalu	2	1
Dormitory	1	1
Edbar's Nanci	1	1
Efishnc	2	1
Eicarl's El Grande	1	1
Elegantimage	1	1
Elena Hanover	1	1
Excella Hanover	3	1
Expressway Hanover	3	1
Farmgirl Hanovder	1	1
Flickering Halo	4	1
Foot Loose	2	1

COLTS

Grand-dam	Sold	$50,000 2 Year Olds
Dual Tracks	7	2
Dutch Love	2	1
Echo Hanover	2	2
Emma Hanover	1	1
Empty Feeling	3	1
Evergreen Sandy	1	1
Falnos Babell	4	2
Fanny Bryce	3	1
Financial Matters	1	1
Forbidden Past	2	1
Foxy Victory	4	1
Frances Lobell	2	1
Freckled Petal	1	1
Ginger Lobell	3	1
Ginger Tree Brenda	2	1
Gold Coast	2	1
Goodtime Kathy	2	1
Gotta Token	1	1
Grand Vitesse	1	1
Grill Now	1	1
Habit	3	1
Happy Doris	2	1
Higher Love	4	1
Idylwood Legend	5	1
I'm Prime Time	1	1
In The Dumps	1	1
Incredible Chic	1	1
Instant Rebate	1	1
Jailhouse Rock	1	1
Jef's Magic Trick	2	1
Jenny M Hanover	1	1
Jollie Dame	2	2
Just Say So	1	1
Justaflirt	4	1
Keystone Sister	1	1
Kisses N Candy	3	1
La Crème	1	1
La Starlet	1	1
Lady Longlegs	2	1
Lady Starlet	2	1
Ladyotra	2	1
Lake Nona	2	1
Life's Highway	1	1
Lifetime Success	1	1

FILLIES

Grand-dam	Sold	$50,000 2 Year Olds
Forbidden Past	1	1
Fortuna Dream	1	1
French Dressing	2	1
Garden Grove	2	2
Gay Filet	1	1
Giant Princess	2	1
Giggle Box	3	1
Gilina	1	1
Gin Daisy	2	1
Hasty Heart	2	1
Hildy Hanover	4	1
Home Treasure	2	1
Hornby Judy	1	1
Hotgeorgianite	1	1
Impress	5	1
Impressive Breeze	1	1
Jate's Strait	1	1
Jef's Celebration	4	1
Jonlin	3	1
Keely Hanover	2	1
Kelsey A	1	1
Kenwood Scamper	4	1
Keystone Chick	2	1
Keystone Myrtle	1	1
Keystone Scent	3	1
Lady Longlegs	4	1
Leap Year Romance	1	1
Legacy Of Glory	2	1
Lhasa Lhasa Lhasa	2	1
Lifelong Victory	3	1
Lights On	2	1
Lindy's Kick Back	1	
Lookslikenorma	2	1
Lou Macs Pride	1	1
Loving Proof	5	2
Lucky Tune	4	1
Malhana Catfur	1	1
Marcella Hanover	3	1
Martine Lobell	2	1
Meadowmiss Hanover	2	1
Mib Hanover	5	1
Midnight Stage	2	1
Miss Donna Mayo	3	1
Miss Flirt	2	1

COLTS

Grand-dam	Sold	$50,000 2 Year Olds
Likeable	2	1
Little Ms Queenie	2	1
Louisa	3	1
Loving Proof	5	1
Madam Christie	1	1
Maeling Hanover	3	2
Making Miracles	1	1
Maple Frosting	4	1
Margarita Miss	3	1
Mary Sue Hanover	2	1
Mattaroni	2	1
Matt's Sunshine	1	1
Me Maggie	7	2
Meadow Ginny	1	1
Meghan's Memories	2	1
Mib Hanover	4	1
Midnight Stage	3	1
Miss Elvira	3	1
Miss Intensity	2	1
Miss Marita	2	1
Miss Photogenic	1	1
Miss Pine Chip	3	2
Missy Will Do It	5	1
Misty Bretta	5	1
Misty Dancer	1	1
Mombassa	1	1
Moonson	1	1
Ms Vic	2	1
My Belle Ami	1	1
Nakiska Lobell	2	1
Napa Valley	2	1
Nicegirlsdont	3	1
Nonpariel M	2	1
Nutcracker Lady	1	1
Ocean Princess	2	1
Odessa Blue Chip	1	1
Open Shut	2	1
Pamella Seelster	1	1
Panned Out	5	1
Perky Almahurst	1	1
Pj Naomi	1	1
Poodle Party	2	1
Pop Art	1	1
Priority Rose	3	2

FILLIES

Grand-dam	Sold	$50,000 2 Year Olds
Monet Blue Chip	3	1
Moonlit Path	1	1
Mostly Super	1	1
My Melissa	3	1
Noble Marty	1	1
Oaklea Ida	1	1
Paisley Yankee	1	1
Panache Lobell	2	1
Panned Out	4	1
Peace A Pie	7	1
Please Polly	1	1
Precious Delight	1	1
Proven Perfect	1	1
Psychiatrist	3	1
Psychologist	2	1
Queen Of Blues	1	1
Queen Of Queens	2	1
Racy Dragon	1	1
Revallee Kathleen	2	1
Roadshow	2	1
Rodine Hanover	3	1
Romantic Victory	2	1
Sabella Lobell	5	1
Santastic	1	1
Santra Lb	1	1
Scarletas Dream	1	1
Scotch Spring	1	1
Sea Style	2	2
Second Act	2	1
Secret Alert	2	1
Secret Passage	2	1
Senorita Sierra	3	1
Seven O'clock	1	1
Shake 'Em Up Suzy	1	1
Shelly Lobell	1	1
She's A Great Lady	2	1
She's The Greatest	3	1
Show Me Leg	1	1
Shy Reflection	5	1
Silksndiamonds	2	2
Singin For Supper	5	1
Slow Dance Hanover	2	1
So Alive	3	1
So Tough	2	1

COLTS

Grand-dam	Sold	$50,000 2 Year Olds
Racing Date	1	1
Reef	1	1
Regression	3	1
Rita Almahurst	3	1
Rodine Hanover	3	1
Royal Lindy	2	1
Rozita Hanover	2	1
Rush Light	2	1
S B Fuchsias Image	1	1
Safety Belle	1	1
Samshu Bluegrass	3	1
Santa Fe	2	1
Santa Royal	2	1
Sara Lawrence	1	1
Sara Loren Rd	1	1
Season's Victory	3	1
Seconds Ahead	2	1
Shake 'Em Up Suzy	3	1
Sharon Again	2	1
Sibyl Hill	3	2
Silksndiamonds	2	1
Simply Ravishing	1	1
Sissy Dee	1	1
Sky Ecstasy	1	1
Smooth Tide	2	1
So Chic	3	1
So Close	4	1
So Easy	2	1
Soignee Kash	1	1
Sole To Sole	3	1
Sonspree	2	1
Spiffey Yankee	2	1
Spurred On	1	1
Stienam's Place	4	1
Sugar	1	1
Supercilious	1	1
Surmise	5	1
Sweet Affection	4	1
Sweet Dahrlin	2	1
Tango Almahurst	3	1
Test Ban	3	1
This Year's Kisses	1	1
Three Diamonds	4	1
Three Mile Island	3	1

FILLIES

Grand-dam	Sold	$50,000 2 Year Olds
Sonspree	2	1
Sos Virago	1	1
Sounds Swell	3	1
Special Measure	1	1
Speedy Beauty	3	1
Stienam's Girl	2	1
Summer Child	3	3
Sunrise Isle	2	1
Super Cool Deal	3	1
Super Shann	3	1
Suydam	1	1
Sweet Affection	5	1
Take Another Puff	3	1
Tessie's Mother	3	1
The Big Enchilada	3	1
Then Again	2	2
Thrill Hill	3	1
Token Gesture	3	1
Too Much Trouble	1	1
Touch Of Jazz	1	1
Toy Poodle	2	1
Tress Hanover	2	1
Trini Hanover	1	1
Two Times Three	1	1
Uniformite J P	2	1
Vernon Blue Chip	2	1
Victory Girl	1	1
Visi D'arte	2	2
Witsend's Nimble	2	1
Yankee Co-Ed	5	1
Yankee Diamond	4	1
Yankee Tomboy	3	1

COLTS

Grand-dam	Sold	$50,000 2 Year Olds
Toni Tyler	2	1
Town Sweetheart	3	1
Treasured Victory	1	1
Tropicana Hanover	2	1
Trudy's Precious	3	1
Valley Regina	2	1
Velvet Sauce	6	1
Vickis Glory	3	1
Victory's Garden	1	1
Viking Princess	2	1
Vodka On Ice	2	1
Wendy Jo Hanover	1	1
Wendymae Hanover	6	1
Wesgate Princess	4	1
Witsend Robin	1	1
Wizzardmania	1	1
Worldclass Victory	1	1
Worldly Woman	2	1
Yagottawanna	1	1
Yankee Tomboy	3	1

Also, we should be aware of those grand-dams that have yet to produce a $50,000 two-year old. To be eligible for Chart 2 a grand-dam must have had at least *four* of her grandchildren of the same gender sold at HB and LEX from 2008–2010 *without* an elite performer credit. The first grand-dam you will notice on the chart is *Peace A Pie* at 0 for 10 with colt grandchildren. She is 1 for 7 with fillies. *Me Maggie* is 0 for 7 with fillies, but 2 for 7 with colts. Then there are grand-dams such as *World Order,* who is 0 for 10, missing with 5 colts and 5 fillies. *Madam Cool* and *Madam Hanover* are both 0 for 9, each missing with 5 fillies and 4 colts.

The 79 grand-dams on the following chart have not produced a single elite performer from 646 sold. Since we will continue to see grandchildren of these mares at future sales, we should be familiar with their records.

Chart 2: Grand-dams with Zero Credits (Minimum of 4 Sold by Gender)

COLTS

Grand-dam	Sold	$50,000 2 Year Olds
Peace A Pie	10	0
Promised Crown	8	0
Melt My Heart	7	0
Trilogy Lobell	7	0
Bedell	6	0
Insideous Charm	6	0
Intercontinental	6	0
On The Day	6	0
Adored Yankee	5	0
Arnies Fortune	5	0
B Cor Tamara	5	0
Bio Bandbox	5	0
Cami Whitestocking	5	0
Candy Crown	5	0
Caressable	5	0
Castleton Molly	5	0
Chatty Hanover	5	0
Cheerful Earful	5	0
Clear Copy	5	0
Crown Starlet	5	0
Dateable	5	0
Harmonics	5	0
Low Places	5	0
Naraculous	5	0
Pirate Laura	5	0
Shipps Dream	5	0
Sonsam's Dream	5	0
Sugarbear Hanover	5	0
Truly A Lady	5	0
World Order	5	0
Ali's Cat	4	0
Allegro	4	0
Angel Park	4	0
Apple Country	4	0
Armbro Intimate	4	0
Art In The Park	4	0
Astro Action	4	0
Beauteous	4	0
Bedeviled	4	0
Candy Victory	4	0
Canne Angus	4	0

FILLIES

Grand-dam	Sold	$50,000 2 Year Olds
Tarbeth Hanover	8	0
Gracious Lobell	7	0
Me Maggie	7	0
Another Choice	6	0
Dawdle	6	0
Missys Goal	6	0
Nukes Magic	6	0
Absolute Martini	5	0
Armbro Éclair	5	0
Keystone Sister	5	0
Luanne Kash	5	0
Madam Cool	5	0
Madam Hanover	5	0
Missy Hadagal	5	0
Sheer Hose	5	0
Shy Devil	5	0
World Order	5	0
Angaal	4	0
Apple Country	4	0
Ariel Lobell	4	0
Armbro Ophelia	4	0
Authentic	4	0
B Cor Tamara	4	0
Balanced Breeze	4	0
Bio Bandbox	4	0
Caviar Please	4	0
Cheer Me Up	4	0
Cirque De Soleil	4	0
Classic Casette	4	0
Classical Beth	4	0
Classical Motion	4	0
Easy To Love	4	0
Emory Girl	4	0
Ever And Again	4	0
Flat Foot Fluzy	4	0
Happy Bottom	4	0
Iminthemoodforlove	4	0
Insideous Charm	4	0
Intercontinental	4	0
Jef's Magic Trick	4	0
Lady Leesun	4	0

COLTS

Grand-dam	Sold	$50,000 2 Year Olds
Central Park West	4	0
Conch	4	0
Coral Glory	4	0
Crown Dream	4	0
Delinquent Account	4	0
Ebony Crown	4	0
Everything Goes	4	0
Flickering Halo	4	0
Grand Lady	4	0
Gypsy Melody	4	0
Jate's Strait	4	0
Keyser's Cousin	4	0
Keystone Shore	4	0
Larjon Heather	4	0
Leah Almahurst	4	0
Lovely Lady	4	0
Madam Cool	4	0
Madam Hanover	4	0
Meadow Good Miss	4	0
Miss Flirt	4	0
Mommy Dear	4	0
Mystical Mood	4	0
Nadia Lobell	4	0
Niajet	4	0
Northern Route	4	0
Rashina	4	0
Rhapsody In Blue	4	0
Set Me Free	4	0
Southbrook Matty	4	0
Storm Tossed	4	0
Tarport Herald	4	0
That Fabulous Face	4	0
The Big Enchilada	4	0
Turola Hanover	4	0
Victorious Tail	4	0
Victory Girl	4	0
Victory Lass	4	0
Vote Getter	4	0
Warrawee Kirra	4	0

FILLIES

Grand-dam	Sold	$50,000 2 Year Olds
Louisa	4	0
Maiden Yankee	4	0
Makin Smiles	4	0
Misty Bretta	4	0
Moll Hanover	4	0
Mt Penn	4	0
My Bell Ami	4	0
Nan Can	4	0
Nan Hanover	4	0
Petrolianna	4	0
Principessa Susi	4	0
Sabra Almahurst	4	0
Satan's Alley	4	0
Shady Katie	4	0
Shipps Dream	4	0
Sign Of Life	4	0
Southtown	4	0
Speedy Moriah	4	0
Swifty But Nifty	4	0
Take Flight	4	0
Town Keeper	4	0
Windsun Dee	4	0

Chapter 11: Birth Order Success Rates

I: The Two-Year Old Performers

In *Profiles of Two-Year-Old Standardbreds Earning $50,000 and Up* we found that *60%* of the *elite performers* from 1993–1998 were early foals (1 to 4) and *78%* were from the first to the sixth foal of their mares. For that reason we have detailed the gender number of foals 1 through 6 to uncover disparities. (Foal and gender numbers work in the following manner: second foal, same gender = 2/2; second foal, different gender = 2/1.) Back in 1999 we did not know the entire population by birth order. Therefore, we were not able to compare Success Rates by birth order. Within the confines of this analysis, we have a population base of 5,685 yearlings so that we can measure the disparities among birth orders. So, let's compare the Success Rate of early foals versus later foals.

Foal Numbers	Sold	$50,000 2 Year Olds	Success Rate	Percent of Sold	Percent of $50,000 2 Year Olds
1 thru 6	4488	333	7.4%	78.9%	82%
7 and up	1197	73	6.1%	21.1%	18%

The productivity is closer than I had imagined even though the early foals have done better. From the two sale venues, foals 1 to 6 have a 21.6% better Success Rate. Of course, by gait, gender and sale venue there are bigger disparities. For example, look at *trotting colts* at LEX:

Foal Numbers	Sold	$50,000 2 Year Olds	Success Rate	Percent of Sold	Percent of $50,000 2 Year Olds
1 thru 6	539	42	7.8%	82.9%	91.3%
7 and up	111	4	3.6%	17.1%	8.7%

Early foals have a *116%* better Success Rate with trotting colts sold at LEX. Conversely, we have *pacing fillies* at LEX:

Foal Numbers	Sold	$50,000 2 Year Olds	Success Rate	Percent of Sold	Percent of $50,000 2 Year Olds
1 thru 6	436	35	8.0%	78.6%	76.1%
7 and up	119	11	9.2%	21.4%	23.9%

Later foals have a 15% better success rate with pacing fillies at LEX.

Yet, we don't place as much emphasis on birth order as we did in the past. There are anomalies to note, but we don't think birth order is as important as sires, farms, and broodmare sires.

When reviewing the charts in this chapter, remember the yearlings were sold from the 2008-2010 Sales and raced as two-year olds in 2009–2011.

Chart 1: Success Rates By Birth Order - Both Gaits

HARRISBURG AND LEXINGTON, 2008-2010

Foal Number	Gender Number	Sold	$50,000 2 Year Olds	Success Rate	Odds 1 in –	Percent of Sold	Percent of $50,0000 2 Year Olds
1	1	1015	76	7.5%	13.4	17.9%	18.7%
2	1	469	38	8.1%	12.3	8.2%	9.4%
2	2	431	24	5.6%	18.0	7.6%	5.9%
All 2nd Foals		900	62	6.9%	14.5	15.8%	15.3%
3	1	203	14	6.9%	14.5	3.6%	3.4%
3	2	424	35	8.3%	12.1	7.5%	8.6%
3	3	230	9	3.9%	25.6	4.0%	2.2%
All 3rd Foals		857	58	6.8%	14.8	15.1%	14.3%
4	1	110	6	5.5%	18.3	1.9%	1.5%
4	2	250	16	6.4%	15.6	4.4%	3.9%
4	3	254	33	13.0%	7.7	4.5%	8.1%
4	4	84	10	11.9%	8.4	1.5%	2.5%
All 4th Foals		698	65	9.3%	10.7	12.3%	16.0%
5	1	36	1	2.8%	36.0	0.6%	0.2%
5	2	143	5	3.5%	28.6	2.5%	1.2%
5	3	193	14	7.3%	13.8	3.4%	3.4%
5	4	144	15	10.4%	9.6	2.5%	3.7%
5	5	34	2	5.9%	17.0	0.6%	0.5%
All 5th Foals		550	37	6.7%	14.9	9.7%	9.1%
6	1	15	2	13.3%	7.5	0.3%	0.5%
6	2	82	3	3.7%	27.3	1.4%	0.7%
6	3	143	10	7.0%	14.3	2.5%	2.5%
6	4	135	13	9.6%	10.4	2.4%	3.2%
6	5	80	6	7.5%	13.3	1.4%	1.5%
6	6	12	1	8.3%	12.0	0.2%	0.2%
6	?*	1	0	0%	0	0%	0%
All 6th Foals		468	35	7.5%	13.4	8.2%	8.6%
Sub Total 1-6		4488	333	7.4%	13.5	78.9%	82.0%
7	All	338	21	6.2%	16.1	5.9%	5.2%
8	All	267	21	7.9%	12.7	4.7%	5.2%
9	All	194	10	5.2%	19.4	3.4%	2.5%
10	All	147	11	7.5%	13.4	2.6%	2.7%
11	All	103	6	5.8%	17.2	1.8%	1.5%
12	All	71	2	2.8%	35.5	1.2%	0.5%
13+	All	77	2	2.6%	38.5	1.4%	0.5%
Sub Total 7-13+		1197	73	6.1%	16.4	21.1%	18.0%
Grand Total		5685	406	7.1%	14.0	100.0%	100.0%

*Note: 6th foal gender number unknown since four of the mare's offspring were raised in Europe and not listed in *Sires and Dams*.

Chart 2: Success Rates By Birth Order – Pacing Colts

HARRISBURG, 2008-2010

Foal Number	Gender Number	Sold	$50,000 2 Year Olds	Success Rate	Percent of Sold	Percent of $50,000 2 Year Olds
1	1	177	12	6.8%	17.2%	17.9%
2	1	82	4	4.9%	8.0%	6.0%
2	2	78	4	5.1%	7.6%	6.0%
All 2nd Foals		160	8	5.0%	15.5%	11.9%
3	1	31	2	6.5%	3.0%	3.0%
3	2	80	5	6.3%	7.8%	7.5%
3	3	44	1	2.3%	4.3%	1.5%
All 3rd Foals		155	8	5.2%	15.0%	11.9%
4	1	22	0	0%	2.1%	0%
4	2	43	1	2.3%	4.2%	1.5%
4	3	46	5	10.9%	4.5%	7.5%
4	4	8	1	12.5%	0.8%	1.5%
All 4th Foals		119	7	5.9%	11.6%	10.4%
5	1	4	0	0%	0.4%	0%
5	2	21	2	9.5%	2.0%	3.0%
5	3	37	4	10.8%	3.6%	6.0%
5	4	27	3	11.1%	2.6%	4.5%
5	5	4	0	0%	0.4%	0%
All 5th Foals		93	9	9.7%	9.0%	13.4%
6	1	3	1	33.3%	0.3%	1.5%
6	2	10	0	0%	1.0%	0%
6	3	20	2	10.0%	1.9%	3.0%
6	4	24	2	8.3%	2.3%	3.0%
6	5	14	2	14.3%	1.4%	3.0%
6	6	0	0	0%	0%	0%
All 6th Foals		71	7	9.9%	6.9%	10.4%
Sub Total 1- 6		775	51	6.6%	75.2%	76.1%
7	All	62	7	11.3%	6.0%	10.4%
8	All	53	3	5.7%	5.1%	4.5%
9	All	41	1	2.4%	4.0%	1.5%
10	All	38	3	7.9%	3.7%	4.5%
11	All	19	1	5.3%	1.8%	1.5%
12	All	20	1	5.0%	1.9%	1.5%
13+	All	22	0	0%	2.1%	0%
Sub Total 7-13+		255	16	6.3%	24.8%	23.9%
Grand Total		1030	67	6.5%	100%	100%

Chart 2a: Success Rates By Birth Order – Pacing Colts

LEXINGTON, 2008-2010

Foal Number	Gender Number	Sold	$50,000 2 Year Olds	Success Rate	Percent of Sold	Percent of $50,000 2 Year Olds
1	1	119	9	7.6%	18.5%	17.9%
2	1	43	1	2.3%	6.7%	6.0%
2	2	56	6	10.7%	8.7%	6.0%
All 2nd Foals		99	7	7.1%	15.4%	13.0%
3	1	34	3	8.8%	5.3%	3.0%
3	2	44	4	9.1%	6.8%	7.5%
3	3	21	0	0%	3.3%	1.5%
All 3rd Foals		99	7	7.1%	15.4%	13.0%
4	1	11	2	18.2%	1.7%	0%
4	2	27	1	3.7%	4.2%	1.5%
4	3	28	6	21.4%	4.3%	7.5%
4	4	10	2	20%	1.6%	1.5%
All 4th Foals		76	11	14.5%	11.8%	20.4%
5	1	6	0	0%	0.9%	0%
5	2	17	1	5.9%	2.6%	3.0%
5	3	20	2	10.0%	3.1%	6.0%
5	4	16	1	6.3%	2.5%	4.5%
5	5	2	0	0%	0.3%	0%
All 5th Foals		61	4	6.6%	9.5%	7.4%
6	1	2	1	50%	0.3%	1.5%
6	2	7	0	0%	1.1%	0%
6	3	15	3	20.0%	2.3%	3.0%
6	4	16	1	6.3%	2.5%	3.0%
6	5	10	0	0%	1.6%	3.0%
6	6	0	0	0%	0%	0%
All 6th Foals		50	5	10.0%	7.8%	9.3%
Sub Total 1-6		504	43	8.5%	78.3%	79.6%
7	All	41	3	7.3%	6.4%	10.4%
8	All	36	4	11.1%	5.6%	4.5%
9	All	13	0	0%	2.0%	1.5%
10	All	19	2	10.5%	3.0%	4.5%
11	All	14	1	7.1%	2.2%	1.5%
12	All	7	0	0%	1.1%	1.5%
13+	All	10	1	10.0%	1.6%	0%
Sub Total 7-13+		140	11	7.9%	21.7%	20.4%
Grand Total		644	54	8.4%	100%	100%

Chart 2b: Success Rates By Birth Order – Pacing Fillies

HARRISBURG, 2008-2010

Foal Number	Gender Number	Sold	$50,000 2 Year Olds	Success Rate	Percent of Sold	Percent of $50,000 2 Year Olds
1	1	139	9	6.5%	16.1%	17.0%
2	1	74	6	8.1%	8.6%	11.3%
2	2	59	4	6.8%	6.8%	7.5%
All 2nd Foals		133	10	7.5%	15.4%	18.9%
3	1	27	2	7.4%	3.1%	3.8%
3	2	68	4	5.9%	7.9%	7.5%
3	3	33	4	12.1%	3.8%	7.5%
All 3rd Foals		128	10	7.8%	14.8%	18.9%
4	1	14	0	0%	1.6%	0%
4	2	37	3	8.1%	4.3%	5.7%
4	3	40	4	10.0%	4.6%	7.5%
4	4	4	2	50.0%	0.5%	3.8%
All 4th Foals		95	9	9.5%	11.0%	17.0%
5	1	4	0	0%	0.5%	0%
5	2	21	0	0%	2.4%	0%
5	3	28	1	3.6%	3.2%	1.9%
5	4	27	1	3.7%	3.1%	1.9%
5	5	3	0	0%	0.3%	0%
All 5th Foals		83	2	2.4%	9.6%	3.8%
6	1	0	0	0%	0%	0%
6	2	10	0	0%	1.2%	0%
6	3	24	1	4.2%	2.8%	1.9%
6	4	23	1	4.4%	2.7%	1.9%
6	5	14	0	0%	1.6%	0%
6	6	2	0	0%	0.2%	0%
All 6th Foals		73	2	2.7%	8.4%	3.8%
Sub Total 1-6		651	42	6.5%	75.3%	79.2%
7	All	59	4	6.8%	6.8%	7.5%
8	All	42	3	7.1%	4.9%	5.7%
9	All	37	1	2.7%	4.3%	1.9%
10	All	17	1	5.9%	2.0%	1.9%
11	All	24	1	4.2%	2.8%	1.9%
12	All	20	1	5.0%	2.3%	1.9%
13+	All	15	0	0%	1.7%	0%
Sub Total 7-13+		214	11	5.1%	24.7%	20.8%
Grand Total		865	53	6.1%	100%	100%

Chart 2c: Success Rates By Birth Order — Pacing Fillies

LEXINGTON, 2008-2010

Foal Number	Gender Number	Sold	$50,000 2 Year Olds	Success Rate	Percent of Sold	Percent of $50,000 2 Year Olds
1	1	90	7	7.8%	16.2%	15.2%
2	1	47	5	10.6%	8.5%	10.9%
2	2	38	3	7.9%	6.8%	6.5%
All 2nd Foals		85	8	9.4%	15.3%	17.4%
3	1	20	1	5.0%	3.6%	2.2%
3	2	39	3	7.7%	7.0%	6.5%
3	3	26	1	3.9%	4.7%	2.2%
All 3rd Foals		85	5	5.9%	15.3%	10.9%
4	1	10	0	0%	1.8%	0%
4	2	21	1	4.8%	3.8%	2.2%
4	3	25	4	16.0%	4.5%	8.7%
4	4	19	3	15.8%	3.4%	6.5%
All 4th Foals		75	8	10.7%	13.5%	17.4%
5	1	3	0	0%	0.5%	0%
5	2	14	0	0%	2.5%	0%
5	3	14	1	7.1%	2.5%	2.2%
5	4	15	2	13.3%	2.7%	4.3%
5	5	4	1	25.0%	0.7%	2.2%
All 5th Foals		50	4	8.0%	9.0%	8.7%
6	1	3	0	0%	0.5%	0%
6	2	10	0	0%	1.8%	0%
6	3	17	1	5.9%	3.1%	2.2%
6	4	12	2	16.7%	2.2%	4.3%
6	5	6	0	0%	1.1%	0%
6	6	3	0	0%	0.5%	0%
All 6th Foals		51	3	5.9%	9.2%	6.5%
Sub Total 1-6		436	35	8.0%	78.6%	76.1%
7	All	29	2	6.9%	5.2%	4.3%
8	All	25	3	12.0%	4.5%	6.5%
9	All	32	4	12.5%	5.8%	8.7%
10	All	15	1	6.7%	2.7%	2.2%
11	All	10	1	10%	1.8%	2.2%
12	All	2	0	0%	0.4%	0%
13+	All	6	0	0%	1.1%	0%
Sub Total 7-13+		119	11	9.2%	21.4%	23.9%
Grand Total		555	46	8.3%	100%	100%

Chart 3: Success Rates By Birth Order – Trotting Colts

HARRISBURG, 2008-2010

Foal Number	Gender Number	Sold	$50,000 2 Year Olds	Success Rate	Percent of Sold	Percent of $50,000 2 Year Olds
1	1	142	11	7.8%	19.7%	20.4%
2	1	69	8	11.6%	9.6%	14.8%
2	2	49	3	6.1%	6.8%	5.6%
All 2nd Foals		118	11	9.3%	16.4%	20.4%
3	1	31	2	6.5%	4.3%	3.7%
3	2	47	5	10.6%	6.5%	9.3%
3	3	26	0	0%	3.6%	0%
All 3rd Foals		104	7	6.7%	14.4%	13.0%
4	1	8	1	12.5%	1.1%	1.9%
4	2	35	3	8.6%	4.9%	5.6%
4	3	30	3	10.0%	4.2%	5.6%
4	4	6	1	16.7%	0.8%	1.9%
All 4th Foals		79	8	10.1%	11.0%	14.8%
5	1	3	0	0%	0.4%	0%
5	2	21	0	0%	2.9%	0%
5	3	29	1	3.5%	4.0%	1.9%
5	4	15	1	6.7%	2.1%	1.9%
5	5	2	0	0%	0.3%	0%
All 5th Foals		70	2	2.9%	9.7%	3.7%
6	1	2	0	0%	0.3%	0%
6	2	12	2	16.7%	1.7%	3.7%
6	3	21	1	4.8%	2.9%	1.9%
6	4	22	3	13.6%	3.1%	5.6%
6	5	7	0	0%	1.0%	0%
6	6	3	1	33.3%	0.4%	1.9%
All 6th Foals		67	7	10.5%	9.3%	13.0%
Sub Total 1-6		580	46	7.9%	80.4%	85.2%
7	All	46	3	6.5%	6.4%	5.6%
8	All	32	2	6.3%	4.4%	3.7%
9	All	21	2	9.5%	2.9%	3.7%
10	All	16	0	0%	2.2%	0%
11	All	11	0	0%	1.5%	0%
12	All	8	0	0%	1.1%	0%
13+	All	7	1	14.3%	1.0%	1.9%
Sub Total 7-13+		141	8	5.7%	19.6%	14.8%
Grand Total		721	54	7.5%	100%	100%

Chart 3a: Success Rates By Birth Order – Trotting Colts

LEXINGTON, 2008-2010

Foal Number	Gender Number	Sold	$50,000 2 Year Olds	Success Rate	Percent of Sold	Percent of $50,000 2 Year Olds
1	1	115	10	8.7%	17.7%	21.7%
2	1	46	3	6.5%	7.1%	6.5%
2	2	51	2	3.9%	7.8%	4.3%
All 2nd Foals		97	5	5.2%	14.9%	10.9%
3	1	21	2	9.5%	3.2%	4.3%
3	2	53	4	7.6%	8.2%	8.7%
3	3	27	1	3.7%	4.2%	2.2%
All 3rd Foals		101	7	6.9%	15.5%	15.2%
4	1	19	1	5.3%	2.9%	2.2%
4	2	34	2	5.9%	5.2%	4.3%
4	3	26	2	7.7%	4.0%	4.3%
4	4	15	0	0%	2.3%	0%
All 4th Foals		94	5	5.3%	14.5%	10.9%
5	1	4	1	25.0%	0.6%	2.2%
5	2	13	1	7.7%	2.0%	2.2%
5	3	28	3	10.7%	4.3%	6.5%
5	4	22	4	18.2%	3.4%	8.7%
5	5	5	1	20.0%	0.8%	2.2%
All 5th Foals		72	10	13.9%	11.1%	21.7%
6	1	3	0	0%	0.5%	0%
6	2	15	1	6.7%	2.3%	2.2%
6	3	19	0	0%	2.9%	0%
6	4	10	2	20.0%	1.5%	4.3%
6	5	10	2	20.0%	1.5%	4.3%
6	6	3	0	0%	0.5%	0%
All 6th Foals		60	5	8.3%	9.2%	10.9%
Sub Total 1-6		539	42	7.8%	82.9%	91.3%
7	All	32	0	0%	4.9%	0%
8	All	24	1	4.2%	3.7%	2.2%
9	All	21	1	4.8%	3.2%	2.2%
10	All	14	1	7.1%	2.2%	2.2%
11	All	9	1	11.1%	1.4%	2.2%
12	All	6	0	0%	0.9%	0%
13+	All	5	0	0%	0.8%	0%
Sub Total 7-13+		111	4	3.6%	17.1%	8.7%
Grand Total		650	46	7.1%	100%	100%

Chart 3b: Success Rates By Birth Order – Trotting Fillies

HARRISBURG, 2008-2010

Foal Number	Gender Number	Sold	$50,000 2 Year Olds	Success Rate	Percent of Sold	Percent of $50,000 2 Year Olds
1	1	128	11	8.6%	18.8%	20.8%
2	1	66	8	12.1%	9.7%	15.1%
2	2	53	0	0%	7.8%	0%
All 2nd Foals		119	8	6.7%	17.5%	15.1%
3	1	24	2	8.3%	3.5%	3.8%
3	2	54	7	13.0%	7.9%	13.2%
3	3	24	1	4.2%	3.5%	1.9%
All 3rd Foals		102	10	9.8%	15.0%	18.9%
4	1	14	2	14.3%	2.1%	3.8%
4	2	29	2	6.9%	4.3%	3.8%
4	3	30	5	16.7%	4.4%	9.4%
4	4	10	1	10%	1.5%	1.9%
All 4th Foals		83	10	12.1%	12.2%	18.9%
5	1	4	0	0%	0.6%	0%
5	2	20	1	5.0%	2.9%	1.9%
5	3	23	2	8.7%	3.4%	3.8%
5	4	13	2	15.4%	1.9%	3.8%
5	5	8	0	0%	1.2%	0%
All 5th Foals		68	5	7.4%	10%	9.4%
6	1	1	0	0%	0.1%	0%
6	2	10	0	0%	1.5%	0%
6	3	16	1	6.3%	2.4%	1.9%
6	4	20	1	5.0%	2.9%	1.9%
6	5	11	1	9.1%	1.6%	1.9%
6	6	1	0	0%	0.1%	0%
6	?*	1	0	0%	0.1%	0%
All 6th Foals		60	3	5.0%	8.8%	5.7%
Sub Total 1-6		560	47	8.4%	82.4%	88.7%
7	All	35	1	2.9%	5.1%	1.9%
8	All	27	2	7.4%	4.0%	3.8%
9	All	17	1	5.9%	2.5%	1.9%
10	All	19	2	10.5%	2.8%	3.8%
11	All	10	0	0%	1.5%	0%
12	All	6	0	0%	0.9%	0%
13+	All	6	0	0%	0.9%	0%
Sub Total 7-13+		120	6	5.0%	17.6%	11.3%
GRAND TOTAL		680	53	7.8%	100%	100%

*Note: 6th foal gender number unknown since four of the mare's offspring were raised in Europe and not listed in *Sires and Dams*.

Chart 3c: Success Rates By Birth Order – Trotting Fillies

LEXINGTON, 2008-2010

Foal Number	Gender Number	Sold	$50,000 2 Year Olds	Success Rate	Percent of Sold	Percent of $50,000 2 Year Olds
1	1	105	7	6.7%	19.4%	21.2%
2	1	42	3	7.1%	7.8%	9.1%
2	2	47	2	4.3%	8.7%	6.1%
All 2nd Foals		89	5	5.6%	16.5%	15.2%
3	1	15	0	0%	2.8%	0%
3	2	39	3	7.7%	7.2%	9.1%
3	3	29	1	3.5%	5.4%	3.0%
All 3rd Foals		83	4	4.8%	15.4%	12.1%
4	1	12	0	0%	2.2%	0%
4	2	24	3	12.5%	4.4%	9.1%
4	3	29	4	13.8%	5.4%	12.1%
4	4	12	0	0%	2.2%	0%
All 4th Foals		77	7	9.1%	14.3%	21.2%
5	1	8	0	0%	1.5%	0%
5	2	16	0	0%	3.0%	0%
5	3	14	0	0%	2.6%	0%
5	4	9	1	11.1%	1.7%	3.0%
5	5	6	0	0%	1.1%	0%
All 5th Foals		53	1	1.9%	9.8%	3.0%
6	1	1	0	0%	0.2%	0%
6	2	8	0	0%	1.5%	0%
6	3	11	1	9.1%	2.0%	3.0%
6	4	8	1	12.5%	1.5%	3.0%
6	5	8	1	12.5%	1.5%	3.0%
6	6	0	0	0%	0%	0%
All 6th Foals		36	3	8.3%	6.7%	9.1%
Sub Total 1-6		443	27	6.1%	82.0%	81.8%
7	All	34	1	2.9%	6.3%	3.0%
8	All	28	3	10.7%	5.2%	9.1%
9	All	12	0	0%	2.2%	0%
10	All	9	1	11.1%	1.7%	3.0%
11	All	6	1	16.7%	1.1%	3.0%
12	All	2	0	0%	0.4%	0%
13+	All	6	0	0%	1.1%	0%
Sub Total 7-13+		97	6	6.2%	18.0%	18.2%
Grand Total		540	33	6.1%	100%	100%

When these numbers are divided by gait, gender and sales venue, some of them can be very small samplings. Where there are larger data, they should be noted. For example, second foal/second filly (2/2) trotters have had *zero* elites out of 53 sold at Harrisburg. They're not much better at Lexington with 2 out of 47. That's a combined 2 for 100 or 2% Success Rate. Can that change? Of course it can. But, a base of 100 is not a small sample by any measure.

With pacing colts the fourth foal/third colt has been very productive. At HB there have been 5 elites from 46 sold. At LEX there have been 6 out of 28 sold. Combined 4/3 pacing colts are 11 out of 74 for a 14.9% Success Rate, or 1 in 6.7.

II: Mare's Success Rates by Birth Order

There is a similar pattern between the performers' birth order and that of their mares. The early foal mares, 1 through 6, have a 14.5 % higher Success Rate at 7.4% versus 6.5% for the later foal mares (7 and up). Only mares of pacing colts at Harrisburg were contrary with a Success Rate of 7.0% for later foal mares versus 6.3% for the earlier foal mares.

There are some strange disparities by gait gender and sale venue. For example, fourth foal mares of trotting fillies at HB are *zero* out of 60. That's unfathomable. But, sixth foal mares of trotting fillies at HB are 9 out of 56 for a 16.1% Success Rate. Within those sixth foal mares, the 6/3 (sixth foal/ third filly) and 6/4 (sixth foal/fourth filly) were 8 out of 36 for an impressive 22.2% Success Rate–or 1 in 4.5. There are numerous anomalies in the birth order charts. Each buyer must weigh the significance on his/her own terms when evaluating a youngster.

Will the results detailed on the following charts continue? That's anybody's guess. But, with so many of the same mares appearing in the HB and LEX catalogs each year, it's prudent to be cognizant of this information.

Once again for clarity, Charts 4, 5 and 6 detail the Success Rates of the Mares (by birth order) of the yearlings sold at LEX and HB from 2008–2010 and raced as two-year olds from 2009–2011.

The Charts are configured in the following order: Chart 4 is the grand total of both sale venues and both gaits. Charts 5, 5a, 5b, and 5c detail the information for pacers by gait and sale venue. Charts 6, 6a, 6b, and 6c are the same, but for trotters.

Chart 4: Success Rates By Mare's Birth Order - Both Gaits

HARRISBURG AND LEXINGTON, 2008-2010

Foal Number	Gender Number	Sold	$50,000 2 Year Olds	Success Rate	Percent of Sold	Percent of $50,000 2 Year Olds
1	1	905	62	6.9%	15.9%	15.3%
2	1	454	38	8.4%	8.0%	9.4%
2	2	383	22	5.7%	6.7%	5.4%
All 2nd Foals		**837**	**60**	**7.1%**	**14.7%**	**14.8%**
3	1	191	15	7.9%	3.4%	3.7%
3	2	375	25	6.7%	6.6%	6.2%
3	3	152	13	8.6%	2.7%	3.2%
All 3rd Foals		**718**	**53**	**7.5%**	**12.7%**	**13.0%**
4	1	68	2	2.9%	1.2%	0.5%
4	2	246	20	8.1%	4.3%	4.9%
4	3	224	17	7.6%	3.9%	4.2%
4	4	62	7	11.3%	1.1%	1.7%
All 4th Foals		**600**	**46**	**7.7%**	**10.6%**	**11.3%**
5	1	29	5	17.2%	0.5%	1.2%
5	2	150	12	8.0%	2.6%	3.0%
5	3	213	19	8.9%	3.8%	4.7%
5	4	103	7	6.8%	1.8%	1.7%
5	5	33	2	6.1%	0.6%	0.5%
All 5th Foals		**528**	**45**	**8.5%**	**9.3%**	**11.1%**
6	1	13	0	0%	0.2%	0%
6	2	73	2	2.7%	1.3%	0.5%
6	3	163	19	11.7%	2.9%	4.7%
6	4	123	7	5.7%	2.2%	1.7%
6	5	57	5	8.8%	1.0%	1.2%
6	6	10	0	0%	0.2%	0%
All 6th Foals		**439**	**33**	**7.5%**	**7.7%**	**8.1%**
Sub Total 1-6		**4027**	**299**	**7.4%**	**70.9%**	**73.6%**
7	All	415	36	8.7%	7.3%	8.9%
8	All	307	18	5.9%	5.4%	4.4%
9	All	248	12	4.8%	4.4%	3.0%
10	All	207	14	6.8%	3.6%	3.4%
11	All	163	8	4.9%	2.9%	2.0%
12	All	99	6	6.1%	1.7%	1.5%
13+	All	212	13	6.1%	3.7%	3.2%
Sub Total 7-13+		**1651**	**107**	**6.5%**	**29.1%**	**26.4%**
Grand Total*		**5678**	**406**	**7.2%**	**100%**	**100%**

*Missing Birth Order for 7 Mares (European)

Chart 5: Success Rates By Mare's Birth Order - Pacing Colts

HARRISBURG, 2008-2010

Foal Number	Gender Number	Sold	$50,000 2 Year Olds	Success Rate	Percent of Sold	Percent of $50,000 2 Year Olds
1	1	155	14	9.0%	15.0%	20.9%
2	1	75	4	5.3%	7.3%	6.0%
2	2	62	4	6.5%	6.0%	6.0%
All 2nd Foals		137	8	5.8%	13.3%	11.9%
3	1	36	1	2.8%	3.5%	1.5%
3	2	69	3	4.4%	6.7%	4.5%
3	3	23	1	4.4%	2.2%	1.5%
All 3rd Foals		128	5	3.9%	12.4%	7.5%
4	1	8	0	0%	0.8%	0%
4	2	47	4	8.5%	4.6%	6.0%
4	3	45	5	11.1%	4.4%	7.5%
4	4	12	0	0%	1.2%	0%
All 4th Foals		112	9	8.0%	10.9%	13.4%
5	1	5	1	20.0%	0.5%	1.5%
5	2	29	2	6.9%	2.8%	3.0%
5	3	38	2	5.3%	3.7%	3.0%
5	4	24	1	4.2%	2.3%	1.5%
5	5	3	0	0%	0.3%	0%
All 5th Foals		99	6	6.1%	9.6%	9.0%
6	1	1	0	0%	0.1%	0%
6	2	12	0	0%	1.2%	0%
6	3	25	0	0%	2.4%	0%
6	4	24	2	8.3%	2.3%	3.0%
6	5	10	0	0%	1.0%	0%
6	6	0	0	0%	0%	0%
All 6th Foals		72	2	2.8%	7.0%	3.0%
Sub Total 1-6		703	44	6.3%	68.3%	65.7%
7	All	87	9	10.3%	8.4%	13.4%
8	All	62	4	6.5%	6.0%	6.0%
9	All	47	2	4.3%	4.6%	3.0%
10	All	35	1	2.9%	3.4%	1.5%
11	All	34	3	8.8%	3.3%	4.5%
12	All	23	3	13.0%	2.2%	4.5%
13+	All	39	1	2.6%	3.8%	1.5%
Sub Total 7-13+		327	23	7.0%	31.7%	34.3%
Grand Total		1030	67	6.5%	100%	100%

Chart 5a: Success Rates By Mare's Birth Order - Pacing Colts

LEXINGTON, 2008-2010

Foal Number	Gender Number	Sold	$50,000 2 Year Olds	Success Rate	Percent of Sold	Percent of $50,000 2 Year Olds
1	1	119	6	5.0%	18.5%	11.1%
2	1	47	4	8.5%	7.3%	7.4%
2	2	39	1	2.6%	6.1%	1.9%
All 2nd Foals		86	5	5.8%	13.4%	9.3%
3	1	21	2	9.5%	3.3%	3.7%
3	2	38	6	15.8%	5.9%	11.1%
3	3	16	2	12.5%	2.5%	3.7%
All 3rd Foals		75	10	13.3%	11.6%	18.5%
4	1	9	1	11.1%	1.4%	1.9%
4	2	22	1	4.6%	3.4%	1.9%
4	3	20	0	0%	3.1%	0%
4	4	8	2	25.0%	1.2%	3.7%
All 4th Foals		59	4	6.8%	9.2%	7.4%
5	1	2	1	50%	0.3%	1.9%
5	2	24	3	12.5%	3.7%	5.6%
5	3	20	4	20.0%	3.1%	7.4%
5	4	12	2	16.7%	1.9%	3.7%
5	5	5	0	0%	0.8%	0%
All 5th Foals		63	10	15.9%	9.8%	18.5%
6	1	4	0	0%	0.6%	0%
6	2	8	0	0%	1.2%	0%
6	3	19	3	15.8%	3.0%	5.6%
6	4	9	0	0%	1.4%	0%
6	5	4	1	25.0%	0.6%	1.9%
6	6	1	0	0%	0.2%	0%
All 6th Foals		45	4	8.9%	7.0%	7.4%
Sub Total 1-6		447	39	8.7%	69.4%	72.2%
7	All	49	3	6.1%	7.6%	5.6%
8	All	35	3	8.6%	5.4%	5.6%
9	All	30	1	3.3%	4.7%	1.9%
10	All	29	3	10.3%	4.5%	5.6%
11	All	15	1	6.7%	2.3%	1.9%
12	All	16	1	6.3%	2.5%	1.9%
13+	All	23	3	13.0%	3.6%	5.6%
Sub Total 7-13+		197	15	7.6%	30.6%	27.8%
Grand Total		644	54	8.4%	100%	100%

Chart 5b: Success Rates By Mare's Birth Order - Pacing Fillies

HARRISBURG, 2008-2010

Foal Number	Gender Number	Sold	$50,000 2 Year Olds	Success Rate	Percent of Sold	Percent of $50,000 2 Year Olds
1	1	128	6	4.7%	14.8%	11.3%
2	1	76	4	5.3%	8.8%	7.5%
2	2	66	5	7.6%	7.6%	9.4%
All 2nd Foals		142	9	6.3%	16.4%	17.0%
3	1	32	3	9.4%	3.7%	5.7%
3	2	51	4	7.8%	5.9%	7.5%
3	3	29	3	10.3%	3.4%	5.7%
All 3rd Foals		112	10	8.9%	12.9%	18.9%
4	1	7	0	0%	0.8%	0%
4	2	41	3	7.3%	4.7%	5.7%
4	3	45	3	6.7%	5.2%	5.7%
4	4	12	1	8.3%	1.4%	1.9%
All 4th Foals		105	7	6.7%	12.1%	13.2%
5	1	3	0	0%	0.3%	0%
5	2	30	3	10.0%	3.5%	5.7%
5	3	30	3	10.0%	3.5%	5.7%
5	4	11	0	0%	1.3%	0%
5	5	3	0	0%	0.3%	0%
All 5th Foals		77	6	7.8%	8.9%	11.3%
6	1	2	0	0%	0.2%	0%
6	2	8	0	0%	0.9%	0%
6	3	23	2	8.7%	2.7%	3.8%
6	4	26	0	0%	3.0%	0%
6	5	12	1	8.3%	1.4%	1.9%
6	6	0	0	0%	0%	0%
All 6th Foals		71	3	4.2%	8.2%	5.7%
Sub Total 1-6		635	41	6.5%	73.4%	77.4%
7	All	51	3	5.9%	5.9%	5.7%
8	All	51	1	2.0%	5.9%	1.9%
9	All	43	3	7.0%	5.0%	5.7%
10	All	22	2	9.1%	2.5%	3.8%
11	All	25	1	4.0%	2.9%	1.9%
12	All	5	0	0%	0.6%	0%
13+	All	33	2	6.1%	3.8%	3.8%
Sub Total 7-13+		230	12	5.2%	26.6%	22.6%
Grand Total		865	53	6.1%	100%	100%

Chart 5c: Success Rates By Mare's Birth Order - Pacing Fillies

LEXINGTON, 2008-2010

Foal Number	Gender Number	Sold	$50,000 2 Year Olds	Success Rate	Percent of Sold	Percent of $50,000 2 Year Olds
1	1	103	9	8.7%	18.6%	19.6%
2	1	39	0	0%	7.0%	0%
2	2	33	1	3.0%	5.9%	2.2%
All 2nd Foals		72	1	1.4%	13.0%	2.2%
3	1	13	0	0%	2.3%	0%
3	2	30	0	0%	5.4%	0%
3	3	18	2	11.1%	3.2%	4.3%
All 3rd Foals		61	2	3.3%	11.0%	4.3%
4	1	6	0	0%	1.1%	0%
4	2	30	6	20%	5.4%	13.0%
4	3	17	3	17.7%	3.1%	6.5%
4	4	3	3	100%	0.5%	6.5%
All 4th Foals		56	12	21.4%	10.1%	26.1%
5	1	5	0	0%	0.9%	0%
5	2	14	2	14.3%	2.5%	4.3%
5	3	20	1	5.0%	3.6%	2.2%
5	4	8	0	0%	1.4%	0%
5	5	1	0	0%	0.2%	0%
All 5th Foals		48	3	6.3%	8.6%	6.5%
6	1	2	0	0%	0.4%	0%
6	2	7	1	14.3%	1.3%	2.2%
6	3	13	3	23.1%	2.3%	6.5%
6	4	12	2	16.7%	2.2%	4.3%
6	5	3	0	0%	0.5%	0%
6	6	2	0	0%	0.4%	0%
All 6th Foals		39	6	15.4%	7.0%	13.0%
Sub Total 1-6		379	33	8.7%	68.3%	71.7%
7	All	52	2	3.9%	9.4%	4.3%
8	All	28	4	14.3%	5.0%	8.7%
9	All	26	3	11.5%	4.7%	6.5%
10	All	21	0	0%	3.8%	0%
11	All	14	0	0%	2.5%	0%
12	All	11	1	9.1%	2.0%	2.2%
13+	All	24	3	12.5%	4.3%	6.5%
Sub Total 7-13+		176	13	7.4%	31.7%	28.3%
Grand Total		555	46	8.3%	100%	100%

Chart 6: Success Rates By Mare's Birth Order – Trotting Colts

HARRISBURG, 2008-2010

Foal Number	Gender Number	Sold	$50,000 2 Year Olds	Success Rate	Percent of Sold	Percent of $50,000 2 Year Olds
1	1	114	9	7.9%	15.8%	16.7%
2	1	69	10	14.5%	9.6%	18.5%
2	2	57	2	3.5%	7.9%	3.7%
All 2nd Foals		126	12	9.5%	17.5%	22.2%
3	1	28	4	14.3%	3.9%	7.4%
3	2	54	3	5.6%	7.5%	5.6%
3	3	26	2	7.7%	3.6%	3.7%
All 3rd Foals		108	9	8.3%	15.0%	16.7%
4	1	8	0	0%	1.1%	0%
4	2	28	4	14.3%	3.9%	7.4%
4	3	36	3	8.3%	5.0%	5.6%
4	4	8	0	0%	1.1%	0%
All 4th Foals		80	7	8.8%	11.1%	13.0%
5	1	2	0	0%	0.3%	0%
5	2	13	0	0%	1.8%	0%
5	3	28	2	7.1%	3.9%	3.7%
5	4	10	1	10%	1.4%	1.9%
5	5	4	0	0%	0.6%	0%
All 5th Foals		57	3	5.3%	7.9%	5.6%
6	1	1	0	0%	0.1%	0%
6	2	11	0	0%	1.5%	0%
6	3	15	0	0%	2.1%	0%
6	4	20	0	0%	2.8%	0%
6	5	7	1	14.3%	1.0%	1.9%
6	6	0	0	0%	0%	0%
All 6th Foals		54	1	1.9%	7.5%	1.9%
Sub Total 1-6		539	41	7.6%	74.9%	75.9%
7	All	50	2	4.0%	6.9%	3.7%
8	All	31	3	9.7%	4.3%	5.6%
9	All	25	1	4.0%	3.5%	1.9%
10	All	27	4	14.8%	3.8%	7.4%
11	All	15	1	6.7%	2.1%	1.9%
12	All	8	0	0%	1.1%	0%
13+	All	25	2	8.0%	3.5%	3.7%
Sub Total 7-13+		181	13	7.2%	25.1%	24.1%
Grand Total		720	54	7.5%	100%	100%

*Missing Birth Order of 1 European Mare

Chart 6a: Success Rates By Mare's Birth Order – Trotting Colts

LEXINGTON, 2008-2010

Foal Number	Gender Number	Sold	$50,000 2 Year Olds	Success Rate	Percent of Sold	Percent of $50,000 2 Year Olds
1	1	95	6	6.3%	14.6%	13.0%
2	1	56	6	10.7%	8.6%	13.0%
2	2	43	3	7.0%	6.6%	6.5%
All 2nd Foals		99	9	9.1%	15.3%	19.6%
3	1	17	1	5.9%	2.6%	2.2%
3	2	54	6	11.1%	8.3%	13.0%
3	3	11	1	9.1%	1.7%	2.2%
All 3rd Foals		82	8	10.8%	12.6%	17.4%
4	1	8	0	0%	1.2%	0%
4	2	33	0	0%	5.1%	0%
4	3	19	2	10.5%	2.9%	4.3%
4	4	4	0	0%	0.6%	0%
All 4th Foals		64	2	3.1%	9.9%	4.3%
5	1	3	0	0%	0.5%	0%
5	2	15	1	6.7%	2.3%	2.2%
5	3	28	3	10.7%	4.3%	6.5%
5	4	12	1	8.3%	1.8%	2.2%
5	5	5	0	0%	0.8%	0%
All 5th Foals		63	5	7.9%	9.7%	10.9%
6	1	0	0	0%	0%	0%
6	2	9	0	0%	1.4%	0%
6	3	23	2	8.7%	3.5%	4.3%
6	4	12	0	0%	1.8%	0%
6	5	8	1	12.5%	1.2%	2.2%
6	6	4	0	0%	0.6%	0%
All 6th Foals		56	3	5.4%	8.6%	6.5%
Sub Total 1-6		459	33	7.2%	70.7%	71.7%
7	All	48	8	16.7%	7.4%	17.4%
8	All	29	2	6.9%	4.5%	4.3%
9	All	25	0	0%	3.9%	0%
10	All	27	2	7.4%	4.2%	4.3%
11	All	24	0	0%	3.7%	0%
12	All	13	0	0%	2.0%	0%
13+	All	24	1	4.2%	3.7%	2.2%
Sub Total 7-13+		190	13	6.8%	29.3%	28.3%
Grand Total		649	46	7.1%	100%	100%

*Missing Birth Order of 1 European Mare

Chart 6b: Success Rates By Mare's Birth Order – Trotting Fillies

HARRISBURG, 2008-2010

Foal Number	Gender Number	Sold	$50,000 2 Year Olds	Success Rate	Percent of Sold	Percent of $50,000 2 Year Olds
1	1	99	7	7.1%	14.6%	13.2%
2	1	56	8	14.3%	8.3%	15.1%
2	2	45	4	8.9%	6.6%	7.5%
All 2nd Foals		101	12	11.9%	14.9%	22.6%
3	1	23	1	4.4%	3.4%	1.9%
3	2	40	3	7.5%	5.9%	5.7%
3	3	16	2	12.5%	2.4%	3.8%
All 3rd Foals		79	6	7.6%	11.7%	11.3%
4	1	11	0	0%	1.6%	0%
4	2	23	0	0%	3.4%	0%
4	3	21	0	0%	3.1%	0%
4	4	5	0	0%	0.7%	0%
All 4th Foals		60	0	0%	8.8%	0%
5	1	5	2	40%	0.7%	3.8%
5	2	19	1	5.3%	2.8%	1.9%
5	3	29	3	10.3%	4.3%	5.7%
5	4	13	1	7.7%	1.9%	1.9%
5	5	7	1	14.3%	1.0%	1.9%
All 5th Foals		73	8	11.0%	10.8%	15.1%
6	1	3	0	0%	0.4%	0%
6	2	11	1	9.1%	1.6%	1.9%
6	3	24	6	25.0%	3.5%	11.3%
6	4	12	2	16.7%	1.8%	3.8%
6	5	5	0	0%	0.7%	0%
6	6	1	0	0%	0.1%	0%
All 6th Foals		56	9	16.1%	8.3%	17.0%
Sub Total 1-6		468	42	9.0%	69.0%	79.2%
7	All	47	5	10.6%	6.9%	9.4%
8	All	44	0	0%	6.5%	0%
9	All	30	2	6.7%	4.4%	3.8%
10	All	29	1	3.5%	4.3%	1.9%
11	All	22	2	9.1%	3.2%	3.8%
12	All	12	0	0%	1.8%	0%
13+	All	26	1	3.9%	3.8%	1.9%
Sub Total 7-13+		210	11	5.2%	31.0%	20.8%
Grand Total		678	53	7.8%	100%	100%

*Missing Birth Order of 2 European Mares

Chart 6c: Success Rates By Mare's Birth Order – Trotting Fillies

LEXINGTON, 2008-2010

Foal Number	Gender Number	Sold	$50,000 2 Year Olds	Success Rate	Percent of Sold	Percent of $50,000 2 Year Olds
1	1	92	5	5.4%	17.1%	15.2%
2	1	36	2	5.6%	6.7%	6.1%
2	2	38	2	5.3%	7.1%	6.1%
All 2nd Foals		74	4	5.4%	13.8%	12.1%
3	1	21	3	14.3%	3.9%	9.1%
3	2	39	0	0%	7.3%	0%
3	3	13	0	0%	2.4%	0%
All 3rd Foals		73	3	4.1%	13.6%	9.1%
4	1	11	1	9.1%	2.0%	3.0%
4	2	22	2	9.1%	4.1%	6.1%
4	3	21	1	4.8%	3.9%	3.0%
4	4	10	1	10.0%	1.9%	3.0%
All 4th Foals		64	5	7.8%	11.9%	15.2%
5	1	4	1	25.0%	0.7%	3.0%
5	2	6	0	0%	1.1%	0%
5	3	20	1	5.0%	3.7%	3.0%
5	4	13	1	7.7%	2.4%	3.0%
5	5	5	1	20.0%	0.9%	3.0%
All 5th Foals		48	4	8.3%	8.9%	12.1%
6	1	0	0	0%	0%	0%
6	2	7	0	0%	1.3%	0%
6	3	21	3	14.3%	3.9%	9.1%
6	4	8	1	12.5%	1.5%	3.0%
6	5	8	1	12.5%	1.5%	3.0%
6	6	2	0	0%	0.4%	0%
All 6th Foals		46	5	10.9%	8.6%	15.2%
Sub Total 1-6		397	26	6.6%	73.9%	78.8%
7	All	31	4	12.9%	5.8%	12.1%
8	All	27	1	3.7%	5.0%	3.0%
9	All	22	0	0%	4.1%	0%
10	All	17	1	5.9%	3.2%	3.0%
11	All	14	0	0%	2.6%	0%
12	All	11	1	9.1%	2.0%	3.0%
13+	All	18	0	0%	3.4%	0%
Sub Total 7-13+		140	7	5.0%	26.1%	21.2%
Grand Total		537	33	6.2%	100%	100%

*Missing Birth Order of 3 European Mares

Conclusion

We realize that there are many, many charts in this work. But, they provide the best method of bringing the data to life. We have reviewed many examples demonstrating the use of this information in preparing for the LEX and HB Sales. If you encounter a striking individual or receive "inside information" about a prospect, you can consult this volume to ascertain the Success Rates of its sire, broodmare sire, farm, cross, birth order, etc. You have that extra dimension at your fingertips, which may give you the edge when bidding or the confidence to refrain from bidding.

By no means is the information presented here definitive. There are many queries that I have edited from this work, and dozens of others that could be explored. However, time and space limitations have precluded their inclusion.

I hope you find the information in this book meaningful. I wish you the best of luck in the purchase of yearlings this fall!

Notes:

The 5,685 yearlings sold were auctioned at Harrisburg and Lexington from 2008–2010. This excludes withdrawn and "out" horses that were never offered to the public. It includes "buy-backs" and "not sold" horses since they were offered for sale, but may not have met the farm or consignor's price threshold.

Sources:

Lexington Select Sales Catalogs, 2008–2010.
The Black Book – Standardbred Horse Sales Company Catalogs, 2008–2010
USTA Sires and Dams (The Register), 1984–2010 editions.
Web sites: The Black Book; Lexington Select Sale; USTA; and Harnessracing.com.

www.ingramcontent.com/pod-product-compliance
Lightning Source LLC
Chambersburg PA
CBHW062037090426

42740CB00016B/2931